Sylvia Topp is the author of numerous essays, including 'Hidden Husbands' and 'You Can't Get to Barnhill from Here'. She has worked in publishing since college, starting as a copy editor on medical journals, then moving to freelance editing at major literary publishing houses. She was the long-time wife and partner of Tuli Kupferberg, a Beat poet who later was a co-founder, in 1964, of the Fugs, a legendary rock and roll band. Together Sylvia and Tuli wrote, edited and designed over thirty books and magazines, including *As They Were*, *1001 Ways to Live Without Working* and *Yeah* magazine. Sylvia joined the staff at *The Soho Weekly News* and later *The Village Voice*, before finishing her publishing career at *Vanity Fair*. *Eileen* is her first book. She lives in Kingston, Ontario.

BY THE SAME AUTHOR

Birth magazine, three issues, each on a different theme,
self-published, 1958–60.
Swing: Writing by Children, four issues, self-published, 1960–61.
Yeah magazine, ten issues, each on a different theme, self-published,
1961–65. All ten issues of *Yeah* were reprinted as facsimile editions in
a box set by Primary Information, Los Angeles, 2017.
All the above magazines were co-edited with Tuli Kupferberg and
designed by Sylvia Topp.

1001 Ways to Live Without Working, self-published, 1961. Reprinted by
Grove Press, New York, 1967.
1001 Ways to Beat the Draft, Oliver Layton Press, New York, 1966.
1001 Ways to Make Love, Grove Press, New York, 1969.
All of the above books were co-written with Tuli Kupferberg and
designed by Sylvia Topp.

Tuli Kupferberg and Sylvia Topp, *As They Were: Celebrated People's
Childhood Pictures*, Links Books, New York, 1973.
Tuli Kupferberg and Sylvia Topp, *As They Were Too: A Collection of
Celebrated People's Childhood Photos*, Quick Fox, New York, 1978.
Tuli Kupferberg and Sylvia Topp, *First Glance: Childhood Creations of
the Famous*, Hammond, Maplewood, N.J., 1978.

Eileen

The Making of

GEORGE ORWELL

SYLVIA TOPP

unbound

First published in 2020
This paperback edition first published in 2021

Unbound
Level 1, Devonshire House, One Mayfair Place, London W1J 8AJ
www.unbound.com

Text Design by PDQ Digital Media Solutions Ltd

A CIP record for this book is available from the British Library

ISBN 978-1-80018-026-0 (paperback)
ISBN 978-1-78352-708-3 (hardback)
ISBN 978-1-78352-750-2 (ebook)

Printed in Great Britain by Clays Ltd, Elcograf S.p.A

1 3 5 7 9 8 6 4 2

For Tuli, my own personal George Orwell

And for Christopher Hitchens, without whose
encouragement this book would not exist

With special thanks to:

Richard Blair
Marie Brown
Richard Sisk

as well as to David Taylor, Gordon Bowker, Peter Davison, and
Quentin Kopp, all of whom supported me from the very beginning

Contents

Foreword

L et me begin at a point that must seem remote from my main purpose here, which is to welcome Sylvia Topp's story of Eileen Blair's life. When, out of the blue, I was telephoned by the late Tom Rosenthal and told by him that he proposed celebrating the year 1984 by bringing out a de luxe edition of Orwell's nine books – that is, those from *Down and Out in Paris and London* to *Nineteen Eighty-Four* – and asked by him to check that there were no misprints in the then available texts, I was surprised. Such expertise as I had was centred on much earlier literature, in particular Shakespeare and his contemporaries. I had, among other books, edited the Penguin editions of *1* and *2 Henry IV*, editions that are still in print. Orwell was a new and potentially very interesting challenge. Of the travails attendant on that task, the lengthy delays and the disastrous changes of programme, I have written in detail and they need no rehearsing here. Despite the problems posed in the production of those nine no longer de luxe editions, Tom then had the imaginative idea of putting into print *all* Orwell's writings. He even despatched me to Boston to negotiate for a facsimile edition of the manuscript of *Nineteen Eighty-Four.* Very significantly, he insisted that I be accompanied – at the publisher's expense – by my wife, Sheila, because he thought, quite correctly as it proved, that she would be an aid in the negotiations. That successfully accomplished, Tom decided that Orwell's writings should be gathered into a single collected and complete edition, fully annotated. At that Tom left the scene and the edition floundered for some years, nearly sinking into the Atlantic as attempts were made to fulfil Tom's enlightened vision.

It soon became apparent as Ian Angus, my wife and I searched through archives that the edition would far outstrip what at first had been thought it might contain, especially when we struggled through the BBC Written Archive at Caversham. The immediate response in Poland Street and in New York was to act like two-fisted Sam with shears in each hand to cut and cut and cut. One first victim would have been letters not by Orwell, merely summarising any to him that might be referred to in his responses. I found much of such correspondence not merely factually informative but often emotionally so or even amusing. Take for example the letter written by the late Labour MP, Jennie Lee, replying to a correspondent a few months after Orwell's death (see Volume XI, item 355A) describing the arrival in Barcelona of a very tall man with large boots slung over his shoulder: 'This,' she wrote, 'was George Orwell and boots arriving to fight in Spain.' Even less priority was to be given to the letters written by his wife, Eileen, especially those to a university friend, Norah Myles, which Orwell would never see but which are wonderfully and emotionally informative.

It was readily apparent that Eileen played a major role in Orwell's creation of what he did. There is the charming account of how each evening Orwell would read to her what he had written that day that would become *Animal Farm*. We knew a little of the important and brave role she played supporting him in Spain. And, deeply personal though it is, I could not but compare the part my late wife played in supporting me during the trials, delays, disappointments, and tribulations over some seventeen years in assembling, editing, and annotating the twenty volumes. While Ian Angus's knowledge and expertise was readily brought to light, as was my indebtedness to him, the part my wife, Sheila, had played, especially in proofreading and in acting as a sounding board to my commentary, was hidden away. This had a mildly amusing aspect.

When the edition was virtually complete, the page proofs for the title pages arrived. It was obvious that Ian Angus's help should be acknowledged but I had also included my wife's name. She was having none of it! She had, she maintained, 'just read the text'. She had done much more but even that expression, 'just read the text', needed qualification. She had, in fact, proofread that text three times, and as it ran to some 9,000 pages, much of it in very small print, she had ploughed through over 27,000 pages. Of course errors got through but she was a far better proofreader than am I. She had obviously made an enormous contribution. Nor was it all she had contributed. When she decided it was inappropriate for her, a 'mere' teacher of deaf children, to be included on the title page, it led to Ian likewise feeling his name should be removed from the title pages. I had obviously to practise a little deception. With the aid of the publisher, a proof without their names was produced – but then ignored – and, as was only proper, both their names were included on the version published. That they only saw on publication day. I leave the reader to imagine their responses!

My concerns so far as Eileen was concerned were twofold. The first was to persuade the publisher to include all she wrote that we could lay our hands on. The second, drawn from my own experience in the light of the assistance my wife gave me, was to ensure that so far as I could Eileen's contribution to what Orwell was doing, whether in his writing or in those tumultuous days in Barcelona, was recognised. Just as my wife provided a vital support to my more mechanical contribution to finding, reproducing and annotating Orwell's work, so I interpreted Eileen's 'hidden' contributions. In this I was only partially successful.

Let me offer one example. Why did Eileen travel to Chapel Ridding in the Lake District (see her letter to Jack Common, 20 July 1938, Volume XI, item 468)? Though I had long-standing family connections to that part of England (my great-uncle Edward Hobley who lived in Penrith was a distinguished painter; his work is featured in Penrith Museum and I have on my walls some seventeen of his paintings), I made absolutely no progress in my enquiries. Even with such contacts as I had I got nowhere, but now, at last, Sylvia Topp has uncovered what I failed to do. And this applies to so much of what she reveals in this volume.

What I am particularly delighted by in this study are the revelations which are brought to light of the partnership underlying so much of Orwell's work, the sort of working partnership I also have been fortunate enough to enjoy.

Peter Hobley Davison

Introduction

'Why a book about Orwell's wife?' a friend asked. 'He would have been a great writer no matter who his wife was, right?' That thought was expressed to me several times as I researched this book. After all, Eileen died in 1945, just before *Animal Farm* was published, and therefore just before Orwell began to be widely recognised as a powerful voice in literature. How important could she have been? Also, 'Why did she do that?' others wondered, after learning that – with a degree in English from Oxford University and a future as a writer and educational psychologist herself – Eileen suddenly decided, in 1936, to give up her own personal aspirations and instead dedicate her life to a struggling, barely recognised, but very ambitious writer.

This book is an attempt at some answers.

Orwell knew well how fragile his own self-confidence was, and how much he needed assurance from others. Towards the end of his life, he confessed to a woman he had asked to marry him after Eileen died: 'It's only that I feel so desperately alone sometimes. I have hundreds of friends, but no woman who takes an interest in me and can encourage me.' And women had indeed 'encouraged' Orwell throughout his life. In fact, the number of women Orwell relied on and cherished will perhaps be surprising to some, especially those who believe him to have been a bit misogynistic. From the very beginning, he felt close to his mother, a kind of kindred spirit. And for many years he relied on her and his two sisters, Marjorie and Avril, to lend him money and share their homes with him, as he constantly needed support. His Aunt Nellie – Elaine Limouzine, his mother's sister – was indispensable to the beginning of his career. She lived in Paris in the late 1920s when Orwell was there, pursuing his desire to become a famous writer. She helped support him financially, while also devising opportunities for him to write for French papers. A few years later she introduced Orwell to the Hampstead bookshop owners for whom he was working in 1935 when he met Eileen. And the following year Aunt Nellie helped Orwell and Eileen find the cottage they lived in just after their wedding.

Then there was Mabel Fierz, a married woman and one-time lover, who believed in Orwell's talent immediately, one of the very first people to do so. She managed to find an agent for his first book, *Down and Out in Paris and London*, just as Orwell was ready to destroy it. Mabel also found him a room in Hampstead, where he could live while he worked at the bookshop. And shortly after he moved in, his flatmate, Rosalind Obermeyer, agreed to hold a party with him when, after having three books published, Orwell felt ready to explore the London literary world. Rosalind was studying psychology at University College London, and she agreed to bring some of her fellow classmates, including Eileen O'Shaughnessy, to their joint party. And thus Orwell met Eileen, who was about to become the most important woman in his life, the one willing to devote herself to 'encouraging' Orwell.

But Eileen was not willing to be a subservient wife, and that wasn't what Orwell was looking for. As David Taylor, a recent Orwell biographer, believes, Eileen was definitely 'a person in her own right – witty, ironic, able to extract humour from the most unpromising situations'. She was not intimidated by Orwell, and she challenged in a playful way some of his most outlandish declarations. Orwell joyfully recreated some of their battles in *Keep the Aspidistra Flying*. 'From time to time [Rosemary and Gordon] quarrelled vigorously, according to their custom,' he wrote. At one point, 'They began a violent argument upon the eternal and idiotic question of Man versus Woman . . . Gordon and Rosemary never grew tired of this kind of thing. Each laughed with delight at the other's absurdities. There was a merry war between them.' Apparently Eileen and Orwell continued their 'merry wars' through their ten years together, while never contemplating divorce because of them.

The belief that Orwell was a self-made man who was reluctant to share his work while in progress is inaccurate. Eileen immediately began typing drafts of Orwell's articles and books, adding emendations to the back of pages as she finished typing them. Her sense of humour and psychological skills aided him in plot development, and with her admiration, unselfishness, and bravery she helped assure his success.

Some friends noticed that Orwell's writing did change in the mid-1930s, but without recognising Eileen's influence. Richard Rees wrote, 'There was such an extraordinary change both in his writing and, in a way also, in his attitude after he'd been to the North [referencing Wigan]' (and of course *The Road to Wigan Pier* was the first book Orwell wrote after his marriage to Eileen). About *Homage to Catalonia*, Rees noted, 'This is the first occasion in any of Orwell's books in which one feels that he really looked at, saw, and paid attention to another human being.' And Rees later declared, 'There are indications in *Coming Up for Air* and elsewhere that [Orwell] was capable of a more contemplative and psychological approach,' describing its mood as 'blithe and sometimes even optimistic' with a 'peculiar buoyancy and vigour'. However, Rees concluded, 'I can't understand it or explain exactly what happened; I just don't know. But I quite agree there was an enormous change.'

Fredric Warburg, one of Orwell's publishers, wrote about *Animal Farm*, 'The writer of rather grey novels . . . had suddenly taken wings and become – a poet . . . There was, after all, little in Orwell's previous work to indicate that he was capable of this supreme effort.' And John Lehman, the editor of *New Writing*, noticed that Orwell had 'hammered out a direct and colloquial style'. However, like Rees, these men were not able to imagine that Eileen's influence could have helped bring about these changes.

Orwell's main biographers did notice that Orwell's writing improved shortly after he met Eileen, but they mentioned this only in short sentences which tended to get lost in 400-page biographies covering all the other aspects of Orwell's adventurous life.

Bernard Crick, Orwell's first biographer, wrote, 'Whether by coincidence or influence, [Orwell's] writing improved greatly after meeting Eileen, becoming a settled, simplified and consistent style', adding, 'After the ordeals of Spain . . . his finest writing, his best essays . . . lay ahead.'

Tosco Fyvel, a friend and biographer, wrote, 'It has so often been remarked that, unlike Orwell's other works, *Animal Farm* is a supremely well-written little satire . . . And if *Animal Farm* is a tale so perfect in its light touch and restraint (almost 'unOrwellian'), I think some credit is due to the conversational influence of Eileen and the light touch of her bright, humorous intelligence.' He added, 'I have two basic thoughts about [Eileen]. The first is that she had a very positive influence on Orwell's writings, especially on *Animal Farm*. The second is that Eileen's death was a blow to him from which in his personal life he never fully recovered.'

In their biography, Peter Stansky and William Abrahams wrote, '"Shooting an Elephant" marks the beginning of the major phase of Orwell's career, and it is not just coincidence that the time of its writing should coincide with the beginning of his marriage [to Eileen].' They added, 'There is an uncramped expression of feeling, a generosity and humaneness, an acknowledgement of the complexity of seemingly simple experience that had been absent from his earlier writing and that would be present in his work thereafter, which can be attributed at least in part to the influence of Eileen.' They concluded, 'It is noteworthy that the vehement bitterness and rancour, so evident in much of [Orwell's] early work, only reassert themselves after [Eileen's] death.'

Two other recent biographers also commented briefly on Eileen's influence. Gordon Bowker wrote, 'Key ideas in [Orwell's] later work may have emerged from mutual observations and discussion with the poetic Eileen', adding, 'It is likely that the transformation in Orwell's work from Wigan onwards owes a great deal to the intellectual stimulus his marriage brought him.' And Peter Davison believed that '*Animal Farm* is a last, and worthy, tribute to Eileen's beneficial influence on Orwell.'

Eileen's friends observed immediately that her personality and skills were improving Orwell's work. Lettice Cooper wrote, 'There was a noticeable increase of light and colour in his writing' after meeting Eileen. Lydia Jackson told people, 'I am certain that [Eileen's] logic, her feeling for accuracy in the use of words influenced [Orwell], perhaps without his being aware of it, in improving his style of writing, which in earlier years had a certain crudity and calculated exaggeration, detracting from its power to carry conviction.' Lydia further elaborated that, at first, Orwell 'was on the defensive against [Eileen's] psychological knowledge, and she was wise enough to keep it in the background, but as time went on, he allowed some of this knowledge to penetrate his defences, and it is clear from his later writings that he had accepted much of what he at first tended to ignore, or brush aside, in modern psychological theory and practice.' When Lydia first read *Animal Farm*, she 'could recognise touches of Eileen's humour in some of the episodes. Whether she had directly suggested them, or George had unconsciously assimilated some of his wife's whimsical ways of talking and viewing things . . . I have little doubt that . . . Eileen had collaborated in the creation of *Animal Farm*.' Edna Bussey, the fifteen-year-old girl who assisted Eileen in her typeshop, believed that Orwell 'owed a tremendous amount to Eileen for his success as a writer . . . It was not until after he had met her that he became famous.' She added, 'She was such a wonderful person and I am sure gave all she had to him to help him to success.'

Eileen's family had always been well aware of how essential she was to the writing of *Animal Farm*. Eileen was not interested in publicly claiming credit for any help she gave Orwell, always using her married name, Eileen Blair, and never Eileen Orwell. However, she did tell her family, including Gwen O'Shaughnessy and Doreen Kopp. According to the children of these women, Orwell had originally written a more traditional essay criticising Stalin and totalitarianism, an unpopular subject at that moment, since Stalin was helping the Allies defeat Hitler. Doreen told her son Quentin that 'Eileen had suggested rewriting the work as an allegory when the issue of Stalin as an ally made it difficult for his publisher in the original format.' As he went on to explain, 'My mother lived in a neighbouring house in Canonbury Square [and] she was close to the Blair household. In consequence that is probably how she was able to say that to me.' Catherine Moncure, Gwen's adopted daughter, remembers that 'there was always a murmur in the background of my youth that [Eileen had a hand in the creation of *Animal Farm*]'. In fact, as he was looking for a publisher, Orwell expected to include a long, explanatory essay, 'The Freedom of the Press', as a Preface, but this idea was later rejected. That essay was perhaps the original book idea that was later changed to an allegory.

Orwell once said that Eileen could have been a writer herself, but, although he certainly appreciated her dedication and encouragement, he did not publicly acknowledge her help. However, after she died, Orwell told a friend, 'It was a terrible shame that Eileen didn't live to see the publication of *Animal Farm*, which she was particularly fond of and even helped in the planning of.' Orwell's second wife, Sonia, said that Orwell 'probably did talk to [Eileen] fully about his works', since she was 'such a nice woman' and had been 'a great help to George'. Orwell himself later gave a very subtle reference to Eileen's importance in his life. In his 1946 essay 'Why I Write', Orwell wrote, 'The Spanish war and other events in 1936–37 turned the scale and thereafter I knew where I stood.' And of course one of those 'other events' in 1936 was his marriage to and future collaboration with Eileen.

Would Orwell have had as much success as he did without Eileen as his wife? Of course his writing would have changed in many ways as he developed his skills, but it's impossible to accurately speculate just how. Certainly he would not have been as prolific. Having Eileen typing drafts of essays and books, as well as using her editing skills from Oxford, was indispensable to Orwell's output. And Eileen's knowledge of psychology definitely helped him develop characters more deeply and convincingly. Also, Eileen constantly stressed how important it was for Orwell to resist taking on so many reviews. She knew his health was deteriorating, and she insisted he concentrate on writing novels in the years he had left.

Just before she died, Eileen and Orwell were arranging to spend the summer in yet another primitive home, this time on the Scottish island of Jura. The idea was to get him so far away from London that he couldn't easily be reached with writing requests and could thus concentrate on his novel. Orwell ended up going to Jura anyway, but if she had lived, Eileen would have been there with him, helping him survive, typing the drafts of *Nineteen Eighty-Four*, and suggesting emendations, as she always had with his other books. This was the first time in many years that Orwell was editing and retyping his drafts alone, and he knew it was killing him. Eileen's presence would definitely have extended his life, perhaps allowing him to write one or two of the other novels he was planning.

I want this book to bring Eileen out of the shadows at last. It's finally time for Eileen to have her own biography.

NOTE: All the above quotations have been credited throughout the book, and details of the sources mentioned are given in full in the Notes.

1

A Complicated Ancestry

*It is probably true that you can't give a really
revealing history of a man's life without saying
something about his parents and probably his
grandparents.*

George Orwell, BBC Radio talk, 1945

'Now *that* is the kind of girl I would like to marry!' George Orwell
told a friend excitedly, the night he met Eileen O'Shaughnessy.[1]
He had just returned from escorting Eileen to Hampstead tube
station after a party he had uncharacteristically suggested hosting with
Rosalind Obermeyer, at the flat they shared at the top end of Parliament
Hill. Orwell was thirty-one at the time, still using his birth name, Eric Blair,
still in the process of transforming himself into his brilliant future persona.
Although he'd had many girlfriends before, some of whom he was still
pursuing, Rosalind believed that this time he was seriously in love.

Eileen O'Shaughnessy, playfully recounting the evening to a friend,
remembered that she was 'rather drunk, behaving my worst, very
rowdy'.[2] Her vivacious party behaviour, added to her beauty, sparkling
wit, serious academic background, and rebellious nature, must have
been overwhelming to Orwell. Even her name was charming.

Rosalind later recalled that, the minute Eileen arrived at the party, Orwell stopped mid-conversation to cross the room and introduce himself, and the two talked together most of the evening. Orwell always vividly remembered this moment; years later he would describe how some of Yeats's poetic images could 'suddenly overwhelm one like a girl's face seen across a room.'[3] Eileen, who was studying psychology with Rosalind at University College London, had not read any of Orwell's three published books – none of them had been hugely successful – but she was intrigued enough to join him for dinner a few days later, and the romance blossomed rapidly.

Whatever Orwell's reason for suddenly wanting to have a party, whatever Eileen's impetus for venturing so far from her Greenwich home – that evening, a man with an obsession to be a great writer and a woman who had been bored for many years with the odd array of jobs available to a female Oxford University graduate connected in a miraculous fashion, one of those lucky accidents that are far too rare in life. They'd both come a very long way to find each other that night.

Within a couple of months Orwell had proposed to Eileen. When her friend and fellow psychology student Lydia Jackson was shocked that Eileen was apparently willing to consider his proposal, she joked, as she was prone to do, 'I told myself that when I was thirty I would accept the first man who asked me to marry him. Well . . . I shall be thirty [this] year.'[4] While making it clear to her friend that she had rejected offers of marriage before, Eileen perhaps wasn't yet sure herself why she was tempted to accept this particular one. Had she instantly recognised that Orwell had exceptional talent that hadn't yet been fully realised? Or had he simply mesmerised her with his piercing blue eyes and ability to concentrate his energies so fully on a person that she felt immediately entwined in his future? He was no doubt the most fascinating man she had ever met, and perhaps she understood instinctively that she had the personal qualities necessary to help him become the great writer he so desired to be.

Lydia thought Orwell was completely unacceptable as a partner for her friend, and Eileen's mother too actively resisted the marriage. But in a little over a year Eileen and Orwell were indeed married. She went on to share nine more years of a sometimes joyful, sometimes gruelling life with Orwell: at first subsisting happily with him in a tiny village where they grew vegetables and tended their own goats and chickens; then following him into the dangers of the Spanish Civil War; nursing him in Morocco after a severe bout of tubercular bleeding; narrowly escaping the destruction of their London flat in the Second World War; and adopting a baby boy with him when it became apparent that they were unable to have their own child. And their partnership through those years produced some of Orwell's greatest works.

Orwell's life before meeting Eileen has been thoroughly documented. Born in India on 25 June 1903 to a father in the Indian Civil Service, he was sent away at the age of eight to St Cyprian's, a school he claimed to have hated, then at thirteen to Eton College, where most of the pupils were expected to proceed to university and then on to rewarding careers. Orwell rejected this future, instead enduring five years in Burma with the Indian Imperial Police, then struggling through his late twenties and early thirties in Paris and London, learning how to write.

But what had Eileen been doing through all her first twenty-nine years?

It turns out she was living a far more interesting early life than had been imagined, a life that developed all the talent and experience and psychological skills to make her a perfect partner for Orwell. He was wise enough to immediately recognise and appreciate those qualities. And, in the course of their marriage, he made great use of them.

Eileen's parents, Laurence O'Shaughnessy and Mary Westgate, were both thirty-four when they married in 1900, and how they found each other in Gravesend is an intriguing mystery.

Laurence O'Shaughnessy died six years before Orwell entered Eileen's life, so he is scarcely a presence in their marriage, or in the

Orwell biographies. But, besides being a dominant person in her upbringing, he had an exceptional history, including a family – a father he had much admired and several interesting brothers and sisters – that Eileen would have definitely told Orwell about. In Ireland the name is pronounced 'O'Shocknessy', a version favoured by Eileen's father as she was growing up. Later, her brother and her nephew each tried to get the family to continue using what they called the 'correct' pronunciation, even as most family members resisted.[5] It's not known what Eileen preferred.

Laurence was born on Valentia Island in County Kerry, a tiny island on the south-western tip of Ireland, on 24 January 1866. The O'Shaughnessy name has been traced back to AD 358,[6] and two O'Shaughnessy castles are still open to visitors near Gort, in County Galway. In the nineteenth century there were some land-owning O'Shaughnessys scattered through Limerick.[7] However, the branch of O'Shaughnessys that Eileen's father was born into was far from those upper classes.

Laurence's father, Edward O'Shaughnessy, was born in 1827. He was a labourer in County Limerick when he enlisted in the Royal Irish Constabulary, the national police organisation, in September 1848, at the age of twenty.[8] Young Catholic men at that time often became policemen when no other jobs were available, and this was a dire time in Ireland: the country was in the midst of the Great Famine, and a strong movement was brewing for Irish independence from Great Britain. The superiors in the Constabulary were most often Protestants, and the police officers, usually Catholics, were there to uphold the status quo and keep control of any potential uprisings. But the young Catholic recruits were often not fully aware of the Constabulary's grand design of maintaining British control of Ireland and saw themselves as just preserving peace and order.[9] If they did have any sympathy for Irish independence, they kept those beliefs to themselves.

The requirements for admission to the Royal Irish Constabulary included a letter of reference from a prominent local resident, a minimum age of twenty, and a minimum height of 5 feet 9 inches. Edward is listed as only 5 feet 7¾, a clear 1¼ inches too short. Custom allowed sons of members of the Constabulary to be 5 feet 8, but there is no record of Edward's father being a policeman. Perhaps the recent famine had wiped out a lot of eligible young men, necessitating a few exceptions to this rule? A large girth is also mentioned as a requirement, so perhaps Edward was exceptionally well built.[10]

Once a young man was accepted and trained in the Constabulary, there were other rules to observe: he was forbidden to get married until he had served seven years, his wife had to be from a different county from his, and he would always be stationed outside his and his wife's native counties. Edward married Mary Doyle, age twenty-seven, a native of County Cork, in 1858. He was stationed in County Kerry, beginning on 1 November 1850, and since the members of the Constabulary and their families were constantly moved from town to town, this couple's seven children were born in different locations.

Edward O'Shaughnessy was continually promoted, going from First Class Sub-Constable to Acting Constable, to full Constable – the highest rank allowed for a Roman Catholic – in July 1867, when he was stationed on Valentia Island. On 24 November 1870, after he had been moved to Shannachill, something must have happened demanding disciplinary action against him, since he was 'Rep. Severely'. While specific records for this kind of 'reprimand' no longer exist, according to an expert at the Police Service of Northern Ireland, this would have been a less severe punishment than a fine, a demotion, or dismissal, however.[11]

The couple had succeeded in bringing three daughters and four sons into the world, the last one in 1871, when Edward died suddenly on 10 August 1872, aged forty-five. His death certificate gives the cause of death as 'Hematemasis' [sic], and the duration of the illness as ten days. Hematemesis is defined as 'the vomiting of blood', often a symptom of acute gastrointestinal bleeding. Considering his job as a police officer, it seems possible that the bleeding could have been caused by a wound of some sort. However, since one of his sons died at thirty-seven and his granddaughter, our Eileen, died at thirty-nine, there might have been a family infirmity that was passed on through the generations. Edward left behind his widow and seven children, aged one to eleven, including Eileen's father, Laurence, who was only six years old when his father died.

Edward O'Shaughnessy and his wife, Mary, who died in 1905, are both buried in the Killorglin Catholic graveyard, in County Kerry. Their tombstone inscription reads: 'Sacred to the memory of Edward O'Shaughnessy, Sgt. R.I.C. died 10 Aug. 1872, age 45 years, and his wife Mary died Apr. 29, 1905, aged 74 years, erected by his sorrowing wife A.D. 1872.'[12]

Eileen's grandmother Mary received a payment of £98 15s 9d at the time of Edward's death, as well as an annual pension of two months' pay for every year of service up to fifteen years.[13] This would amount to between £86 and £104 a year, on account of his over twenty years of service,[14] a sum which can be roughly converted to £4,500 today. With this income, Mary O'Shaughnessy was able to provide her children with some education, and their lives consequently developed in intriguing directions. Each of them was proud of their father, listing him variously as 'Royal Irish Constabulary', 'Police Constable', and 'Sargeant'. A few of these six aunts and uncles of Eileen's became quite prominent citizens, and Eileen would surely have entertained Orwell with stories of their distinguished lives.

Edward and Mary O'Shaughnessy's first child, Mary Anne (sometimes spelled Marianne), born in 1861, was perhaps the most conventional. She married John C. O'Sullivan on 21 August 1890, and produced nine children. One was called Eileen, a name used by other family members too. No doubt there was a favourite Aunt Eileen somewhere in their lives.

Edward and Mary's second child, Lizzie, was born in 1863 on Valentia Island, where she lived for many years. She was head teacher at the National School in Knightstown[15] before she married Thomas

O'Donoghue, around 1892. O'Donoghue was a 'telegraphist', an occupation introduced on Valentia Island when the first transatlantic telegraph cable was successfully laid there in 1858, connecting the island and Heart's Content, Newfoundland, thereby establishing for the first time a permanent communication link between Europe and America. Valentia was thus transformed from a remote island of farmers to an essential centre for telegraph transmissions. In 1901, Lizzie was living at 57 Farranreagh in Knightstown, with her husband and their three children, along with two servants.

Also in the household, alive and well and listed in the census as age sixty-four, was old Mary O'Shaughnessy, Eileen's grandmother. Since she was seventy-four when she died in 1905, she would have been seventy in 1901, so either the census taker made a mistake or she was lying about her age.[16]

The third child and daughter, Margaret, born on 8 February 1864, had a spectacular life. In 1883 the Reverend Mother of the Charity of the Incarnate Word, based in San Antonio, Texas, was in dire need of new members for her mission. She made a trip through Europe that year and recruited fifteen girls from Ireland to take back to Texas with her. One of them was nineteen-year-old Margaret O'Shaughnessy. Margaret was being educated by the Presentation nuns to be a teacher in the schools of her district when she signed up to go to Texas.[17] The Irish priests tried to discourage the young girls from going to Texas, frightening them with tales of the hardships of mission life, but Margaret was not deterred.[18]

In a 1925 account of the mission in Texas, Margaret was described as having a 'versatile mind' and was praised for encouraging the sisters of the congregation in the study of 'science, letters, and arts' throughout her fifty-five years there.[19] She was remembered as 'dignified in her speech, proper in her bearing, and exacting and strict about observance of the rule'. Because she was also said to be 'very nervous and demands too much perfection of the sisters . . . perhaps a little too severe', many of her students 'avoided passing the door of her office to offset the chance of another correction' for their failings.[20] These personality traits resemble those of her brother Laurence, Eileen's father, as well as those of Eileen's brother, Eric.

Margaret took the name Mother Mary John, and she visited the continent and Ireland in 1900, returning to Texas with sixty-three young girls as 'candidates',[21] and again in 1923, when she brought back eleven girls from Ireland.[22] From 1911 to 1922, 160 young women made the journey to Texas from Ireland, far more than from any other country. When Eileen was in high school she was intrigued by mission work, and of course knew many details about her Aunt Margaret.

In June 1918, when the current Reverend Mother retired, Margaret, aged fifty-four, was elected to the highest office, Superioress General of the Congregation,[23] the first Irish woman ever to attain this office. A photograph of her just after she was promoted shows a woman with the attractive looks that were common in her family, with features and a slight smirk reminiscent of her niece Eileen, including her need for glasses for short-sightedness, although Eileen hardly ever wore hers. Margaret served in this capacity until 1930, when her second term was completed. Her influence on the mission was so strong that the next four heads of the Congregation were Irish.[24]

By 1925, when a history of the Congregation of the Sisters of Charity of the Incarnate Word was written, it had grown to 'seven hundred and eighty-three members employed in seventy-four establishments'.[25] Margaret was a prime founder of the College of the Incarnate Word, as well as of several other new institutions, and the University of the Incarnate Word is now the largest Catholic university in Texas. So by any standards, little Margaret O'Shaughnessy, the daughter of an Irish constable, had made a huge success of her life. When she died in 1938, aged seventy-four, she was considered so distinguished that her death was recorded in the newspapers: 'She accomplished great work for the Congregation and was beloved by the nuns at San Antonio.'[26]

Her two Irish sisters, Mary Anne and Lizzie, were both considered prominent enough to be mentioned in one newspaper article, as was her brother Edward, Laurence's younger brother, who had died in 1905. Eileen's father, Laurence, had died nine years earlier and was not listed as a brother in the papers. Nor had he been mentioned in his brother Edward's newspaper memorials thirty-three years earlier. He was a judgmental and demanding man, and not easy to live with.[27] He was also the only brother who worked for the British government and the only one who married a Protestant English woman, apparently not practising his Catholic faith. So perhaps he wasn't a favourite member of the family.

Eileen's father, Laurence, was the fourth child, born in 1866; his story will be dealt with later. Next was Edward and Mary's second son, Edward, who was born in July 1868 in Shannachill, in County Kerry, shortly after his father was commissioned there. Like their sister Margaret, Edward also achieved some prominence. He moved to London around 1889, and was quickly married on 13 June 1891, to Mary Egan, the daughter of a 'Customs Officer'. (Accidental research uncovered the curious detail that Edward's wife-to-be lived at 11 Maidman Street, Burdett Road, only a few doors away from 19 Maidman Street, the home of one of Jack the Ripper's attempted murder victims, in 1888.) Edward, then aged twenty-two, had a literary calling, listing himself as a 'Journalist' on the wedding certificate.

Edward's journalistic ambitions were swiftly rewarded, and by 1901 the couple were living at 133 Elms Road, in the genteel district of Clapham, in south-west London, with one son and five daughters, one of them another Eileen. Edward was so well loved by his colleagues that '[H]e was elected Chairman of the Press Gallery in the House of Commons [in 1904], being the youngest member and the only Irishman ever elected to the position.'[28] In that job he transcribed everything that was said in Parliament every day it was in session, and his typed copies were published in the *Official Report*.[29]

Edward's career advanced swiftly, and by 1905 he was the London correspondent for the *Irish Independent*, a newspaper just founded that January, a direct successor of the *Daily Irish Independent*, where he had been a reporter. The *Irish Independent* favoured self-government for

Ireland and was geared to predominantly middle-class Catholic readers. In his first column that January, Edward tackled twelve different topics with ease and fluidity of style, beginning with: 'The opening of the New Year is being greeted very optimistically in London, especially in commercial circles. Truth to tell, 1904 was desperately disappointing . . . An immense crowd congregated in the vicinity of St Paul's Cathedral to await the midnight chimes [but] police interference, except in the capture of the almost inevitable pickpocket, was not required. The joy of the jubilators when a member of the slim-fingered fraternity was being marched off was immense.' He continued with a report on a new music hall: 'The Lyceum Theatre . . . was opened as a music hall on Saturday. Regret at its artistic decadence is tempered with the knowledge that as a music hall it is exceptionally entertaining.'[30] To write such a column every day, plus act as a reporter at Parliament and transcribe all his shorthand notes must have taken considerable skill and energy.

But luck abruptly ran out for Edward on 18 July 1905, just a few days after his thirty-seventh birthday. His death certificate lists 'Cardiac Dilatation, Hepatic Congestion Syncope' as the cause of death, while one newspaper reported 'heart failure, following an illness of the heart, due to two attacks of rheumatic fever'. According to another article, 'His health up to a short time ago had been as robust as his life had been active. But then came an illness that made him just a shadow of his former self. He came over to Ireland and spent some time in his native town of Cahirciveen trying to recruit [sic].'[31] While most of his brothers and sisters lived into their seventies and eighties, he must have inherited the weak constitution that ran in his family, the same fragility that was passed on to Eileen.

Newspaper articles reporting on Edward's sudden death were extravagant in their praise of him. He was described as 'one of the finest types of Irish journalists in the great English Metropolis, and one of the most popular'; 'a splendid specimen of Irish manhood, tall, athletically built, of gentlemanly deportment, and with all the brightness of intellect peculiar to the sons of his native "Kingdom" of Kerry'. For many years a photograph of him hung in one of the journalists' rooms in the House of Commons Press Gallery. The newspaper reports went on to say, 'He was one of the earliest members of the Irish Literary Society [founded in 1892 by William Butler Yeats, as an avenue to introduce Irish literature to the English public].'[32]

Edward's funeral, the papers noted, 'was found to be simply packed – another tribute to the popularity of our late colleague. It was noticeable, too, that there were several poor old Irish women present to whom in his life-time Mr. O'Shaughnessy had been a benefactor.'[33]

Besides apparently possessing all the glorious attributes it was possible to bestow on an Irishman, Edward exhibited one other unusual skill: 'As a stenographer he was probably one of the most expert, if not, indeed, the most expert in the Three Kingdoms, his speed in writing the mystic characters being something phenomenal . . . His speed reached the extraordinary rate of 263 words a minute.'[34] These days, a speed of 100 words a minute is considered quite respectable.

This is a fascinating titbit. We know that Eileen – besides inheriting this Irish charm, as well as, perhaps, a very weak constitution – was also, coincidentally, an exceptional stenographer. Edward died just two months before Eileen was born, and a case could perhaps be made that she took the place of this beloved brother in her father Laurence's eyes.

Edward and Mary O'Shaughnessy's sixth child, Michael, was baptised on 27 March 1870, while his father was still stationed in Shannachill. He went to London at an early age to join his two older brothers, working first in the offices of the British South Africa Company and later for the London Tramway Department. Birth records state that on 29 May 1900 a daughter, Eileen Gertrude Frances, was born to a Michael O'Shaughnessy and Hannah Ronaye (possibly a misspelling of 'Ronayne') in Greenwich, close to where Michael's brother Laurence had married Eileen's mother three months earlier. Neither Hannah nor Eileen Gertrude Frances is easily found in any other ancestry records, and by 1901 our Michael was living alone at 41 Ravensdon Street in Lambeth. Perhaps his wife and daughter had suddenly died.

In 1905, when Michael was living at 1 Jeffreys Road, South Lambeth, he was the 'informant' of his brother Edward's death. That was a terrible spring for Michael, who, less than three months earlier, had gone to Ireland to be a witness at his mother's (Eileen's grandmother's) death. His newspaper obituary, on 17 January 1930, described him as 'a well-known and much respected member of the London-Irish community . . . He was unmarried . . . His passing will be widely deplored in London.' The fact that he was unmarried when he died lends credence to the possibility that his wife and daughter had indeed died years earlier.

Patrick, the last of the O'Shaughnessy children, was born on 8 October 1871. On 29 December 1872, only four months after his father had died, his mother reported Patrick's death from a two-month bout of measles and whooping cough.

The middle child of Edward O'Shaughnessy and Mary Doyle was Laurence, Eileen's father, born on 24 January 1866. He first showed up in England in 1885, the year of his entrance, aged nineteen, into Her Majesty's Customs Department as a 'First Class Out-Doors Officer'. In 1891, by then twenty-five, he was living in Limehouse, at 19 East India Dock Road, boarding with the family of Thomas Ducas, a 'Retired Lighterman' (a highly skilled operator of a barge called a lighter, onto which boats unloaded their goods while anchored in the middle of the Thames). Laurence and two other Irish boarders were 'Clerks in Her Majesty's Customs'.

While living there, Laurence acted as a witness at the wedding of his brother Edward, the journalist. Edward's wife was the daughter of a Customs Officer, suggesting that Laurence might have introduced the couple. According to the 1892 *Ham's Book* (which records information about members of the Customs Department, but always relevant to the preceding year, therefore 1891), Laurence was still an 'Out-Door Officer, First Class'. No exact location was recorded, but as an Out-Door Officer, he would have spent much time on the water, and at that point Mary Westgate, his future wife and Eileen's mother, was working as a teacher right across the Thames.

However, the following year, now a second-class clerk, Laurence was transferred to the Customs Department in Hartlepool, way north on the County Durham coast, and he remained there through 1898. The next year, he was transferred even farther north, to Sunderland, still as a second-class clerk. By 1900, Laurence had spent fifteen years in the Customs Department, with a consistent annual increase in salary. If he did meet Mary years earlier, when he was living across the river from where she worked, his promotion to Sunderland might have convinced him that he was finally financially stable enough to propose to her, and they were married on 7 February 1900. He believed he had a future in Sunderland, and he was ready to settle down there with a wife and children. But there was a huge shock in store for his family: almost immediately after setting up house with his new wife, Laurence was instead transferred to a remote outpost.

Eileen's mother, Mary Westgate, had had an unusual life before she married Laurence. Her parents, Mary Ann Mickleburgh, age twenty-five, and David Westgate, age twenty-four, were married in Hempnall, just outside Norwich, on 30 March 1865, and Eileen's mother was born soon after, on 27 December 1865. Tragically, Mary Ann died on 10 January 1866, just two weeks after giving birth, with the cause of death listed as 'Confinement, Exhaustion 14 days'.

David Westgate – who was born on 28 August 1840, and listed himself as a 'Farmer' on his daughter's birth certificate – was perhaps a completely unknown grandfather for Eileen. After his wife's sudden death, David decided not to stay in the community to raise his infant daughter by himself. Instead, he left Eileen's mother Mary to be brought up by his deceased wife's parents, James and Ann Mickleburgh. In 1871, James, a prominent member of the community, owned 265 acres, employing nine men, two boys, and two women. In 1883 he and, interestingly, David's own father, Samuel Westgate, a 'Maltster' (a master in the production of malt for alcoholic beverages), were listed as two of the thirteen most influential people of their area.[35]

It appears that David Westgate made a complete separation from his daughter. By 1881, he was living in Nottingham and working as an 'Ostler' (a man who looked after horses at an inn). In 1883, then forty-three and working as an 'Omnibus driver', he married a widow, Susannah Tingey.[36] On 27 May 1910, at the age of sixty-nine, David died in the Nottingham Union Workhouse, of 'Bronchitis, Emphesema [sic], and Heart Failure'. However, he had been admitted straight into the infirmary; there is no record of his ever being admitted to the workhouse as a pauper. He was buried in the Dissenters section of the Nottingham General Cemetery,[37] the section set aside for those who were not members of the Church of England.

Eileen's grandfather, therefore, did not live the life of the 'Gentleman' that Mary Westgate listed him to be on her wedding certificate. In fact, she also gave him the wrong first name, leading to a few questions. Had Eileen's grandmother, Mary Ann, precipitously married David Westgate after getting pregnant, and had the Mickleburghs kept his history secret from their granddaughter? Did David leave his comfortable life voluntarily, or was he perhaps disinherited by his family? Although he didn't die until Eileen was four, sadly there's no record of David's having kept track of his daughter and two grandchildren.

Mary Westgate, Eileen's mother, was sent off to boarding school in Great Yarmouth, in 1881, at the age of fifteen. Also in the school household were four other girls, including her cousin Annie Westgate, the daughter of David's brother, so it appears that David's relatives back in Norwich were prospering. By 1891, at the age of twenty-five, Mary was one of two assistant teachers at the Lewisham High Road School in Deptford, south-east London, with a total of sixty-eight female pupils, mostly between the ages of fourteen and eighteen. This was the school where Mary was teaching when Laurence O'Shaughnessy was living and stationed just across the Thames.

Sometime before her marriage, in 1900, Mary Westgate moved to a small boarding house at 46 Harmer Street in Gravesend.[38] The Holy Trinity Church, where the couple were married, was around the corner from this house. Built in 1845, it soon became 'the fashionable church in the town', with a congregation that 'included a large proportion of the more prosperous waterside community – pilots, customs officers, and watermen, with their families'.[39] At the turn of the century the town of Gravesend was dominated by people dependent, in one way or another, upon the Thames.

Many theories could be developed for exactly how Eileen's parents met. However the particulars developed, in 1900 two attractive, intelligent, well-educated people from opposite ends of the British Isles found themselves together in the small town of Gravesend. They were both thirty-four when they married, with respectable, well-paying jobs, and they each must have had ample opportunity to marry earlier. Judging from pictures of her in her sixties, Mary would have been a beautiful young woman, and Laurence, if he at all resembled his brother Edward or his sister Margaret, was surely an attractive catch.

It would not have been uncommon for a man like Laurence to wait until he was thirty-four and settled in a job before getting married. It was less usual for a woman, but Mary might have been hesitating about choosing a life of marriage and children with the troubling knowledge that her own mother had died in childbirth. Whatever the reasons, the pairing of these two complicated people with their difficult backgrounds and strong personalities resulted in the creation of two extraordinary children.

Laurence O'Shaughnessy and Mary Westgate were married in the Holy Trinity Church in Gravesend on 7 February 1900, by Vicar Francis Clement Naish. It was Church of England, not Catholic, as Laurence had been raised, but that was Mary's religion and the church of her choice, and Laurence went along with her wishes. If he was still a Catholic, he would have asked for a 'dispensation' in order to marry a non-Catholic.[40]

This unlikely couple never intended to make their home in Gravesend, an unfortunate name for any town, no matter how insistent today's inhabitants are that it derives its name from 'grafs-ham', a place 'at the end of the grove.' At the time of the wedding, Laurence was working in Sunderland, 269 miles north of London, and living at 62 Herrington Street, where Miss Jane Bell was letting out furnished apartments. Mary joined him there.

Their son, Laurence Frederick, was born in Sunderland on 24 December 1900. He got his second name from his mother's cousin, Frederick Mickleburgh, and went all his life by the name Eric. By 31 March 1901, Laurence and Mary and their infant son had set up home in Sunderland at 109 Cleveland Road, no doubt expecting some stability in their lives. But things were not going to be so easy: almost immediately Laurence was transferred back to Hartlepool for a year. That must have been upsetting enough, but it was minor compared to the shock that came next. Unexpectedly, Laurence was 'promoted' to 'Clerk in Charge' of the tiny Customs Department at Lerwick, in the Shetland Islands. Laurence and his family arrived in Lerwick on 12 July 1902.[41] They were to live on this remote northern outpost for the next three years.

As 'Clerk in Charge', Laurence had only one assistant and one or two boatmen on his staff. The job consisted mainly of navigating the island's coastline, trying to stop any illegal movement of goods or alcohol. The community depended partially on smuggled material, and Laurence's job would often entail stopping small boats while still at sea and confiscating, or at least charging a fine for, anything he deemed illegal. Obviously the customs official would not have been overly popular, and in a book published at that time, a piece of dialogue includes this warning: 'The Customs man has wind of your eight boxes. He'll be aboard of you in fifteen minutes.'[42] A history of Shetland points out that citizens at that time would define 'outsiders' 'not as foreigners but as the military officers, the Customs Collectors and the kirk minister.'[43] Therefore the O'Shaughnessy family, already extreme outsiders, would not have been generously accepted into this inward-looking community. Laurence was promoted to 'Chief Officer' in his last year there, but he still had only one assistant and two boatmen on his staff.

Mary O'Shaughnessy, with her background as a respected teacher, and so elegant in the photo that has survived of her, could not have been prepared for the rugged, challenging life that awaited her family in Lerwick. This era of the O'Shaughnessy saga is nowhere mentioned, and perhaps they thought it better forgotten. Yet, although there is no family record of those adventurous first years of her parents' marriage, Eileen would surely have heard stories. Eric most likely had a few vivid memories of his three years as a small child on that wild island, and it would be wonderful to know details of his adventures. It can only be a coincidence that Eileen and Orwell's adopted son, Richard Blair, spent a similar spell of isolation as a small child, on a similar gorgeous but desolate island, Jura.

Scarcely two months after the O'Shaughnessys' arrival in Lerwick, no doubt because of the dangers involved in the job, Laurence made out his will:

> *This is the Will of me, Laurence O'Shaughnessy of H. M. Customs Lerwick Shetland Islands. I appoint my wife Mary O'Shaughnessy of Lerwick Shetland Islands Executrix of this my Will. I give and devise all my remaining Estate and effects real and personal of which I may die possessed or entitled to including any moneys due from the Customs Annuity and Benevolent fund unto my said wife for her sole and separate use. And I hereby revoke all former Wills, and Codicils.*

Far away in County Kerry, Laurence's mother died on 29 April 1905. But Laurence, still mastering his skills in the far north, would not have been able to get enough time off to travel the many days it would have taken to attend her funeral.

After three years in the Shetland Islands, Laurence, now with a young son and a pregnant wife, petitioned for a more civilised post for his growing family. And as a result, he was happily promoted to Head Collector and Surveyor of Customs in South Shields, back in northeast England. At this port, customs officials regulated traffic at the mouth of the River Tyne, a few miles downriver from the important shipping city of Newcastle. Counting back the months, Eileen must have been conceived on a freezing December night in Lerwick.

A page from Eileen's father's South Shields Customs Ledger, listing expenses for the Customs House plus charges for certain 'offences' by ships he had checked.

Laurence, his very pregnant wife, and four-year-old Eric arrived in South Shields in June 1905 and settled temporarily into an apartment that a minister was renting out. But their troubles were not over. On the night of 19 July, barely a month later, Laurence precipitately left South Shields for London, sending a hurried telegram the following day:

> *Honourable Sirs,*
> *I respectfully request leave of absence for five days,*
> *commencing on this date and ending on Tuesday the 25th inst.*
> *I submit that Mr. A. Rhind, Second Class Clerk and*

Second Officer, may act as Collector, and that Mr. G. A. Smith,
Examining Officer, Second Class, may act as second officer.

In the event of assistance being needed, I submit that
a Second Class Clerk may be sent to South Shields by the
Collector at Newcastle, who is aware of my absence.

I respectfully request that a telegram may be sent to me at
the under-mentioned address, should the above arrangements
be approved.

Respectfully submitted, L. O'Shaughnessy, Collector.

This infuriated his new bosses, who demanded an explanation when he returned, one of them saying, 'The Collector at South Shields should have given longer notice of his proposed absence to enable the proper arrangements to be made,' while another added, 'I quite agree & think we should have a full explanation of the very inconvenient & unusual action taken by the Collector.'

But Laurence had an excellent explanation. Edward, his talented, popular younger brother, had died, aged just thirty-seven. Laurence had clearly stayed in close touch with his brother and, perhaps dismayed that he had missed his mother's funeral a few months earlier, had risked his new promotion to be with his brother one more time.

On 24 July 1905 he left a long report in the Collector's Manual, beginning:

Honourable Sirs,

In accordance with your order of the 21st inst, I beg to report
that I have resumed duty on this date.

The circs that have given rise to my request for leave are as
follows:–

On Tuesday evg, the 18th inst, I received a telegram
informing me of the unexpected death of a brother in London.
On Wednesday, I made arrangements for my temporary
absence during the 20th & 21st inst, in anticipation that

> *the funeral would be over and that I could resume duty on*
> *the 22nd. I was satisfied that the work of the port would be*
> *efficiently carried on during my short absence.*[44]

Laurence O'Shaughnessy's excuse proved good enough to assuage his superiors, and he settled down for twenty years as head of the South Shields Customs Department, giving him job security and instantly making his family one of the most prominent in town.

2

Head Girl at High School

*Full of commonsense and initiative; Eileen has
developed in a very satisfactory way.*
Sunderland High School report, 1922

Eileen Maud O'Shaughnessy was born on 25 September 1905, and her father's promotion in June of that year happened at exactly the right moment to allow Eileen to begin her life in the booming town of South Shields rather than in the isolation of the Shetland Islands. She was the fourth girl to be named Eileen in this family of at least eighteen cousins: one Eileen was born in Dublin and two others in London. Her second name can't be definitely traced. Maud was the middle name of one of the Westgate cousins on Eileen's mother's side of the family. Also, Maud Gonne was an activist for Irish home rule around that time. But it was possibly just a romantic choice by her mother, after a popular turn-of-the-century love song based on Tennyson's poem 'Maud'.

South Shields is still a small city, even smaller now than it was in 1905. A visitor today might be told of Muhammad Ali's thrilling visit in 1977, or about Sting being born in Newcastle, and Eric Idle in South Shields itself. But the fact that George Orwell's first wife, Eileen

O'Shaughnessy, spent the first nineteen years of her life there is not commonly known.

It was a fairly recent policy in 1905 to give the job of Collector of Customs to a professional civil servant who had spent his career being moved from city to city rather than to promote a local man. It was assumed that this outside person would not get caught up in local prejudices and would be more able to handle problems from a professional distance. Thus, the O'Shaughnessy family arrived in town as strangers, with no local connections or friends. However, after already serving twenty years in the Customs Department, Laurence had acquired a healthy income, a small staff to lead, the high standing that came with his new position, and total job security. The village son of an Irish policeman was now a prosperous man. Orwell liked to microdefine his own class as 'lower-upper-middle', and 'the O'Shaughnessys were a shade more securely placed than the Blairs', as one biographer put it.[1] Eileen's parents were both thirty-nine when they finally settled in South Shields, and the family remained there until Laurence's retirement, in 1925.

The day Eileen was born, her family were temporarily residing at 3 Park Terrace (now part of Lawe Road), a short-rental establishment, with furnished rooms for newcomers or visitors to town. In 1901, a 'commercial traveller' was also staying there with his wife and four children, while two other rooms were let to a 'theatre proprietor' and to a man 'living on own means'. The building faced the newly developed North Marine Park, with its bowling green, tennis ground, and bandstand, and was a short walk from North Sea beaches and the glorious mile-long promenade to the lighthouse at the far end of the South Pier. But the block Eileen was born on was losing its prestige, with the houses next door also renting out apartments to commercial travellers. Just around the corner, on what is now Ocean Road, private homes were being transformed into small hotels and boarding houses to handle the increase of visitors attracted by the new swimming and sunbathing possibilities that South Shields was creating on its way to a future as a seaside resort town. Popular Middle Eastern restaurants also began opening in this area, run by descendants of the Yemeni British seamen who had settled there in the early 1900s.

A more fashionable district was developing a little farther south, where the streets were 'wide, well lighted with gas and electricity and paved'.[2] And within a year the O'Shaughnessy family was ensconced in a large Victorian house at 2 Ravensbourne Terrace (now part of Beach Road). In the early 1900s, each residential block in South Shields had its own individual name, almost always with the elegant ending 'Terrace'. It's impossible to find most of these 'Terrace' addresses today without consulting old maps and business directories, since those original 'Terrace' names have been combined into long streets, with consecutive house numbers. Current South Shields residents aren't familiar with most of the old 'Terrace' names, and even taxi drivers who have been working there for many years have no idea how to find them.

The house on Ravensbourne Terrace was impressive, but somehow not satisfactory for this aspiring family. They wanted a brand-new home, and they chose one being built on the empty site between Nos 2 and 3 Wellington Terrace, just a few streets away. When the O'Shaughnessys moved in, in 1908, it was one of the newest homes in town. The eleven-room house was spacious and elegant, three storeys high, with magnificent arched windows facing the street. The property was situated right in the centre of the most fashionable part of South Shields and included grand side and back gardens, as well as stables in the rear, with a separate entrance, with its own bell, for the servants.[3]

Circumstances demanded that the new building have the address 2½ Wellington Terrace, and that's how it was listed in the roll books of city residents. Their nearest neighbours, at 2 Wellington Terrace, were six single, middle-aged sisters, and attached to that building was the Society of Friends Meeting House, a large hall seating 250 people. But the O'Shaughnessy family never bothered to use that awkward number 2½. Instead, their luxurious new home was called 'Westgate House', using Eileen's mother's maiden name. Perhaps she regretted having to give up the name she'd used for thirty-four years, not having the option then of keeping it after marriage. Christening their new home Westgate House must have been a proud moment for Mary. It was somewhat audacious for the family to eliminate any street number for their new home; the majority of South Shields houses of that time were listed simply with the owner's name and the street number on the Terrace.[4] But Eileen always wrote her address as: Westgate House, Wellington Terrace, South Shields, sometimes even leaving out the Terrace name, and with no mention ever of that 2½.

The name Westgate House is still engraved in the glass over the front door of the old O'Shaughnessy home, although its correct address today is 35 Beach Road. The present owner kindly allowed visitors into his home, proudly pointing out one of the gorgeous arched windows that the O'Shaughnessys had requested, although the others had been replaced and were stored on the top floor.[5]

Laurence O'Shaughnessy worked diligently. The large customs ledgers are full of his hand-written notes about activities and ideas for improvement. His handwriting suggests a man with a strong will who was 'tough, persistent, diligent, and determined.'[6] He expected a lot of himself and just as much of others. He got fully involved in the minutiae of his responsibilities and wasn't afraid to suggest innovative changes to the wasteful way the office had been run before his arrival.

One of his early concerns was the inefficiency of the Uniform Committee. After two of his assistants' coats had to be returned for 'necessary alterations', he complained that '[N]o record of such alterations is made in the original measurements kept by the Contractors.' His logical suggestion was: 'In cases in which the officers desire it, they should be allowed to forward . . . a record of their measurements taken by a local tailor. This procedure would conduce to a better fit and would probably in many cases eliminate the necessity of returning misfits to the Contractor.'[7] His most common activities involved taxing imports and apprehending smugglers. At one point he detailed the discovery of 'a cask of spirits' hidden on an incoming ship, a fairly typical occurrence. As he wrote in the ledger: 'The cask formed part of a consignment of stones brought from Norway . . . bound to Algoa Bay.' The solution in this case was a five-shilling fine.[8]

The old Customs House where Laurence worked all those years has been transformed today into 'one of the leading cultural venues in the North', with a popular bar/restaurant, a large theatre where touring bands perform, an art gallery, and a cinema. But there are many rugged individuals left in South Shields. When the New York Dolls went there recently to perform, one owner of a bed and breakfast proudly refused to book them because they wouldn't guarantee not to smoke in their rooms.

In the census taken in 1911, when Eileen was six, the family is listed as employing a twenty-five-year-old governess, Florence Watt, as well as one 'domestic servant'. In that census, as well as in 1901, Eileen's mother was listed as Marie, possibly a mistake caused by Laurence's Irish accent, or else yet another attempt by Mary to add elegance to the household.

Eileen's mother centred her life around her children, making sure they got the best education available. Having been a schoolteacher, she had strict ideas about how she wanted them raised. Laurence Frederick, who went by the name Eric, was always considered brilliant. He was close to his mother, who was remembered as 'domineering'.[9] As an adult, Eric was described as stern and demanding, traits his father too displayed, perhaps causing friction between father and son. Eileen, on the other hand, was closer to their father. She had a vivacious sense of humour, full of irony and teasing playfulness, apparent in her vibrant letters as well as in the memories of her friends. Although their father could be assertive and judgmental, he was also a lively, dynamic storyteller who could easily command an audience;[10] he and Eileen shared this trait. Perhaps she reminded him of his beloved brother Edward, full of 'brightness of intellect' and 'joyous spirits',[11] who had died just two months before Eileen was born.

Eileen's Irish father was clearly an outsider in South Shields, while her mother never lost her heavy Norfolk accent. So Eileen, starting with a bit of a local Geordie accent, had to develop her own northeast England approach to the world. Perhaps the area's soft lilting accent that she used through her early years helped create her calm, confident persona, what her friends perceived as her sometimes 'meandering' a bit, seemingly without purpose, yet always getting things done efficiently. However, after arriving as a student at Sunderland High School, aged ten, or perhaps even earlier, she would likely have been taught the strictly cultured accent known as Received Pronunciation.

Eileen's friend Lydia Jackson recorded her memories of Eileen and her family before they met Orwell, but Lydia never knew Eileen's father. He died in 1929, and some biographers assumed wrongly that he was a nonentity. Although Eileen's mother was remembered by others as a serious, unforgiving woman, Lydia saw her as 'a benevolent-looking, soft-spoken person', and she 'found it difficult to imagine that she and Eileen did not get on as Eileen had told me'.[12] She understood that Eileen's mother favoured her son, while Eileen was her father's favourite, and that apparently Eileen and her brother had a few conflicts when they were children. However, it seems they became quite close as adults.[13]

With Eric off at boarding school from an early age, coming home only for holidays, Eileen was alone with her mother much of the time, and the friction between them that was obvious later on no doubt started in South Shields. Eileen, who was very much a rebel as an adult, must have been a difficult child. Even then her brilliance and individuality would have been prominent. Both her parents demanded excellence from her, as she did from herself. Although she was expected to control her diverse moods, they quite likely erupted into occasional outbursts. Her untidy habits, which were evident throughout her life, started in these early years, as her school reports would show.

South Shields provided many possibilities for fun for a young girl of that time, including 'a bowling-green, tennis-ground and a band-stand, where music is provided twice weekly during the summer months', as well as 'an artificial lake two and a half acres in extent, used in the summer time for model yacht sailing and in winter for skating'.[14] The remains of a large Roman fort had been excavated in the north part of town, and the town museum during Eileen's time there contained intriguing articles gathered from the ruins of the fort, including sculpture, coins, cameos, and rings that indicated that the occupants of the original settlement had been quite well-to-do. South Shields was also proud of its imposing Theatre Royal, capable of seating an audience of 2,000, along with a renovated luxury cinema – called the Scala, after the just-opened grand cinema in London – with 'three cafés, a palm court, and hair-dressing rooms for both sexes'.[15] It's easy to imagine Eileen and her family watching Rudolph Valentino in *The Sheik* or Charlie Chaplin in *The Kid* in that upmarket setting. Photos of the time portray a lively, bustling town, with a large variety of shops bursting with goods, and mazes of tram tracks and their overhead electric wires crisscrossing at all the busy corners.

And of course there were the magnificent beaches, 'broad and clean', stretching many miles down the shore of the North Sea, with grand rock formations scattered along it. Marsden Rocks, the most spectacular, were 'of a bold, precipitous and romantic character', perhaps 100 feet at the base and over 70 feet high.[16] A photo of that time shows a precarious wooden staircase climbing up to the top of one rock formation, and from this high perch religious choirs would serenade worshippers gathered below. A huge number of early photos and picture postcards of South Shields have survived, including a lovely one showing a group of girls smiling as they climb a sandy hill from the beach, the North Sea spreading into the distance behind them. But the girls all have coats on, so it's not clear how much swimming was possible that day, though some people in the far distance do have their feet in the water.[17]

At some point well before she was ten, Eileen was enrolled in South Shields High School, a private school for girls, where she proved to be an excellent student. A newspaper reporting the results of the 'Cam. Local Examination, Dec. 15, South Shields High School' listed several names under 'Senior Honours', including 'E. O'Shaughnessy, distinguished in English' and 'passed in Spoken French'.[18]

The First World War did not cause much damage in South Shields, but over the night of 15 June 1915, Zeppelin airships attempted a strike on the town. The attack was diverted at the last minute, presumably because the skies barely got dark during the short summer nights. Of course the town's young men had enlisted to fight in the war, and an old photo shows hundreds of uniformed troops in a closely packed march along Ocean Road, a main street leading to the North Sea, where they were set to embark.

Eileen's father, close to fifty, was too old, and Eric, at fourteen, was too young to join at the beginning of the war. However, when he was fifteen, Eric 'insisted on leaving school, to do war work, and studied in coastguards' huts until he was old enough to begin reading medicine at Newcastle'.[19] He was a brilliant student and later won many scholarships, although he graduated with only second-class honours as Bachelor of Medicine and Bachelor of Surgery, in 1923.[20] When he was twenty-six, Eric was elected a Fellow of the Royal College of Surgeons, which meant that he was qualified to practise as a surgeon anywhere in the United Kingdom or Ireland.[21]

One of the legacies of Eileen's many years in the northeast was her relationship with weather. Knowing that part of the world intimately for nineteen years, she learned to endure, with a spirit of aplomb, the constant winds and rain and damp cheerlessness of the winters. The mile-long North and South Piers extending far out into the North Sea, at the entrance to the River Tyne, were there 'to protect vessels from the prevalent and destructive gales'. Her father's job was closely connected to the vagaries of the sea, and Eileen was aware of 'a watch-house [for use] on stormy nights, a room for ship-wrecked crews, and one containing a bath, drying closet and warm clothing'.[22] Dreadful weather was far more common than calm sunny days. Those constant wailing winds of her early life would have helped prepare Eileen for the rugged winters she and Orwell endured in their ill-equipped cottage during the early years of their marriage.

The weather is still a constant subject in South Shields, accepted always with a knowing chuckle, certainly not enough of a worry to cause a resident to take the trouble of moving away. Young girls like to dress in sleeveless blouses and scant sandals even though the wild wild ocean is only metres away. They frolic through the bleak evenings, past the weathered faces of their older neighbours, through the rain-soaked winds, laughing in accompaniment with the constant squawking seagulls. As in the Shetland Islands and other wild northern lands, there's a spirit, a determination to be thrilled, that's hard to resist. Eileen, as a young South Shields teenager, would have danced with her friends through the rainy evenings, daring anything as inconsequential as weather to make her miserable.

In September 1915, after some years with a governess and then at the junior school of South Shields High School, and just before her tenth birthday, Eileen was sent to the Sunderland Church High School, seven miles south, a school that was just beginning to make a name for itself in County Durham, under the headship of the Dickensianly named Edith Ironsides. By 1915, when Eileen arrived, there were over 200 girls enrolled in the school. On page 28 of the giant registry book, Eileen is listed as the 1,005th girl to enrol since the school had opened in 1884. The fathers of girls who joined the school the same year Eileen did were, like her own father, ambitious professionals: they included a Ship Merchant, Mechanical Engineer, Doctor of Medicine, Solicitor, and Brewer, as well as a couple of Clerks in Holy Orders. Regrettably, at the beginning of 2016, one hundred years after Eileen attended, it was decided to close the school for ever, owing to a large decrease in student enrolment. In July 2016, an

'Online Auction for Memorabilia' was held, and whatever objects were considered valuable were randomly scattered around the world.

Sunderland High School had the facilities for a small number of boarders, mostly for students from far-off cities, but Eileen had only a short distance to travel back and forth each day. Her family had a stable behind their home where they kept a horse and carriage. But Eileen probably walked to the nearby station every morning and boarded the Sunderland train with her fellow students from South Shields.

As was often the case with intelligent, educated women at that time, Miss Ironsides had opted for teaching over marriage. One former pupil remembered that she 'combined the organising ability of a Napoleon with the persuasive powers of a Delilah and the resistless energy of a steam-hammer'.[23] Her early 'Manifesto' stated: 'Our highest hope is to send out into the world a race of women of sane balanced mind . . . eager to read and form judgements for themselves . . . able to reason, able to listen; in short, women with training, and not ignorant, gossiping idle beings.' She also believed that 'happiness was an essential; without it children's work became mechanical and dull.' Miss Ironsides was rewarded by receiving the love of the students, being remembered by many for her personal kindness and her 'sheer unfaltering joy in the job itself'.[24]

The year Eileen arrived at the school, Miss Ironsides and her staff were in the process of developing a house system for the first time. The students in four different houses, each one including girls of all different ages and scholarly ability, would compete with each other in every possible field. Miss Ironsides had perceived a 'lack of cooperation and enthusiasm' of some of the girls, and this was an attempt to correct that. A map was drawn of Sunderland town and the areas nearby, with the High School at the centre. The surrounding areas were then divided into four pie shapes, extending out from the school centre – north, east, south, and west – and each given a name of an animal or bird: Swift, Drake, Tiger, and Panther. Eileen, living north of the school, was assigned to the 'Swift House', and that's where she stayed throughout her nine years as a pupil at the school.

A distinctive badge was designed for each house, and in the best surviving picture of Eileen as a young teenage schoolgirl, she is shown with the Swift House badge on her left chest. (Years later, when Orwell described Rosemary and Julia – two characters based partly on Eileen – as having 'swift movements', could this have been a secret signal to Eileen?) In this photo, Eileen and her classmate are wearing the new uniforms that were introduced just after the end of the First World War: navy blue box-pleated gym tunics, ending quite a bit above the knee, with loose bowed sashes around the waist, white blouses, and dark stockings. The girls are pictured without the ties that were sometimes required and without the white panama hats designed for summer wear. We can clearly see Eileen's inquisitive, confident personality; her legs are poised as if she is ready to dash away the minute the shot was taken.

Miss Ironsides encouraged constant competition among the four houses, and a large part of the *Chronicle*, the school magazine, was devoted to their rivalry, in such areas as Honours, singing, reading, acting, art, French, domestic science, conduct, and deportment, as well as in games, gymnastics, and other sports. A beautifully designed mahogany board, painted and decorated for each house, hung over a table where the cups most recently won by that house were proudly displayed. These much-desired cups, ranging in size from ones easily held in one hand to others a foot high, were awarded weekly in the endless competitions. Cup-winning contests became less important through the years, but the once precious cups themselves were never discarded. Instead, they were randomly tossed into huge cardboard boxes and sat sadly for years in an upstairs room full of other remnants of the school's past glories, all waiting for a patient historian to catalogue them. They were not listed as part of the auction memorabilia, and perhaps the decision was finally made to dispose of them.

It would have been difficult for some ten-year-olds to be suddenly thrust into this competitive world, but Eileen, with her lively sense of humour and intelligence, was quickly absorbed into the rhythms of the school. In the massive ledger that the teachers used for hand-written comments on students, to which they added twice a year, Eileen first appears in the Christmas 1915 report, shortly after she arrived at the school. She has assessments by three teachers: 'V. good: she has made a most promising beginning,' 'V.G.; untidiness lowers her standard,' and 'V.G. and her work is most promising but she spoils it with the extraordinarily careless habits of her every-day life.'

This is fascinating because these comments were made when Eileen was only ten years old, yet years later her friends were still constantly surprised by her apparent lack of concern for clothes and appearance in general. Other students were also judged, often with criticisms, such as 'inclined to be disobedient at times,' 'extraordinarily absent-minded,' 'a lazy girl,' 'so far she has not shown the slightest interest in her work or in the school,' and 'she still talks unduly.'

Two years later, Eileen's teachers were still frustrated by her slapdash ways: 'V.G. but really promising work is spoiled by lack of finish and of tidiness; at times this also applies to her personal appearance,' and 'Very good, but still dreadfully untidy.' Was Eileen being rebellious, as a pretty girl might be, pretending a disregard for appearance to upset her teachers and, perhaps more importantly, her mother? Or did she truly believe that her physical appearance was insignificant, and that putting

One teacher's assessment of Eileen, in the Sunderland High School 1917 Ledger. She notes that Eileen's work is 'spoiled by lack of finish and of tidiness,' adding, 'at times this also applies to her personal appearance.'

all her energy into her studies and moral development was far more important? Whatever her motives, she never changed, even long after she'd left home. When Orwell commented near the end of his life on the 'incorrigible dirtiness & untidiness' of women, he might very well have been remembering Eileen.

Throughout the school year there were many activities the girls were expected to participate in, but the only compulsory physical exercise was drill, taken outdoors every morning that the weather permitted.[25] New classes were introduced each year, and in 1914, at the beginning of the First World War, Miss Ironsides had added 'sewing and knitting soldiers' comforts' to the daily activities. She insisted that everyone take sewing lessons, explaining, 'The day surely is past when it was accepted that an educated woman was loftily "above" sewing and other home arts and crafts.'[26] So throughout the war Eileen helped supply clothing and small bags for various army needs.[27] And sewing was a handy skill for her later life with Orwell, when she made some of her own clothes in order to save money.

In 1916, the school proudly announced that class work had not been disrupted by the war, and as a demonstration of keeping strong in times of adversity, a grand performance of *A Midsummer Night's Dream* was staged to celebrate the tricentenary of Shakespeare's death. No record exists of which students took which roles, but Eileen performed in plays when she was at Oxford University and, with her vivacious personality, she most likely took part.

In 1918, when Eileen was thirteen, just as the war was ending, she was absent from school for many months, exactly at the time when a worldwide epidemic of what was labelled 'Spanish Flu' had broken out. It was assumed that ships full of soldiers returning to England from mainland Europe introduced the virus to their communities, and there was no real treatment for this devastating illness. Glasgow, a little over 100 miles to the northwest, was the first British city to suffer from this epidemic, and 228,000 people died in Britain within a few months. Overall, twenty to forty million people died of Spanish flu throughout the world, many more than had been killed in the war itself.

Eileen's teachers were upset that she had been absent from school for some time, and, as they recorded in the school ledger of 1918, they were afraid their brilliant student would fall behind: 'We much hope for an uninterrupted term,' and 'We much regret her absence which has made progress impossible.' Her illness was not identified, but it can be assumed that Eileen was home for some time suffering with a severe case of influenza.

By 1919, when Eileen had been back at school a while, her health recovered, her teachers were enthusiastic, writing: 'V.G. She has worked splendidly to make up for last term's absence as is clearly shown by her exam results.' But perhaps that illness contributed to her later health problems, and even to her possible infertility, which so disappointed her and Orwell after their marriage.

Eileen continued to develop her intellectual agility, pleasing her teachers, one of whom reported at Christmas 1920: 'Very good; she is growing in depth and strength.' In June 1921, under 'Prizes and Certificates, 1920,' Eileen won 'Senior Divinity. No refusals. Certificate in Inspector's Exam on Church Catechism.' According to recent officials at the school, her concentration on religious study was not required and would have been her personal choice. Since Eileen's parents don't appear to have been active churchgoers, this was an early exploration into which life choices Eileen might find acceptable, a quest she continued earnestly throughout her life. Her Aunt Margaret had recently been chosen as Superioress General of the Congregation of the Sisters of Charity of the Incarnate Word, in Texas. Eileen would have heard this news from her father and no doubt been impressed.

The first mention of Eileen in the *Chronicle*, the school magazine published every June and November, is in the 'Roll Call' section of the November 1916 issue, where her name is listed among twenty girls in Form IIIb. Starting with the November 1921 *Chronicle*, when Eileen was sixteen, her name began to appear more regularly. She was then sub-librarian as well as sub-prefect – an assistant to the teacher in charge of the library. And Swift House began to succeed in sports competitions, gaining possession of the much-desired Relay Race Cup as well as winning assorted creative competitions, from the Bean Bag File Race to Jumping the Shoe, although individual participants were not listed. In the Christmas 1921 ledger, Eileen's impressive development began to be noticed and praised effusively. One teacher wrote, '[Eileen] is growing in depth and in effectiveness and is achieving much in consequence,' while another, with a few reservations, added, 'Still somewhat immature for the VIth but she is beginning to [illegible] her work and will soon understand what is wanted from one of the School's leaders.' By the summer of 1922, when she was not quite seventeen, Eileen was described as, '[F]ull of commonsense and initiative; she has developed in a very satisfactory way.' And indeed she had. That spring, the Senior Reading Team, made up of Eileen and three other students, participated in the North England Competition and won second prize. Eileen also won the Durham School Certificate, and had her first poem published in the *Chronicle*.[28]

SONG

Oh a rose sky and a gay sky,
Is the sky of the dawning day;
And a gold sky and a bright sky
Is the sky when the sun holds sway;
But the sky of skies is pearly grey,
With a rift to show its colour by,
And if it be August or if it be May,
Soft winds will whisper a lullaby,
And the things of the earth will rest.

Apparently, after living her whole life in a part of England where the sun rarely shines, Eileen was insisting that she actually preferred grey skies.

At the beginning of her eighth year at Sunderland High School, aged seventeen, Eileen became the sub-editor of *The Chronicle*, a position she held until she left for Oxford University. As chief student editor, she acted as assistant to the main editor. Eileen's job was to write the 'Notes' section, usually a rather dull accounting of school events that had taken place during the six months since the last issue. Eileen stuck to the format for the most part, listing the new 'table-decorating competition', and the recipients of various scholarships, including ones she would later receive herself.

But what most impressed her during 1922 were two lectures that had been given to the students. In her Notes section in the November issue, Eileen wrote: 'We were fortunate enough to have Miss Bruce with us on Empire Day [24 May]. [She] took for her subject St Francis of Assisi. She told us of the little hill-town where he lived, but she spoke chiefly of St Francis himself – his wondrous gaiety and charm, his influence which has lasted through the ages, his love for his fellow creatures. Through his cheerful endurance of the hardships which fell on him after his conversion, she brought us the message of faith and hope in the perplexities which now beset the nation.' A similar event also caught her attention: 'In June we much enjoyed a most unusual lecture on "The principles of Greek Balance" . . . [The speaker] told us of the strenuous life the Greeks led, and pointed out how the very struggle for existence increased their mental and physical alertness, so strengthening the harmony between body and mind.'

Eileen clearly concluded that the difficult life choices she heard described were to be admired rather than avoided. It's impossible not to connect her early attraction to these ideas about deprivation and struggle to her later deliberate choice of a life of personal sacrifice and individual integrity with Orwell. Like the ancient Greeks, she, and perhaps Orwell also, saw physical hardship as a road toward 'mental and physical alertness'.

At the same time as she was evaluating these new life-changing ideas, Eileen continued to write her light-hearted, mostly upbeat poems, another of which was published in the *Chronicle* that year.

SATIS!

It was a day, a sunlit day
That silvered a late winter's snow,
And those who once had been so gay
Sat vainly wondering what to say,
    With heads bowed low.

And one pen squeaked and one went dry,
And one sighed loud and one sighed soft;
Both panic-stricken wondered why
The cuckoo in the clock its cry
    Must voice so oft.

And History with its complex scheme,
And English with its too deep thought,
And Essays with unwieldy theme,
And French and Latin, made them deem
    They were distraught.

But not e'en swift impending doom,
Nor minds as blank as minds may be
Bring uniformly settled gloom;
One joy remained – entered the room
    Two cups of tea.

The November 1922 issue of the *Chronicle* mentioned Eileen's prowess in school sports, listing her as 'Hockey Captain' of the Swifts. However, the report added, sadly, 'This last year has not been very successful for the Swifts, for we have only one cup left, for Examination Honours, and our shelf looks deserted and bare.'

During this time an attempt was made to encourage interest and participation in a Debating Society, and the first debate, 'The Savage Is Happier than the Civilised Man', was a lively success, with the motion being defeated thirteen votes to ten. 'The Pen Is Mightier Than the Sword' was proposed as a debate topic by Eileen, and she and her partner must have made a very convincing argument for the pen, since the motion was carried thirteen to four. Eileen made an even stronger case in what was called '[a] sharp-shooting debate' when she spoke alone on the subject 'Ignorance Is Not Bliss'. This time her motion was carried twelve to none.

In her final year at school, Eileen continued to write the Notes section of the *Chronicle*. Impressed by a speech on Missions, Eileen wrote: 'Miss Graham . . . said that Missionary work solved the problem of how to live side by side with the rest of the people in the world, and . . . Western peoples must . . . conquer the prejudices of the East, which arose merely from social misunderstanding. This applied specially to India – the dim and mysterious – which was composed of many races united by a common hatred of the white peoples, and which was the special responsibility of Great Britain.' Could this early curiosity have enhanced Eileen's interest in Orwell when she discovered that he had been born in India and had spent five years working in Burma? In the same issue, Eileen wrote about one visitor who had lectured on the education of girls in China: 'The position of women in China was changing rapidly since the influence of Christianity had made itself felt.'[29] Her Aunt Margaret by then had been at her Mission in Texas for forty years, and Eileen was clearly still intrigued by this choice of work.

Another visitor spoke about the current situation in Serbia, which, 'with a population of four million, turned back the Austrian forces three times before she was finally overcome, her land devastated, her people murdered', as Eileen described it. Slowly her politics were forming.

During all these years of study, Eileen had been preparing to go to university, a decision that her parents encouraged. In those days the majority of Oxford students came from schools which catered for university entrance,[30] and Eileen's parents had chosen just such a school for her. Her mother, herself once a teacher in a girls' secondary school, no doubt encouraged Eileen to aspire to the university education that had not been available to women when she was young. In the spring of 1923, Eileen passed the London matriculation test, a necessary requirement for enrolment in a university, and was subsequently interviewed as part of the process. One alumna remembered an entrance-exam question that 'revealed one of the purposes of Oxford, to give the ability to find out and realise the many sides to a question', and perhaps in that way the examiners were evaluating the likelihood of an individual being suited to an Oxford education.[31]

By this time Eileen had proceeded to the top of almost every school category, being listed in the Roll Call section as 'Head Girl, Head Prefect, sub-editor of Chronicle, Swift House Captain, and President of the League of Nations Branch', which had incorporated the Debating Society. Her final term ended in June 1924, and the Prize List showed Eileen winning honours for 'Good Conduct (the Lord Bishop of Durham)', 'The Whitaker Thompson Memorial Prize', and 'English Exhibitioner, St Hugh's Coll., Oxford', while five other pupils won one prize each. Eileen's being listed as an Exhibitioner at Oxford was misleading since Sunderland High School gave her a partial scholarship, not Oxford University.

In October 1924, Eileen headed south to Oxford University with substantial funds in her pocket and a whole new world ahead of her. It's not clear how many times she ever returned to South Shields. A notice in a later *Chronicle*, mentioning Eileen and a few other pupils, stated,

'Among the girls some real props of the School left,' while another announced, 'We were sorry to have to say good-bye to three Swifts last term, and especially to Eileen O'Shaughnessy who captained us so splendidly during the year.'

3

Honours at Oxford

I consider her work at its best really first rate,
with keen insight . . . There is a quiet controlled
enthusiasm about her which is very attractive.
Mr Ridley, one of Eileen's Oxford tutors

E
ileen O'Shaughnessy arrived at St Hugh's College, one of the
four women's colleges at Oxford University, on 10 October
1924, at the beginning of the Michaelmas, or autumn, term, and
just two weeks after her nineteenth birthday. She put her name and
personal information into the official registry, which had one oversize
page dedicated to each new student. Her address was listed simply as
'Westgate House, South Shields,' with no mention even of the street
name. She was one of fifty new students to register at St Hugh's that
term.

Eileen would have had a fairly simple day of travel, from South
Shields to London, and then on to Oxford, and she left no record of the
circumstances of her arrival. However, other students did share some
of the intricacies of those first days. Kathleen Hobbs, arriving from
France on the same day as Eileen – after a very hectic trip requiring
train, boat, and train again – discovered, once in Oxford, that 'the

station was piled with trunks & cases of all shapes & sizes from end to end.'[1] Hansom cabs with thin, old horses were waiting at the station, and most of the new students rode behind one of these miserable animals on the short trip from the station to St Hugh's, she reported.

Esther Power, an American, recorded her difficult first day. She arrived so late that evening that the college gates were already locked. When she did finally manage to get inside the building, she was told that she would be boarded for the year in a house nearby. She then 'taxied around to my digs, not far away, and found them rather typical of the north Oxford buildings of the less spectacular kind . . . My "bedder" was on the third floor, an unheated room, and had a washstand. My hostess had put a heated brick in my bed.' But her disappointment over the rather unstylish neighbourhood where she was to be housed, as well as the primitive state of her 'digs', was quickly mitigated when she was introduced to the two students who would be her housemates. As she remembered it, 'I met two of the liveliest English girls, Eileen O'Shaughnessy and Norah Symes, who shared with me the same digs.'[2]

One student, whose last name began with an 'H', discovered that all her roommates had last names starting with 'G', 'H', or 'I', so perhaps because the three girls' last names started with an 'O', a 'P', and an 'S', they were assigned a house together. If so, in that very arbitrary way, Eileen and Norah had found each other. They quickly became close friends and remained in touch for many years after their Oxford life ended. In fact, Eileen's newly discovered letters to Norah reveal some of the most fascinating puzzlements about Eileen's adventures and life choices. Her cheerful personality had been immediately obvious to a stranger, and, perhaps helping explain the two girls' immediate closeness, Norah was also characterised by Esther as lively. Since Eileen saved none of Norah's letters, her personality had never been evident before.

The following day, 11 October, was Matriculation Day. All the new students were given detailed information on where and when the service would take place, and just before the appointed time, dressed in the compulsory caps and gowns, they were all 'paraded in front of Miss Gwyer [the principal] so that she knew we looked alright'.[3] A photograph titled 'Matriculation, 1920s' shows a line of young women students, all dressed in caps and gowns, and one of them is clearly Eileen.[4] Lancelot Phelps, provost of Oriel College, performed the ceremony, and one woman student was shocked when he stopped suddenly in the middle of reading his Latin lines, which he had been performing rather by rote. Apparently he had suddenly realised there were females present as well as males. 'He pulled up short and went back to the beginning turning the Latin into the feminine,' she wrote, then added, 'He was not notably pro woman!'[5]

These students and many others, very old ladies by 1986, were pleased to send in their memories of their three years of university life to the editor of *St Hugh's: 100 Years of Women's Education in Oxford*. Eleven of those who reported back had been at St Hugh's at the same time as Eileen, and a complete set of their reports is in the St Hugh's archives. These were all unusual women for their time, smart enough and bold enough in their late teens to be excited about the challenge of acquiring a university degree, so excited in fact that they were willing to put off the idea of marriage for at least three years. And of course they had supportive parents, who believed that their daughters deserved the same chance to excel as their sons did, parents who thought the expense of educating a daughter was entirely justified. These women who sent in their memories had walked the grounds of St Hugh's with Eileen, sat with her at lectures, and shared her afternoons of spirited conversation and complaints at local tearooms. And we can imagine them playing hockey with her, punting with her on the river in the spring, and spending evenings listening to gramophone records with cocoa and sweet biscuits when all the young women were locked in after eleven. Since St Hugh's was located on St Margaret's Road, in north Oxford, far from the other colleges, it was necessary for them to bike to central Oxford to attend some classes and special events, and many memories involve their bike adventures. In her novel *Neapolitan Ice*, Renée Haynes, one of

Eileen's classmates, and the mother of Crispin Tickell, the former diplomat and environmentalist, described her main character's 'ideas of Oxford, which was in her mind a place of people, free, young, ready to experiment, ready to find out what living was like, people . . . continually and successfully in flight from the commonplace, people perpetually brilliant, perpetually exotic, alive.'[6] Crispin Tickell revealed that he has a drawer full of letters to his mother, but it wasn't possible to check whether there might be one or two from Eileen buried in that drawer.[7]

A glorious photograph of St Hugh's students taken around 1925 shows the huge variety of women – in age and dress and physical appearance – who studied there with Eileen. Although she is not definitively recognisable in the photo, two young women standing side by side in the third row may well be Eileen and Norah. Another class photo, from 1927, with annotations on the back, identifies a student with a stylish haircut and glasses as Eileen. This is a rather shocking image of Eileen when compared with the other existing photographs, and some will have a hard time accepting its veracity.

S t Hugh's College was founded by Dame Elizabeth Wordsworth, the great-niece of the poet. Using money she inherited in 1886, she set up a college for female undergraduates who couldn't afford to go to university. That year there were only four students, but by 1912 the number had expanded to forty-three, and it continued to increase, until reaching what was deemed a logical limit of 150, in 1923. Those first students were from poorer families, but by the time Eileen arrived they had wealthy parents for the most part. In a study of 742 students from 1920 to 1939, of the twenty-one categories of occupations of fathers that were included, 14 per cent were from industry, 11 per cent were clergy, 10 per cent were school teachers, 9.6 per cent were doctors, and 5.3 per cent were in the civil service. At the time, there were no opportunities for young women to support themselves with a job as they studied for a degree.

Although women had been accepted as students for many years, Oxford University had refused to grant them any degrees until 1920. The First World War emptied the university of most of the male students, who, along with a few women students, had enlisted in the war. But most of the women continued their studies, gaining the respect of university officials. In 1918, when the war ended, women over thirty were granted the vote in Britain. And, after much controversy, a statute of 17 February 1920 admitted them to full membership of Oxford University. Then, in the Michaelmas term of 1920, for the first time women were allowed to enrol towards receiving a degree in three years, the same privilege that men already had.[8] As another result of the new statute, on 14 October 1920, fifty women who had been studying unofficially at Oxford for many years finally received degrees, including Vera Brittain and Dorothy L. Sayers. At that ceremony, an MA in History was presented to Miss Eleanor Frances Jourdain, the then principal of St Hugh's.[9] During the next months, nearly a thousand women, often middle-aged and already tutors or professors, received their degrees, based on their earlier studies.

The year before Eileen began her Oxford education, a scandal, commonly called 'the Row', had been developing at St Hugh's, and it came to a rather tragic conclusion in the spring of 1924. Years earlier, before she became principal, Miss Jourdain had befriended the much younger Cecilia Mary Ady, a tutor. Some of her letters to Miss Ady have survived – letters written in an extremely affectionate tone, calling her 'Baby Don' and 'Cara Mia Cecilia'.[10] In 1915, when Miss Jourdain was chosen to be principal of St Hugh's, she persuaded the Oxford officials to appoint Miss Ady as her vice-principal. But, as the years had gone by, something went seriously wrong with the friendship. Finally, shocking everyone, Miss Jourdain suddenly fired Miss Ady in 1923, accusing her of undermining her authority and of long-standing 'disloyalty'. Miss Ady was extremely popular with the students, some of whom boycotted classes, as well as with her fellow tutors, and some senior tutors resigned in protest.[11] Many believed that, although Miss

Ady had 'frequently disagreed with the Principal on matters of Business and discipline, and discussed her disagreements with other tutors', the charge of disloyalty 'seemed to rest on the flimsiest of evidence'.[12] As a result of all this controversy, Miss Jourdain's health began to deteriorate, but she remained adamant, threatening to resign herself if her decision about firing Miss Ady were overturned.

When it became clear that there was no easy resolution to the conflict, some high Oxford University officials reluctantly got involved. Lord George Curzon, the Chancellor of the University, sent a letter to Miss Jourdain, 'putting the blame for "the Row" firmly on her shoulders', according to one student.[13] This proved too much of a shock for her, and Miss Jourdain died of a heart attack on 6 April 1924. The aftermath of the affair lingered on for years, and St Hugh's began to lose some of its prestige. As one of Eileen's 1924 fellow intake put it, 'We were entering St Hugh's at the worst time in its history. College fortunes, morale, and its standing in the University were probably at their nadir . . . A number of distinguished dons left the college.'[14]

Eileen would have had an interview with Miss Jourdain in the spring of 1924, shortly before her death. This interview was customary for incoming students, and although it wasn't openly discussed, all the September intake knew about 'the Row' and about Miss Jourdain's sudden death. One new student, who had her interview the afternoon Miss Jourdain died, was afraid that she might have been the last person to see her alive. 'I went to take leave of her before going to catch my train . . . The College parlour maid brought the afternoon post in just before I left. I only knew afterwards that in it was the letter from Lord Curzon.'[15]

When Eileen arrived on 10 October, a brand-new principal, Miss Barbara Elizabeth Gwyer, had just been instated. She was remembered by one student as 'a tall, angular English woman' with a rather gruff manner. She had been carefully chosen to oversee the new St Hugh's, and the routines of settling in, which had long been enforced, continued more or less as usual. And Miss Cecilia Mary Ady was still part of her staff.

Eileen received a scholarship of £20 a year for five years from Sunderland High School, as well as an extra £30 a year for the last two years from the Old Girls Scholarship Fund.[16] (£50 would be equivalent to around £3,000 today.) Cheque stubs have curiously survived that record two of the payments to Eileen through those years: an undated one for £10 from the Old Girls Scholarship Fund and another dated 13 May 1927, for £16 13s 4d. In 1933, the average annual cost for a woman to study at Oxford ranged between £160 and £240, and this would not have been considerably less in 1924.[17] So Eileen's father paid for a large portion of her education.

Eileen studied English Language and Literature. Her syllabus included: Gothic and German Philology; Old English Philology; Middle English Philology; the History of the English Language, with special reference to the period since Chaucer; Old English Texts (Old English Poetry and Prose, with special attention to *Beowulf*, Exodus, Judith, the Lyrical Poets); Old English, with special reference to *Sweet's Anglo-Saxon Reader*; and Middle English Texts, with special reference to Morris and Skeat's *Specimens of Middle English* and Sisam's *Fourteenth Century Verse and Prose*. And she would have been judged for her written essays on: Outlines of the History of the English Language; Shakespeare and Milton; Old English and Middle English Literature; Chaucer and His Contemporaries; and the Fifteenth to Nineteenth Centuries.[18]

How would Eileen have handled this rather elaborate range of subjects, to say nothing of the drastic move from the protected, Head Girl atmosphere of Sunderland High School to being one of many bright new girls at St Hugh's? She was an ambitious, hard-working young woman who wanted to prove that she deserved the opportunity of studying at Oxford. Her main goal was to receive a first-class degree at the end of her three years of study. Her older brother was already a success in his field, but he had received only a second-class degree. Eileen was always in competition with him, and this knowledge might also have goaded her into trying harder.

There had definitely been rules and restrictions at Sunderland High School, but each evening and weekend Eileen was at home enjoying whatever freedoms her parents allowed. Now she had to learn to deal with the rather limiting restrictions for young Oxford women. To begin with, the rules for 'Academic Dress' were strict, requiring the students to always wear 'the cap and gown approved by the Vice-Chancellor and Proctors', even when bicycling to classes in central Oxford. This creates the humorous spectacle of the roads full of young women in caps and gowns manoeuvring their bikes through heavy horse and buggy traffic. Since some lectures and other events took place after dark, the bikes were equipped with oil lamps, with wicks that needed constant trimming.[19] There were pages and pages of other rules – dedicated to curfew time, visits with men, dances, and appropriate chaperones – that the young women were expected to honour. Students often made formal requests to change some of the harshest restrictions, but they were almost always denied.

There were many groups for students to join, including 'a fairly flourishing Literary Society which on one occasion was addressed by G. K. Chesterton whose advent was spectacular for he was then at his greatest girth';[20] the English Club, where one student remembered seeing 'the dazzling, dashing Vita Sackville-West';[21] and a Debating Club. All of these would have interested Eileen, but no details of membership are given.

The students had to present weekly essays, and one St Hugh's student recalled, 'Many were the times I sat up until 2 a.m. to complete an essay.' She was amused by how one of her tutors then treated her hard work: 'My tutor stopped me after I had read only one sentence, and spent the rest of the tutorial discussing those few words, while the rest of the essay for which I had burned the midnight oil was consigned to oblivion! But such was her method, and I gained more inspiration from those discussions than I should have from a more orthodox approach. I learned to think.'[22]

October. 14th

The Nature & Value of Logic

The study of logic is an enquiry into the conditions of correct reasoning. Various definitions have been formulated

(i) *Logic is the science of the laws of thought* –

This, which is the commonest definition, states what is most essential: namely, that Logic is a science differentiated from all other sciences in that it investigates those fundamental principles subject to which we all think & reason; laws which we sometimes defy or ignorantly disregard with the result of fallacy & failure. Putting on one side the results of immediate intuition every correct conclusion we ever reached, or any knowledge we ever acquired depended upon our conforming to certain laws, & it is the investigation of those laws which

constitutes the province of logic.

Logic has been called 'scientia scientiarum as artium' because the individual arts & sciences are necessarily subordinate to the science which investigates the laws governing man's supreme faculty – his reason.

But it has been thought that we have not a complete definition in the above statement, for sciences are not always used by speculation; some are practical sciences. Is not Logic one of these and therefore in some sense an art?

(ii) *Logic is the science & the art of reasoning*

A definition given by Whately & which met with the approval of J. S. Mill. Their own definitions embody the same idea.

The first two pages of Eileen's 123-page treatise, 'The Nature & Value of Logic', written for one of her classes at Oxford.

Throughout her three years at Oxford, Eileen had a number of colourful tutors. One of the prominent professors in Eileen's field was J. R. R. Tolkien, who began teaching English Language and Literature at Oxford in 1925, and whose lectures were popular and widely attended. He was one of the tutors hired when others had resigned in protest over 'the Row', during a period when some prominent scholars were reluctant to tie themselves to St Hugh's because of the scandal. Tolkien was then only thirty-two and it would be many years before he wrote the novels that made him world-famous. Esther Power, Eileen and Norah's housemate, who also studied English, remembered that Tolkien 'began his lectures with the explosive Anglo-Saxon word "hwaet", a word which began almost every Anglo-Saxon poem and meant something like "lo!" and sounded very much like "quiet!"'[23] Although no tutor reports have survived from Tolkien, Eileen must have attended his lectures with Esther. And at graduation time, Tolkien was one of Eileen's four 'examiners'.

Tolkien befriended Clive Staples (C. S.) Lewis, who began teaching

English Language and Literature at Oxford at the same time. Esther Power remembered him also, saying, 'He lectured on Spenser to just a dozen or so students. My friend [perhaps Eileen] and I were obviously visitors and attended the class just one day. Lewis sat behind a desk and I could see his broad chest. He merely glanced at us and paid us no more attention,'[24] presumably because they were women. Another student had even harsher words for Lewis, saying that, although his lectures were inspiring, 'it was difficult to stand up to C. S. Lewis's dislike of our presence – as women.'[25] There was still resentment against women intruding 'into the spheres of men instead of keeping within their proper roles as wives and mothers.'[26] Two young women who were studying law had a curious, but more positive, reception at their first lecture. One remarked that '[T]he men got up and cheered, which embarrassed us a bit.'[27]

Another of Eileen's English tutors, Mary Ethel Seaton, was one of the many strong, distinguished women scholars at St Hugh's. A fellow student described her as a 'conscientious and interested' tutor 'who cheered me along with wise talk and tea.'[28] When Miss Seaton died, in 1974, her obituary noted, 'She affected the dress of an earlier period, long-skirted, be-capped, and often carrying an umbrella and a capacious carpet-bag . . . She was full of surprises.' Yet, '[S]he was cool, firm, and shrewd in her judgement of her pupils' work.' In her two surviving reports on Eileen, she was mostly positive, being one of the few to appreciate Eileen's sense of humour.

And then there was H. F. B. Brett-Smith, another of the large assortment of unusual tutors Eileen studied with. Before teaching at Oxford, he was employed in First World War military hospitals, advising on reading matter for the war-wounded. He had an unusual approach to his assignment: 'For the severely shell-shocked he selected Jane Austen.'[29]

The St Hugh's librarian during Eileen's years was Winifred Mammatt, an odd woman whom Eileen remembered well and joked about years later. In Mammatt's obituary, one of her fellows wrote:

'She possessed a keen sense of humour, a readiness to be amused, and was full of enthusiasm for her work.' But then, after allowing that there was 'a certain simplicity in her nature, a child-like-ness,' the obituary continued, 'She cannot be said to have had an academic mind. She was neither highly intellectual nor a real scholar, but she was cultured, appreciative, and eager to learn, and her desire for knowledge did not cease with her Oxford days.'[30] Eileen wasn't always kind in her conclusions about people, and when she ran into the old Oxford librarian years later she clearly dismissed her as not worthy of respect.

But it wasn't all work at Oxford. There seemed to be plenty of time in the afternoons for adventure. The food in the St Hugh's dining room, which was the compulsory place for dinner, was deemed so atrocious that many hours were spent chatting and complaining, all the while enjoying tea and chocolate desserts in the many different tearooms that were favourites – the Candied Friend, the Cadena, and the Super Cinema among them.

Apparently the fashionable women of London believed that the Oxford students were hopelessly out of style, buried as they were in small-town academia. Mary Grigs, on assignment for a London newspaper in 1926, went to Oxford 'to track down the phenomenon of whom we have heard so much lately – the ill-dressed Undergraduate.' In her pursuit of women students in unstylish costumes, she 'braved the dangers of the highways of Oxford at the full tide of bicycle traffic' and 'hid behind gates' to spy on passers-by. While acknowledging that she 'saw none of the "policeman" hats, the "luxuriously lined wraps", the shoes with the "new spiked heel and decorative vamp" that have been pronounced to be the height of fashion' in London, she concluded nonetheless that 'the girls I saw wore unostentatious, up-to-date, becoming country clothes.' And this should be no surprise, she concluded, 'for, after all, Oxford is not Oxford-street.'[31]

However, the student body did contain a number of eccentric young women. One South American undergraduate 'strung up to dry 25 pairs of silk stockings, corner to corner in her room', which her roommates considered an ostentatious show of her great wealth.[32] Another young woman 'trailed around in a cloak and toga, and was said to have been found sitting in a room lit only by a ring of various coloured candle flames'.[33] Many of the female dons were also unorthodox, and their quirky clothing choices were smiled at by the students.

Esther Power remembered the spring terms as 'full of beauty, romance and adventure . . . a world of green seen through the mist or rain, a perfect background for romance'.[34] In her recollections, she went on in some detail about young men who were constantly falling in love with her, but regrettably she never mentioned Eileen being involved in any particular romance of her own. However, it has been rumoured that Eileen did have an affair with a fellow student who years later worked at the BBC when Eileen was working at the Ministry of Food. Eileen is also on record saying she turned down a few offers of marriage before she met Orwell.

Dating men while at St Hugh's was not at all simple. Chaperones had to be taken on any date, and this person had to be a don or a don's wife, not just another fellow student. This arrangement was given a clever twist by one woman, and no doubt others copied her scheme. When a male undergraduate asked her to tea one day, she told him that she would 'have to drag a don along with me, so he thoughtfully provided another man from his own college'. She was never sure 'whether the [man] had been previously primed as to his duties or whether it was a case of mutual attraction . . . but he and my don got into a huddle and remained deep in earnest conversation during the entire visit', allowing the young couple to enjoy their time together in private.[35] Another amusing date involved a young woman and her brother sitting in her room with the door open while her date 'was provided with a chair in the corridor'.[36] Obviously, Eileen and the other students were forced to develop ingenious manoeuvres around these constricting rules. One young woman was not cautious enough, though she clearly didn't mind getting caught. She was 'seen and recognised coming out of New

College [a male college] in the early hours of the morning'. Because 'she was quite outstanding in appearance and had been indulging in rather flamboyant behaviour with her male admirers,' she ended up being disciplined.[37]

When there were no activities to attend in town, the evenings were spent in the students' rooms. Most of them had been used to warm homes, and at St Hugh's the bedrooms were bitterly cold. One had an attic room that 'was heated (or supposed to be) by a very small coal fire, but this firmly refused to burn'.[38] One remedy was for a group of students to all gather together in one room, creating some human warmth while they enjoyed cocoa and whatever snacks were available. In one report after another, cocoa in the evenings is mentioned as one of the highlights of the students' memories. No alcohol was allowed in the rooms and no one mentioned any heavy drinking, but one student was known by all to keep a hidden stash of sherry. Another, who had lived for some time in France, thought it was a silly rule, and she claimed that she and others found no difficulty in quietly bringing wine into their rooms.[39]

One former student remembered enjoying gramophone records along with the cocoa, 'and I still have a few of the old 78s with which we amused ourselves on those hilarious evenings'. She added, 'We had never heard a radio' while there.[40] But another did not appreciate the late-night hilarity. 'In my third year I had a particularly pleasant room on the second floor overlooking the terrace. Halfway through the year a student who lived just round the corner and who afterwards became well known in the literary world had a gramophone. She gathered her friends together and they had parties at which they played the loudest records imaginable. On one or two occasions they also burnt some kind of cheap incenses which drifted far and wide through the college'. Could this have been Eileen? Apparently the annoyed student complained to the authorities, causing 'a stormy crisis after which the use of gramophones was better regulated'.[41]

There didn't seem to be any 'lights out' rules, and many other evenings were spent writing essays for the next-day tutorials. Evenings spent cramming were part of everyone's memories. Then, early in the morning, there would be a knock on each door, and 'some nice maids brought hot water to our rooms . . . and laid fires with sticks and paper and coal and how cold Oxford was in winter'.[42]

Twenty-one tutor reports about Eileen's work at Oxford have survived, nine from her first year. During her first three months, in the Michaelmas Term of 1924, Miss E. A. Francis was dubious in her first report, writing:

Prose Class C: Miss O'Shaughnessy is very weak, but she has given the impression of willing & steady work. I am afraid she will have difficulty in making much progress.

But later in the same term, she had some second thoughts, writing:

Set Books: Miss O'Shaughnessy has a sense of style and when she translates correctly her work is quite good. But the weakness, which her prose composition discloses, is a hindrance to her in a general way. She is a hard worker, and I hope will get up to standard on her set books.

Another tutor, Joan Evans, who was remembered for wearing brocade and velvet dresses to dinner and who held Dante evenings,[43] made the shortest comment:

Unseen [translating Latin into English]: *Very fair*

while Miss Evelyn Dorothy Ritchie had great optimism for Eileen's future, writing:

Latin Prose [translating English into Latin] *& Unseen: Miss O'Shaughnessy's work is clear-headed & intelligent, & she seems to be*

well grounded. Her prose is on the whole better than her unseen; but she should pass in both without difficulty.
Pliny & Virgil: Both papers were satisfactory & pleasant to read. Miss O'Shaughnessy's style is good. Her knowledge of the subject matter might have been better.
Pliny S; Virgil VS+

In the following Hilary Term, from January to March 1925, Miss Ritchie is still enthusiastic:

Latin Prose & Unseen: Good work showing a sense of style; occasionally however marred by elementary grammatical blunders.
Set Books: Miss O'Shaughnessy's work, besides showing knowledge of her texts, is interesting & original. Her literary style is pleasing.

Miss L. Biden wrote succinctly:

Very satisfactory work – promises well.

But Miss Francis was still critical:

Set Books: A good collection paper. Miss O'Shaughnessy has distinct ability.
Prose: Unfortunately this is very weak. Miss O'Shaughnessy has a sense of style and often selects her vocabulary well; but her work is constantly marred by careless errors of a very serious kind. I am very much afraid this may plough her.

In the final Trinity Term, April to June 1925, Miss Eveleen Emily Stopford, one of the tutors hired after 'the Row', was much more encouraging:

Miss O'Shaughnessy's work has been most satisfactory. Her essays show

wide reading & appreciation. She has a certain sense of style and her
work, on the whole, is promising.

E. M. Wright had only a brief comment:

Translation well prepared. Grammar needs further work in
the vacation.

Interestingly, three of her tutors highlighted Eileen's sense of style. Neither L. Biden nor E. M. Wright could be identified. Probably they were filling in during the time that St Hugh's was having trouble finding tutors willing to work there.

In June all the students headed off to their diverse home towns and countries for a working summer vacation. On Eileen's way north to South Shields, there was a London wedding to attend, at St Joseph's Roman Catholic church. John Kingdon (sometimes spelled Kingston) O'Donoghue, one of her Irish cousins, then working in London as a civil servant in the Foreign Office, got married that June. His mother was Aunt Lizzie O'Shaughnessy, one of Eileen's father's three older sisters. Even though John worked in the British Civil Service, he kept his Catholic religion, unlike Eileen's father.

The Imp, the St Hugh's literary magazine, was published three times a year. And when Eileen came back from vacation in the autumn of 1925, she was listed as *The Imp*'s 'Second Year Representative', while Norah Symes was Treasurer. Most of the poems, playlets, and reviews were printed with no attribution, so it's only possible to guess at Eileen's contributions. However, the sole surviving page, part of Act II, Scene 2, of a comic play Eileen wrote while at Oxford[44] does resemble in style the ones printed in *The Imp*. The only other writing by Eileen that has been preserved from her time at Oxford is an eighty-page hand-written treatise on logic.[45]

The March 1926 issue of *The Imp* reviewed a performance of the comic Elizabethan-era play *Frier Bacon and Frier Bungay*, which was performed by St Hugh's students, with all the roles – including 'men' with pasted-on beards – being played by women. *The Imp* review began, 'I believe St Hugh's is becoming famous for its presentation of old plays.' The reviewer continued, 'Although my seat was near the back of the hall, I heard almost every word (except for a few sentences that were drowned by a too-appreciative audience) – an unexpected pleasure at an amateur show.' One student of that time, who took her three great-aunts to the show, remembered that '[t]hey were clearly non-plussed.'[46] After praising all the actors profusely, the review ended: 'The programmes were delightful, although the names of two of the *Dramatis Personae* sounded rather oddly – *A Post*, E. O'Shaughnessy; and the *Brazen Head*, J. Sargeant. I hope that the latter has not been permanently injured by being broken in so many pieces.' So Eileen was performing in plays at Oxford, albeit, at least in this case, in a rather minor role.

Noah's Flood, a medieval English mystery play, was also presented by St Hugh's students while Eileen was there.[47] The review doesn't mention Eileen by name, but much of the cast was made up of the animals chosen for the ark. While at Oxford, and therefore long before she met Orwell, Eileen developed the unusual nickname 'Pig', signing all her letters to Norah with this name. So, besides playing 'A Post' at St Hugh's, she may well have played a 'Pig' in *Noah's Flood*. This is an interesting speculation in light of the fact that her current relatives insist that she was actively involved in the creation of the characters and concept of *Animal Farm*.

The June 1926 issue of *The Imp* had a section called 'If the Cap Fits'. A list of twelve quotations appeared – such as 'The loud laugh that spoke the vacant mind' – and the reader was asked to guess which student epitomised each quotation. In the copy of that issue in the St Hugh's Archives, someone had filled in by hand some of her guesses. And after:

'Tis the voice of the sluggard, I hear him complain,
'You have waked me too soon; I must slumber again.'

she wrote, 'Fania & Eileen'. If this is our Eileen, it would appear that rising early was not one of her virtues.

In the springtime, punting and canoeing on the Isis, the section of the Thames as it passes through Oxford, was a popular activity, and Eileen, with her athletic ability and the river adventures of her childhood with her father's job on the River Tyne, would surely have taken part. As usual the women had to be chaperoned, and as usual they found ways to avoid surveillance. One of the students of Eileen's time remembered 'bumping into another punt concealed under a willow. It contained two of our seniors, in company with two men.'[48] One comic story of capsizing was fondly retold. The student who fell into the river 'was wearing a summer dress made of double chiffon in pale green. When wet, this material shrinks to far less than its original dimensions, so it was a mermaid who was bundled into a hastily summoned taxi and hurried back to college.'[49] A more tragic outing was also recalled. At the time, students were allowed to ride in the boats even when they couldn't swim. But that changed quickly when 'a punt was capsized, and about three people who could not swim were drowned, chiefly because they were caught in the weed, which was then very thick in parts of the river, and dragged down before anyone could get to them.'[50]

One exciting annual spring event was Lady Astor's Ball, held in London for Rhodes Scholars. Esther Power was invited, and she believed this was the first time women had attended. She wrote that some of her friends went with her, and since she and Eileen were often together, there's a good chance Eileen was at this event too. Esther met the Prince of Wales at the Ball, with 'his usual hangdog look', as well as the Prime Minister. Many years later, after their marriage, Orwell was impressed that Eileen seemed to know everyone important and could always manage to reach the right people to get what she wanted. Being an Oxford graduate definitely had its perks.

In the evening the students were allowed to attend plays, and quite a few of them remembered seeing Gyles Isham in *Hamlet* and John Gielgud in *The Cherry Orchard*, before he had a reputation outside the provinces. The plays often continued past the St Hugh's curfew time of 11 p.m., and many of the former students remembered having to leave the theatre before the plays had ended in order to dash home in time. One described in detail 'the simultaneous uprising of all the female undergraduates, treading on people's feet in the dark, dashing out of the theatre, before cycling like mad to their respective colleges or digs'. She concluded, 'We must have been very unpopular'.[51]

Often it proved impossible to get back before the doors were locked, and many ingenious ways of climbing in after 11 p.m. were devised. On one occasion, a late arriver, seeing a light in a don's sitting room, 'tapped on her window. She kindly forgot to be a don, and helped me to climb in – not too easy, as I happened to be wearing an ankle-length dress'.[52] Another woman remembered that it was a simple job to climb the fence and get into the garden, where the bars on the windows on the ground floor could somehow be removed, leaving 'enough space for most people to get through'.[53] Eileen was an adventurous enough person to have likely tried one of these stunts.

In the spring of 1926, the General Strike, as it became known, brought England to a standstill. A million miners, asking for pay increases and better working conditions, were locked out of their jobs, and the conflict speedily escalated. In a very short time four million British workers were on strike, including builders, printers, and dockworkers, and London transportation was almost completely shut down. Many feared a countrywide revolution. Worries about the strike spread throughout Oxford as supplies such as coal and food were rationed. Most of the young students weren't informed in any detail about conditions throughout the rest of the country. Some, like the American Rhodes Scholars, 'were loyal to Labour as they thought

Americans should be.'[54] But, among the mostly well-to-do students, anger at the strikers was also common, with one recalling that she felt distressed when she 'began to be conscious of the political leanings of certain members of college mostly dons and found some of them very disconcerting, even worrying [presumably referring to socialist beliefs she thought they possessed]. I had a glimpse of the destructive agencies that have wreaked so much havoc over the last 50 years.'[55] Notes transcribed in the 'Minutes Book' that month, offering no opinion on the strike, stated: 'The President said that on account of the General Strike the Bursar wished students to be very sparing in their use of coal, to keep strictly to the bath ration of three baths a week and not to grumble if the food was not up to the usual standard.'[56]

Seven tutor reports about Eileen have survived from her second year at Oxford. In the Michaelmas Term of 1925, after summer vacation was over, Eileen's tutors weighed in on her progress. The two that have survived for that term were very favourable.

Miss H. Buckhurst wrote:

Miss O'Shaughnessy is a capable student, & has been quick to grasp linguistic principles. Her translation is good, combining accuracy with spirit.

And Miss Seaton was quite encouraging:

Miss O'Shaughnessy is a capable student; in two essays only has she fallen below a steady level of excellence, without, as yet, brilliance. She has a detached attitude which aids her criticism, but not perhaps her appreciation. Her style is already formed, & is lucid & well-balanced. If her powers expand proportionately to her reading, she should promise very well.

However, during the Hilary (spring) 1926 term, Miss Buckhurst became somewhat disappointed in Eileen, writing:

Miss O'Shaughnessy is capable of very good work but does not always produce it. A more sustained effort is needed, both in phonology and translation.
Papers β4, β-, β4, α-, β+, α-.

But Miss Seaton was still positive about Eileen's work:

Miss O'Shaughnessy did some good work in her Collections papers & has worked with capability, & some enthusiasm & humour. She needs to read even more widely to bring her matter up to the level of her excellent arrangement & style.
Collections β+, γ, α- -.

In the Trinity (summer) 1926 term, Miss Buckhurst again had reservations:

I still feel that Miss O'Shaughnessy does not always give of her best in her language work; she generally seems content with a moderate achievement, but at times shows that she is capable of almost first-class work. Her fluent style in translation sometimes covers a slight uncertainty as to the exact meaning.

Mary S. Serjeantson wrote simply:

Translation usually good; written work good in places but with many gaps.

In contrast, Mr Ridley was very impressed by everything about Eileen:

I consider her work at its best really first rate, with keen insight and a knack of trenchant expression which never descends to the mostly clever. She cannot always keep this level up throughout an essay. There is a quiet controlled enthusiasm about her which is very attractive.

Eileen and Esther Power went together to a tutorial given by Mr Ridley of Balliol. As Esther explained, 'It would have been considered inappropriate at that time to attend a tutorial with a young man without a female companion.' The subject was nineteenth-century poetry, and Esther remembered Mr Ridley as 'a very good-looking man with a high-bridged nose' who would 'stand in front of the fireplace

ST. HUGH'S COLLEGE.

REPORT ON Miss O'Shaughnessy

Trinity TERM, 1926.

I consider her work of the best really first rate, with keen insight and a knack of trenchant expression which was demand to the mostly clever. She cannot always keep this last up through out an essay. There is a quiet controlled enthusiasm about her which is very attractive.

(Mr Ridley)

Please return to Miss Seaton. Buckhurst.

THE PRINCIPAL, St. Hugh's College.

Report from Mr Ridley, one of Eileen's tutors at Oxford, Trinity Term, 1926. By kind permission of the Principal and Fellows of St Hugh's College, Oxford.

and listen very attentively as we read the weekly essays . . . [He] was very flattering in his attention and seeming interest.'

On the whole, these tutors were impressed with Eileen's style of writing, which they called 'fluent' and 'lucid', with 'excellent arrangement'. And their mentions of her 'humour', 'enthusiasm', 'spirit', and 'keen insight' all show that Eileen's essays were in many ways remarkable. Although she was submitting serious compositions, hoping for excellent grades, she did not suppress her natural sense of humour, which sustained her throughout her life. But the references to her being a 'capable student' doing 'almost first-class work' must have been disappointing to Eileen. Unfortunately, none of her essays were preserved.

Eileen's name disappeared from *The Imp* masthead in the autumn of 1926, suggesting she moved on to other publications. The *Fritillary* was a strongly suffragist magazine, run jointly by representatives of the four women's colleges, and Eileen most likely began writing for it in her third year. In a photograph of four masked women parading in Oxford with placards urging people to buy the magazine, one is the editor, Renée Haynes, and another resembles Eileen.[57] Working at this magazine for a year would have helped form Eileen's later beliefs. The *Fritillary* contained mostly anonymous poetry, short stories, and reviews composed by female students. It also reported on the various debating societies, with topics such as 'The Woman of to-day has more liberty than sense to make use of it' and 'The essential elements of the Irish sense of humour are lacking in the Anglo-Saxon',[58] topics that would have appealed to Eileen, especially with her debating success in high school. Occasionally separate news columns from each college appeared, similar to the 'Notes' column Eileen wrote for the *Chronicle* at Sunderland High School, and some were simply attributed by the letter O. However, there is no proof any of them were written by Eileen.

Eileen's brother said that she had a few articles published in a popular newspaper, and some possibilities have been discovered. In

1926, the *London Evening News* – the largest evening newspaper in London at the time, and the publisher of short stories by the likes of D. H. Lawrence and F. Scott Fitzgerald – began a long series of weekly articles called 'My Day'. Women of all occupations, ages, and walks of life were invited to describe a typical day in their lives. The women were assured that the articles would be printed anonymously so that they could feel free to reveal secrets without worrying about adverse reactions from husbands or fellow workers. There is no way this many years later to trace who the real authors were.

'My Day IX: Work and Play of a Woman Undergraduate', in the 12 November issue, was promoted as 'written by a woman undergraduate at Oxford', and it has quite a flavour of Eileen's sense of playfulness. If it is not hers, it certainly gives us a rewarding look at what was probably a typical day of study for a student.

'And his head was severed at one blow.'

It is 4 a.m.; King Charles has died. But my essay is finished and I am too tired to anticipate the sarcasms of a tutor well-feared for his ruthlessness. Numb and shivering, I stumble into bed. It is cold: oh why didn't I write the essay last night instead of going to a show? I must look up Clarendon again to-morrow . . . To-morrow – to-day . . .

With a vague feeling of having been wronged, I open my eyes. 'Seven o'clock, Miss'. But that does not, cannot, concern me; nor can the sounds of a gong and a bell, and the pattering of feet towards chapel and hall. Beatitude . . .

A knock at the door: a well-fed friend looks in casually.

'Hullo! Day in bed?'

'No. I'm being tutored at ten.'

'Oh, well you've got quite fifteen minutes before you.'

Bang! goes the door. There ensues a mad struggle with clothes: the cap is pulled low over an untidy coiffure: gown – pencil – paper – and I dash doorwards.

Within ten minutes I rush, panting and out of temper, into a study devoid of all tutorial presence and adorned only by two bored undergraduates, who add to my discomfort by their detached examination of my person. It is twenty past before the wonderful old Don enters, with a kindly and witty apology for having forgotten his nine o'clock 'tutorial' with the two young men. He offers to take the three of us together; and, full of embarrassment, we know not how to decline.

As we watch him light the well-known pipe it occurs to me that, if we can induce the great man to talk, I may be spared the pains of reading my ill-prepared essay in the hearing of these supercilious young men. They, doubtless as bashful as myself, place no obstacle in my path, and my efforts are rewarded. For an hour a flow of profound and witty instruction makes us feel somewhat akin to those animals before which pearls are proverbially cast.

After hall-lunch some half-dozen fellow sufferers assemble to rid me of fruit and cigarettes, and we are able to give rein to our gossiping tongues, for it is Saturday and life is glorious.

About four o'clock I begin to change, and an hour later I am installed on a chintz-covered window-seat, amid the cheery gossip and laughter of young men and women friends. Outside, in the Meadows, the yellow leaves are falling; and here are crumpets brought up in relays by the incredibly dignified 'scouts' of Christ Church. When it grows dark we gather nearer to the fire to discuss the latest achievements of the fifteen, or tell the oldest ghost stories in the world.

As seven o'clock booms out, a few yards from the window, I remember dinner.

Somebody takes me in a car and deposits me at the college gate. I search the pigeon-holes for letters and find invitations, a paper to be done for a tutor ('show up Tuesday by 7 p.m.'), an envelope containing 'Doriola' powder, and garnished with a suitable poem, more advertisements and a bill. To my room I go and change into evening dress: at dinner I sit next to a Don, a lady Don, of course, who talks of the weather, Italy, the garden, and examinations . . .

Then, dismissing thoughts of chapel, I do my week-end shopping in the college shop and retire to have a bath and wrap myself in my favourite dressing gown for a couple of hours' work.

At ten o'clock I fetch milk from the pantry and make ready biscuits and cake and fruit and chocolate for a hungry party of girls who, also wrapped in dressing gowns, crouch by the fire on cushions, footstools, and even pillows until the chimes of St Mary's ring midnight. Eating, smoking and arguing, we give ourselves over to 'that week-end feeling': to-morrow is Sunday – peaceful Oxford Sunday; and then – bed; and a good sound sleep.

A few details in this lively description of a day in the life of an Oxford woman undergraduate remind us of Eileen. She was known for oversleeping and dressing haphazardly, her hair was described as unruly by friends, and of course she was a heavy smoker. Then there's the reference to pigs, 'those animals before which pearls are proverbially cast'. And she definitely possessed the ability to charm.

Only four tutor reports have survived from Eileen's last year at Oxford, all rather short. In the Michaelmas term of 1926, Mr H. F. B. Brett-Smith, the man who had promoted reading Jane Austen in unusual First World War circumstances, wrote:

Miss O'Shaughnessy has done good work for me, and writes quite well and with some sense of style.

E. M. Wright added:

Very good work – both Class & Paper-work.

In the Hilary Term of 1927, Miss Buckhurst had finally come around, having only praise for Eileen:

Miss O'Shaughnessy has produced extremely good work in language, both in translation and written papers. Her work is clear and accurate and is generally well arranged.

However, a new tutor, Frank Percy Wilson – another man who, along with Tolkien, would be Eileen's 'examiner' in the final oral exams – also weighed in:

Her work has no great depth or penetration, but it is pleasant and attractively fresh. She writes with point and edge and with good taste and discrimination.

While not wholly negative, Mr Wilson doesn't sound here like someone who was likely to recommend Eileen for the first-class degree for which she longed.

Among the dated and signed tutor reports that have survived, one containing no tutor's name or date must have given Eileen confidence that she was developing into an estimable writer and critic:

A--. A well written thoughtful paper, showing independence of judgment & sound taste. The answer on Coleridge as a critic was excellently presented, that of Keats & Shelley unusually sane & discriminating. She writes from a full knowledge & has a real critical gift

```
E.O'Shaughnessy.
            A--. a well written thoughtful paper,showing independence of
judgment & sound taste. The answer on Coleridge as a critic was excellently
presented,that of Keats & Shelley unusually sane & discriminating. She
writes from a full knowledge& has a real critical gift.
```

Report from an unidentified Oxford tutor, undated. By kind permission of the Principal and Fellows of St Hugh's College, Oxford.

After three years of intense preparation, 'Examination week finally arrived,' as Esther Power remembered. 'It was the climax of . . . tutorials, lectures and "collector papers". All the weekly essays and other reading and writing did not contribute at all to a degree – only the final exams counted.'[59] This was the most important week of the three years at Oxford, and the students had to overcome their fears and prove their excellence. Esther continued: 'Everyone in the examination room appeared pale. The room was divided in two with men on one side and women on the other. I sat in the last row by the window. I managed to spend some time adjusting my clothes, with my printed book before me of the examination questions. There were also blue covered notebooks which I was to fill up with answers.' She had earlier mentioned, 'I'm so mad with my stomach,' and now, as she looked around the room, she 'saw Eileen O'Shaughnessy sitting at the end of the next row. She was opening a little box and eating aspirins, apparently trying to assuage her neuralgia pains.' Eileen rarely complained of her own discomforts through the years, but the fact that she suffered from neuralgia, which might have been a mistaken diagnosis of migraine headaches, was apparently common knowledge to her good friends. Although Eileen usually presented a light-hearted demeanour, getting a first, after three years of serious dedication to that result, was extremely important to her. And Esther was well aware of that.

After almost a week of filling up the blue books with answers, the students then took 'the *viva*, the oral examination. This examination was held in a small room where some other girls were seated . . . waiting to be called to the tables in front of the examiners.' The four men who acted as Eileen's examiners all went on to illustrious careers; they made a very imposing panel for a twenty-one-year-old woman to face. One of them was A. O. Balfour, who later edited *Twelfth Century Homilies*; another was Tolkien. Frank Percy Wilson, Eileen's third examiner, was the author of *The English Drama 1485–1585*. Biographers have called him 'the most learned Elizabethan scholar of his generation, as well as a master of social graces and a witty conversationalist'. The fourth examiner was Ernest de Selincourt, a professor of poetry who later edited Wordsworth's *Guide to the Lakes* and *The Journals of Dorothy Wordsworth*, among many other books. He went on to play a significant role in Eileen's future. Apart from the note by Frank Percy Wilson, no tutor reports survive from these men.

Finally, after those excruciating hours answering oral questions, there was the long anxious wait for the results to be posted on the bulletin board. 'The results were on the four honours – first, second, third and fourth. If one did not receive an honour, one received a "pass" degree; otherwise one failed.'[60] Eileen must have devoured many more aspirins as she waited. Then, when she finally did search the bulletin board, she was devastated to discover that she had received only a Class II BA in English Language and Literature. It was no comfort to her to learn that, of her class of 1924–7 at St Hugh's, no one had managed to graduate with the coveted first-class degree. Instead, there were ten with Class II degrees, seventeen with Class III, and six with Class IV. Only thirty-three of the original fifty women students at St Hugh's with Eileen had received honours degrees. Perhaps the fact that the four examiners were all men, and Eileen's intake was only the fifth since women had been allowed to graduate, was a factor in the results. Some of the women students were all too aware that they had received different treatment from their professors through the years of study, and it's entirely possible they were still not being graded as equal in ability to the male students.

Only one woman studying at Oxford during Eileen's years there received a first-class degree. Kathleen Constable, a Somerville student in English, stayed on to do postgraduate work, along with her husband, Geoffrey Tillotson, who had been an undergraduate along with Eileen and Kathleen. This couple went on to become distinguished literary scholars, a life that Eileen had perhaps dreamed of.

Throughout those three years, quite a few of the fifty undergraduates who had begun their study at St Hugh's with Eileen had dropped out. Some students just didn't thrive in such a competitive environment and – like Margaret Munro Ellis, a scholastic competitor of Eileen's at Sunderland High School – they left Oxford when they failed. Others, like Eileen's good friend Phyllis Guimaraens, whom she kept up with after graduation, left Oxford early to get married. And Norah Symes, who saved Eileen's delightful letters after they graduated, managed only a third-class degree. One student, who hadn't done well academically, was nevertheless appreciative of her three years at St Hugh's: 'I came down in 1927 with nothing more distinguished than a Third, but with a lifelong gratitude to Oxford in general, and to St Hugh's in particular for all the happiness, the lively thought, the companionship I knew there, and for all they gave me to feed on in later years.'[61]

But Eileen was disillusioned. Her tutor reports suggest that her qualities were perhaps not fully appreciated at Oxford. Some of the weaknesses she later became aware of in her own writing were apparent then. But she also did not present the arrogant, self-confident façade her female dons exhibited. Would the talkative, lively, teasing Eileen ever have been happy in the restricted, rather dour atmosphere of academia? Possibly not. But that was what she wanted then, and with a second-class degree, that world was now closed to her. She was on her own.

By all later accounts, Eileen was an attractive, brilliant, humorous, captivating young woman at a time when those qualities were often valued only as attributes to flaunt in an auspicious marriage. And Eileen wanted more. She had made many influential friends during her three years at Oxford, and she would soon realise how important those friendships would become in her search for a fulfilling future.

4

Between Oxford and Orwell

Eileen's eyes could dance with amusement,
like a kitten's watching a dangling object.

Lydia Jackson

Eileen had taken her Oxford opportunity very seriously, hoping to get that first-class degree which would have set her up for an academic career. Her second-class degree pleased her family and her Sunderland teachers, and it was better than all her friends had managed, but Eileen was 'bitterly disappointed'.[1] She had always expected to be successful in her pursuits, and now, perhaps for the first time, she had failed. She thought life as a scholar was what she wanted. But, instead, she was forced to search for another satisfactory direction for her life.

Her position as a woman with a second-class degree was a confusing one. Most women with a third-class degree ended up getting married, but Eileen had much grander ambitions. So when she left Oxford she was in a bit of a no-man's-land. Were there jobs that she would enjoy and that would support her, so she didn't have to live at home with her parents? It was the late 1920s and young women were just beginning to get a taste of what it meant to be independent, to live

71

a fulfilling life without requiring a man to support them. And Eileen had the enthusiasm to make the most of it.

Thus, with curiosity, and with great faith in her skills as well as support from her parents, but without any decisive direction, Eileen began drifting in and out of the odd assortment of jobs available to an educated, intelligent woman of the time. She didn't realise it, but she was just at the very beginning of what would turn out to be an eight-year quest to find a meaningful purpose to which she could dedicate her life.

The most obvious career for a woman with a second-class university degree was teaching girls in one of the many private boarding schools set up for the well-to-do, and this is what Eileen tried first, perhaps influenced by the strong will of her mother, who had chosen that path herself. Eileen's first paying job was as an assistant mistress (the very title her mother had just before her marriage) at Silchester House, a school for girls, in Taplow, Buckinghamshire. After her father's retirement, her parents had moved south, to the village of Harefield in the borough of Hillingdon, northwest of London. The new house, Ravensdene, was close enough to Taplow to allow Eileen to commute to work while living with her parents. The headmistress was Miss Beatrice Roberts, who had opened the manor house as a girls' school around 1911, after the owner, Jonathan Bond, had died. The school continued to function until about a decade ago, when a day nursery took its place.[2] However, Eileen lasted there only one term before being courageous enough to inform her parents that this was not the career for her. She told a friend that, while there, she was 'engaged mainly in making a humorous study of the species of female who own and staff such schools'.[3] Taplow is within ten miles of Henley-on-Thames, Orwell's childhood home, and for the first of many times throughout those eight years, Eileen's path passed close to Orwell's, though the timing was always off.

As we know, another of Eileen's assortment of odd jobs through the years was writing and publishing a number of articles, another possible career she might have considered. A second piece possibly by Eileen was discovered in the *London Evening News*. On 4 December 1928, the paper printed an article entitled 'Looking Back on the Michaelmas Term', by 'A Woman Graduate'. Eileen visited Oxford often through the years, and this article, published a year after she graduated, and therefore just months after she had decided not to return to the job as schoolmistress, contains vivid memories, perhaps indicating that its author was still struggling to find herself after a year at a disagreeable job. It began:

> *The Michaelmas term at Oxford is drawing rapidly to its close, and the women especially are busy crowding their numerous activities into these last weeks.*
>
> *Most women undergraduates find Michaelmas term the best of all . . . Perfect autumn weather has shown Oxford at her best, a rapturous revelation to 'freshers', an ever-increasing beauty to those who know her already.*

Then, after reminiscing about all the special and thrilling activities the 'fresher' women students had the opportunity to participate in, as well as the 'new freedom' they were experiencing for the first time away from home, the author closed with:

> *Not the least pleasant hours of the Michaelmas term are those when, work finished, games and amusements ended, and the college gates securely shut, the women finish their happy, crowded day with a late coffee party . . . If much good talk goes up the chimney, enough remains to add a lasting fragrance to the memory of the Michaelmas terms.*

This article recalls many of the same pleasures mentioned in the piece published by the same newspaper a couple of years earlier, and is likely written by the same person, quite possibly Eileen.

A postcard to Eileen from an unidentified friend in Baden-Baden, Germany, 27 July 1930.

Eileen's father became ill with tuberculosis around this time, causing her brother Eric to return briefly from the Sudan, where he had gone in 1924 to practise medicine. Laurence O'Shaughnessy died on 5 November 1929, at the age of sixty-three, and the cause of his death no doubt influenced Eric's further medical studies in the field of tuberculosis. In Laurence's will, which he had made out in 1902 when he was stationed in the Shetland Islands (with later revisions), all his belongings, including the Harefield house and 'any moneys due from the customs Annuity Benevolent fund', were left to his wife. The gross value of the estate was listed as £1,024 10s 3d but the net value was only £166 9s 4d. Although he had been a well-paid civil servant, he had apparently accumulated no savings. At that point, with Eric back in the Sudan, the care of her mother fell totally to Eileen. Mary O'Shaughnessy was sixty-three, and would live another twelve years, so she became completely entangled in Eileen's life, even well after Eileen's marriage to Orwell.

Eileen and her mother continued to live in Harefield through 1930. That summer, Eileen received a postcard addressed simply to 'Eileen O'Shaughnessy, Harefield, Middlesex', and dated 27 July 1930. It was from Baden-Baden, Germany, and stated simply, though in poor English, 'Here is very old England. No lady with less than 60. Yours WB.'[4] This postcard, mysteriously preserved, is one of the very few sent to Eileen that have survived, which could imply a special interest in this person. During his years in the Sudan, her brother had made trips to Germany to study with experts in his field, so possibly Eileen had visited him in Germany and met a colleague of his there.

Oxford University asked its students to keep it informed of their activities after graduation, and Eileen dutifully kept in touch, though not in much detail. In 1930 she informed the university that she was on the 'Archbishop's Advisory Board for Prevention and Rescue Work'. This has generally been assumed to mean that she worked in some manner with London's prostitutes. However, extensive records of the work of the 'Archbishops' Advisory Board for Preventive and Rescue Work' (as it is correctly worded) have been preserved in the Lambeth Palace Library, and Eileen's name cannot be found anywhere in the Board's records. However, there is a far more likely explanation of the type of work she did.

In 1930, after ten years in existence, the Board was being criticised by its own staff members for not providing the proper moral and sexual advice. An attempt was made to reconstitute its operation, and on 13 March a letter went out to prominent citizens, including 'experienced physicians, psychologists, educationalists, social workers, and theologians', stating: 'The Archbishop of York and I are anxious to invite the assistance of some who have special knowledge of the important subject of Sex and its bearing on all human relationships.' The cumbersome name of the Board was also debated, and it was later changed to the hardly more simple 'Church of England Advisory Board for Moral Welfare Work'.

To help with all the note-taking and typing that would be required to transcribe the events at the Lambeth Conference that summer, it was decided to hire 'a Shorthand typist (half time)', and on 30 June 1930, a letter stated that 'W. B. Gurney & Sons, Shorthand Writers, of 47, Victoria St.', had been chosen as the 'official shorthand writers'.[5] This date coincides exactly with Eileen's note to Oxford informing them of what she was doing in 1930. She had developed into an excellent shorthand writer, like her late Uncle Edward.

We know from a friend that, after her year of teaching, Eileen had worked 'in an office run by a neurotically sadistic woman' who 'took pleasure in humiliating her employees, criticising their work in a most severe, destructive way and keeping them under a permanent threat of dismissal',[6] and this job with W. B. Gurney[7] must be the one Eileen told her friend about. Another woman employee had almost had a nervous breakdown while working for this same boss, 'who revelled in reducing all her female staff to tears'.[8] Eileen found it impossible to continue working for this malicious woman after the job with the Archbishops' Advisory Board was completed, and she decided to call it quits. But not in a quiet way. She bragged to her friend that she planned the dramatic occasion ahead of time, and 'led a successful "revolt of the oppressed" against [the boss] before she walked out in triumph'.[9] Eileen left no further details of her 'revolt', but she was obviously proud of it.

Her experience at Oxford fighting against the traditional assumptions about women was now influencing her activity in the working world. And throughout the rest of her life, Eileen proudly resisted orders from her bosses that she found repugnant to obey.

Eileen told Oxford that her next job, in 1931, was as 'reader to Mrs George Cadbury of Birmingham'. A friend later remembered that 'curiosity and a wish to get away from home prompted [Eileen] to accept' this offer to work with 'the doyenne of that well-known family, who had become almost blind in her old age'.[10] Being a companion or reader for a wealthy older woman was quite a common occupation for someone in Eileen's situation. Perhaps a member of the Archbishops' Board had introduced Eileen to Dame Elizabeth Mary Cadbury while she was working there, and that gave her the courage to walk out in defiance from W. B. Gurney. It's also possible that Ernest de Selincourt, one of her Oxford tutors, facilitated an introduction, since at that time he was a professor at the University of Birmingham.

Dame Elizabeth, the widow of the chocolate manufacturer, was seventy-three at the time, and she was living in the Manor House, Northfield, Birmingham, today a hall of residence for the University of Birmingham. She was a highly educated woman, the child of former temperance crusaders, and as a young woman had done social work in poor areas of London and Paris. When Eileen took the job, Dame Elizabeth was well known for her philanthropic work on behalf of women, acting at one point as Britain's representative at the World Congress of the International Council of Women. She believed that a life of service should be a requirement for a woman with a higher education, an echo of Miss Ironsides, back in Sunderland High School. Eileen's skills would have been valuable to Dame Elizabeth, and her life's work no doubt impressed Eileen, but the job was short-lived. Perhaps her lonely mother convinced her to leave this job, or perhaps being isolated in a Birmingham manor house lost its charm, although her friend said Eileen 'seemed to have enjoyed the experience'.[11] Working with this influential woman, Eileen began to discover that there was a stimulating and honourable way to use her talents.

By the end of 1931, Eileen had returned to London and was sharing a flat with her mother at 22 Albany Mansions, on Albert Bridge Road, in southwest London. However, they retained the Harefield house, renting it out for extra income. Eileen inherited it when her mother died, and for a few years she and Orwell benefited from its rent. When Eileen died, Orwell sold the house as quickly as he could. Eileen informed Oxford University that, as of December 1931, she was 'Proprietor of an office in Victoria Street for translation, typing and secretarial services'. This was Murrells Typewriting Bureau, a business created by Grace Murrell and taken over by Eileen, located in the basement of 49 Victoria Street, right next door to W. B. Gurney & Sons.

Eileen's fifteen-year-old assistant, Edna, who called herself the 'oil rag' – which must have been something like today's 'gofer' – worked there with Eileen for two years. When information was being collected for the Orwell archives, Edna (whose married name was Bussey) offered an early personal description of Eileen, a loving recollection of a generous woman genuinely trying to help clients, and with no apparent drive to make the bureau a financial success. Fortunately, Eileen was from the class of working women who didn't have to completely support themselves by their jobs. As Edna remembered: 'They were very happy days as [Eileen] was a very happy person and had a very vivid personality. I don't think she ever made very much money as she was too generous and I fear most unbusinesslike. She was untiring in her efforts to help people.' Edna recalled, as an example, 'a Mr Tereshenko, he was a white Russian, who was writing a thesis for his professorship, being taken under [Eileen's] wing. She literally re-wrote his thesis for him and I have always felt that it was she who earned the professorship.' And another friend remembered that a Nikolai Tereschenko, with some influence at Oxford, helped her get a job there in 1941.[12] Edna concluded, 'Writing was her love I think.'[13]

On 20 November 1933, the *London Evening News* printed the following article: 'Queer Clients Who Come to Me,' by 'A London Typist'.

It is since I wrote 'Typewriting Bureau' on my office door that I have fully realised the truth of the saying: 'All the world's queer . . .' [This quote, by Robert Owen, goes, in full: 'All the world is queer save thee and me, and even thou art a little queer.'] For my machine is what the scribe's pen used to be – a link between cranks, crooks and geniuses, and the powers-with-the-money who can make the day-dreams of all these queer folk come true.

My first surprise was from the old Irishman, clad in frayed trousers and what had once been a chauffeur's tunic, who ordered thus: 'A draft of a letter asking for nine million pounds. Not for meself, Miss. A door-to-door appeal to start an allotment scheme that will finish unemployment in ten months.'

I suggested that nine million was a lot to hope for.

'Too much, d'ye think? Then make it six, or one, or just a few thou . . . Oi leave it to you.'

A one-shilling bill for the draft, and the information that I could not make five thousand copies 'on tick' settled that client.

More profitable but more provoking too was the Russian student who knows so much more about English than does the Oxford Dictionary. As for punctuation, he arranges it frankly for artistic effect. A week after I had typed his examination thesis, he brought it back: 'Just for a little re-adjustment of the commas. They are too stereotyped. I prefer them so . . . and so . . .'

Young inventors are hard cases. Natural boastfulness about their brain-children, when combined with the technical language that the Patents Office approves, results in what is so much double Dutch to the mere lay typist. Once, after typing three foolscap pages of a descriptive report about 'junctions,' 'cross-sections at thirty-five degrees' and 'remarkable improvements,' I asked: 'Does this apparatus look very complicated?'

> *'Oh, well, it doesn't appear so very different from the old,*
> *unimproved hat-stand,' admitted my client.*
>
> *The most eager to make confidences are unlaunched authors. One,*
> *a shabby-looking individual, came in to look up a telephone number,*
> *stayed to dictate a letter asking for a loan – 'the words "money badly*
> *needed" in the biggest letters of your machine, please' – and finally*
> *explained that he was looking for a philanthropist to publish his book.*
> *A book which would revolutionise the whole world. He has written it on*
> *odd scraps of paper, everywhere between Newfoundland and Borneo,*
> *during the last thirty years; and it settles the man-from-apes question*
> *once and for all. I was promised the typing of it. But the MSS hasn't*
> *arrived yet . . . perhaps philanthropists are rather scarce.*

The mention of a Russian student whose examination thesis the article's author typed coincides directly with Edna Bussey's memory, making it distinctly possible that this was written by Eileen. At the bottom of this piece are typed the letters S.O.: perhaps a mistake, although it is possible that Eileen used an alternative first name for her creative writing, as she did later with one good Oxford friend, as well as when she worked at the Ministry of Food. The newspaper did not save original manuscripts from that time, so the actual author cannot be traced.

While she worked with Eileen, Edna met Eileen's family and left the earliest description of them: 'Her mother . . . was a Norfolk woman, with a very pronounced accent,' she remembered. 'They were a mad, gay family and I was very fond of them.' She also recalled that Eileen wanted to help her get an education. 'We got along together so very well, we seemed to know each other's thoughts and sometimes even the next moves,' Edna said. '[Eileen] wanted me to go and live with her and her mother and continue studying English. She thought I had potential and took a great interest. Her idea was for me eventually to try to enter a university.' But Edna divulged that she believed her own mother was 'very jealous' of her friendship with Eileen, and when her parents decided to move to the country, they insisted that she leave the business and move with them. 'Eileen was very disturbed as she had grown very fond of me,' she recalled. Edna ended her letter of remembrance saying, 'Probably you may think I am biased – well I am. I am sure you too would have been under [Eileen's] spell – she was truly Irish.' We can only guess what she meant by 'truly Irish'. The two stayed in contact for some years, and Edna appears from her letter to have become quite competent in her use of English, perhaps studying further after leaving her job with Eileen.

In this letter, Edna also admitted that she was upset when Eileen married Orwell. 'I didn't like the idea of him. I may be very wrong but I have always had the feeling that he didn't take enough care of her. She should never have died from just a simple operation nor so young,' she wrote. She believed that Orwell 'owed a tremendous amount to Eileen for his success as a writer . . . It was not until after he had met her that he became famous . . . Poor Eileen, it seems such a pity that she should just be known to the world as his "first wife". She was such a wonderful person and I am sure gave all she had to him to help him to success.' Edna is here supposing that Eileen helped edit and rewrite Orwell's creative work, an assumption she might easily make after having observed Eileen perfect the thesis of the Russian student. '[Eileen] and I corresponded for several years,' Edna wrote, 'but unhappily for me I was deprived of [her letters] by one of Hitler's land mines.'[14]

In 1932, Eric O'Shaughnessy and his wife, Gwen, decided to return permanently to London from the Sudan. They had joined the Sudan Medical Service in 1924 and worked in Africa together for seven years, getting married there in 1926. After his father's death from tuberculosis, in 1929, Eric became seriously involved in the treatment of that disease. At the Omdurman Civic Hospital, in the Sudan, he began developing 'his aptitude as an "experimental" surgeon . . . In his desire to do something for the cases of pulmonary tuberculosis he met with, he carried out at that early stage at least 200 phrenic avulsions [partial extraction of the phrenic nerve, causing collapse of the infected lung].'[15] According to the doctor he had assisted, Eric 'was hard-working, persevering and extremely intelligent. He was apt to be off-hand and abrupt in his manner and did not suffer gladly those he considered fools. Consequently he made enemies, but learning the hard way he gradually acquired a more tolerant and courteous attitude.'[16] This abrasive quality to Eric's personality was commented on throughout his life.

Eric's wife Gwen, herself a doctor, worked first in the Church Missionary Society Hospital, in Omdurman, which was 'a well equipped hospital of thirty-five beds in charge of a highly qualified surgeon assisted by a lady doctor [Gwen Hunton, her maiden name] . . . Two hundred and fifty major operations were performed [during that year].'[17] Gwen was remembered as 'an excellent doctor, with first-class clinical judgment and a good pair of hands. It was a pleasure to watch her do cataract extractions. She was gentle in her approach to people, which appealed to the Sudanese women.'[18]

On their way back to England, the couple spent six months in Germany, where Eric worked with Ferdinand Sauerbruch, a man he had studied with on his leaves from the Sudan. Sauerbruch was a renowned German surgeon who specialised in experimental work in thoracic surgery, and later had connections to Hitler and the Nazi regime. When the couple arrived in England, Eric continued to work on, among other things, improving the surgical treatment of pulmonary tuberculosis. And later, as we shall see, when his sister's husband, George Orwell, began struggling with tuberculosis, Eric's expertise allowed him to be of great assistance to them. But for a while Eric 'found it extremely difficult to establish himself as he was anxious to do in London.'[19]

Eric and Gwen set up house at 59 Trafalgar Road in Greenwich, where Eileen and her mother joined them, at 59A Trafalgar Road, probably the upstairs flat, in 1933. Although her brother became acclaimed for his innovative surgical techniques, like many scientific geniuses he had neglected to perfect his knowledge of the grammatical subtleties of the

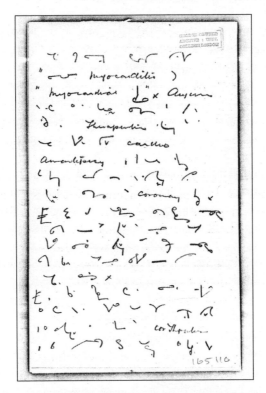

A sample of Eileen's shorthand for one of her brother Eric's books.

English language. As Eileen told a friend, tactfully, Eric 'had difficulty in putting his findings into clear language.'[20] So when he started writing medical articles and books, Eileen acquired yet another time-consuming job, that of editing, proofreading, and typing her brother's work. She would also take dictation from him, and copies of her shorthand notes have been preserved in the Orwell archives. Throughout the following years, even as she had her own jobs and a Master's in psychology to pursue, Eileen was on constant call to her brother.

Eric never credited Eileen in his many articles in the *Lancet* and other journals, nor in the books he worked on with Sauerbruch, including, according to one review, the 'magnificent volume' *Thoracic Surgery*, published in 1937. But we never hear Eileen complain. Throughout all her attempts at finding fulfilling work, she realised that being of crucial assistance to her brilliant brother, one of the people she most admired, was an occupation that satisfied her. She did not require any acknowledged praise for her help; she believed being needed, and using the skills she prized in herself, was reward enough.

Eileen's high school in Sunderland celebrated its fiftieth anniversary, in 1934, with gatherings and dinners both on the school grounds and in London. Eileen is not obvious in some surviving photos of the celebrations, but she was well aware of the significance of the anniversary. Looking fifty years ahead, to the school's 100th anniversary, she wrote a poem titled 'End of the Century, 1984', which was published in the Sunderland High School magazine in 1934, the year before she met Orwell.[21]

END OF THE CENTURY, 1984

Death

Synthetic winds have blown away
Material dust, but this one room
Rebukes the constant violet ray
And dustless sheds a dusty doom.
Wrecked on the outmoded past
Lie North and Hillard, Virgil, Horace,
Shakespeare's bones are quiet at last.
Dead as Yeats or William Morris.
Have not the inmates earned their rest?
A hundred circles traversed they
Complaining of the classic quest
And, each inevitable day,
Illogically trying to place
A ball within an empty space.

Birth

Every loss is now a gain
For every chance must follow reason.
A crystal palace meets the rain
That falls at its appointed season.
No book disturbs the lucid line
For sun-bronzed scholars tune their thought
To Telepathic Station 9
From which they know just what they ought:
The useful sciences; the arts
Of telesalesmanship and Spanish
As registered in Western parts;
Mental cremation that shall banish
Relics, philosophies and colds –
Mañana-minded ten-year-olds.

The Phoenix

Worlds have died that they may live,
May plume again their fairest feathers
And in their clearest songs may give
Welcome to all spontaneous weathers.
Bacon's colleague is called Einstein,
Huxley shares Platonic food,
Violet rays are only sunshine
Christened in the modern mood.
In this house if in no other
Past and future may agree,
Each herself, but each the other
In a curious harmony,
Finding both a proper place
In the silken gown's embrace.

As Eileen wrote this poem, she was engulfed by news of the growing horrors of governments close by, those led by Hitler, Mussolini, and Stalin. She feared that the world of scholarship and cultural life that she so loved – represented by some interesting choices of writers in the poem – was being destroyed by the designs of men she abhorred.

Her typing and stenographic work had deprived her of the time to glory in the poetry of the past, and she wrote this poem in memory of her days of study at school, regretting that in the present time there was no use for her beloved poets – they had become 'outmoded'. She was critical of the present, with its emphasis on science, technology, and rationality, where 'sun-bronzed scholars,' without the need for books, 'know just what they ought', leading to 'mental cremation'. This vision foreshadows Orwell's vision, expressed in *Nineteen Eighty-Four*, of a world where the only accepted thought is prescribed by Big Brother. Orwell saw his novel as a warning, not a prediction, about the future. Eileen envisioned a 'curious harmony' of the past and future. Because she was eternally optimistic, she decided to look forward another fifty years, to 1984, and imagine that the world would right itself. She believed that knowledge of the past could not be completely wiped out and that, at least at institutes of learning, the past glories would be resurrected. Orwell's thoughts about how the world might transform itself years later were not as optimistic as his wife's. He hoped she was right, but he feared she was wrong.

Through all her various attempts to find some worthy way to use the talents and energy she knew she possessed, Eileen constantly missed her engrossing studies at Oxford. She bemoaned the fact that in London she was never relaxed enough to enjoy reading poetry, one of her great loves. She recalled many years later, 'When I lived in London before I was married I used to go away certainly once a month with a suitcase full of poetry and that consoled me until the next time – or I used to go up to Oxford and read in the Bodleian and take a punt up the Cher if it was summer or walk in Port Meadow or to Godstow if it was winter.'[22] She dreamed of a future life outside of London, but she hadn't yet found anyone who shared this desire. In the meantime, she chose yet another defiantly new direction.

Bored with correcting other people's attempts at creativity, and accepting that she was not advancing quickly enough as a writer herself, Eileen became intrigued by the relatively new field of educational psychology. University College London promoted its psychology classes taught by Professor Cyril Burt and his staff, hoping to broaden interest in the field, and in the autumn of 1934, Eileen signed up for a two-year course towards an MA. She had been mentally cataloguing different human types since childhood and she was already astute in understanding human behaviour. Now she decided to put it all together for a career.

Cyril Burt, fifty-one in 1934 and a prominent and influential educational psychologist, was described as 'short in stature and brisk in manner . . . always eloquent, witty and stimulating.'[23] He had conducted tests in 1912 establishing that girls were equal to boys in general intelligence, and had later acquired a reputation as an expert on IQ testing. He specialised in investigating whether there was a correlation between heredity and intelligence, believing that all children should be given the chance for a good education. Eileen was 'urged on by Burt, who recognised in her a more than ordinary aptitude. She was particularly attracted to intelligence-testing in children,'[24] according to someone who interviewed him later. In later years Burt was accused of fabricating some of his data, but there has been no definitive conclusion that he did.

The Department of Psychology was located on the top floor of one wing of the college, and lectures were held 'in the large room with the leaking ceiling,'[25] suggesting that these classes were not yet considered important subjects of pursuit. Most of the study involved lectures, but twice a week the students participated in experiments in a psychological 'laboratory', to teach them 'the scientific method

– observation, accurate measurements, presentation of results'. As a classmate remembered, 'This we did in pairs, for one student had to act as "experimenter" and the other as a "guinea-pig", the two changing roles when the process was repeated.' These experiments later included 'word association' and 'reliability of eye-witness' tests 'which involved imagination and feeling rather than mere sensation'.[26] This more in-depth training, added to her intuitive personality, became of great use later in Eileen's life, when she constantly had to deal with her difficult brother and sometimes more difficult husband.

During her first year of study, Eileen signed up for sixteen courses, divided into three terms, many of them taught by Cyril Burt. The catalogue lists Eileen's courses as:

General Courses.

Z1. Psychology: its General Principles and Methods.

Z2. General Seminar. This will consist in discussion and in written work based on the preceding course of lectures (Z1).

Z4. A short Laboratory Course especially to meet the needs of students of Education.

Z5. Technique of Experimentation. A Course in the methods used, and the ground covered, by the experiments of Courses Z3 and Z4.

Intercollegiate Courses.

A1. A Seminar on the recent results and views in contemporary Psychology.

A2. Fundamental Problems and Controversies. This will consist of advanced lectures and discussions on selected topics of fundamental importance in Psychology.

A3. Correlational Methods in Psychology: An acquaintance with advanced mathematics will not be presupposed.

A6. Psychophysics, Oscillation and Fatigue.

A9. The Psycho-Analytic Study of Conduct and Character.

A10(i). Psychopathology.

A10(ii). Mental Hygiene.

A11. Psychology of the Learning Process.

A12(i). The Psychology of the Child under Nine.

A12(ii). Seminar. Special methods of Research with Infants and young Children.

A13. Individual Differences in Mental Characteristics. This Course includes the general theory and chief experimental results.

A14. Higher Mental Processes.[27]

In addition, as part of her curriculum, Eileen conducted three meetings for Young Workers' organisations, the first year in Tottenham and the second in Camberwell.[28] Each meeting included a short course in psychology.

It is at this point that Lydia Jackson (who sometimes wrote under the name Elisaveta Fen) entered Eileen's life. Lydia was a fellow MA student who left us vast amounts of intimate information about Eileen. Born in Russia, recently divorced, and ten years older than Eileen, Lydia was one of an odd range of interesting people who chose to study psychology that year. Eileen immediately befriended Lydia, who, in her own self-description, 'could not refrain from asking [the lecturers] questions, no matter how pointed, or naïve they might sound'. Eileen found Lydia's behaviour amusing, and early on, as Lydia remembered, Eileen turned 'to look at me, her large, short-sighted, blue eyes narrowed, a smile raising the corners of her mouth'.[29] Although most photographs of Eileen show her without glasses, a few friends do mention her need of them. And recently a class photo at Oxford was discovered showing her sporting a pair. Eileen introduced herself in a break, and Lydia soon became one of her closest friends – and, later on, perhaps a little too close a friend of Orwell's.

Lydia often sounds a bit peevish and overcritical in her characterisations of others, and a rarely seen photograph of her shows a woman with a stern glare and a severe centre parting in her brushed-back hair. But one of their fellow students, John Cohen, who later became a psychology professor at the University of Manchester, remembered Lydia as 'a very jolly type, with huge teeth . . . and blonde hair with a huge coil bound round her head: very companionable and pleasant'. He continued his friendship with her after graduation, including visits to her flat in Bloomsbury.[30] Lydia, for her part, remembered Cohen as showing off in class 'by involving lecturers in hair-splitting arguments about minor points of theory', suggesting that she might not have returned his interest in her.

Lydia believed, while watching them interact in class, that 'Eileen was amused by [Cohen's] cleverness and persistence.'[31] However, Cohen was not, at least in his later memory, equally amused by Eileen. He said that he 'had a very vivid memory of Eileen', and 'knew [her] very well indeed', as she was for a time his partner in experiments. He described Eileen's behaviour in class as 'bright, rather tough, could be argumentative and "provocative"'.[32] But he also remembered her as 'rather prim and stiff, very unlike [Lydia] . . . Nothing voluptuous about her'.[33] Although Cohen dined regularly at Bertorelli's and the Fitzroy Tavern, the meeting places for 'everyone that counted . . . all the Bloomsbury literati', he apparently did not continue a friendship with Eileen, who also frequented these places later on with Orwell. However, with this being a rare divergence from the usual description of Eileen's personality – and with her, at least at first, being 'amused' by Cohen's 'cleverness' – one is tempted to imagine an unrequited love on his part.

Lydia also described in great detail some of the other students in the class, revealing a curious collection of the type of person attracted by the study of psychology at the time. She remembered especially two young Jewish girls, Miriam and Jenny, whose 'looks and behaviour were very different from the image of "Jewishness" I had brought with me from Russia'. Miriam, from what was then Palestine, was 'slow-moving, with cow-like eyes and fresh complexion . . . [She] was somewhat at sea among the sophisticated crowd of psychology students . . . and failed the examinations at the end of the first year.' On the other hand, Jenny, a Londoner, and the daughter of a rabbi, 'looked very English with her blue eyes, light-brown hair and rosy complexion . . . But she was very shy and unsure of herself – character traits not commonly associated with Jewishness,' as Lydia believed. She went on to inform us that 'Eileen had a theory that Jenny was terrified of falling in love with a Gentile,' adding, 'I do not know what grounds she had for thinking that.' After qualifying, Jenny decided to change fields, and Lydia mused that her 'flight from psychology into neurology might have been a result of her fear of emotion and "the unconscious" which Eileen had perceived earlier on.'[34]

And then there was Rosalind Obermeyer, a student from South Africa. Lydia did not leave a description of her in her memoirs, but she was soon to become a momentous force in Eileen's future.

Eileen's chosen thesis 'involved giving intelligence tests to a large, unselected sample of children,'[35] and as Lydia remembered, 'She was a brilliant student and was greatly encouraged to go on with this work by the Head of the Department [Cyril Burt].'[36] However, Eileen never completed her second year of study, and never did receive her MA, as we will see. Lydia was very happy to be accepted immediately by Eileen. She found her 'outgoing and curious about people,'[37] as was Lydia herself, and their friendship developed quickly. Eileen preferred friends who were as lively and outspoken and as self-confident as she was. Lydia appreciated Eileen's mischievous sense of humour, what others called her Irishness, and noticed that, when she told you something amusing, her 'eyes could dance . . . like a kitten's watching a dangling object,'[38] even as 'you knew that she habitually embroidered her stories, that things did not happen quite as amusingly or unexpectedly as she described.' Nevertheless, Lydia added, Eileen's 'exaggerations were rarely malicious.'[39] Occasionally, however, they were. In some of her letters, Eileen barely conceals her scorn for certain kinds of human behaviour, though she tries to disguise these critiques in her constant teasing descriptions. And she was always outgoing and competitive, especially when dealing with her brilliant brother. According to a professional analysis of her handwriting, she had a need for attention and sometimes put on an act to impress others with her intellect, which she highly valued. The analysis also predicts that Eileen could be persistent in getting her version of things understood, since she felt she wasn't always being listened to, and one way she attracted attention to herself was by being inventive and charming and full of teasing humour. But she often chose to hide her deeper real feelings.[40]

Through Lydia, we get an extensive description of Eileen's appearance at that time. 'Physically, she was very attractive . . . tall [by which Lydia meant about 5 feet 5 inches] and slender,' and she had 'what is commonly regarded as Irish colouring: dark hair, light-blue eyes and [a] delicate white and pink complexion.'[41] However, 'her shoulders [were] rather broad and high, giving an impression of a slight stoop,'[42] and making her 'rather gawky in the way she moved'. When Lydia was surprised that Eileen used rouge, she explained, 'If I didn't I'd look as if I were about to pass out.'[43] One night, when Lydia stayed over in Eileen's room, she 'was struck and strangely moved by Eileen's exceptional thinness when I saw her standing in her nightdress before a looking-glass and shivering with cold.'[44] Lydia came to believe that the 'milky whiteness' of Eileen's skin was an early sign of her weak constitution, although '[S]he somehow succeeded in doing more work than many strong women.'[45]

Gradually, as Eric O'Shaughnessy worked hard to establish himself in England, success and recognition began coming his way. As he and his wife moved to larger and more impressive houses, they always had room for Eileen and old Mrs O'Shaughnessy. Gwen was remembered by everyone as kind and good-hearted, rather quiet, and constantly unselfish. But taking her rather difficult mother-in-law and her vibrant sister-in-law into her home could not have been easy for her. Her adopted daughter, Catherine Moncure, said recently that Gwen herself 'never commented on her [mother-in-law's] personality or whether she did or didn't like living with her'. However, she got the impression from other people in the household 'that Mrs O'Shaughnessy had a domineering or forceful character'.[46] Eileen told Lydia that 'she was her father's favourite [while Eric was] the apple of their mother's eye',[47] implying a division in the family's early affections.

Of course, Gwen was also living with a difficult husband. One heart-specialist friend remembered Eric as 'an Irishman, quick and determined'.[48] According to another report, 'O'Shaughnessy would have no truck with pompous mediocrity and tolerated badly those who put form before deed.'[49] Eileen herself later described him as 'a Nature's Fascist',[50] though she meant this somewhat lovingly, since she clearly admired him greatly. Although Eric was a busy doctor, Eileen could always charm him into doing any favour she needed. Perhaps they hadn't always got along well as youngsters, but as adults they had grown very close.

Lydia immediately became intimately involved with the vivacious family that Edna Bussey had so appreciated. Lydia and Eileen's class lectures on 'Psychopathology' and 'Mental Hygiene' were given by Dr Hadfield on Friday evenings at King's College. One evening after class, Eileen's brother picked her up in his 'large, important-looking car'. Lydia 'was struck by the resemblance between [them]: the shape of his face, rather wide at the cheek-bones . . . and he carried himself in the same way, with shoulders raised and a slight stoop'. From his photographs it's clear that Eric was a strikingly handsome man. When Eileen introduced Lydia to her brother, she was greatly impressed that he gave her 'a penetrating look straight in the eye'. Eileen then announced to her brother, 'We'll drive Lydia home', and he replied, 'Of course.'[51] Clearly Eric was willing to help out whenever Eileen needed him, but, for her part, she expected her wishes to be followed without question. She, of course, had been helping Eric for a couple of years with his scientific papers and books, and she would continue to do so for many years to come.

Around this time, Eric and Gwen moved into a pretty three-storey house at 18 Montpelier Row, in Blackheath, close to Greenwich Park, and Eileen and her mother must have moved with them since this is the address Eileen gave when registering for her MA in psychology in the autumn of 1934. Shortly after meeting Eileen's brother, Lydia was invited to dinner with the O'Shaughnessys. She felt she already knew a lot about them because '[Eileen] talked of her family with what seemed to be an utter and deliberate frankness, revealing their relationships with one another as if she were discussing people in a book.' At first Lydia dismissed Gwen as 'a person of little significance', believing she was 'displaced in her own home by her husband's brilliant sister'. Eileen, displaying her occasional tendency to reject people, was also a bit dismissive of Gwen, telling Lydia, with 'some satisfaction', Lydia thought, that 'his wife can't help him. He doesn't discuss his work with her. Anyway, she rarely says anything at all.'[52] Perhaps in this case Eileen was feeling a little jealous about losing her much admired brother to another woman. Gwen would have sensed a negative attitude from Eileen, and yet she continued willingly to share her home with her husband's sister and mother. She was a brilliant doctor in her own right, as well as a generous, courageous woman, and Lydia learned eventually to appreciate how exceptional she was, as did almost everyone who met her.

The O'Shaughnessy home became a gathering place for many visitors. Lydia wrote, 'New faces were always welcomed in the O'Shaughnessies' household. Eric had a curiosity about people almost as great as Eileen's.' She added that she 'noticed with some surprise and admiration the composure with which Gwen went on accepting various young females he brought into the house from time to time. She must have been sure of his unswerving attachment to herself to accept so much rivalry without protest.'[53] We know that Eileen and Orwell had a somewhat open marriage, but there is no record of such an agreement between Eric and Gwen. However, in a much later diary entry, Lydia included Eric in her list of 'male friends and lovers'.[54]

Catherine Moncure remembered that Florrie Taylor – who was then the household cook, but later became her nanny – told her that she 'used to get so upset because Eric would invite people over for dinner and not tell anyone and Florrie would have to go to her brother, a butcher, and beg for some extra meat . . . Feeding everyone . . . wasn't easy as it seemed to be a revolving door.'[55]

At one of these parties, Eileen met Karl Schnetzler, a friend of Eric's, a man Lydia described as 'blond, with blue eyes, over six foot tall . . . pleasant-looking without being handsome'. According to Lydia, Karl 'came from a well-to-do family [in Germany] and had studied at Heidelberg, [but] as he disliked living under the Nazi régime, he decided to settle in England.' He had apparently done well in his new country, since 'his specialty was electrical engineering and he had no difficulty in obtaining a job with a large English firm.'[56] Karl wrote later that he had 'worked in England as an Electrical (Research) Engineer from 1935 to 1956, except for the war years, when I was interned (from 1939 to 1943)'. He remembered that he 'was introduced to George Orwell's first wife Eileen at a party at her brother's house at Greenwich.'[57] He didn't mention any romance, even though Lydia felt sure that Karl was in love with Eileen. They kept in touch for many years, as Eileen did with other male friends. When Karl first visited Eileen at the Wallington cottage after she was married, he was, according to Lydia, upset at the way Orwell was treating her. He later went to the cottage 'from time to time', and also accompanied Eileen on visits to see Orwell when he was recuperating from a serious attack of tuberculosis in 1938. But Eileen always denied any romantic relationship between them.

A s the spring term at University College London began, in 1935, Rosalind Obermeyer invited her classmates Eileen and Lydia and a few others to a party she was co-hosting in her flat at 77 Parliament Hill, in Hampstead. Her new flatmate, Eric Blair, who had just begun living in a small room attached to Rosalind's larger flat, was a relatively unknown writer who wrote under the pen name George Orwell. He had long awaited the moment when he would have enough books published to consider himself 'lancé'[58] (successfully launched into a writing career), and he now felt that time had arrived. So he asked Rosalind whether they could 'give a joint party, as his bed-sitter was too small'.[59] To entice Eileen and Lydia to accept the invitation, Rosalind mentioned that two published authors would be at the party. When they agreed to go, they were both totally unaware that their lives were about to be irrevocably changed.

5

A Whirlwind Courtship

Now that *is the kind of girl I would like to marry!*
Orwell to a friend, the evening he met Eileen

As Eileen and Lydia walked up Parliament Hill Road to the last house before the climb onto Hampstead Heath, Lydia slipped and scraped her knee, which started to bleed. So she was in 'a far from festive mood' as they neared the house where the party was being held. But that was not uncommon for her. Her ex-husband had left her for another woman, which had shocked and depressed her, and Eileen might even have had to persuade her friend to venture out that night. Eileen, who would turn thirty soon, hadn't yet found anyone she cared enough about to marry, and she'd been intrigued when Rosalind had promised they would meet some published authors at the party. Being occasional writers themselves, she and Lydia were curious enough to make the long trip, although neither of them had heard of the two authors mentioned, Richard Rees and George Orwell.

The party soon spread from Orwell's small room into Rosalind's larger quarters across the hall. When Eileen and Lydia entered what Lydia remembered as a 'sparsely furnished and poorly lit' room, they noticed in particular, among the dozen or so guests, two very tall men 'draped over an unlit fireplace' in deep conversation. Lydia was not at all impressed with their appearance, saying, 'Their clothes were drab and their faces lined and unhealthy.' Russian was her native language, and she went on to elaborate that they looked, 'in Chekhov's immortal phrase, rather "moth-eaten".'[1] However, the description 'moth-eaten' does not appear in the English versions of any of Chekhov's plays. It has recently been suggested that this was Lydia's own translation of *'oblezly barin'* from *The Cherry Orchard*, meaning literally a 'shabby-looking gentleman.'[2]

One of these tall men stopped in mid-conversation to admire Eileen as he watched her for a moment from across the room. He then quickly approached her and introduced himself as Eric Blair, the name Orwell still used with his friends and for all his writing except his novels. Orwell must have been remembering this electric moment when he compared, a few years later, beautiful images in Yeats's poetry to the overwhelming feeling of seeing a girl's face across a room.[3] Lydia didn't record what she did the rest of the evening, but Rosalind noticed that Orwell 'paid a good bit of attention to Eileen', and that Eileen welcomed it.[4] It is significant, considering later events, that when seeing the two women for the first time Orwell immediately chose Eileen. Perhaps his initial preference for her helped shape Lydia's early distaste for the man.

Eileen and Orwell liked each other immediately. Just her name, Eileen O'Shaughnessy, was delightful. Gwen, Eileen's brother's wife, joked that his surname had been one of his main attractions. And their adopted daughter, Catherine, regretted having to give up the O'Shaughnessy name when she got married.[5] Although Eileen grew up under her mother's Church of England beliefs, she had inherited her Irish Catholic father's sense of playfulness. As Lydia noted, 'One could never be certain whether she was being serious or facetious . . . Her Irishness was revealed most clearly in the ease with which [rather outlandish] remarks rolled off her tongue . . . with a slant and a degree of whimsicality all her own.'[6] Orwell shared and appreciated her wry sense of humour. As one friend summed it up, 'Orwell's genuine streak of old-fashioned conventionality sometimes bordered on whimsy and you could not always be quite certain if he was serious or not.'[7]

Eileen and Orwell spent the evening in earnest conversation. He had his three published novels to show his success as a writer, even though he was still poor enough at thirty-one to be working part-time in a bookshop. And she had many Oxford tales with which to charm him, including her interactions with Tolkien and C. S. Lewis, both of whom had become well known since their time as her tutors. Their evening together was likely also punctuated with joyous laughter because, as we know, Eileen believed she had been 'rather drunk, behaving my worst, very rowdy' when they met.[8] As Eileen revealed much later, in those early years she had a capacity for large amounts of alcohol, regularly drinking 'four glasses of sherry, half a bottle of claret and some brandy.'[9] Her self-described party personality shows clearly the charm she could turn on with ease, and Orwell was love-struck immediately. Perhaps she was the first woman he had met who really appreciated his dry wit.

When the party ended and he had returned from walking the guests down the hill to nearby buses and trains, Orwell excitedly told Rosalind, 'Now *that* is the kind of girl I would like to marry!' Rosalind 'was delighted to hear this, as [she,] too, felt they had much to give each other.' She described Eileen as 'a very attractive, very feminine Irish woman, with lively interests and [a] gay, infectious laugh'. Orwell was thrilled when Rosalind suggested inviting Eileen to dinner the next time she saw her at college.[10]

At their next class together, Eileen told Rosalind that she had found Orwell 'very interesting'.[11] She was already reading *Burmese Days*, Orwell's second book, most likely at his suggestion. His third book, *A Clergyman's Daughter*, had been published a few months earlier, and although it had received more favourable reviews than he expected, Orwell himself was quite critical of it, while *Down and Out in Paris and London*, his first book, was a wild, original creation that he perhaps feared Eileen might not appreciate. *Burmese Days* had recently been published in America, though not yet in England, and Orwell had received very positive reviews for it. Geoffrey Gorer, a social anthropologist who would later become a close friend of the couple's, wrote, 'It seems to me an absolutely admirable statement of fact told as vividly and with as little bitterness as possible.'[12] And Orwell's Eton classmate Cyril Connolly recommended it 'to anyone who enjoys a spate of efficient indignation, graphic description, excellent narrative, excitement, and irony tempered with vitriol.'[13] As she read this novel, Eileen had the literary knowledge and skills to realise right away that she had met a man with the potential to become a great writer.

Eileen agreed to meet Orwell again, and Rosalind remembered that 'our small dinner-party two days after was a very gay affair. I left them quite soon (after the meal) in my sitting-room and went out to near-by friends.'[14] Left alone, as Rosalind had so wisely allowed, Eileen and Orwell continued to explore their initial intrigue with each other. Orwell realised that at last he'd met a woman who was his intellectual equal, perhaps the most intelligent woman he would ever know, a woman who had actually gone to Oxford while he felt he had 'wasted' those years as a policeman in Burma. She had the education and background to be able to take him and his writing as seriously as he did, one of his most important requirements in a wife.

Eileen was glad to have found a man who was not intimidated by her intelligence, a man with as intricate a past as her own. As one of her friends remembered, 'She had the kind of mind that was always grinding. She was interested in most things, but especially in people.'[15] And of course Orwell also had an exceedingly 'grinding' kind of mind. Eileen, just finishing the first year of her MA in psychology, would have found the sometimes gloomy Orwell an intriguing personality to explore. She shared his humorous, sceptical approach to the inanities of the world, and they both loved twisting language in teasing ways. Although he was often deliberately provocative, Eileen was capable of countering with her own quips when his exaggerations were too extreme, and he enjoyed her attempts to outwit him. Her friends thought she understood people better than Orwell did, and had an equal and expansive range of interests.

Richard Rees, one of Orwell's closest friends, believed that '[He] had something else, something other than literary genius, which made him a very remarkable man,'[16] and Eileen sensed this immediately. She also shared Geoffrey Gorer's belief that Orwell 'was one of the most interesting people I've ever known. I was never bored in his company.'[17] Cyril Connolly said, 'You have this feeling that you're in the presence of a great man without being able to say why. I mean he's just outside the ordinary human failings.'[18] Even Lydia, who at first believed, 'It must have been his outspokenness that attracted her,' eventually understood Eileen's fascination. 'George talked in a way that intrigued [Eileen], interested her, because he was an unusual person.'[19] A later friend of Eileen's who didn't really care for Orwell admitted that he nonetheless possessed an 'intense charm that was difficult to define.'[20] He 'projected more than most writers the image of a deeply moral man,'[21] another friend believed, the kind of personal morality that Eileen shared and highly valued. When Orwell summed up Dickens as a writer who 'is laughing, with a touch of anger to his laughter, but no triumph, no malignity. It is the face of a man who is always fighting against something, but who fights in the open and is not frightened, the face of a man who is *generously angry* . . . a type hated with equal hatred by all the smelly little orthodoxies which are now contending for our souls,'[22] he could well have been describing the man Eileen quickly fell in love with.

These two highly intelligent but restless people, immersed in their separate searches for fulfilling futures, had found each other at an auspicious moment. Before they met, they had each been drifting from partner to partner and from one life choice to another, but shortly after they met, they became an almost inseparable couple, with a combined and evolving life goal.

At first Eileen would meet Orwell on Sundays at his room on Parliament Hill, but there was very little privacy for them there. According to one friend, Orwell was not much of a housekeeper. His small room was 'not merely dingy, but rather sordid. Half-eaten food lying around and very dusty.'[23] His sister Avril complained that, when he got back from Burma, after being used to having servants there, he would throw matches and cigarette stubs on the floor and expect others to sweep them up.[24] But, then, Eileen had always been messy herself, so perhaps she didn't notice. Instead of worrying about the dust, Orwell would concentrate, as Rosalind remembered fondly, on 'a butterfly in his room, or in the movements of a caterpillar he had found on his windowsill.'[25]

The fact that Eileen and Rosalind were students in classes together would have made meeting at her flat awkward, forcing Eileen and Orwell to whisper their developing love. So they began packing a rucksack on Sunday afternoons and taking the train to the country for the long walks so exquisitely recreated in *Keep the Aspidistra Flying*, the novel Orwell was in the midst of writing. In this book, he romantically had Gordon and Rosemary, the two lovers, lie in each other's arms on the bare ground, crushing the fragrant wild flowers in the woods. However, according to one friend, he and Eileen often took 'shooting sticks' with them on their walks, objects which opened up into small chairs, with one pointed end stuck deep into the earth – a rather prim contraption used by privileged people to avoid sitting directly on the grass.[26] But Orwell and Eileen, within the privacy of the countryside, also surely spent enticing moments entwined on beds of wild flowers.

Eileen was an exceedingly attractive woman whom most men would notice right away. Orwell told people she had 'a cat's face', which Lydia elaborated on, saying, 'It was rather short, soft in outline, the nose slightly uptilted, the eyes large and round with a look of disarming innocence.'[27] There are very few photographs of Eileen, but after she came into Orwell's life, many friends commented on her looks. Denys

King-Farlow, an Eton classmate of Orwell's, described her as 'pretty and dark-haired – I don't know whether it was because her name was Eileen – I thought she had rather an Irish look.'[28] Connolly found Eileen 'very charming . . . intelligent . . . and she loved him, and she was independent, and although she didn't wear make-up or anything like that, she was very pretty.'[29] And Gorer remembered her as 'one of those plain women who give you the impression of being beautiful – serene and yet vital, calm yet animated.'[30] Even the sometimes critical Humphrey Dakin, the husband of Orwell's older sister, thought Eileen was 'a good-looking woman of character (not warmth) and assurance.'[31] Dakin's son, Henry, who lived with the couple for a few weeks in London during the war, took note of Eileen in the way a young man would, and he now recalls that when she decided to dress up Eileen could become 'quite dazzling.'[32]

Because Orwell had always chosen intelligent girlfriends, a more important requirement for him than physical beauty, one friend claimed he had an 'incredible taste for ugly girls, not just plain girls, but absolutely downright ugly girls, with warts, pimples, anything going.'[33] But, in fact, Orwell's girlfriends were never ugly. He was 'absolutely not seduced by second-rate glamour', Sonia Orwell – his second wife, whom he married shortly before he died – said years later. Instead, he was 'attracted to character and performance.'[34] But the fact that Eileen was pretty certainly didn't bother him. When Lydia was surprised by Eileen's 'exceptional thinness', she said, 'I felt sorry for her and wondered what kind of man would lust after a body as ethereal as that.'[35] But, according to another friend, one woman to whom Orwell had been seriously attracted before he met Eileen 'was a little trollop he picked up in a café in Paris [who] was beautiful, and had a figure like a boy . . . and was in every way desirable.'[36]

Gorer believed that 'Orwell was a lonely man until he met Eileen, a very lonely man. He was fairly well convinced that nobody would like him, which made him prickly.'[37] Malcolm Muggeridge thought the 'division between the romantic lover and the wry realist made

[Orwell's] relations with women difficult.'[38] And Mabel Fierz, Orwell's first literary champion, said, 'He went to bed with women as if to prove his masculinity and virility [and] found it difficult to form deep relationships with women.'[39] Indeed, Orwell always claimed he was unattractive to women. But that was quite likely a ploy for sympathy, since he never had any difficulty finding girlfriends. He was the kind of shy, slightly awkward man to whom many women are drawn. 'You mustn't underestimate how attractive he seemed – so tall, so austere, so withdrawn, so puritanical, so unlike most of the other men who overdid it, who overwooed,' Sonia Orwell said, 'so gnarled, so totally sexy without trying to be in any way.'[40] He had a rare ability to convince his girlfriends that he found them special, almost hypnotising them with the haunting, piercing blue eyes that gaze out from his photos. And, contrary to some assumptions, he was very careful about his personal appearance, choosing just the right sort of casual clothes, wearing his hair rather long and unruly, and sporting that thin Hollywood-style moustache of the thirties popularised by William Powell and Clark Gable. Throughout his adult life, Orwell continued to order custom-made clothes from the family tailor in Southwold: pairs of flannel trousers and sports jackets – even pyjamas and overcoats – all fashioned from the best materials. As the tailor recalled, 'It dates back to the 1920s when we first made clothes for him here,' and 'from that time we went on making clothes until he died. He kept in touch all the time.' He continued, 'We kept patterns for him here so if he wrote in and said he wanted anything specially made, well they were just . . . sent off to him.'[41] Unfortunately, he added, 'He was one of those people who put on a suit and don't look well-dressed even when they put it on new.'[42] This man assumed that Orwell wasn't as poor as he claimed, considering how much he spent on clothes. Perhaps his family continued to pay his clothing bills as they always had, and somehow that didn't count to him as part of being self-sufficient.

One girlfriend remembered Orwell as good company on their walks, often discussing unusual topics, although, she added, 'He could be a bit boring at times.'[43] Orwell was at that time engrossed in composing an epic poem inspired by his love of Chaucer,[44] and Eileen, with her English degree, was able to admire as well as critique his efforts. She had learned to love Wordsworth's poetry at Oxford, and Orwell resembled in many ways Wordsworth's glorious description of a poet as a person 'endued with more lively sensibility, more enthusiasm and tenderness, who has a greater knowledge of human nature, and a more comprehensive soul, than are supposed to be common among mankind'.[45] Eileen, who had published her poem 'End of the Century, 1984' the year before, and who was justifiably proud of it, would certainly have shared it with another aspiring poet. He told friends that she could have had a successful literary career on her own.[46] Eileen's poem was not discovered until 2001, after many Orwell biographies had been published. So those authors weren't aware of the obvious connection between the title of her poem and the title of his great last novel, *Nineteen Eighty-Four.* Scholars made wild guesses about why he had chosen that title, including the idea that he had simply inverted the numbers of the year 1948, one of the many years during which he had worked on it. But, with this new knowledge, it is hard today not to accept that Orwell's final choice of title for his final book was a tacit tribute to Eileen's memory.

As his courtship of Eileen progressed, Orwell continued to take long walks with Brenda Salkeld, a close friend he had met many years earlier, when he was still living with his parents. She saved all his long, detailed, chatty letters, giving us a good idea of the type of letter he could easily knock out. He certainly wrote such letters to Eileen as they were courting, though she didn't bother keeping them. Orwell had joked to Brenda that '[U]gly women make love best,'[47] but Brenda was attractive, as were Orwell's other known girlfriends. Perhaps this was a dig at Brenda's constant refusal of a sexual affair. His 'Dearest Brenda' letter in May, two months after meeting Eileen, is full of his usual wildly diverse interests. But the last sentence reveals a response to what must have been Brenda's fine instincts. She had apparently sensed something new about Orwell. 'As to your presentiment, or "curious feeling" about me', he wrote, 'I don't know that I have been particularly unhappy lately – at least, not more than usual.' Not yet willing to reveal his relationship with Eileen, nor willing to give up what would turn out to be his lifelong attachment to Brenda, he had signed his letter, reassuringly, 'With much love and many kisses.'[48] When he did finally tell Brenda months later about his coming marriage to Eileen, he naïvely assumed she would support his decision and remain a close friend – the way he evidently thought of her since she had always rejected his advances. She was, remarkably, the person he chose to tell, in a letter the day after the wedding, many details about how the service had been conducted.

But Orwell was deceiving himself about Brenda's real feelings. Throughout the years before he met Eileen, they had kept up an intense friendship full of long, descriptive letters about their shared interest in literature as well as nature, and in them he had often referred to the time 'when we are married.'[49] Although Brenda realised Orwell 'would [not] have been an easy person to be married to at all', she had apparently continued to expect that eventuality, and he had not given much effort to convincing her he was not entirely serious. When an interviewer asked her many years later whether she had wanted to marry Orwell, she refused to give a direct response, answering only that she 'wouldn't like to say.'[50] Brenda stayed in touch with Orwell throughout his life but, although she hid it well, she never forgave him for marrying someone else. She carried her broken heart to the unmarried age of ninety-eight,[51] keeping her intimate love letters from Orwell secret until she died, in 2001, at which time they amazingly came to light.

Orwell was also keeping up an affair – a sexual one – with Kay Ekevall, who remembered him as 'a nice looking fellow.'[52] He took long walks with her on Hampstead Heath during the week, while saving Sundays for Eileen. Kay, who was eight years younger than Orwell, was at the party where he first fell for Eileen, and she was not surprised when his meetings with her grew less frequent. When Orwell finally told Kay that he had decided to marry Eileen, a friend reported that 'from Orwell's room the two voices seemed to be raised in continuous argument until after midnight'.[53] But Kay denied this version, claiming that she and Orwell had an agreement to tell each other honestly if they found someone else, and Orwell had made good on his promise when he told her casually, 'Look, I've met a girl I want to marry'. Kay, who considered herself a feminist, recalled, 'Most of my women friends in those days weren't looking for marriage or anything like that. I think we rather despised marriage'. She thought Eileen was 'gay and lively and interesting, and much more his level' than she was.[54] She later reported in a bit more detail, 'He told me that he was keen on Eileen and so I said OK, that's it, cheerio'.[55] There was, however, an unsubstantiated rumour that she had later attempted suicide.[56]

Orwell had been truly in love once before. He was hoping to marry Jacintha Buddicom, a Shiplake girl he had met when he was eleven years old and had an intense teenage relationship with. But just before he left for Burma, she had become infuriated when, overcome by his sexual desires while they were in the woods together, he had torn her skirt and bruised her shoulder and hip. She refused to ever see him again.[57] He was distraught for some time, and sent her a final disappointed poem with the last line, 'My love can't reach your heedless heart at all'. Only in the final months of his life, when he was in a hospital being treated for tuberculosis, did Orwell hear from Jacintha again. She had just been shocked to discover that her childhood friend Eric Blair was the now famous George Orwell. Rather tragically, he died before they could reunite. But the thought must be entertained that, had Jacintha accepted Orwell's love and made him a happy husband and father years earlier, would Eric Blair ever have become George Orwell?

Within weeks of meeting Eileen, Orwell had asked her to marry him. He made no secret of his wishes, sharing them with Rayner Heppenstall, who became one of his roommates when he moved a few months later. Heppenstall remembered, 'Orwell's letters had made it plain that the important person now was Eileen O'Shaughnessy . . . I was in favour of her and had ventured to say as much to Eric'.[58] Heppenstall thought Eileen was 'a beautiful woman and a most interesting one, most good for George'.[59] Eileen astounded Lydia when she told her she had accepted Orwell's early offer of marriage, even though she was confused by its rather muddled wording. She explained casually, 'Though I'm not sure it was a proposal of marriage. He talked about "not being eligible" . . . I didn't really know what he wanted me to say to that'.[60] Orwell was perhaps referring to the fact that he had very little money or income. But some friends thought that word referred to his belief that he was sterile, a conclusion based on nothing concrete. He told one girlfriend who questioned this assumption, 'Well . . . I've never had any [children]'.[61]

Eileen playfully recounted her thinking to Lydia. 'You see,' she explained, 'I told myself that when I was thirty I would accept the first man who asked me to marry him,'[62] and, as she reminded her friend, she would turn thirty that September. Some people have mistakenly interpreted this to mean that no one had yet proposed to Eileen. But this is not a joke a woman would make who had never had an offer of marriage. Eileen was simply informing her friend that she was indeed taking Orwell's proposal seriously. Eileen used the name Eric for Orwell, and Lydia later wrote: 'Being psychology students, we commented on and agreed about the significance of her marrying a man whose first name was the same as her brother's'.[63] Lydia much preferred Eileen's brother's friend Karl Schnetzler as a mate for Eileen, and she made sure she knew it. But clearly Eileen now found Orwell the most fascinating, original, and exciting man she had yet met, and she began withdrawing from Karl. Lydia 'could not believe [Eileen] had fallen in love with Eric Blair; I did not think him at all attractive,'[64] she recalled many years later. But this comment is curiously confusing, since barely two years after the wedding Lydia herself chose to accept Orwell's sexual advances towards her, exchanging many kisses, at least, with him.

At first Eileen was quite open to the idea of a quick marriage, but she then began to hesitate, perhaps because her mother and Lydia were so definitely against it. Eileen knew her family would have a hard time understanding her choice of husband. They would not see Orwell as she saw him, a genius with all the peculiarities that geniuses often have. But she hoped, given a bit of time, they would be convinced that she was making the right decision, so she agreed to wait until she had completed her MA in psychology, the following spring.

Money was also an issue. Years earlier, Orwell had gone off to Burma as a policeman instead of to university, a completely different pathway from most of his Eton friends. Some thought his father was unwilling to put up the money for a university education, while others believed Orwell wasn't really interested in a traditional education, opting for five years of adventure instead. Now, eight years after returning to England, and after using up all his savings from that job, he was still not earning enough to easily support himself, let alone a wife. In Orwell's first written mention of his wife-to-be, only a few months after meeting her, he told Heppenstall, 'You are right about Eileen. She is the nicest person I have met for a long time. However, at present alas! I can't afford a ring, except perhaps a Woolworth's one.'[65] Like Eileen, he used humour to soften his distress. In October, Orwell told his friend, 'Eileen says she won't marry me as yet (of course you won't repeat these things I tell you about E. etc.) as she is not earning any money at present and doesn't want to be a drag on me'[66] – perhaps her gentle way of putting the marriage off for a while.

Orwell also had a grand plan he needed time to develop. He hoped to convince Eileen to isolate herself in the country with him, sharing an attempt to subsist outside society's traditional expectations for an educated urban couple – to at last escape what he called the 'money-god'. Ever since he had returned from Burma, he told a friend, 'What I profoundly wanted was to find some way of getting out of the respectable world altogether.'[67]

In the meantime, he had to save up enough money to afford this dream. Despite his occasional doubts about the artistic success of his novels, he was secure in his creative ability, and Eileen was well aware of his expectation that he would soon be recognised as a respected author. When the reviews of *A Clergyman's Daughter* were mostly positive, he began to believe more strongly in his transformation from obscure poet to novelist of renown. He was in fact quite proud of parts of this novel, and just around this time he signed a book review 'George Orwell' for the first time,[68] instead of using his customary 'Eric Blair' byline for everything he wrote except the novels. When his literary agent, Leonard Moore, informed him that Victor Gollancz, his publisher, had said, 'In my opinion, [Orwell] is likely to be in years to come one of the half dozen most important authors on our lists,'[69] his confidence soared. At this point new friends started to call him George, but Eileen continued to call him Eric through all their years together, except when it was occasionally necessary to differentiate him from her brother Eric.

Orwell wanted his books to sell well and he wasn't reluctant to promote himself, suggesting to his agent at one point that *Burmese Days* might have a readership in Burma and India. After the success of a lecture he gave in the autumn to about 500 people on the topic 'Confessions of a Down and Out',[70] he was thrilled to report to a friend, 'Lecture on Wed. went over *big*. Was surprised to find how easy it is.'[71] So he asked that more lectures be arranged, 'since I am anxious to earn all I can,'[72] no doubt in order to hasten the beginning of his dream life with Eileen. He also believed that any mention of his work, good or bad, was valuable, assuring his agent, 'It is worth getting some serious (though not necessarily favourable) reviews in papers where I am known.'[73] Unlike some authors, he made a point of reading all the reviews of his books, even preserving them in a special scrapbook.[74] He was also reviewing other people's books, which he understood was another important way to keep his name in the news as well as earn a bit of money. Being a voracious reader capable of forming strong, immediate opinions, he managed to review nine books in March, the month he met Eileen,[75] but that number dwindled drastically throughout the time he was wooing her.

Later in the year, he wrote a very positive review of Henry Miller's *Tropic of Cancer*,[76] and his praise of this controversial book added to his own reputation. Miller's book had been published in Paris in 1934 but was banned in England because of its candid depiction of sex, then considered pornography. Orwell managed to get hold of a smuggled copy and wrote, 'There is much in it that is remarkable, but its most immediately noticeable and perhaps essential feature is its descriptions of sexual encounters . . . with a callous coarseness which is unparalleled in fiction, though common enough in real life.'[77] Orwell's review led to further correspondence between the two men, as well as an auspicious meeting in Paris a year later, when Orwell was on his way to fight in Spain.

When Lydia finally understood that Eileen was indeed serious about marrying Orwell, she called their meeting at the party 'doom-laden'. She later wrote that she 'did not like it at all. I admired [Eileen] and thought she deserved someone better than an unknown and impecunious writer.'[78] She wanted Eileen to make 'her mark in child psychology' and 'to have a secure and comfortable life . . . I hated to think of her talents being wasted and of her studies abandoned half way through.'[79] Orwell's old girlfriend Kay agreed: Eileen 'had an intellectual standing in her own right, and I thought it was rather tragic that she should give it all up. I don't think I would have.'[80] Although in the end Lydia reluctantly accepted Eileen's decision, the only way she could justify it was by believing that 'Eileen was not really interested in shaping her own life, in becoming someone – a writer, a psychologist – in her own right: she was out for a variety of experience, for change, for meeting and observing people.'[81] Lydia saw this as a 'lack of ambition', and Eileen would not have been able to convince her otherwise.

In the middle of the summer of 1935, Orwell arranged through his great friend and facilitator, Mabel Fierz, to move to a three-room flat on the top floor of a three-storey brick house at 50 Lawford Road, now in Kentish Town, remembered as 'a quiet, pleasant street' by Rayner Heppenstall, one of his two roommates there,[82] and as 'a road with an air of decay about it' by the other.[83] Today the road is calm, with rows of attractive houses, and a plaque adorns the front of the building where Orwell lived for only five months. The wide outdoor staircase leads to a private indoor stairway to the upper floor. Two small rooms facing the street were given to the roommates, who often used the flat simply as a place to bring girlfriends or to sleep after drunken nights out. Orwell took for himself the large open room at the top of the stairs, with the kitchen attached and a picture window onto the pleasant back garden.[84] At last Orwell and Eileen could be together without any worries of being overheard in their lovemaking. Neither of them was aware that the two other tenants in the building, a plumber and a tram driver, disapproved of Orwell. According to Heppenstall, the tram driver's wife once told him, 'We never did think much of that Mr Blair. Keeps us awake till three and four o'clock in the morning he does sometimes with his typing.'[85]

Orwell, who considered himself something of a gourmet by this time, enjoyed having dinner gatherings in his rooms where he prepared meals on his new 'Bachelor Griller'. He boasted to Brenda, 'I can cook not too badly, and I have already given a dinner-party to three people all at once and cooked everything myself.'[86] Cyril Connolly – who hadn't seen Orwell since their Eton days and was 'absolutely horrified' by the 'deep, deep lines' in his face – claimed he enjoyed 'chips and onions and steak and beer' that Orwell had served him,[87] though other guests were a bit more critical of Orwell's attempts. Lydia, of course, was one of those who believed Orwell to be bereft of a chef's skills. She remembered going with Eileen to Lawford Road several times, writing much later about 'the depressing dinginess of the street, the house and the rooms'. Recalling one evening, when she and Eileen had been invited for dinner, Lydia wrote, 'He must have cooked the meal himself and it must have been something hardly edible – for he was no cook.'[88]

Eileen never mentioned Orwell's cooking skills or lack thereof, but perhaps we can assume something from the fact that after the marriage she took over that job completely. Although that could also have been a sign of the couple's conventionality.

Sometime that same summer, Eileen's brother, who was now doing exceedingly well in his medical career, purchased 24 Croom's Hill, across the park from their last home. It had once been owned by an astronomer who worked at the Royal Observatory,[89] and fortunately Eric and Gwen were not superstitious, since they had been warned that the house 'had an unfortunate history'. In Lydia's words, 'The previous owner, a medical man, had been killed in a car accident. His wife had died in strange circumstances, probably a case of suicide.'[90] This tragic personal history might have made the building a bargain, however.

It was a large Georgian house on a quiet curving road bordering Greenwich Park, and it was spacious enough to hold the whole O'Shaughnessy family. Lydia described it lovingly as 'a very pleasant house, inside and outside. The long and lofty ground floor room had bow windows at both ends and was used as a dining-room. The drawing-room above it was loftier still, with French windows at each end.' She got to know this house well, and added more details. 'On the left of the large entrance hall a door led to Gwen's surgery with a small dispensary attached. On the first floor immediately above it was Eric's [Eileen's brother's] study. There were three or four bedrooms on the second floor, and a vast kitchen on the ground floor.'[91] This magnificent corner house is still one of the most elegant on the road, with gorgeous bow windows and a walled-off back garden, and it was most likely quite expensive to buy, since in 2018 it was valued at £3,500,000.

Throughout the autumn, as their love progressed, Eileen would often enjoy time with Orwell in his Lawford Road rooms before they set off on their long country walks. On other weekends, he would pick her up at her brother's home and they would go horse riding or skating at a nearby Ice Club. Lydia, a self-proclaimed expert skater, remembered that Orwell wasn't at all agile on the ice, and in her opinion even Eileen and her brother 'always looked rather awkward on skates'.[92] After these weekend outings, they would return to the O'Shaughnessy house to share a crowded Sunday dinner, which always included the assorted friends whom Eileen's brother spontaneously invited. Eric O'Shaughnessy had become aware of Hitler's rise to power when he was working in Germany in the early 1930s,[93] and political discussions developed between the two Erics. Lydia remembered conversations where 'Eric [O'Shaughnessy] spoke very forcefully of the necessity of "stopping Hitler"', a name she wasn't familiar with in 1935, but a name Eileen must have heard many times. And when Orwell decided to fight in the Spanish Civil War a year later, Eileen's brother was one of the few people who approved of his action.

The affluence of Eileen's home life would not have escaped Orwell's notice. Although she was intrigued by the idea of a career in psychology, she had never been encouraged to make her own living. Her childhood had been more materially comfortable than his, although their fathers were both civil servants. Heppenstall believed, perhaps unfairly, that Orwell 'considered [Eileen's] family background more suitable' for a wife than that of his former girlfriends.[94]

Eileen and Orwell continued their outdoor adventures even though what Heppenstall called Orwell's 'winter cough' continued to trouble him. He got this dismissive phrase from Orwell himself, who always minimised what he well knew was a symptom of his seriously weak lungs. He used this term with Eileen too, not wanting her to know that he often suffered from bronchitis and that he had already endured several bouts of pneumonia, with a couple of near-fatal attacks. In fact, when he was only a year old, his mother had written in her diary: 'Baby not at all well, so I sent for the doctor who said that he had bronchitis.'[95] But when Eileen met him, she was unaware of his health history. A year later, in the first letter by her that has survived, she told a friend how surprised she had been when she discovered how often he suffered from 'bronchitis', which she put in quotes. The fact that her brother was a specialist in the treatment of tuberculosis proved to be a helpful coincidence for Orwell.

Orwell was far from the type of person who restricts his behaviour to accommodate the weakness he was born with. On the contrary, he constantly pushed himself beyond what his body could stand. One old girlfriend remembered that he was always trying to be a 'he-man'. Eileen also pushed herself beyond her capacities, trying to ignore her own sickly constitution. It seems likely that she smoked before she met Orwell, and she soon acquired his habit of preferring the strongest black tobacco available. They formed an immediate bond over their shared belief that challenging their bodies' inadequacies was a crucial choice.

Orwell's physical awkwardness, which Lydia had noticed when he was skating, was obvious in other ways. As his friend Gorer remembered, 'He was awfully likely to knock things off tables, to trip over things. I mean he was a gangling, physically badly coordinated young man.'[96] Muggeridge was kinder, saying Orwell had 'a lack of grace'.[97] And his friends insisted he had always had 'a rather peculiar voice'[98] even before his vocal chords were damaged in Spain. Brenda believed that what Connolly called his 'dry wheezy voice'[99] 'stopped him from mixing easily'.[100] Others commented on his laugh, one calling it 'painfully snickering'[101] while another softened this description to 'a dry, vibrant, somehow rusty chuckle, very characteristic and very endearing'.[102] He was also rather socially awkward, often unable to be heard in a large group, and he was known for sometimes sitting in a bar sipping his beer while friends all around him chatted loudly. Eileen noticed these shortcomings right away, and she was well aware how important her companionship would become to him. He needed an outgoing, gregarious woman to help him overcome these social deficiencies, and Eileen had no insecurities of this type. She could also help him even in simple ways, as when he absent-mindedly lost track of important addresses and phone numbers,[103] even though she could sometimes be quite absent-minded herself.

She loved his ability to concentrate avidly on minuscule details that hardly anyone else noticed, although at times, like a brilliant child full of exciting thoughts, his attention could quickly scatter. As one of her friends summed it up, '[Eileen] loved George deeply but with a tender amusement: she admired his work; she shared his views; she was ready to accept the haphazard austerity of his life-style.'[104]

Eileen told a friend that she was 'very much like [Orwell] in temperament which is an asset once one has accepted the fact.'[105] They fell in love so quickly because they immediately recognised these similarities. Eileen was seen by her friends as 'a vivacious young woman, at times looking a little eccentric,'[106] and she admired what others saw as Orwell's unorthodox behaviour. They were both free-thinkers with an appetite for risk, and they enjoyed delving into underlying truths that were often disregarded by others. They could both be quite stubborn and opinionated, and were almost oblivious to the fact that they sometimes upset those close to them. Eileen could be dismissive of anyone she didn't admire or who had angered her, so she came across as rude to some people. Not everyone warranted the full force of her charm. Eileen and Orwell were known to have quite boisterous arguments with each other, though they always seemed able to reconcile. It was also helpful that they shared a similar pace as they went through life. Rather surprisingly, one of Eileen's friends said, 'I never saw her in a hurry, but her work was always finished up to time,'[107] while one of Orwell's friends said almost exactly the same thing: 'He was never rushing about in a hurry but seemed able to get things done immediately.'[108]

A distant acquaintance reported that Eileen had a 'curiously elusive personality', and you have to read between the lines of Eileen's sometimes over-the-top, chatty letters to find her more serious concerns. Heppenstall once called her 'giddy', and it's possible that at times her high-energy personality might have been wearying. In her surviving letters to Orwell just before she died, Eileen honestly expressed her wishes and her worries in huge detail. We don't know whether she always wrote to him in a more serious voice than she used with friends and family because he didn't save most of her letters. And we can't know how revealing he was in his letters to her, because she threw them all away.

The question is always puzzled over by Orwell scholars: why would an intelligent woman like Eileen, right on the verge of a highly respected degree in psychology, decide to just suddenly give up her chances for a career of her own? But Eileen had already turned down other possibilities for success. She had also rejected the idea of marrying a man who could have given her the type of family life and home she had grown up with. She had always known – and this belief was increasingly reinforced in those eight years after she graduated from Oxford – that such traditional goals had no interest for her. Since her teenage years, perhaps influenced by her aunt, she'd been intrigued by missionaries and saints, and the rewarding life choices they had made. Instead of being tempted by comfort and common pleasures, she admired the values of self-denial, rejection of worldly greed, and devotion to moral causes. For a well-to-do woman of her time, Eileen was a rebel, but she was not a true feminist as Orwell's ex-girlfriend Kay and her younger friends considered themselves. She shared with Orwell a more traditional understanding of marriage. However, since she had by then spent over ten years making her own life decisions, it was impossible for her to become a complete second fiddle to him. And, at any rate, that wasn't really what he wanted. They were both social rebels, uninterested in a mundane marriage. Although her choice might be criticised by young women of today, Eileen was acting in a very defiant manner.

She had enjoyed her years before moving to London and was easily charmed by Orwell's idea of a self-sufficient country life, with a garden and animals to provide the food they needed, and very few other necessary expenses. Her friends remembered her as 'a woman careless of creature comforts herself',[109] and as a child she had always been criticised for not being neat enough. Now she had a man who didn't seem at first to care about or even notice these things. And he in turn was relieved to find an attractive, refined woman who was as excited as he was to experiment with a primitive lifestyle. So they began to develop the dream of the married life they hoped to create. Eileen believed she'd finally found the purpose in her life that had so far eluded her, a way to use her extensive talents towards the goal of helping this brilliant yet still insecure man attain the literary heights they both believed he was capable of. She could see that Orwell would be a difficult man to live with, but life with him promised the thrills and surprises for which many women constantly yearn. And Eileen was old-fashioned enough to want to help her husband succeed instead of being admired for excelling on her own. In agreeing to move to a primitive cottage with Orwell, she was thoroughly rejecting both the comfortable married life and the professional career that could be expected of a woman like her. And it's entirely possible that Orwell himself might not have been brave enough to venture into a risky new life in the country without Eileen's encouragement and willingness to try the experiment with him. However, together they were acting more like saints than bohemians.

6

Orwell in Love

I would like to stay a good long time in the North . . . only it means being away from my girl.

Orwell, just before the wedding

Duering the first nine months of Orwell's courtship of Eileen, he was working on his fourth book, *Keep the Aspidistra Flying*. As in all his early novels, the characters he created were largely based on people he knew, and the incidents in this book were based on real-life ones. The adventures of the protagonist, Gordon, were written as a comical exaggeration of Orwell's own pursuit of recognition as a published writer. (In *Down and Out* he had also made his self-based character quite a bit wilder than he was in person, and his Aunt Nellie – another of the many women who came to Orwell's rescue over the years – had to assure the bookshop owner who hired Orwell that he was 'not a bit like his book.'[1]) Orwell also allowed Gordon to display some of Orwell's own usually hidden emotions, though again in high gear. The character Rosemary was originally based on earlier girlfriends, but when Orwell met Eileen, Rosemary soon began to take on Eileen's personality, and some of the humorous scenes also strongly suggest input from Eileen. Rosemary has often been dismissed as a superficial stereotype, but her decisions when she gets pregnant are quite radical, suggesting possible help from an independent woman. These scenes seem mild now, but they no doubt shocked some readers at the time.

Orwell always wrote long letters to his girlfriends, and some of them saved what they considered his precious ramblings, leaving us some illuminating details about his romantic character, which was quite similar to that of his creation, Gordon. Eileen also wrote rambling letters, many of which *her* friends thought worthy of saving, and these letters give us our clearest understanding of how she used wit and exaggeration to distract from serious events. In the novel, Gordon is endlessly obsessed with whether or not Rosemary has written to him, telling her, 'Your letters are the only things that keep me going.' Once, after waiting what he considers too long before hearing from her, he sends her a mock tragic letter, saying simply, 'You have broken my heart.' There's no doubt that Orwell and Eileen exchanged many letters during these months, even though they were seeing each other almost every week. In those days, that was the only way to set up times and places to meet. One of the great regrets of anyone trying to delve into the development of Orwell and Eileen's love for each other is the realisation that neither of them saw any importance in saving the other's letters.

As Gordon attempts to create a life for himself free of the 'money-god', Rosemary is always sympathetic. 'How patiently [Rosemary] put up with his almost intolerable ways,' Orwell wrote. She 'did not try to prevent him from throwing up his job. It was against her code to interfere – "You've got to live your own life," was always her attitude.' And of course this was Eileen's attitude when Orwell eventually quit his bookshop job as the couple dreamed of creating their own form of adventurous marriage. As Orwell was writing the novel, he and Eileen engaged in complicated conversations about the future, and she began to understand the needs of this eccentric man and to admire him for these goals. But Orwell had trouble accepting the fact that women found him attractive, and he has Gordon constantly doubting Rosemary's love, questioning her feelings over and over again. Gordon worries that Rosemary 'knew all about him and considered him a bit of a joke', that she was 'a callous creature who was amused by him and yet half despised him'. These appear to be interesting insights into Eileen, reflecting the 'tender amusement' one of her friends noted about Eileen's feelings towards Orwell.

Although she joked a lot, Orwell began to realise that Eileen was indeed falling in love with him, and he had Rosemary say, 'Gordon, you are such a dear old ass! I can't help loving you.' Rosemary's love for Gordon is somewhat inexplicable to him, and possibly to some readers, but Orwell wrote, 'They were very happy. Indeed, they adored one another. Each was to the other a standing joke and an object infinitely precious.' As Orwell summed it up, with a lovely romantic sentiment that any woman would treasure, 'There was a deep intimacy between them. They could have sat there for hours, just looking at one another and talking of trivial things that had meanings for them and for nobody else.'² At this point, Orwell was recording his growing love for Eileen.

At least one piece of psychological insight inserted itself into the novel, somewhat awkwardly: 'The thought that [Gordon] was merely objectifying his own inner misery hardly troubled him', Orwell wrote. Eileen might have presented this as a psychological interpretation of his anti-hero, but Orwell seems to have rejected her suggestion. Interestingly, Orwell called Gordon 'moth-eaten' at least ten times in this novel – exactly the term Lydia had used to describe Orwell himself when she first saw him at the party. Might Eileen have shared this information with Orwell? If so, it seemed to have resounded very strongly with him.

When Rosemary gets pregnant in the novel, Orwell used that development to create a complicated interaction between his two young protagonists. Rosemary does not insist that Gordon marry her, as he assumes she will, and as no doubt readers of that time would also have expected. When Gordon says, 'We shall have to get married, I suppose,' Rosemary answers bravely, 'Not unless you want to. I'm not going to tie you down. I know it's against your ideas to marry. You must decide for yourself.' She does not allow him to escape making a decision, even though he might have wished she had forced marriage on him. When Rosemary suggests an abortion as a solution, Gordon flips out, accusing her of forcing him into an impossible dilemma. 'It comes down to this. Either I marry you . . . or you go to one of those filthy doctors and get yourself messed about for five pounds,' he complains. But Rosemary immediately rejects what she calls 'a sort of beastly blackmail' by Gordon. Instead, she surprises him with what he is forced to acknowledge is an honourable resolution: 'Marry me or don't marry me, just as you like. But I'll have the baby, anyway.' Rosemary's willingness to make quite unconventional choices seems consistent with Eileen's personality. Eileen no doubt also had some input on Gordon's development into 'an amusing, wickedly comic, rumbustious, profane and dissolute'[3] character. As one biographer noted, this type of personality is 'not normally on display'[4] in Orwell's work, and this trait appeared at the very moment when humorous, cheerful Eileen entered Orwell's life. She might also have helped Orwell create the hilarious final pages of the novel, in which Gordon gets a job composing clever slogans for an advertising agency. Harman Grisewood, a friend of Eileen's from Oxford, was writing slogans for an advertising agency at that time, and she might have consulted him.

As Orwell was writing these closing pages, he was becoming more optimistic in his personal life. Eileen had agreed to marry him, and they were thinking ahead about having their own child, a joyful future for Orwell since having a son was one of his greatest wishes. He decided on a conventional and rather unsatisfactory ending for his rebellious characters, allowing Gordon to surrender his poetic life for a dull job in an advertising agency, at the exact moment when Orwell knew for sure that he himself no longer had to consider such a choice. Unlike Gordon, Orwell now had an idea of just how he might be able to live a life 'where money does not rule', without having to sink down into 'muck', and without selling out and being forced to throw 'between the bars of the drain' the hoped-for masterpiece he'd been working on for two years. Another biographer thought this book was 'clearly therapeutic, purging [Orwell's] extreme bitterness, jealousy and sense of failure'.[5]

Orwell was now able to attempt what Gordon had failed to do in *Keep the Aspidistra Flying*: contrive a way to somehow be self-sufficient, a way to concentrate his energies on his writing, married to the woman he loved, the perfect partner with whom to share the adventure. Some people have called Orwell a masochist, but that hardly describes a man who convinced a beautiful woman to dedicate herself to his career as they planned a creative life in the country together. It helped that, as part of her Oxford education, Eileen had read Dorothy Wordsworth's letters and journals describing her ecstasy at being asked to share an isolated life with her brother in the remoteness of the Lake District. They would become 'pilgrims in search of healing and enlightenment who had turned their backs for ever on their former lives',[6] Dorothy declared, and this idea appealed strongly to Eileen. She identified with Dorothy's excitement when she wrote, 'An opportunity now presents itself of obtaining this satisfaction, an opportunity which I could not see pass from me without unspeakable pain.'[7] Eileen was now going to commit herself to Orwell, which meant transforming herself into part of his dream.

In January 1936 *Keep the Aspidistra Flying* was finished, and after Orwell had made a few reluctant changes to his product inventions and slogans – which were deemed too close to actual goods being advertised at that time – the book was sent to the printer, scheduled to arrive in bookshops on 20 April. Now Orwell had to decide what he would write next, having, as always, his goal of one book a year. He had given up the Lawford Road flat at the end of December, with both his roommates gone, and was at a loose end. At this point, to his happy surprise, his publisher suggested that he take on a brand-new type of book, a non-fiction report on unemployment and general living conditions in the industrial north of England. This idea immediately intrigued Orwell, and the small advance gave him new assurance that he would soon be financially ready to marry Eileen. He quit his job at the bookshop and left for the north on 31 January, planning two months of intensive research.

Orwell took the assignment very seriously and continued what became a lifelong custom of preserving, in an extremely detailed diary, what Christopher Hitchens called his 'meticulous and occasionally laborious jottings'.[8] Not a healthy man to begin with, he put his body through tremendous hardships during this research, staying in the homes of impoverished workers and ignoring the limits of his fragile constitution. He crawled miles underground with the coalminers on three occasions, telling a friend casually that it once 'was enough to put my legs out of action for four days'.[9] According to a man who was with him on one trip underground, Orwell passed out completely three times.[10] And, at another point, he spent three days in bed with what some believed was pneumonia.[11] But, as usual, Orwell presented these problems as less serious than they were. In fact, by pushing himself beyond his endurance time after time, he was knowingly sacrificing his own health for this book.

While he was away in the north, Orwell missed being with Eileen, and they kept in constant touch, though, as usual, none of their letters to each other were saved. We have his old schoolmate Cyril Connolly to thank for one small titbit of news: 'I would like to stay a good long time in the North,' Orwell wrote to Connolly, 'only it means being away from my girl.'[12] This was one of the last times for nine years that Orwell would be all alone during his bouts of self-neglect and over-exertion. Luckily for him, Eileen had chosen to be constantly at his side, protecting him as best she could. She saved his life at least once during the terrifying episodes of tubercular bleeding that she endured with him. Yet, throughout those years with Eileen, Orwell continued to insist that there was nothing seriously wrong with his lungs.

While Orwell was away, Eileen was in charge of finding them a small house in the country to which he could return in early April. Then they would plan a spring wedding after her psychology classes were finished. It turned out that Orwell's Aunt Nellie was moving out of a house in the Hertfordshire village of Wallington, and, after a visit, Eileen gave Orwell all the gritty details of what they both called 'the cottage'. However, she assured him that she was willing to accept its obvious difficulties at his side. So, at the end of February, Orwell told a friend, 'I am arranging to take a cottage at Wallington near Baldock in Herts, rather a pig in a poke because I have never seen it, but I am trusting the friends who have chosen it for me, and it is very cheap.'[13] Wallington was about thirty-five miles north of London, and less than four miles away from Baldock, where the train stopped. However, there was a bus service to Baldock only twice a week, requiring many long walks from 'cottage' to train. This inconvenience was treated as minor by the two dreamers. According to town legend, 'People live in Wallington as long as they please,'[14] a detail that would have appealed to the romantic couple.

When Orwell got back from the north at the beginning of April, he immediately moved into the house in Wallington, a village of perhaps a hundred inhabitants,[15] with 'thirty-four houses, two pubs, and a church'.[16] The main part of the cottage had been built in the sixteenth century[17] and it was even more primitive than Orwell had expected. He told one friend, with his usual understatement, 'This is quite a nice little cottage, but with absolutely no conveniences.'[18] In fact, the house was not wired for electricity, the toilet – with a poorly functioning cesspool that backed up when the wrong brand of toilet paper was used – was located outside the back door and 'was a ramshackle-looking place' with ivy growing inside,[19] the only running water came from a single cold-water tap, and the fireplace constantly smoked. Nevertheless, Orwell was enchanted, telling friends that he expected to stay there for a very long time.

The tiny cottage, only eleven feet deep, was two storeys high. You entered through a badly fitting wooden front door, which was variously remembered as three feet nine inches or four feet six inches high[20] – an obvious annoyance for Orwell's six-foot-four-inch frame – then down a few steps into the original structure, an eleven-by-eleven-foot room, apparently the exact size needed for a yoke of oxen.[21] A door from this original room led to a central room, with a small kitchen attached. This middle room, which Orwell used as his studio while he was living there alone, contained a basic fireplace, which caused endless problems for the couple for many years. Huge oak ceiling beams throughout the ground-floor rooms were so low as to risk splitting the heads of unwary visitors. Behind a wooden inside door was an ancient 'narrow, twisting elm stairway, so unusual it is listed [for preservation].'[22] It was 'curved and badly worn, with treads being minimal in places, making it pretty dangerous,'[23] according to the woman who bought the house years later. The stairway ended on a landing with entrances on one side to what would become the couple's bedroom and on the other to a much-used small guest bedroom. The whole structure was topped by a corrugated-iron roof, which had recently been added over the original thatch that was rotting. This roof made a colossal racket every time it rained, which was often. When Eileen moved in after the wedding, Orwell started using the upstairs landing, an open area at the top of the stairway between the two bedrooms, as his studio.

Some of these guessed-at details were clarified recently when the current owners kindly permitted some visitors inside the cottage. These days the main entrance is through a side door, with the ridiculously low front door, measured by the owner at 4 feet 9¼ inches, having been wisely abandoned. Once inside the old 'store', a visitor is overwhelmed with astonishment at how low the actual ceiling is. The inside floor has been lowered a bit, but the owner estimates that in Eileen and Orwell's time the ground-floor ceilings would have been around 5 feet 9½ inches high, and a little lower under the ceiling beams. The internal doorways are 5 feet 6 inches at the tallest. Thus one can only assume that the six-foot-four-inch Orwell would have necessarily been bent over at every moment he was standing up downstairs. The ceiling heights upstairs actually reach 8½ feet in some places, allowing him a bit more comfort when up there. And then there's the ancient twisting staircase to contemplate, with only ten or so extremely narrow stairs needed to reach the upstairs rooms. One can easily imagine Orwell's head popping though the opening to the upper floor before he took his first step up. And the long-legged Orwell would probably have needed only two strides to get to the top. Sadly, this precarious heritage staircase is now enclosed behind a cupboard door, with the narrow steps used as shelves for groceries.[24]

Orwell immediately realised he had an epic amount of fixing-up to do before the cottage would be presentable to his in-laws as a fit home for his new bride. But he was undaunted. As usual, he put his huge energy into action. His first concern was getting the garden started, a project that excited him. Growing their own vegetables was one of the ways he and Eileen had agreed on to reduce living costs. But Orwell was devastated by what a bad state the grounds were in. He wrote various accounts to friends, saying, 'The garden is potentially good but has been left in the most frightful state I have ever seen.' He said it was 'a pigsty at present',[25] and 'a wilderness of tin cans',[26] though perhaps he was exaggerating a bit when he claimed in one letter, 'I have dug up twelve boots in two days.'[27] But he thoroughly enjoyed this preparation because, as he often told friends, 'Outside of my work the thing I care most about is gardening.'

The building was called 'The Stores' because the largest ground-floor room had served this purpose until recently. The couple had agreed that they would reopen the shop as a small source of income, and Orwell surveyed the village to get ideas of what local customers might need, settling at first on 'groceries, sweets, packets of aspirins etc.'[28] Eileen claimed optimistically to Lydia that their own costs would be reduced since running the shop would entitle them to buy goods wholesale. And, from the moment he moved in, Orwell used 'The Stores', Wallington, as his new address, a habit that Eileen copied and which they both continued long after the shop had been closed down. Orwell sought advice from his friend Jack Common, who had once run a shop and now lived eleven miles away, and one Sunday Orwell biked over. Common wrote later about watching him approach up a steep hill, 'a tall man on a tall bike'. He thought Orwell might be better off walking the bicycle up the steepest inclines, but, as Common recorded, 'Not he. This Don Quixote weaved and wandered this side, that side, defeating windmills of gravity till he grew tall on the hillbrow'.[29] Once again, Orwell had provided a charming example of his stubborn refusal to ever appear weak, even when he thought himself unobserved.

It didn't take Orwell much time to get the shop set up. And, when open, it turned out to be 'very little trouble', as he told a friend, since 'in a grocer's shop people come in to buy something, [while] in a bookshop they come in to make a nuisance of themselves'.[30] He made some holes in the door between his original studio and the shop so he could see when customers came in, and these openings are still evident in that door today.

Eileen could easily make weekend visits as she attempted to finish her final college year. They had to choose furniture for the house, and she helped by doing some of the cooking and some of the garden work. She would bring a variety of city food with her because while he was alone at the cottage, as she told a friend, he lived almost exclusively on boiled eggs. At last Eileen and Orwell were able to spend comfortable nights together, and he could realise the charming dream he had written for Gordon to say to Rosemary in *Keep the Aspidistra Flying*: 'What I like best of all is to think of having breakfast together. You opposite me on the other side of the table, pouring out coffee. How queer it is! We've known each other all these years and we've never once had breakfast together.'

Besides getting the cottage and garden in order and working in the shop, Orwell was beginning to write *The Road to Wigan Pier*, his book based on the research he had done up north. On 11 April he told his agent that he was 'making out the scenario for my new book, and shall be beginning it in a day or two.'[31] Writing was always his biggest compulsion. Even the hectic research for this new book didn't count as 'work' to him, and by mid-April he was complaining to a friend, 'It is awful to think that for nearly three months I have not done a stroke of work.'[32]

Eileen and Orwell expected their friends to approve of their daring new life. Even before the wedding Orwell began inviting people to stay overnight, and Jack Common was his earliest guest.[33] Then, in mid-April he asked Cyril Connolly and his wife to visit, and, a week later, Richard Rees, though it's not clear whether either took up the offer. But the endless round of guests making use of the spare bedroom started almost immediately, with hosting apparently a pleasure they both thoroughly enjoyed.

When Eileen and Orwell chose 9 June for their wedding day, he explained that they were 'telling as few people as possible till the deed is done, lest our relatives combine against us in some way & prevent it.'[34] One might assume that Orwell's family would feel relieved that their eccentric son had found someone who agreed to share his meagre life. But a Blair family friend later revealed that 'Avril [one of Orwell's sisters] did not like Eileen – they didn't "cog". There was something about Eileen that Avril and Ida Blair [Orwell's mother] didn't cotton to. They suspected something.'[35] Perhaps they had a hard time simply believing that an educated, sophisticated woman could actually fall in love with such an odd man. Or perhaps they had devoted so much of their own energy to his care that they resented his decision to leave them for a wife. In later years, however, Avril came to appreciate how well Eileen had looked after Orwell.[36] And then, of course, she got her old job back, taking over the care of her brother once again when Eileen so suddenly died. Orwell was also well aware that Eileen's mother wasn't exactly thrilled about her daughter's coming marriage to an impecunious, barely known writer who had no ambitions towards a money-making career. He understood, as he confided to a friend, that marriage at this point was 'very rash of course but we talked it over & decided I should never be economically justified in marrying so might as well be unjustified now as later.' He expected that 'we shall rub along all right – as to money I mean – but it will always be hand to mouth.'[37]

One day that spring, as plans were proceeding for the coming wedding, Eileen brought her mother, her brother, and her sister-in-law up to inspect her new home. She and Orwell had fixed the place up as much as they could, but they were nervous about how such a rustic home would appear to her family, accustomed as they were to the grandeur of Greenwich. Eileen brought Lydia too, perhaps hoping she would finally support her friend's decision. We 'went there together in Eric's [Eileen's brother's] large car, arriving in time for Sunday lunch,' Lydia wrote. They ate 'in the downstairs middle room, somehow managing to squeeze ourselves [six people] round the gate-legged oak table.' Lydia didn't mention what they had for lunch, but no doubt, instead of Orwell trying to prepare such a large meal by himself, they brought dishes made at home in Greenwich. Lydia appreciated the cottage's 'genuinely ancient appearance', but couldn't resist adding that the charm 'was spoiled by a new, corrugated iron roof'.[38]

She was a little more enthusiastic about the surrounding countryside, through which Orwell led the entourage after lunch, hoping to highlight what he and Eileen believed were the most appealing features of their new home. Everything seemed to be going well until Eileen, who had been unusually silent during the walk, suddenly began to run ahead of everyone. Lydia was shocked, but Mrs O'Shaughnessy 'was the only one to murmur some remark on her daughter's eccentric behaviour'. Eileen eventually came back to the house, looking 'defensive and somewhat out of breath,'[39] according to Lydia. But she offered no explanation of what had caused her to dash off, and the matter was not discussed any further.

Eileen later confided to Lydia, 'I just couldn't bear it any longer . . . I had to run.'[40] Though neither of them divulged any particulars at the time, Lydia thought she instinctively understood that Eileen had some lingering doubts about her choice for her future. However, Eileen later told another friend, 'Mother drove me so hard in the first week of June [before the wedding] that I cried all the time from pure exhaustion.'[41] So her mother's reservations about her marriage and the cottage set-up were probably what she couldn't bear any longer. Eileen knew her family would not see Orwell as she saw him, but she had hoped they would at least be as charmed with the cottage as she was. Nevertheless, Lydia was partly right. On that afternoon, so close to the wedding day, the visit by her family had made Eileen vividly aware that by marrying Orwell she was about to start a precarious and unpredictable new life, many miles from the family then visiting her, and so far from the comforts to which she had been accustomed for thirty years.

Orwell was clearly excited about the coming wedding. Early in May, when asked by his American publisher for 'a picturesque detail' about his life, he said that he was 'thinking very seriously about getting married.'[42] On 8 June, the day before the wedding, he wrote to his agent rather succinctly, 'Just a line to let you know I am being married tomorrow – very quietly, at the parish church here.'[43] Neither Eileen nor Orwell were churchgoers, yet they had agreed on an old-fashioned wedding at St Mary's, the village church, which had recently been repaired after being 'in a ruinous state.'[44] Perhaps the fact that it was a lovely twelfth-century church was seductive, but it might also have been an attempt by Eileen to placate her mother. She had chosen John Woods to perform the ceremony, the parson she knew from her childhood days in South Shields, the man who had christened her thirty years earlier. But also, in order to separate herself from tradition, she had secretly written up some as yet undisclosed words to modernise the ceremony in her own way.

On the morning of 9 June, as Eileen was upstairs preparing herself, with the help – and no doubt continuing apprehension – of her mother,

Orwell found time to jot off a letter to Denys King-Farlow, an old Eton friend who had just got back in touch. 'Curiously enough I am getting married this very morning,'[45] he wrote, adding as a tease, 'I am writing this with one eye on the clock & the other on the Prayer Book, which I have been studying for some days past in hopes of steeling myself against the obscenities of the wedding service.'[46] Even so, Orwell didn't put up much of a fuss about having a more or less traditional marriage. There is no record of what kind of wedding gown Eileen wore since no pictures of the ceremony survived. A sole photograph, speculated by some to have been taken on their wedding day, shows Orwell standing alone in front of the church, rather spiffily dressed, with a flower in his lapel.

Finally, the hour had arrived. Orwell emerged from his study and Eileen, having withstood her mother's expressed reservations for the last time, came down the narrow winding staircase at just the right moment. The couple then set off together on the long walk to the church.

7

Six Happy Months of Marriage

I think the only year that I ever knew Orwell
really happy was that first year with Eileen.

Geoffrey Gorer

Eileen O'Shaughnessy and Eric Blair set off together on the morning of 9 June 1936, walking joyfully hand in hand along the dirt lanes towards St Mary's church. The day they had chosen for their wedding was a Tuesday, so from the very beginning this had the touches of an unconventional event. That very morning they were gleefully breaking a common custom, that of bride and groom not seeing each other on their wedding day until the moment she walks down the aisle on her father's arm and joins him, waiting admiringly at the altar with the ring. And this was not the only wedding tradition they had decided ahead of time to change or ignore. They both enjoyed shocking people, and that day they had planned surprises for their families as well as for each other.

Eric Blair was beginning the process of transforming himself into George Orwell, but on the wedding certificate he entered his birth name. Under 'Rank or Profession' he listed 'Author' while Eileen simply drew a line through that space, an admission that she didn't take seriously any of her preceding attempts at a career. With his sometimes conventional beliefs, and in agreement with the custom of the time, Orwell no doubt approved of Eileen's willingness to change her exotic 'O'Shaughnessy' to the bland 'Blair'.

Marriage was a major decision for both of them. They were older than the average couple of the time, and they had each rejected previous chances to be married. Nevertheless, when they finally made up their minds to take this serious step, they still had to stubbornly resist attempts to convince them to wait even longer – at least until Eileen got her master's degree in psychology and Orwell had begun to earn what they would need to support themselves. With all the turmoil surrounding them during the months before the wedding, it had taken all Eileen's huge reserves of energy and courage to push back. A conventional life would have been so easy for her. It was all set up: the looks and personality to entice an attractive, well-to-do man; a smart home in prosperous Greenwich; a highly successful and well-regarded older brother. The fact that she wanted to rebel against tradition and was able to resist all kinds of negative pressure was part of what Orwell loved in her. And she never showed any sign of regretting her choice through all her years with Orwell.

Lydia was aghast when she some time later overheard an Orwell admirer enthusiastically proclaim, 'Here's a man for you – he practises what he preaches! He's married to a woman of the people, and leads the life of a labourer!' She declared, 'No two words could be less appropriate in describing Eileen.' Instead, her friend was 'sophisticated, fastidious, highly intelligent and intellectual . . . perhaps no less gifted, though in different ways, than the man she married.'[1]

The O'Shaughnessys and the Blairs were seated in the ancient pews of the church when the wedding couple approached the churchyard gate. But then – perhaps forgetting the timing of another marriage custom, or perhaps just so full of exuberance he felt the urge to rush ahead – Orwell suddenly vaulted over the high stone wall surrounding the churchyard and ran ahead to the gateway. When Eileen caught up to him, he decided 'to pick [her] up and carry her to the church door, having plainly got his folk-lore muddled,' according to a villager who attended the event.[2] Having fallen in love with such an eccentric man, Eileen of course enjoyed this playful disruption of yet another tradition.

Eileen's brother might have taken her late father's role in walking her down the aisle, but it is likely the couple walked the short distance to the altar together. Orwell had managed to acquire something fancier than the 'Woolworth's ring' he had teased about using some months earlier, though it's not clear that Eileen would have minded. And, as he somehow found the time to inform Brenda in a letter the very next day, the marriage took place 'in correct style . . . but not with the correct marriage services'. Apparently Eileen had arranged for the minister to leave out 'the "obey" clause among other things,'[3] without telling Orwell. He shouldn't have been surprised, however, since he'd written just such a scene in *Keep the Aspidistra Flying*, in which Rosemary rejects the idea that marriage must include a 'promise to obey' – an idea he may well have got from Eileen at the time. Orwell did not divulge the 'other things' Eileen had convinced the minister to change.

Just before he died, Orwell wrote some lines for a new story he was working on that might have referred to this day. 'Coming back from church after the wedding, he did manage to make her come by the lane so as to see the chaffinch's nest on the trunk of the elm-tree. She wanted to go in the car with the others, but he was so anxious for her to see the nest that she rather impatiently did come with him. And it was a beautiful early June morning, & the mother chaffinch was doing her stuff, sitting there on the nest & not budging even when they were standing only a couple of yards away from her.' Up to this point, this could be read as a sad but fond memory of his and Eileen's wedding day. But then Orwell ended the segment on a downbeat note: 'The only bit of real married life that they ever had.'[4] Could this have been added to make a more dramatic storyline?

After the ceremony, no matter how the couple got back to the cottage, the wedding party of eight – Orwell's parents and sister Avril, and Eileen's mother, brother, and sister-in-law – crowded into the cottage's small central room for a wedding luncheon.[5] Most of the food must have been transported from Greenwich that morning, since the dishes on the strangely formal, typed 'Menu' would not have been available anywhere in Wallington. Copies of this charming wedding invitation, with a reproduction of a romantic painting of an upper-class eighteenth-century man and woman on the cover, and tied with a pink ribbon,[6] were sent to the select group of guests. This would seem to be a whimsical choice of illustration by Eileen, considering the primitive life they were planning to embark on. These invitations could have been shop-bought cards, with the typed menu pasted inside, or possibly they were made individually by Eileen with picture cutouts from magazines. Only one copy has survived, and it does present a bit of a mystery. The menu inside this card has always been presumed to be the one from their wedding day, but the card contains no mention of a wedding at all. Some believe this luncheon took place at the Plough – the pub next door to the cottage – but people who remembered the pub in those days said such an elaborate menu could not have been prepared there or anywhere else in the village.

One hopes the new couple filled up on the abundant lunch of 'Minestrone Soup, Fried Fillet of Sole with Tartare Sauce, Roast Aylesbury Duckling with Sage & Onion Stuffing, Orange Salad, New Potatoes and Garden Peas' followed by 'Sherry Cream Trifle, Fruit Salad & Cream, Biscuits & Cheese, and Coffee,'[7] since it would be their last extravagant meal for quite a while. As Orwell later wrote to a friend, rather romantically, 'When Eileen and I were first married . . . we had so little money that sometimes we hardly knew where the next meal was coming from, but we found we could rub along in a remarkable manner with spuds and so forth'[8] – an admission that setting up a productive garden took much longer than they had hoped.

Eileen described the wedding feast to a friend in great humorous detail, including the odd revelation that 'old Mrs. Blair talked without stopping, while Avril said not a word the whole day'.[9] At some point these two women took Eileen upstairs and gave her their condolences. As she told another friend, 'Mrs. Blair shook her head & said that I'd be a brave girl if I knew what I was in for,' and Avril added that 'obviously I didn't know . . . or I shouldn't be there'.[10] But Eileen wasn't worried at all. She was thrilled by the challenges and couldn't wait for this new adventure to begin.

After presenting the couple with the entirely inappropriate wedding present of some Blair family silver, and leaving Hector, a dog they had hopefully asked for, in their care, the relatives all piled into Eric's large car, leaving Eileen and Orwell alone in their rustic cottage. The newlyweds had no money or plans for a honeymoon, although beginning a loving life in a 300-year-old cottage, together at last, could perhaps have counted as one.

But if Eileen had expected to start their new life together with a couple of restful honeymoon days, she was mistaken. Immediately after the wedding, before the many shortcomings of the cottage could even be addressed, the importance of Orwell's writing schedule strongly asserted itself. Throughout his life, he had demanded of himself superhuman outputs of writing, and while living alone at the cottage for two months before the wedding, he had made a good start on his fifth book, *The Road to Wigan Pier*. Throughout that time, besides getting some of the garden planted and fielding the requirements of the shop, he had also written reviews of eleven books and at least fourteen letters – not counting the many he surely wrote to Eileen – but including two sent the day before the wedding and one more, to Denys King-Farlow, on the actual morning. That last letter had been quickly answered by his friend: 'Hearty congratulations! Will be looking you up before very long – but will give you time to get over it first.'[11] He assumed Orwell would allow himself a few days to savour life with his new wife. Orwell, however, had an immediate writing assignment to complete.

On 27 May, just two weeks before the wedding, he had responded to John Lehmann, the editor of *New Writing*, a literary magazine committed to anti-Fascism. Lehmann had asked for a contribution and Orwell had humbly suggested writing a 'sketch' about an elephant, although he hadn't managed to see a copy of the magazine, since a friend in London (probably Eileen) had been unable to find one. This subject would appear to be a surprising detour from his Wigan Pier book. As he explained in his letter, 'It all came back to me very vividly the other day.' Possibly, during one of Eileen's cottage visits, Orwell had regaled Eileen with some stunning memories from his years in Burma. There is a mention in *Burmese Days* of Flory entertaining his girlfriend with a tale about shooting a tiger. '*Do* tell me some more about tiger-shooting. It's so awfully interesting!' she had said. So Orwell had already concluded that women would be thrilled by such tales.

Orwell was worried about the story's appropriateness, however; he wrote apologetically, 'It might be too lowbrow for your paper & I doubt whether there is anything anti-Fascist in the shooting of an elephant!'[12] Luckily, Lehmann was intrigued. But the rush to get the article finished in time for the new issue caused some friction in the early days of their marriage. His 'sketch' was due just three days after the wedding, and Orwell did manage to complete in time what turned out to be one of his most beloved essays, 'Shooting an Elephant'.

The first extant letter by Eileen, written about five months after the wedding, was saved by Norah Symes Myles, one of her best friends at Oxford University. In it, Eileen rather dramatically reported: 'I lost my habit of punctual correspondence during the first few weeks of marriage because we quarrelled so continuously & really bitterly that I thought I'd save time & just write one letter to everyone when the murder or separation had been accomplished.' She went on to explain that the arguments arose 'partly because Eric had decided that he mustn't let his work be interrupted & complained bitterly when we'd been married a week that he'd only done two good days' work out of seven.'[13] This choice of words caused some later readers to worry that the couple actually came close to breaking up in those first weeks of married life. But that reading ignores the light-hearted exaggerations in all of Eileen's letters. Besides implying gloriously that she herself would be the murderer in the imagined crime, rather than the victim, Eileen dramatically displayed her lifelong ability to extract humour from possible disaster. However, she did quickly realise that she would have to learn how to deal with Orwell's stubborn rigidity on certain matters – his reacting 'bitterly', as she repeats twice – and some of the arguments no doubt involved Eileen's resistance to Orwell's insisting that his order of daily events must be followed absolutely. This trait of Orwell's was noted by his friend Malcolm Muggeridge: 'He had in him a strain of almost insensate obstinacy behind which he would retreat and refuse to be dislodged.'[14] However, this letter shows that Eileen was not at all discouraged by the inauspicious start to cottage life.

These fights may be put in perspective when we remember that Orwell portrayed his lovers' disagreements in *Keep the Aspidistra Flying* as joyful squabbles between two intelligent, eccentric individuals who seemed to love each other even more because of them. As his fictitious lovers explored the countryside, Orwell wrote, 'From time to time they quarrelled vigorously, according to their custom.' At one point, 'They began a violent argument upon the eternal and idiotic question of Man versus Woman . . . Gordon and Rosemary never grew tired of this kind of thing. Each laughed with delight at the other's absurdities. There was a merry war between them.' In her letter to Norah, Eileen's comical approach to their fighting suggests that at least some of their disagreements were cheerful bantering between two strong-willed individuals who had to learn to live together in a tiny, uncomfortable space. However, Orwell had perhaps expected a more traditional division of marital duties than Eileen was willing to accede to. Her perpetual untidiness was probably part of the problem. Eileen would not have been willing to pick up after Orwell, especially since a messy house didn't really bother her. In his last notebook, just before he died, Orwell mused in a general way about the 'incorrigible dirtiness & untidiness' of women, which a man only discovers after getting married.[15] He does not explicitly mention Eileen, but he did indeed marry a messy woman.

There's ample reason to believe that this 'merry war' continued throughout Eileen and Orwell's nearly ten years together. Sonia Orwell, his second wife, said, 'Certainly they had the most stupendous rows,' but she thought he viewed that as part of being married.[16] And Richard Blair, their adopted son, grew up believing that their rows weren't 'stormy' but instead were 'powerful arguments,' because she was 'his intellectual equal.'[17] David Astor, another friend of Orwell's, talked a good deal about 'what a remarkable woman Eileen was . . . a great character, matching George very much in face and mannerisms – occasionally uncanny . . . how much they seemed alike and how much they spoke alike.' But, he added, 'they had their quarrels, two distinct personalities despite her very great respect for him.'[18]

Eileen's six marvellously descriptive letters to Norah miraculously surfaced in

The first two pages of Eileen's first extant letter, twelve pages long in total, to Norah Symes Myles, an Oxford friend, November 1936.

letter to everyone when the murder or separation had been accomplished. Then Eric's aunt came to stay (who stayed two months) that we stopped quarrelling – that quieted. Then he went away – now all our troubles are over. They arose partly because we'll drove me so hard to the first week of June that I cried all the time – pure exhaustion – partly because Eric had decided that he must not let his work be interrupted

2005, being discovered by one of Norah's relatives, and they are now part of the Orwell Archive. In them Eileen's independent personality and her wry approach to any troubles shine through. Apparently Norah only started saving these letters after Eileen had married Orwell, even though they must have written to each other many times between 1927 and the marriage. The fact that these letters are all signed 'Pig' has been the subject of scholarly speculation, but the discovery that Eileen might have played a pig in an Oxford play could resolve this conundrum. Since Eileen didn't save Norah's letters, we have no way of knowing Norah's private nickname.

The very first sentence of her first letter is a fine example of Eileen's rambling, playful, light-hearted approach to a subject: 'I wrote the address quite a long time ago & have since played with three cats, made a cigarette (I make them now but not with the naked hand), poked the fire & driven Eric (i.e. George) nearly mad – all because I didn't really know what to say.' These letters to Norah reveal in many delightful ways Eileen's optimism and intelligence and pure charm. But they also show, although thinly veiled, that at times she was capable of feeling exasperation, annoyance, and even anger at Orwell. She never wanted to appear as a nagging complainer, but at the same time she wanted her friends to know that she did suffer sometimes. These letters help us to understand that, even with all the tedious chores and discomforts of the cottage, Eileen remained intently focused on the goal of expanding the pleasures of the idyllic country life she and Orwell had spent so many months planning.

There were many problems the couple had to deal with at the beginning of married life. In that first letter to Norah, Eileen disclosed, in typically jaunty yet slightly hysterical detail, some of the unexpected horrors. Almost as soon as they'd settled in, she wrote, 'Eric's aunt [Aunt Nellie] came to stay & was so dreadful (she stayed <u>two months</u>) that we stopped quarrelling and just repined. Then she went away & now all our troubles are over' – an ironic touch if there's any truth at all to the rest of her letter. Among the early cottage difficulties Eileen detailed was the discovery that she 'couldn't make the oven cook anything & boiled eggs (on which Eric had lived almost exclusively) made me sick'. As she explained to another friend, 'The fireplace in the living-room had an oven on one side, but it had a large crack in it and could not be used for cooking with any reliable results.' As a result, '[T]he hearth itself smoked dreadfully whenever a fire was lit, and the front door had to be opened to get rid of the smoke.'[19] But that was incidental considering that during the summer, as she told Norah, 'It rained every day for six weeks during the whole of which the kitchen was flooded & all food went mouldy in a few hours.' Then of course there was the hard work of setting up the garden with ripe vegetables to eat, and looking after chickens and goats. But, still, the couple shared a kind of hubris that everything would eventually be all right. Many months later, when friends Mark Benney and Richard Rees visited the cottage 'one bleak October afternoon', they found Orwell, 'face and clothes covered with coal smuts', trying to light a fire in the problematic fireplace, which never got properly repaired. Some bricks were missing in the chimney, the likely cause of the problem, and the two men brought back some blocks of granite from the yard that seemed to be a perfect fit. But Orwell 'shook his head regretfully [since] the bits of granite . . . were fragments of old tombstones'. He explained that 'he wouldn't feel right' about using stones from a graveyard to patch his faulty chimney,[20] an explanation that impressed Rees but caused Benney to shrug in disbelief.

The bad times, no doubt somewhat embellished by Eileen, were greatly overshadowed by the good times enjoyed at the cottage. At last they were living the honourable life they had dreamed of for so long, and the next weeks and months were filled with joy. They perhaps even welcomed some of the constant annoyances: having to struggle to achieve their dream only made it more valuable. As Orwell's Eton classmate Cyril Connolly concluded later, 'I was a stage rebel, Orwell was a real one'.[21] Of course, he should have added Eileen's name. Although they couldn't have realised it at the time, those six months together in Wallington, when they were newly in love and still relatively healthy, would turn out to be perhaps the happiest period in their nine years of married life.

They both relished visitors, and friends started arriving for weekend stays in their tiny guest bedroom. Different friends had different takes on the couple, but they could all sense a deep attachment between them. And they were all amazed to find a complete change in Orwell. Mabel Fierz believed, 'He was very happy. That was the only time in his life when he was really happy. He was devoted to [Eileen].'[22] Gorer agreed: 'I think the only year that I ever knew [Orwell] really happy was that first year with Eileen.'[23] He continued, 'They were obviously so happy together. She was just right for him . . . Wallington was not sordid like the Hampstead rooms, very simple but very clean. There was a feeling of contentment.'[24] Eileen fitted comfortably into this dream world. Connolly said she was 'totally worthy of him as a wife; he was very proud of her'.[25] Gorer remembered that '[S]he didn't actually say much in conversations, but listened to him and prompted him and looked after him and his guests very well, or as well as they could afford; she seemed to accept his way of life entirely.'[26] Mabel remembered that Orwell had 'always wished to find a good wife who would be a companion, and a presentable wife, pretty and intelligent. He would never have allied himself to anyone less than that . . . He thought a lot of her and she thought a lot of him.'[27] Humphrey Dakin, Orwell's brother-in-law, agreed. 'I don't recall that she ever let lack of money worry her unduly and of course she always spoilt Eric.'[28] One of Eileen's friends believed, 'Both [Orwell] and Eileen were among the most fearless people I met . . . That he could have found anybody who would have fitted in with him better over a term of years I doubt.'[29] A woman from Eileen's psychology studies had a few reservations, but concluded, 'Eileen was a dreamer. To marry Orwell and share his curious life-style at Wallington, she had to have a streak of mystical dream.'[30] And a friend of Orwell's agreed. She 'shared her husband's sense of humour and his odd ideas.'[31]

However, their life choice continued to stun some of their friends. A man from his Southwold days thought Eileen 'effaced herself', and Orwell was 'sort of a God about the place'. He didn't believe Orwell was being 'unpleasantly dominant', but 'if a woman was going to worship him', he would accept that role.[32] But Eileen was no subjugated wife willing to quietly suffer Orwell's peculiar needs and demands. Although her friends continued to disagree with her radical decision, they were well aware of her own eccentricities. This dream of subsisting on their own produce, far from sophisticated city dwellers, was as exhilarating to Eileen as it was to Orwell. Though neither of them mentioned Henry David Thoreau, they seem to have shared his belief that each person has a moral obligation to follow his or her conscience.

Of course, the whole experiment had always been partly a game for Eileen and Orwell, as it had been for Thoreau. Their hardships were romantic and self-inflicted. They knew they were never going to really starve. Their well-to-do families were always within easy reach for a favour. They often visited London and Southwold, where they were well fed. The dramatic contrast between the hard-scrabble life at the cottage and the luxurious conditions at her brother's Greenwich home, with servants and dinner gongs, is impossible to overstate. Yet they both managed to discount these breaks from self-sufficiency as minor blips, continuing to believe that they were actually setting up a life independent of 'the money-god'. They were two brilliant, privileged children who had always been treated as beloved heroes at home, and they often seemed naïvely unaware of the degree to which they were exploiting their families. However, just because they could wander into comfort whenever they chose doesn't diminish the original challenge they had set for themselves.

Lydia had a dissenting view of the couple, complaining that 'I did not detect any fond glances, or small gestures of attention from him to her,'[33] and believing that 'Eileen was not happy in that marriage from the very beginning.'[34] She continued to regret the marriage years later, saying, 'I was always sorry that Eileen married George. She deserved someone who would support her. I think his work was all to him, human relationships just a background. She really needed and deserved devotion, I think.'[35] Another prominent friend, Jack Common, who knew the couple very well, agreed more with Lydia. He and his wife 'thought that Orwell and Eileen's marriage was not a true one (this not meant in a sex sense), but that it seemed somehow wrong for them to be together.'[36] The Commons took over the cottage while Eileen and Orwell were in Morocco, and Eileen and Mary Common exchanged letters, but they don't seem to have been social friends in any extensive way. Perhaps, as a more conventional couple, the Commons didn't approve of Eileen and Orwell's somewhat open marriage in later years. However, for those first months in Wallington they were faithful to each other and very much in love.

Eileen had agreed from the beginning that Orwell's writing was the essential core around which all cottage life would revolve. For years she had acted as an assistant to her brother, being called on to take dictation and do the final editing and typing of his medical books and articles. Now she hoped to create this same kind of essential partnership with Orwell, where she could contribute her thoughts and insights as she retyped various versions of his work, though she probably knew better than to state this wish overtly. She understood, as Mabel Fierz did, that Orwell 'needed a lot of encouragement . . . He was rather a pessimistic person by nature.'[37] And Orwell was well aware of this need himself. Eileen told Lydia that at first she was disappointed not to be helping Orwell more, but she soon convinced him that he could be much more efficient if she did some of his typing during the hours when he was involved with the goats and garden. And of course he took advantage of a wife who was an excellent typist and a very willing assistant. Eileen told Norah that she would give Orwell her 'typescripts the reverse side of which are covered with manuscript emendations', and that Orwell read her suggestions and took them seriously.[38] Friends believed she was a perceptive critic and could make intelligent suggestions for improvement as she typed his work.[39] In her first letter to Norah, Eileen wrote that Orwell's family 'are all quite penniless but still on the shivering verge of gentility as Eric calls it in his new book which I cannot think will be popular with the family'. This line never appeared in print, but it makes it clear that Eileen was intimately involved in his work. Perhaps she even convinced him to delete that comment. Years later – when Orwell was pleased to discover that he could knock out book reviews and some of his casual columns straight from the typewriter – he recalled that he had often written five drafts of parts of his work. He welcomed Eileen's dedication, and he told friends that she understood the importance of his work.

After writing, Orwell's second favourite occupation was working in the garden. He had been distressed by the condition of the grounds around the cottage when he arrived, but many weeks of gruelling work meant there was no longer the 'wilderness of tin cans, boots and nettles' he had reported to Brenda, with whom he kept in constant touch. Rows of vegetables were planted as well as apple and plum trees and gooseberry and loganberry bushes. Soon they were able to grow much of the food they needed from day to day, banishing for good their initial simple diet of spuds and eggs. Hollyhocks, lilac bushes, and rose bushes soon decorated the grounds around the house, including the much written-about Albertine, a rambling rose that Orwell bought at Woolworth's for sixpence, along with 'a beautiful little white rose with a yellow heart'.[40] On a visit to the cottage in the late forties, after Eileen had died and Orwell was ready at last to give the place up, he was so thrilled to find that the rambling rose 'had grown into a huge vigorous bush'[41] that he wrote a column about it. Some of the roses still blossoming at the front of the house eighty years later might be descendants of the ones Orwell originally planted.

Another part of the dream of self-sufficiency included raising chickens and goats. Any excess eggs could be sold as a source of income, while they used goats' milk regularly. Muriel, their first goat, was named with Eileen's sense of mischief after one of Orwell's aunts.[42] A lovely photograph has survived of Orwell, dressed as a country gentleman, squatting patiently in front of Muriel, holding a large pot of goodies for her to eat. Orwell built a henhouse in the backyard, but when he discovered that the grassy plot of land across the street from their house was designated 'common land', he 'exercised his rights as a sort of English peasant', as one friend described it,[43] and grazed the goats there. When Denys King-Farlow visited the cottage that first summer, he noticed that there was 'in the garden and on the verge by the roadside, room for a couple of goats and also for geese and chickens which he and his wife were rearing'. Orwell himself 'was burnt a deep brown and looked terribly weedy, with his loose, shabby corduroys and grey shirt'.[44] Apparently Orwell was able to enjoy his beloved gardening chores during the hours Eileen spent typing revised drafts of his book and articles, although he was probably pushing himself to extremes as usual.

If all this wasn't enough to easily fill all their waking hours, there was also the shop to run. Part of their reasoning for re-opening it was to be eligible for wholesale food for themselves, but it might also have been an attempt to fit in to the new neighbourhood as equals by providing a welcome service for the villagers. Further, although bringing in minimal income, the profits did cover their tiny rent, as they had hoped. Along with the rather mundane products they stocked, Orwell fulfilled one of his cherished dreams by setting up a bacon slicer, presumably acquiring the necessary meat to slice from nearby farms. Local people had fond memories of their unusual new neighbours and their shop. 'There was no end of bacon there; they had a proper bacon slicer. Beautiful bacon they used to have. And sugar and everything else,' said one. 'Grandfather Hatchett used to go and milk [the goat] twice a day' when the couple were away. This neighbour added that Orwell and Eileen 'wanted me to taste the goat's milk . . . I just had a sip of it, and it was horrible'.[45]

Nevertheless, as it eventually turned out, most of the villagers preferred to go to nearby Baldock to shop, and soon it was mostly children who came by the shop. As grown-ups, they still remembered the lady who would give them liquorice allsorts and mint humbugs at a halfpenny for four, a better price and a closer walk than in town. Of course the shop quickly became another of Eileen's chores, although a man who still lives in Wallington remembers that his mother sometimes worked there, giving Eileen a break from time to time.[46] Paydays were irregular, one longtime resident remembered, always happening just after the mail had brought a cheque for Orwell's writing.[47] There must not have been very precise opening hours, since one visitor remembered that the newly installed bell – which had taken the place of the original peepholes in the door between the living room and the shop[48] – would ring at all hours, and Eileen would dash off to answer it, even jumping up during a meal.[49] Years later Orwell told a friend that 'when he and Eileen tried to lie in on a Sunday morning there might be a customer banging on the door and what did he want? Most likely a sixpenny mousetrap'.[50]

The shop eventually proved to be too much of a bother to continue operating, but, according to the woman who took over the lease when Orwell finally gave up the cottage, in 1948, the bacon slicer was still there. She reported that she also inherited 'a lot of correspondence lying on the floor among his boots and scraps. It had disintegrated over the years so I just had to burn it.'[51] One can only regret that she didn't think of at least showing the correspondence to someone.

As Eileen settled in to cottage life, she still had a huge decision to make. When she met Orwell, she had another year of her MA in educational psychology to go, and a dissertation to write. At first she considered putting off the wedding until she had completed her degree, but with Orwell's eager insistence and her own excitement about the life they were preparing together, she changed her mind. But she still wanted to prove to her mother and to Lydia, as well as to herself, that both those dreams were possible. She completed her second-year coursework before the wedding, and with Lydia's help she was intending to complete her thesis, 'The Use of Imagination in School Essays,'[52] by working with Wallington children. However, there were only five or six children living in Wallington at the time,[53] and Eileen would need a much larger sample to do a proper comparison.

There's a poignant story of Eileen and Peter, a ten-year-old local boy she had befriended who, according to Lydia, was judged backward and quite below the standards needed to get a scholarship for a secondary school. Eileen decided to challenge this conclusion by giving him an IQ test. And, indeed, the results showed Peter possessed a superior intelligence. Eileen 'then volunteered to coach him in reading and arithmetic for several months, which resulted in his winning the coveted scholarship,'[54] Lydia remembered. Eileen was very proud of her success with Peter and hoped for further similar satisfactions in the future if she continued in this career. So she worked on her thesis with Lydia in London through the autumn. She told Norah she hoped to visit her in Bristol, but first she had to 'see Eric (brother) a bit about his book, the proofs of which I'm now correcting, & also have some intelligence testing to do with Lydia'. She joked about Lydia's strong will, adding, 'I want passionately to see you [but] Lydia must have a bit of notice & indeed at any minute is going to descend on me in wrath (against Eric [Orwell] on social grounds not against me, for I am perfection in her eyes) & force me to go to London exactly when I don't want to.' [55]

Before the wedding, when Orwell explained to his old flatmate Rayner Heppenstall that Eileen 'is not earning any money at present and doesn't want to be a drag on me,' he had added, 'However, that will arrange itself later when she has finished her course at London University.'[56] But, as her chores at the cottage intensified, Eileen began to accept that finishing her thesis was an almost impossible task. Also, since the couple had settled on their dream of a self-sufficient country life, Eileen's ability to earn money ceased to be a factor. Orwell probably had no regrets that Eileen had given up a moneymaking career. It would have cut dreadfully into her time with him, which he was already reluctantly sharing with his brother-in-law as well as with her London friends. So Eileen turned her attention away from helping troubled children and towards helping her husband.

Having two important Erics in her life led to a perceptive discussion with Lydia, who once asked Eileen 'whether brother Eric was jealous of husband Eric, and Eileen replied that her brother certainly found it hard to do without her'. She had hoped, perhaps naïvely, to continue her work with her brother, especially since at first Orwell had implied he wouldn't need her help with his writing. Her brother on the other hand 'had come to depend on her help so much that he drove over only a couple of weeks after the wedding and carried her off to Greenwich in order to go over with her a piece of writing he dared not send to the printers without her reading it first'.[57] And she certainly hadn't expected Orwell to be ill as often as he was. Eileen knew in general terms about his poor health, but she seemed surprised when she told Norah that he 'had his "bronchitis" for three weeks in July', putting in quotation marks Orwell's own oversimplification of his illness. She soon discovered that helping her brother was complicated by the fact that 'Eric [Orwell] always gets something if I'm going away if he has notice of the fact.' And 'if he has no notice (when Eric my brother arrives & removes me as he has done twice) he gets something when I've gone so that I have to come home again.'[58] Although Eileen presented all this with a psychological slant, she didn't directly accuse Orwell of faking any illness. But she did begin to sense that acting as nurse for a needy husband Eric might eventually conflict with her editorial chores for a needy brother Eric. And, as Orwell's needs grew, the stress of dividing her duties between the two men she loved became more of a burden.

Eileen understood their different personalities, telling Lydia, 'If we were at opposite ends of the earth and I sent [brother Eric] a telegram saying "Come at once", he would come. George would not do that. For him work comes before anything.'[59] When Lydia later asked Eileen, 'Would not Eric Blair resent his wife being whisked away from time to time to make life easier for Eric O'Shaughnessy?' Eileen said 'she saw no signs of it, so far. "I don't think he really minds."'[60] This contradicts her previous report of Orwell getting sick every time she left the cottage to help her brother. But Eileen loved her brother, and had spent many years helping him with his writing, and maybe she did not want to see those signs. Or perhaps the truth lay somewhere in between. Perhaps she was flattered that Orwell sometimes used his illnesses as a way to keep her at home with him. But in the end, when forced to choose between them, she always went along with Orwell's wishes. However, she never cut herself off from the rest of the world, nor did Orwell ever request that. They each visited London regularly while the other one stayed at the cottage managing the chores alone. In this they had a true partnership where they both thrived.

There was no average day during these six months, of course, but Orwell was a stickler for routine, and he was always able to segment his multiple activities efficiently. A typical day at the cottage would start with a 6:30 a.m. alarm clock, marking the time for him to feed the chickens. At the same time in the morning, he would wake the goats, believing, according to his neighbours, that getting them up before sunrise was good for the quality of their milk.[61]

When Lydia was a guest in the spare bedroom, she suffered from this early alarm, whose sound, she said, 'reached you through two closed doors and a room between'[62] and 'nearly made you jump out of your skin.'[63] When she questioned why there had to be an alarm even on Sundays, she was not impressed by Orwell's deadpan explanation: 'Hens don't know it's Sunday.' She also complained that '[T]he spare bedroom was as cold as an ice-box,'[64] elaborating about 'the cold seeping through the [very thin] mattress from below, as well as from around, while I shivered under the heavy but quite inadequate blankets'.[65] Lydia repeated a couple of times another memory that had obviously impressed her. 'Birds built their nests between the ceiling and the roof, and . . . at night they would sometimes stamp and struggle overhead like an army of demons,'[66] she wrote. When Orwell tried to shock her by suggesting the racket might be made by rats running around in the rafters, she was not amused. Yet she seemed to have been a constant visitor. And she did actually enjoy some of her visits.

On another weekend, Lydia was charmed by the guest bedroom, 'a wonderful place for hearing the dawn chorus [of birds]. Nowhere else have I ever heard such [a] splendid, multi-voiced, vociferous and protracted dawn chorus as I did there.'[67] She also noticed that Eileen had added some nice touches to the cottage, hanging some bright yellow-and-white-check curtains at the windows and putting coconut matting on the floor over yellow tiles.[68] Eileen had somehow mingled these improvements attractively among Orwell's treasures, including a couple of swords from Burma, Blair family silverware, heirloom brass candlesticks, 'furniture dating from more prosperous generations of bygone Blairs,'[69] and eighteenth-century portraits of Blair ancestors, from back when the Blairs were part of the aristocracy, including one of Lady Mary Blair. Eileen also moved her extensive book collection of Elizabethan and Lake District poets to the cottage, much-loved relics of her university days, though one wonders if she ever found time to read them. By chance, one book with her name on the flyleaf, *The Country House* by John Galsworthy, was left with a relative.[70] Of the hundreds of books Orwell owned at his death, over twenty are inscribed with Eileen's name, most of them from her Oxford years, including the complete works of Chaucer.[71]

Every morning Eileen would make one of those huge English breakfasts they both loved. She had somehow mastered the smoking oven, and as she told Norah, 'Now I can make the oven cook a reasonable number of things.' She was an inventive cook and, besides making delicious breakfasts in her tiny kitchen, she would concoct creative dinners worthy of compliments from friends. Denys King-Farlow, when he visited shortly after the wedding, said he had 'some very good pickles that Blair and his wife were very proud of that they'd made together,'[72] and a later visitor told of having 'some of Eileen's very nice apple meringue pie; she was an excellent cook.'[73] A funny marmalade story has persisted through the years, showing that Orwell insisted on practising some of his fastidious customs even in this rustic setting. One of Eileen's friends remembered the incident in excruciating detail: 'The only story I heard about their honeymoon was that somebody had given them a special pot of marmalade, and Eileen put the pot on the table,' the friend said. 'George objected solemnly that the marmalade should have been decanted into a jam dish. Eileen said that they hadn't got one. George said that they must get one, jam and marmalade should always go in a jam dish.' Even if we read this as one of Eileen's comic exaggerations to a friend, there must be some truth to it. As her friend continued, 'This amused Eileen very much as George had warned her that they were going to live like the working class, but she discovered that there were a lot of gentilities that George set great store by.'[74]

After breakfast, Orwell would climb the ancient twisting staircase to the often cold upstairs room to work on his book or his reviews while Eileen cleaned up after the meal, not a simple task considering water had to be drawn from the outside tap and then heated on the old-fashioned stove. She once joked to a friend that 'she reckoned there were only twenty-five minutes between the clearing up of one meal and the start of preparations for another.'[75] Years later, when they were considering renting a similarly rustic house on the Scottish island of Jura, Eileen reminded Orwell that living a primitive life often wasted a lot of time.

Orwell's main occupation was working on *The Road to Wigan Pier*, but during the six months at the cottage after the wedding he somehow managed to fit in writing three important essays as well as reading and reviewing thirty other books. And there was also the strenuous garden work, since the vegetables they grew were an essential part of their diet. He was the designated goat-milker, as well, an activity he greatly enjoyed. He took huge pride in the amount of milk he collected as well as in the speed with which he could complete this complicated task. He adamantly believed that goats' milk not only tasted better but was better for you than cows' milk, a belief that some swear to eighty years later, though no one has yet credited Orwell for this trend. Eileen never quite acquired a shared taste, but she went along with his strong belief as one of her many concessions to him. Milking the goats was such an important chore to Orwell that he once interrupted a letter to Henry Miller to write, 'I have got to go and milk the goat now but will continue this letter when I come back.'[76] Counting the number of eggs the chickens laid each day was another of his 'charming' compulsions, and he later kept a Domestic Diary that included that count every evening, even having Eileen fill in the data when he was too ill to go outside himself. As Anthony Powell noted, 'He was not without a love of detail.'[77] And then, of course, he was the master of the bacon slicer, somehow managing to fit that into his busy day.

In her 'twenty-five minutes' between cleaning up after one meal and preparing for the next one, Eileen worked in the garden, fed the chickens and goats, made jams and pickles, cleaned the house (though, as we know, that wasn't a big concern of hers), filled the lanterns, sold sweets to the children when they arrived suddenly at the shop, entertained visitors when Orwell was writing, and contacted neighbours for help with any special problems. Whenever Orwell needed her to type his work, that job would of course supersede any other she might have planned. She passionately championed his writing and exerted every bit of energy it took to keep his revisions moving rapidly. At this point she might have had a stronger belief in his talent than Orwell had himself. As Connolly said, 'He didn't think he was a great writer then . . . He was quite without that sort of vanity . . . I really do think he was not conscious at that time that he had very, very remarkable powers as a writer.'[78]

Some saw their cottage life as masochistic. Certainly they pushed themselves to the extreme, wanting to fill each day completely with fulfilling work. But they didn't see this as suffering, or get any pleasure from the pain of it. They got pleasure from the rewards of accomplishment: the garden grew, the eggs and milk fed them, the books and articles were perfected and appreciated.

The Wallington residents reported seeing the couple walking the goats slowly along the village lanes in the evenings before dinner, both of them constantly smoking the harsh black tobacco they rolled into cigarettes themselves, never seeming to consider that smoking could damage his already weak lungs. Perhaps this was when they found the time to collect newts at the disused village reservoir, as Orwell told a friend years later. 'We used to have a small aquarium made of a 7-pound pickle jar each year and watch the newts grow from little black blobs in the spawn to full-grown creatures, and we also used to have snails and caddis flies.'[79]

Another of Orwell's reversions to his genteel past appeared at dinnertime which, when guests were present, was usually an elegant, complicated meal created by Eileen. As one remembered, Orwell would 'go around looking like a damn tramp during the day, but when dinnertime came he'd go upstairs and he'd wash himself and do his hair and he'd dress, and you'd sit down to the linen and all the rest.'[80] Orwell later left a list of his gentlemanly food and life preferences: 'I like English cookery and English beer, French red wines, Spanish white wines, Indian tea, strong tobacco, coal fires, candle light and comfortable chairs. I dislike big towns, noise, motor cars, the radio, tinned food, central heating and "modern" furniture.' Then he added thoughtfully, 'My wife's tastes fit in almost perfectly with my own.'[81] We can't help but notice that 'almost.'

After dinner, one hopes, there would be a restful pause in chores, a time to read, or talk over the next day's plans, or discuss the progress of whatever Orwell was in the midst of writing. He no doubt appreciated a chance to run over some difficult parts of his day's work with a sympathetic, intelligent listener, as most writers do. Brenda remembered that 'he liked to work out his ideas in letters. Then we might discuss them when we met.'[82] There were two typewriters in the house and Eileen and Orwell were both impressive letter writers, each able to compose charming re-creations of whatever exciting events had interrupted the daily routine, and quiet evenings would have been a good time to catch up. Music, however, was not a part of their evening entertainment. Brenda said Orwell was 'tone deaf' and 'didn't enjoy music or concerts',[83] and his niece Jane Morgan, herself tone deaf, said it was not a musical family.[84] Eileen had enough of a musical ear to tease him about this. When he joked the next year that he might never sing again, after a bullet had pierced his neck, Eileen assured him that his singing voice would not be missed.

Some evenings, especially at weekends when they had visitors – and they almost always had visitors – they would go next door to the Plough for drinks, or possibly to the nearby Derby, since the Plough often had a mangle (a machine for ironing damp sheets) running in the taproom, making it 'seem to be always washing-day there'. The owner, after hearing complaints, later moved the mangle out of the room and started to keep 'a huge fire burning every night, and two oil-lamps.'[85] But, even on these friendly outings, Orwell could show his stubborn side. He was a stickler for his own preferences in alcohol over anyone else's, and one of Eileen's friends remembered how, even when she had specifically ordered lager, Orwell would always bring her dark ale. When she finally protested, Eileen explained the situation: 'It's no use. Once you are established as a friend of his, you become the kind of person who wouldn't drink lager or light ale if you could have dark ale, and nothing will shake him.'[86] Eileen was learning to treat Orwell's often thoughtless stubbornness with quiet acceptance. Sometimes they would bring jugs of ale back to the cottage from the Plough and share stories with their visitors. One surviving jug from this time, white ceramic with a blue stripe, is in the possession of a woman who worked at the Plough as a teenager. She remembered that Orwell drank Simpson's ale, brewed in Baldock.[87] And, when the spare room was taken, some guests stayed overnight at the Plough, where they were served elaborate breakfasts.[88] The neighbours in general reported liking the couple but, according to one report, 'they loathed his friends.'[89]

Orwell was prone to dramatically overstating his beliefs, and sometimes Eileen, a clear, logical thinker, would enjoy challenging him. Adrian Fierz, Mabel's son, recalled two of Orwell's broad generalities that 'he just sort of threw off, partly as a joke': 'All scoutmasters are homosexuals,' and 'All tobacconists are fascists.'[90] Lydia preserved one perhaps typical example of an Orwell 'non sequitur', what she called the 'bacon story'. Orwell had proposed that 'every villager ought to have his own pig and cure his own bacon. "But," he added, "they are not allowed to keep pigs unless they satisfy a set of complex sanitary regulations. Bacon manufacturers had seen to this."' As Lydia remembered it, Eileen, after giving Lydia 'a quick glance and a smile', had exclaimed, '"Now what made you say this? Isn't it rather a sweeping statement to make?"' Lydia watched carefully for Orwell's reaction to Eileen's criticism and reported, 'The look in George's face showed that he was both amused and a little embarrassed but he stuck to his guns. "It is in the interests of bacon manufacturers . . ." he began.' Eileen immediately responded, ' "Yes, I know, but have you any evidence to show that they were responsible for the sanitary regulations?" He had not', and Eileen rubbed it in a bit: ' "That's the kind of statement an irresponsible journalist would make." ' Lydia seemed pleased to conclude that 'George had enough sense of humour not to mind this kind of challenge, and

Eileen often challenged him in these ways.'[91]

Another friend who often visited them at the cottage verified the teasing interaction between the two. Eileen 'had a good sense of humour and was given to telling funny stories. And funny stories about George, which he didn't seem to mind. In fact I think he rather liked being made fun of by Eileen. I don't think George was an easy man to live with, but they did get on quite well. I had the impression it was a very happy marriage.'[92]

All in all, they both seemed to thoroughly enjoy the 'merry war' they had chosen to indulge in, and their evenings of ale and conversation would end in their pleasant bedroom in a bed they shared throughout their lives together.

One extremely important subject infringed upon their happiness during these months. The very first thing Eileen and Orwell had expected to happen after the marriage, the one event they both most looked forward to, was for Eileen to get pregnant. Orwell often told her and others how much he wanted to have a son, and they were both intent on producing one. They had never suggested theirs was an intellectual marriage only, and both families were no doubt awaiting an announcement. Heppenstall remembered that Orwell 'badly wanted children and was miserable about [Eileen's not getting pregnant]'.[93] Orwell had warned Eileen that he might be sterile, but she hadn't taken this seriously. At this point she was generally healthy, but the fact that she later suffered greatly from vaginal bleeding might imply some medical problem. At any rate, realising month after month that a child was not on the way must have been the subject of many late-night talks between them, a tragic blemish on their marriage.

Orwell's musings a few months before he died about the 'terrible, devouring sexuality' of women add some confusion. His thoughts about the subject in his last literary notebook are striking. These are written in the third person, in a separate paragraph in the notebook, but they don't seem to be part of a future novel. He wrote, 'In his experience women were quite insatiable & never seemed to be fatigued by no matter how much love-making . . . Intercourse was thought of as a duty, a service owed by the man to the woman. And he suspected that in every marriage the struggle was always the same – the man trying to escape from sexual intercourse, to do it only when he felt like it (or with other women), the woman demanding it more & more, & more & more consciously despising her husband for his lack of virility.'[94] Eileen told a friend that she believed 'Orwell had had too much sex before marriage,'[95] and there can be no doubt that some of their early arguments involved their sex life. When he and Eileen had made love in the woods before their marriage, sex was the planned result of the adventure, and during the months of courting Orwell seemed anxious for sex whenever possible. No doubt Eileen expected even more love-making when they shared a double bed after marriage. But Orwell apparently was conventional enough to think that making love happened when the man was in the mood, and the woman shouldn't initiate it or expect it at random times. After all, as he had told her many times, writing was more important than anything else. However, in these happy six months of marriage, Eileen perhaps got her way more often than she did later.

During the summer of 1936, the real world started to rudely intrude, and Orwell and Eileen began to pay closer attention. In Moscow, Stalin succumbed further to his paranoia about losing power and began for the first time executing men he suspected were helping Trotsky try to take over the country.[96] In Germany, Hitler decided to remilitarise the Rhineland, in violation of the Treaty of Versailles. In Italy, Mussolini, fresh from conquering Ethiopia, agreed to a pact with Hitler, increasing the dread of these two Fascist dictators throughout the democratic world. And in Spain, Franco and other generals began a long march towards Madrid, hoping to overthrow the newly formed Popular Front socialist government. Earning the praise of left-leaning citizens around the world, the Spanish workers took up arms in resistance to Franco, and a prolonged civil war began. Seeing that Franco needed help, Germany and Italy quickly came to his aid, and in reaction to that move, the Soviet Union began sending support to the Popular Front. Many were worried about the possibility of war in Europe, and a year earlier Orwell had already imagined 'the humming of the aeroplanes and the crash of the bombs'.[97] If England and the United States had chosen to get involved in the resistance to Franco in Spain, he might have been quickly stopped. But they opted instead to remain neutral.

Throughout the summer and autumn, as they handled all the cottage chores, Orwell and Eileen were well aware of the escalating civil war in Spain. He spoke at a nearby Marxist conference and 'astonished everybody . . . by his interventions in the discussions', according to a friend. 'He produced breathtaking Marxist paradoxes and epigrams, in such a way as to make the sacred mysteries seem almost too obvious and simple.'[98] Orwell admired some of those attending the conference, and apparently Eileen did also, since Orwell told Common, 'My wife almost fell in love with [E. C. Large, one of the speakers] when he came to tea here.'[99] They understood that opposing Franco, an honourable position in itself, would have the added value of curbing Hitler and Mussolini, who were supporting him. Orwell was only eleven when the First World War started, and he told a friend that 'his generation must be marked for ever by the humiliation of not having taken part in [that war]'.[100] When idealistic young men from all over the world began to pour into Spain, believing that they, as individuals, had the obligation to stop Franco, Orwell got caught up in their hopes. 'Socialism is the only real enemy that Fascism has to face,' he wrote at the time, since he believed that capitalist governments would eventually choose to appease Hitler.[101] Denys King-Farlow remembered that Orwell talked with great interest about Spain on his Sunday visits to the cottage, and he wasn't surprised when Orwell dropped him a note 'saying that he was going to do some journalism abroad'.[102]

But at this point Orwell was enjoying the happiest time of his life, newly married and trying to have a child with Eileen. Rees thought that consideration 'might have kept Eric away from Spain. However, he's an adventurer type. Or rather an adventurous type.'[103] If Eileen had become pregnant during those first six months, would that have changed Orwell's thinking? Would he have resisted his strong drive to fight in the Spanish Civil War and stayed instead with his pregnant wife? Impossible questions, of course. But, as is often the case in life, one seeming tragedy – Eileen not getting pregnant then – perhaps prevented another worse one, since it meant she was in Spain when he needed her most.

In November, in the middle of all this Spanish discussion, Eileen and Orwell spent two weeks with his parents. Eileen enjoyed the visit, telling Norah, 'The family on the whole is fun & I imagine unusual in their attitude to me because they all adore Eric & consider him quite impossible to live with.'[104] By then Orwell had almost finished the final draft of *The Road to Wigan Pier*, and a few weeks later he told his agent, 'The book will be typed in ten days or so,'[105] the passive tense implying that Eileen was busy typing the final copy. Eileen told Norah in November that they would be 'completely broke . . . until Christmas' because this latest book 'won't earn its advance until December'.[106] With her help, Orwell presented it to his agent on 15 December.

Perhaps Eileen could have talked him out of going to Spain – there were many arguments to be made against it, including his own poor health. But she herself got caught up in all the excitement and honour of the war. She supported the Spanish cause as strongly as Orwell did, and was proud of him for being anxious to help however he could. She told Norah later that he had gone there 'with my full approval'.[107] Some friends believed Orwell was going to Spain as a journalist, and he did of course intend to write about his experience there. But he had made it clear to Eileen from the beginning that he planned to actually go into the hills and fight. In fact, as Orwell wrote in 1947, 'My wife and I both wanted to go to Spain and fight for the Spanish government.'[108] Now all that remained to be done was the tedious preparation that the trip required.

8

Escape from Catalonia

In Eileen Blair I had seen for the first time the symptoms of a human being living under a political Terror.

Richard Rees

Once Orwell had made up his mind to go to Spain, everything moved very quickly. On 23 December, while the couple were visiting Eileen's brother's home for Christmas, Orwell made the shocking announcement that he was leaving immediately. He tried to calm any fears they had by falsely claiming he planned to stay away from any actual fighting. He seemed cheerful about going, but then he'd been in a happy mood ever since his wedding day. Lydia was with Eileen at her brother's home that day, and she was dismayed when Orwell, 'with a wry smile', said to Eileen, 'Shan't be kissing you under the mistletoe this Christmas.'[1] She noticed that Eileen showed no sign of disagreement about his decision, but she thought this meant that she was afraid to speak up. Lydia recalled later that her own reaction was 'one of dismay, then of anger – at Eric Blair'.[2] After all, he and Eileen had only been married a short time, and he seemed not the least bit concerned about the burden his absence from the cottage would place on Eileen. Lydia even tried to get Eileen's brother to intercede, but he told her, in admiration, that Orwell had 'a warrior's cast of mind'.[3] Indeed, there was no way to keep him from going. As he had declared to one of his magazine editors, 'This fascism, somebody's got to stop it.'[4]

Lydia vastly underestimated Eileen. The final draft of *The Road to Wigan Pier* was already with Orwell's agent. But there were still some dangling decisions to be made before its publication in March, and Orwell felt entirely confident leaving Eileen in charge of everything. In the formal letter he sent his agent just before he left, he wrote, 'During my absence abroad will you please communicate with my wife on all subjects relating to my literary affairs and accept her decision as my own. In the event of any alterations being required in my manuscript or proofs before publication, my wife has my authority to make them on my behalf.'[5] Then, packing his Spanish phrase book, a pair of rare size-twelve boots, and a letter of introduction to John McNair, who represented the Independent Labour Party (ILP) in Spain, Orwell set off for Barcelona at Christmastime in 1936, joining a growing number of idealistic people from many countries around the world who believed the Spanish Civil War warranted personal involvement.

He first needed a safe-conduct pass from the Spanish Embassy in Paris, and while he was waiting for that to be processed he decided to drop in on Henry Miller. The two had been in contact already after Orwell wrote some words of admiration for *Tropic of Cancer*, and they had considerable respect for one another. But Miller, outspoken as always, did not hide his belief that 'to go to Spain at that moment was the act of an idiot,' later branding Orwell 'a foolish idealist'.[6] However, when Miller became convinced that Orwell was really going on this 'stupid' mission, he gave him a jacket to keep him warm on the front lines. Scholars disagree on whether the jacket was corduroy or leather, and the blurry pictures of Orwell at the trenches don't help to clarify the question. But whichever it was, it was clearly more suitable attire for the front lines than the blue suit and tie in which Orwell was heading to Spain.

As the 'Red' train packed full of international volunteers lumbered through the French countryside on the thirty-six-hour trip to Barcelona, Orwell was thrilled to see that 'every peasant working in the fields turned round, stood solemnly upright', and gave them the communist raised-fist anti-fascist salute as they passed by.[7] And when he finally arrived, he found the atmosphere in Barcelona immediately intoxicating. As he wrote, 'Waiters and shop-walkers looked you in the face and treated you as an equal', while 'many of the normal motives of civilised life – selfishness, money-grubbing, fear of the boss – had simply ceased to exist.' He added, 'I recognised it immediately as a state of affairs worth fighting for.'[8] It took him a very short time to decide, if indeed he had not before he got there, that merely reporting on the conflict would not be enough for him.

He arrived early in the morning at McNair's Barcelona office, as yet unfamiliar with the distinctions among all the left factions arrayed against Franco. With McNair's help, he decided to join the small POUM (Workers' Party of Marxist Unification) anarchist militia rather than the communist-controlled International Brigade in Madrid. Orwell seemed glad for a chance to get so quickly to the front lines, where he was sent after some minor training at the barracks in Barcelona. He had no idea at that point how inefficient and ill-equipped this particular group of volunteers would turn out to be, or that he'd end up spending almost four months at the front, in alternating periods of boredom and disorganised danger, before finally getting some leave at the end of April.

Meanwhile, back in England, Eileen was busy. Besides being alone at the cottage with the goats and chickens and garden and shop, she was now in complete charge of Orwell's literary affairs. He knew very well how competent she would be, and she indeed handled everything efficiently. In a letter to Orwell's agent in January regarding the publishing contract for *The Road to Wigan Pier*, which particulars she had overseen, she wrote, 'I enclose the signed agreement . . . I was delighted, as I know my husband will be when he hears the details.'[9] She also managed a comical exchange with great aplomb. Apparently in the sentence, 'For the first time in my life . . . I saw rooks copulating', the publisher had changed the word 'copulating' to 'courting'. But, as Eileen explained wryly, the sentence had then become nonsensical, since Orwell had certainly 'seen rooks courting hundreds of times'. If any change absolutely had to be made (though she much preferred going back to the original 'copulating'), Eileen insisted, on Orwell's suggestion, that they use the word 'treading' instead.[10] And 'treading' it became.

She also had to figure out how they were going to support themselves with no new writing income imminent, another 'bother' that Orwell seemed barely to consider as he took off so precipitously. Before he left, 'we panicked at the last moment that he hadn't enough money with him, so we pawned all the Blair spoons and forks,' Eileen told a friend. Unfortunately, Orwell's mother and sister noticed the missing cutlery when they visited the cottage. 'I had to think of something on the spur of the moment, so I said it seemed a good opportunity, George being away, to have the crest engraved on it,' she explained.[11] If Mrs Blair fell for this story, accepting that her son had the money for such trivialities, she was indeed in some fantasy world about how the couple were getting along financially. As Eileen was trying to discover some further sources of income, she got the 'splendid . . . news that [*The Road to Wigan Pier* had been] definitely chosen for the Left Book Club,'[12] which meant sales closer to 50,000 than 3,000 – a considerable increase in their royalties, though they wouldn't see that money for some months. The choice of Orwell's book was somewhat surprising, and had been doubted by Orwell himself, since, as he believed, the book was 'not very left-wing'.[13]

When Eileen had finished all the business letters and been alone with the shop and the animals for some weeks, she decided that she would much rather be in Spain with her husband. Life all alone at the cottage was mostly dreadful, and she wasn't about to isolate herself at the cottage with the goats while he was having his Spanish adventure. She'd heard from Orwell that, as she joked to her Oxford friend Norah, the Spanish government was feeding him 'bread without butter and "rather <u>rough</u> food" and has arranged that he doesn't sleep at all, so he has no anxieties'.[14] As one biographer noted, 'Already there is a characteristic tone at work in Eileen's reflections on [Orwell]: affectionate, exasperated, its incidental comedy not always disguising straightforward annoyance and deep-seated anxiety over Orwell's health.'[15] Eileen went on to hide her worries with more conjectures: 'He's on the Aragon front, where I cannot help knowing that the Government ought to be attacking or hoping that that is a sufficient safeguard against their doing so'.[16] This is perhaps an ironic suggestion that the government might be afraid to attack the Aragon front if it were known that Orwell was there defending it. Or perhaps just a cynical belief that governments rarely do what they 'ought to'. At first the war seemed more of an entertainment than a dangerous event for her, making her capable of such a frivolous joke. Still, she wanted to be closer to him, where she could help with his comfort. She wasn't making any money in England, she figured, so she might as well be poor in Barcelona instead. And Orwell wanted her there too. Eileen told his agent that '[He] thinks he may get some leave at the end of this month and wants me to be in Barcelona as soon as possible'.[17]

So Eileen now concentrated on how to get to Spain. A friend said later, '[Orwell's] wife came to see me . . . Perhaps I was able to facilitate her plan (which she courageously carried out) to go to France and get [Orwell] out of Spain'.[18] However she managed it, Eileen soon discovered that a volunteer was needed as an English–French shorthand-typist to John McNair. She immediately offered herself and, being well over-qualified for the job, she was chosen. She laughed about the situation to Norah, telling her, 'I suddenly became a kind of secretary perhaps to the ILP in Barcelona. They hardly seem to be amused at all. If Franco had engaged me as a manicurist I would have agreed to that too'. John McNair, Eileen continued, 'has an unfortunate telephone voice and a quite calamitous prose style in which he writes articles that I perhaps shall type.'[19]

Lydia visited Eileen at the cottage at weekends before she left, 'usually bringing a chicken as a gift,'[20] a strange choice it would seem since the cottage chicken population at that time was quite vast and Eileen had no shortage of prospects for dinner. With some more devious plan in mind, perhaps, Lydia also brought Karl Schnetzler with her, an old friend of Eileen's from before her marriage. As Lydia later remembered, 'There was a look which came over his face when Eileen appeared on the scene which left me in no doubt that he was in love with her.' Karl was highly critical of Orwell, angrily telling Lydia, 'If I were married, I would have worked hard in the garden and in the house, to make the place nice for my wife.'[21]

But Eileen had made up her mind to leave for Barcelona. She had two difficult final jobs to do before she could depart. First, she had to convince her local bank to let her and Orwell withdraw royalties from a branch in Barcelona after they had been deposited in London by Orwell's agent. And, so as not to abandon the cottage completely, she had to persuade Orwell's Aunt Nellie, who was subletting the cottage to them, to come over from France to look after the shop, milk the goats, etc., etc. Although Aunt Nellie accepted this responsibility willingly at first, she later complained bitterly about it.

On her last day in London, Eileen informed Norah, with her usual jaunty tone: 'Supposing that the Fascist air force goes on missing its objectives and the railway line to Barcelona is still working, you'll probably hear from there some day . . . I am staying at the Continental too to begin with, but as we have now spent practically all the money we shall have until November . . . I think I may be doing what the Esperantists call sleeping on straw – and as they are Esperantists they mean sleeping on straw.'[22] The possibility of living in Barcelona without much money seemed to delight rather than worry her, just as a typical rich woman might approach that condition. Eileen was spending her last night in England at her brother Eric's elegant Greenwich home, and she ended her letter to Norah on a fanciful note, apparently oblivious of the huge contrast between the frugal cottage life she had chosen and the very civilised home life she'd grown up with: 'The dinner gong is going. Is it not touching to think that this may be the last dinner unrationed available for Pig.'[23]

Eileen left for Spain in the middle of February, less than two months after Orwell had gone, travelling alone through France and needing McNair's assistance before she was allowed to cross the border into Spain. And when she climbed the long stairway to McNair's fourth-floor office in Barcelona, bearing gifts for Orwell of his beloved Typhoo tea, chocolates, Havana cigars, and some of the strong black tobacco he enjoyed, she caused quite a stir. Charles Orr, McNair's assistant, was quite shocked to discover that Orwell had a beautiful wife. He remembered Eileen as 'a round-faced Irish girl, prim and pretty, with black hair and big dark eyes'. He thought she was 'friendly, gregarious and unpretentious', the complete opposite to her husband, whom Orr described as 'tongue-tied', a man who 'stammered and seemed to be afraid of people'. Orr also found Eileen at first to be 'very vaguish when she talks', a quality others had noticed before. A lot of Eileen's work would be as an assistant to Orr, and he found her to be 'an excellent secretary . . . intelligent and self-confident. Everyone liked her, women as well as men.' He felt she stood out as 'a superior person . . . not too proud to accept a job as secretary-typist'.[24] Another office volunteer described her as 'a remarkably even-tempered young Englishwoman . . . as she efficiently handled the affairs and finances of half a dozen members of the ILP contingent.'

Orr was also impressed by Eileen's open admiration for Orwell, saying, 'At the office, Eileen just could not resist talking about Eric – her hero husband, whom she obviously loved and admired,' adding, perhaps ironically, 'It was my privilege to hear about him day after day.' Orr decided that '[A] man who could win a woman of such quality must have some value.' He understood why Orwell, whom he saw as socially awkward, would be 'attracted to this outgoing gregarious Irish girl . . . apart from her natural beauty,' believing that Orwell needed 'a socially extrovert wife as a window to the world. Eileen helped this inarticulate man to communicate with others.'[25] And another friend recalled, 'Eileen was very much a figure in ILP quarters [in Barcelona], holding what in other circumstances . . . would have been called "a salon" in the Hotel Continentale.' He remembered her as 'an elegant person' and 'scoffed at the notion of her somehow being untidy and frumpish.'[26] However, Orr did complain that Eileen was 'eternally smoking cigarettes.'[27] And although his wife Lois's first impression of Eileen was as a 'nice dainty little English girl,' she too complained that, during a cigarette shortage, Eileen was constantly 'smoking the most horrible big cigars, which smell simply terrible.'[28]

In mid-March, after Eileen had been in Barcelona only a few weeks, she talked Georges Kopp, Orwell's commander, into taking her along when a trip was planned to the front-line trenches, since Orwell had not yet been given leave. On the way, they visited a small hospital near where Orwell was stationed. Feeling perhaps a little guilty about all the good food and drink she was enjoying in Barcelona while Orwell, as she knew from his letters, was suffering sometimes from dangerous missions his militia struggled through and sometimes just from boredom, Eileen told her mother that she would 'have moved heaven & earth to stay . . . as a nurse,' and thus be even closer to him. But this tour of the hospital shocked her enough to change her mind. 'The doctor is quite ignorant & incredibly dirty . . . Used dressings are thrown out of the window unless the window happens to be shut when they rebound onto the floor.'[29] Unfortunately, it was to this very hospital that Orwell was sent a few days later, suffering from a hand so badly infected he had to remain there ten days, an infection that recurred months later when they were safely back in England.

Eileen stayed at the front with Orwell for three days, getting her picture taken with the gang of volunteers, posing near a machine gun, then sleeping with Orwell at night in the outbuildings of a rambling farmhouse that served as a barracks. She described some of the scary details to Orwell's agent: 'I was allowed to stay in the front line dugouts all day. The Fascists threw in a small bombardment and quite a lot of machine gun fire.' Then she added, 'It was quite an interesting visit – indeed I never enjoyed anything more.'[30] It's not clear whether she was purposefully making light of Orwell's danger to keep from worrying too much, or whether she was still just so naïve about war that she could be nonchalant.

In a letter to her mother, Eileen said simply, 'I thoroughly enjoyed being at the front.' She also added a detailed account of her last night there with Orwell, with hints at the titillating parts: 'My visit to the front ended in a suitable way because Kopp decided I must have "a few more hours" [with Orwell in his bedroom] . . . 'We went to bed at 10 or so & at 3 Kopp came & shouted & I got up & George went to sleep again I hope.'[31] So after a couple of months apart, they had a few pleasant hours together before she had to leave him in danger again. Eileen, always the trooper, didn't ask Orwell to get out of bed to accompany her to Kopp's car, and apparently he didn't offer to. She told her mother, in her exuberant way, 'I emerged in black dark & waded knee deep in mud in & out of strange buildings until I saw the faint glow . . . where Kopp was waiting with his car.'[32] Although she didn't tell her mother, she was well aware of the favour Kopp was doing her, later calling his behaviour 'extraordinarily magnanimous'.[33]

She left some greatly appreciated goodies for Orwell, and his only letter to her that has survived was one written after that visit: 'Dearest, You really are a wonderful wife. When I saw the cigars my heart melted away. They will solve all tobacco problems for a long time to come . . . & you should have seen their faces when they saw the margarine.' Then he added, in a personal touch, 'The weather is much better . . . & the look of the earth makes me think of our garden at home & wonder whether the wallflowers are coming out & whether old Hatchett is sowing the potatoes.' Orwell was looking forward to his leave, which he knew might still be weeks away, '& then what a rest we will have, &

go fishing too if it is in any way possible.' He ended his letter, 'Goodbye, love. I'll write again soon. With all my love, Eric.'[34] This is a beautiful letter from a man obviously very much in love. It's not clear why this one survived – possibly it got mixed in with McNair's files – while so many other letters between them had been discarded. Perhaps they were so confident in their mutual love that they didn't need to hold on to the written proof.

Eileen worked in the Barcelona office for over two months before Orwell finally got the long-promised leave from the front. She had gone to Spain to be near him but, while waiting week after week for Orwell

An example of Eileen's handwriting, 22 March 1937.

to arrive on leave, she was having a marvellous time. It wasn't her fault that Barcelona was full of exciting people. The contrast for her couldn't have been sharper between lonely days and nights at the cottage with all the mundane chores and the heady life she discovered in Barcelona. She was no doubt entirely ready for some social fun. As she wrote to her mother a little over a month after arriving in Barcelona, 'I've had 3 superb dinners in succession . . . I have coffee about three times a day & drinks oftener, & . . . at least six times a week I get headed off into one of about four places where the food is really quite good by any standards . . . Every night I mean to go home early & write letters or

An example of Orwell's handwriting, 5 April 1937.

something & every night I get home the next morning.'[35] She quickly became good friends with Lois Orr, and they shared many adventures together. Some of the splendid meals Eileen described to her mother were the result of an invitation by a journalist from the *Daily Express* – 'a reactionary sensational paper in England' – who Lois felt 'was always trying to pump us for information' as he treated the two women to 'swell dinners in all the fine places at his expense.'[36] Of course neither of them divulged any useful information to him.

In this strange city of constant fluctuations, being a pretty woman, a vivacious conversationalist, and someone who appreciated good food and drink, Eileen became a flame that attracted a few of the Barcelona bachelors. And she certainly enjoyed the attention. One of her constant companions was Georgio Tioli, a handsome man who Lois described as an 'elegant, spare, Italian gentleman, immaculate in his white linens', who was frequently in Eileen's company during George's absence at the front. She was also pursued by David Crook, who, along with Tioli and two other men, turned out to be spies working for the Soviet Union. The suggestion has been made that Eileen was considered a more important person to observe than Orwell, since she had a high-level job with McNair and the Independent Labour Party.[37]

One idyllic day spent in the hills surrounding Barcelona was a highlight of the peaceful months before the horrendous events in June. Eileen and Tioli joined Lois and Charles Orr one Sunday, lounging in the sun for hours on a hill overlooking a spectacular view of Barcelona while they joked about where they might settle if a European war started. Eileen surprisingly suggested Mexico while Tioli, Lois recalled, preferred Iceland. After a luxurious lunch in a nearby village, they 'crossed vine fields and meadows' and followed wagon trails as they laughed about founding an organisation that reflected Eileen and Tioli's supposed hatred of the Catalan language. The four friends went so far as to imagine acquiring 'a rubber stamp, two flats, three cars, a bath, an office, three typewriters, etc.',[38] a list that suggests Eileen's fanciful wit. And wouldn't 'two flats' have meant she would share one with Tioli?

Eileen and Tioli had adjoining rooms at the Hotel Continental and they were in constant touch. Charles Orr came to believe that Tioli was a communist agent assigned 'to gather information from the talkative, but non-political Eileen'.[39] The fact that he claimed he was a child psychologist was a good ploy for a connection with her. The suspicion that he had been spying on them was later proved true, but some speculated that he had grown to admire Eileen and the Orr couple so much that he eventually stopped reporting on them. Later he was somewhat forgiven when he managed to provide peaches to Lois and blankets to Charles while they were in jail, and it's possible he helped keep Eileen from being arrested at all.

Eileen's most curious and enigmatic relationship was with Orwell's commander, Georges Kopp. During the four months she was in Barcelona, Kopp would spend time with her whenever he visited headquarters in town, and he quickly fell in love with her. Apparently he was not conventionally handsome, although he was described rather extravagantly by one of the men who served at the front with him as having 'a strong, dimpled chin, laughing lips and blue mischievous eyes surmounted by a broad, smooth brow'.[40] Orr described him as 'a big, heavy, ruddy, blond Belgian, jolly, not very sophisticated, but an educated man. Everyone liked him.'[41] Kopp was enormously charming, and didn't try to hide his attraction to Eileen, no doubt flattering her with his compliments and intriguing her with his fabulous – though, as it turned out, partly fictitious – life story. He had presented himself as a Belgian, but it was discovered later that he had been born in Russia and left a wife and five children behind in Belgium when he decided to fight in Spain. Perhaps as part of his Russian nature, he 'had a tendency to gush', and 'his charm, sense of humour and boyish enthusiasm did the trick' with women,[42] making him a strong contrast to Orwell. Those seeing Eileen and Kopp constantly together believed he was trying to seduce her behind Orwell's back, one of them calling it 'a rotten business'.[43]

It was not unheard of during the war in Spain for wives to have affairs while their husbands were at the front, but Lois didn't approve. She remembered with disdain one German wife who, although 'deeply in love with her husband', was 'having an affair, before God and everybody'. Lois left no comment on the possibility of an affair between Eileen and Kopp, possibly because she didn't find him at all attractive, describing him as 'gross, ruddy [and] pot-bellied'.[44] For her part, Eileen didn't hide her close friendship with Kopp, telling her mother that, when she 'discovered by accident' that he 'longed for Lea & Perrins Worcester Sauce I . . . found some in Barcelona'[45] – apparently yet another man she felt needed looking after. And as fodder for at least another giggle with her psychology friends back home, Kopp's first name was Georges. So, including Georgio Tioli, she now had three Georges along with her two Erics, though of course Orwell was one of the Erics as well as one of the Georges. David Crook, one of the spies who escorted Eileen around Barcelona, wrote in his reports that he was '95 per cent certain that Kopp and Eileen were on intimate terms'.[46] Back in England, much later, their friend Rosalind Obermeyer, speculating on the rumours, said, 'Eileen was attractive to men . . . Her eyes always lit up whenever Georges Kopp's name was mentioned, so there may have been some truth in the belief that she and Kopp had an affair'.[47]

While enjoying her very eventful Barcelona nightlife, Eileen continued to fulfil her duties as secretary to McNair. In addition, Orwell was sending her notes on scraps of paper, backs of envelopes, even toilet paper, and Eileen would type those up. It was easy for him to find time to jot down brief accounts of his thoughts and observations, sometimes at 5:30 in the morning, before the day's activities got started, and again at night, by candlelight, before going to bed. Eileen told Orwell's agent that 'there is apparently no "proper" fighting as neither side has efficient artillery or even rifles,' so Orwell spent some of his time in his 'dug-out in which he can make tea'.[48] He also smoked constantly, and even the rugged front-line volunteers complained about his 'incessant smoking of cigarettes . . . rolled from the strongest, coarsest black shag pipe tobacco. He kept a rope cigarette lighter hanging from his belt all the time.'

Then there was Orwell's phobia of rats, which nearly caused a disaster. As he wrote later, 'If there is one thing I hate more than another it is a rat running over me in the darkness. However, I had the satisfaction of catching one of them a good punch [his euphemism for a bullet from his gun] that sent him flying.'[49] That satisfying moment of shooting a particularly annoying rat in the sleeping quarters was not so relished by others, however. By one account, 'The Fascists thought this is the attack, you see. Shells came over, bombing planes came at us . . . It was a very costly shot at a rat, that was.'[50] But when his group was called into action, those who fought with Orwell were impressed by his bravery. He was always modest about the skirmishes, but he famously described one incident when he saved one of the short supply of bullets by deciding not to shoot a Fascist soldier. This particular man was holding up his trousers as he ran away, and as Orwell recalled later, 'I had come here to shoot at "Fascists"; but a man who is holding up his trousers isn't a "Fascist", he is visibly a fellow creature.'[51]

Finally, near the end of April, Orwell arrived in Barcelona on his first leave, after 115 days at the front, his only other break being the ten days he spent in the horrendous nearby hospital with a hand infection. He was exhausted, but what he needed most was a very hot bath, since, as he later wrote, 'The lice were multiplying in my trousers faster than I could massacre them.' Eileen told her brother that Orwell 'arrived completely ragged, almost barefoot, a little lousy, dark brown, & looking really very well. For the previous 12 hours he had been in trains consuming anis, muscatel out of anis bottles, sardines & chocolate . . . Now after two days in bed he is really cured.'[52] But Orwell noticed right away that the joyous atmosphere in Barcelona that had first delighted him had changed.

John Dos Passos, a left-wing American author, and a man Orwell was anxious to meet, was also in Barcelona at the end of April. Eileen was working with Charles Orr to schedule some interviews and prepare an itinerary for him, and Orwell got her to ask Orr if he could 'find some excuse or some way' for him to get together with Dos Passos. In Orr's words, 'Though married for less than a year, [Eileen] had already become [Orwell's] spokesman.'[53] Orr set up a meeting in the lobby of the Hotel Continental, and as Dos Passos remembered that day, Orwell rushed over from the wicker chair he'd been patiently waiting in and said, 'Things I've heard lead me to believe that you are one of the few who understand what's going on.' Dos Passos liked Orwell right away, and he was able to overlook his tattered uniform and ragged cap to appreciate that he 'had a bloody-but-unbowed air that was almost a swagger'. Dos Passos realised, after weeks of talking to people he thought were lying to him, that '[H]e was talking to an honest man.' The two men settled in armchairs for a long exchange about their disappointment at how things were going in the revolution they had supported. Agreeing with Dos Passos, Orwell said they were witnessing 'a Fascist victory. And it won't be the last.'[54] Afterwards, instead of thanking Orr personally for arranging the meeting, Orwell sent Eileen with the message: 'Eric wants me to thank you from the bottom of his heart. He asked me to thank you for him, because he knows he can't talk.'[55] And this was before Orwell got shot in the neck, when he actually did lose his voice for a while.

Orwell's dreams of resting and going fishing during his leave were quickly dashed. He had expected two weeks of good food, soft sheets, and wifely pleasures and instead was soon immersed in confusing skirmishes on the streets near their hotel. At one point, with gunfire erupting along the main Barcelona avenues, Orwell found himself camped on the roof of a cinema with a rifle for three days and nights, not quite sure whom he was protecting. He believed those attacking were Spanish policemen, and he later explained, 'When I see an actual flesh-and-blood worker in conflict with his natural enemy, the policeman, I do not have to ask myself which side I am on.'[56]

At this very inopportune time, Aunt Nellie suddenly decided that she could no longer manage the many demands of keeping the cottage going. During her months in Barcelona, Eileen had scarcely given a thought to the Wallington cottage, but suddenly she had to send a flurry of letters to sort out the problem. Again and again, both Eileen and Orwell expected their families to come through for them when difficulties arose, either with money or with solutions that would consume their personal time and energy. Orwell's mother was the one who had informed them of Aunt Nellie's wish to bail out of caring for the cottage. So Eileen quickly involved her brother, writing, 'The aunt is not only tiring but tired & I have written to her suggesting evacuation.' Eileen went on to outline all the complicated arrangements she now expected her brother, a busy physician, to handle for her, although perhaps she felt she deserved a few return favours from him. Of course the shop would have to be closed, leaving many perishables that apparently Aunt Nellie couldn't deal with. So Eileen suggested that Eric give the aunt money for these and later 'dump doubtful stuff in the car & dispose of it anyhow you like'. Then Eileen's mother was expected to 'perhaps go over after the aunt is out & see that there is nothing to attract <u>mice</u>'.[57] However, we never hear any complaints from the families. Eileen and Orwell were obviously both well loved and well coddled.

Meanwhile, rumours were flying that Russia had decided to eliminate the very group Orwell was fighting with, calling the POUM members Trotskyist while at the same time accusing them of supporting Franco and the Fascists. Some of the street battles were between factions of the left who were technically all there to keep Franco from taking over the country. Orwell had considered resigning from the POUM and joining the communist International Brigade in Madrid, where the main fighting against Franco was taking place, but, bitterly disappointed by the behaviour of some of the communist supporters he witnessed on his leave, he decided instead to stay with his old anarchist militia. So on 10 May he set off back into the hills, carrying his newly cobbled boots (his large size not being available in

Barcelona shops), and still believing all the volunteers were on the same honourable side. As he later wrote, 'My attitude always was, "Why can't we drop all this political nonsense and get on with the war?"'

But he wasn't at the front for long. Ten days later, on 20 May, at 5 a.m. – while, according to one contested version, he was entertaining the others with tales of his experiences in Paris brothels – a Fascist bullet got him clear through his neck. His head was visible above the parapet as he talked, but he mocked his companions' fears that he was tempting fate. It's interesting to speculate about that shooter, presented with a fairly easy target that early morning, probably proud of his good aim, but with absolutely no knowledge of the man he came so close to destroying.

Orwell crashed hard to the ground, not in much pain yet, but pretty sure he was a goner. 'My first thought, conventionally enough,' he later said, 'was for my wife.'[58] Before assuming he was fatally wounded, he had mused, 'This ought to please my wife, I thought; she had always wanted me to be wounded, which would save me from being killed.'[59] One American, at his side at the moment he was hit, remembered Orwell whispering, 'I've had it. I'm done for. Please tell Eileen I love her.'[60] But then he quickly felt 'a violent resentment at having to leave this world which, when all is said and done, suits me so well.'[61] Somehow the other fighters, with extraordinary strength and strong hope, lugged him, first on a stretcher and later draped over a donkey's back,[62] some miles to the closest field hospital. Still conscious and not bleeding much but unable to use his vocal cords above a whisper, and hurting more in his right arm and left side than in his neck, Orwell was given some preliminary treatment before being taken by stages to a larger hospital in Lerida for more tests.

When Eileen heard that Orwell had been injured, she rushed to the hospital, with Kopp's help, getting there fifty hours after he had been wounded. She hadn't taken the war seriously enough until that moment, once joking that she hoped he would be injured soon, and thus avoid being killed. But, after finding Orwell with such a severe injury, her whole attitude changed. She stayed constantly by his side as she arranged to have him moved closer to Barcelona, where more expert doctors could attend him. As Kopp explained in a letter to Eileen's brother, 'Eileen was with her husband all the time and states his comportment was absolutely peace-timely,'[63] his enigmatic translation from his native language. With all the jostling Orwell had gone through in the last hours, just seeing Eileen at that dangerous point must have buoyed his spirits and he began to improve much more quickly than expected.

Eileen knew she had to inform his family immediately. Her telegram to Orwell's parents, probably partly following his request to downplay the seriousness of his injury, but mostly due to her own wish to keep them calm, read: 'ERIC SLIGHTLY WOUNDED   PROGRESS EXCELLENT   SENDS LOVE   NO NEED FOR ANXIETY   EILEEN.'[64] Meanwhile, Kopp wrote to Eileen's brother asking for treatment advice, enclosing a detailed description of Orwell's injuries and a drawing of the bullet entry and exit wounds, revealing a medical knowledge that surprised the others. Kopp's long letter included an odd side comment, 'Sense of humour untouched.'[65]

Towards the end of May, Eileen had Orwell transferred to the Sanatorium Maurin, once an elegant estate, on the outskirts of Barcelona. The goal now became to get him back to England as quickly as possible for more professional treatment, but first he had to improve to a state where travelling would be possible. About ten days after he had been shot, he felt so much better that he decided to go into Barcelona on his own. As Kopp described Orwell's surprise morning arrival: 'Eric travelled by tram and tube, on his own initiative . . . He explained his escapade by the want of cocktails and decent lunch, which were duly produced by Eileen's tender care (with help of a barman and several waiters).'[66] Again we see Kopp graciously helping Orwell as a friend even though he was in love with Orwell's wife. And Eileen was appreciative of this, as she told Norah, even while feeling guilty because Orwell was as yet oblivious to Kopp's feelings about her, as well as to Eileen's somewhat reciprocal behaviour.

Miraculously, the bullet, which had passed through Orwell's throat, had just barely missed his carotid artery,[67] and his voice slowly improved beyond the initial whisper. But he continued to complain about an aching left side and 'nervous pains in the right arm',[68] and the Spanish doctors prescribed bi-weekly electrotherapy shocks. Eileen could easily visit him at the sanatorium, and on 9 June they celebrated their first wedding anniversary in a location they could hardly have guessed at a year earlier, happy to be together and safe. Soon, they supposed, they would be on their way back to England.

On 10 June, Eileen wrote to her brother about their plans: 'Eric is I think much better though he cannot be brought to admit any improvement . . . He is <u>violently</u> depressed, which I think encouraging. I have now agreed to spend two or three days on the Mediterranean (in France) on the way home . . . go on to Paris & spend there two nights & the day between, & then get the morning train to England.' She had tried to dissuade Orwell, preferring to return directly to London, but finally gave in, explaining to her brother, 'I do not altogether like this protracted travel, but . . . he has an overwhelming desire to follow this programme – anyway it has overwhelmed me.'[69]

When the hospital released Orwell a few days later with the notation 'declared useless', he decided that it was important to first obtain an honourable discharge before heading back to England. His timing could not have been worse. He spent five crucial days, from 15 to 20 June, on trucks and trains, going in frustration from one dysfunctional front-line outpost to another as he gathered all the properly signed releases. It doesn't seem from her letters that Eileen had been following the politics all that closely, but in those five days she got a frightening lesson, as everything in Barcelona began to collapse.

On 16 June, the POUM party that Orwell had been fighting with was declared illegal by the communists. Although this was not unexpected, the way it was enforced shocked everyone. While Orwell was off in the hills, Eileen had one last peaceful dinner with Kopp and the Orrs. Lois remembered 'a marvelously and exquisitely prepared meal', but she complained that 'Kopp, being a gourmet, talked about food the whole meal. Eileen too.' She added, 'Funny people, don't want to talk politics in the middle of the world's most exciting and interesting situation.'[70] But perhaps they were purposely avoiding reflecting on what they knew was about to happen.

In fact, Georges Kopp and the Orrs, along with many others associated with the POUM, were thrown into jail the next day. A report to 'The Tribunal for Espionage and High Treason', which was discovered in Madrid's archives fifty years later, listed Orwell and Eileen as 'rabid Trotskyists', and contained more than enough information to justify their arrest. Although she couldn't know those details, Eileen saw clearly what was happening around her and, although terrified, she continued bravely to stay in her room at the Hotel Continental, believing she was being left alone as a decoy for the police searching for Orwell. She hoped she would be able to warn him in time when he returned.

During these last days in Barcelona, Richard Rees arrived to volunteer as an ambulance driver, completely unaware of the deteriorating situation, since the British left-wing papers were distorting the facts and favouring the Stalinist viewpoint. When Rees ran into Eileen he was shocked at her fearful behaviour, describing her as 'absent-minded, preoccupied, and dazed', and at first he had no idea how to interpret this. She refused an offer of lunch, but, when he insisted, she finally explained that she was worried 'about the risk, for [him], of being seen in the street with her'.[71] Rees wrote later that 'in Eileen Blair I had seen for the first time the symptoms of a human being living under a political Terror.' He was shocked to find that the couple 'that one associated . . . with their cosy little village shop at Wallington . . . had suddenly transplanted themselves to the front line of . . . resistance against fascism, thereby also exposing themselves to a Communist reign of terror.'[72] At that time, the *New York Times* was repeating the lies being spread by the Stalinists, with an article headlined: 'Fascist Spy Ring Uncovered in Barcelona,' referring to the arrest of the POUM members.

Adding to Eileen's agitation was the harrowing late-night visit by six plain-clothes policemen who had burst into her hotel room while she was asleep. She stayed lying in bed, courageously feigning unconcern as the police barked questions and ransacked the room, grabbing every book and loose piece of paper they could find. They took 'my diaries, all our books, all the press-cuttings . . . all my war souvenirs, and all our letters,'[73] as Orwell remembered. They left behind only the passports and cheque book, because Eileen had cleverly put them underneath her in the bed for safekeeping. Of course they would have been confiscated if she had got up, so she had to continue pretending to be calm even as she must surely have been lying there in a state of panic. As she later explained to Lydia back in England, she knew the police were Spanish, and although they were very officious and had been well trained in procedure by the Russians, she trusted they would not be so impolite as to order a lady in her nightclothes to get out of bed.[74]

It is suspected, though yet to be proved, that some of Orwell's papers and notes confiscated that night are still being held in Moscow files. Other of Eileen's transcriptions had been stored in the POUM office and were thankfully saved by McNair. When Orr was released from jail with the help of the American consul, he met Eileen and Tioli in the streets of Barcelona, and they told him a strange story: 'Eileen had permitted [Tioli] to store a roll of supposedly incriminating maps on her balcony. When he noticed that the police were searching Eileen's room, he reached across from his balcony and took the maps . . . Were these maps intended to incriminate Eileen and the POUM? Did George, then, try to protect Eileen?' Orr wondered. 'Or was this just another ploy – an episode contrived to cover George's role as an inter-party spy?'[75]

When Orwell finally arrived back with his discharge papers on

20 June, he had no inkling of the last five days' atrocities. Fortunately, Eileen was sitting in the hotel lobby when he came in, giving her the opportunity to protect him from arrest. 'She got up and came towards me in what struck me as a very unconcerned manner; then she put an arm round my neck and, with a sweet smile for the benefit of the other people in the lounge, hissed in my ear: "*Get out!*"' he wrote later. Orwell immediately sensed Eileen's fear and listened intently to her description of what dangers had developed while he was gone, including Kopp's arrest and her frightening night visit by the police. 'I was badly in need of a proper night's sleep. I wanted to risk it and go back to the hotel,' Orwell remembered, but 'patiently she explained the state of affairs . . . The fact that I had served in the POUM militia was quite enough to get me into prison.' Among other things, 'My wife made me tear up my militiaman's card,' since it showed he had fought with POUM.[76] She also worked with Lois Orr, after her release from jail, to make lists of all those who had been arrested.

In the daytime they were able to mingle with the tourists in the cafés and shops, tourists who were somehow still visiting Barcelona, apparently oblivious to all the ongoing horror of arrests and imprisonments and torture. Eileen immediately started the process of getting travel papers prepared at the British Consulate, a task that consumed three difficult days. At night it seemed wise for her to continue staying alone at the hotel, to give the impression that Orwell had not yet arrived back. He, on the other hand, spent the nights sleeping 'in ruined churches' and in a cemetery. When he ran into another volunteer arriving in town on leave, Orwell warned him, 'They're after me. I've left my hotel.' As they waited for their travel papers to be prepared, Orwell and Eileen made the courageous decision to visit Kopp a few times in jail, risking great danger to themselves as they made attempts, unfortunately in vain, to get him released. Orwell was still unaware of the romance between the two, but Eileen assumed that he was fond enough of Kopp to want to help him no matter the personal situation.

It wasn't until Eileen's letters to Norah were discovered in 2005 that we could be fairly certain that she and Kopp had an affair. She seemed to imply this in a very long letter, written about six months after she had returned to England, as she recalled the tragic events that had disrupted the blissful Barcelona life. She began by mentioning, 'I found a bit of a letter to you, a very odd hysterical little letter' about her experiences in Spain and, being reminded of those months, she wrote, 'Georges Kopp is still in jail but has somehow managed to get several letters out to me, one of which George opened and read because I was away.'[77] In an attempt to keep his letters to Eileen from Orwell's view, Kopp was sending them care of her brother, explaining to him that 'I agreed with your sister to communicate to her through you. Tell her I am intensely thinking of her and give her my love.' Then he thought to add, 'Shake hands to Eric.'[78] But somehow one letter had got through to the cottage, and Eileen and Orwell always opened each other's mail when convenient. After reading the letter from Kopp, Orwell mentioned it to Eileen, no doubt prompting some intense discussion. In her letter to Norah, Eileen tried to explain just how complicated her relationship with the Georges had become.

'[George] is very fond of Georges . . . and he is extraordinarily magnanimous about the whole business – just as Georges was extraordinarily magnanimous,' she explained. 'Indeed they went about saving each other's lives or trying to in a way that was almost horrible to me, though George had not then noticed that Georges was more than "a bit gone on" me. I sometimes think no one ever had such a sense of guilt before.' She tried to clarify the situation, continuing, 'It was always understood that I wasn't what they call in love with Georges . . . but the last time I saw him he was in jail waiting, as we were both confident, to be shot, and I simply couldn't explain to him again as a kind of farewell that he could never be a rival to George.' She concluded, 'So he has rotted in a filthy prison for more than six months with nothing to do but remember me in my most pliant moments. If he never gets out, which is indeed most probable, it's good that he has managed to have some thoughts in a way pleasant, but if he does get out I don't know how one reminds a man immediately he is a free man again that one has only once missed the cue for saying that nothing on earth would induce one to marry him.'[79]

This is an amazing confession, filled with obvious guilt and contradictions. And her use of the word 'pliant' seems to suggest a sexual relationship. Eileen had already told Kopp many times, when he was still a free man in Barcelona, that she was not going to leave Orwell for him, but she wasn't willing to repeat this on her last visit to his jail cell, when she believed he was about to be shot. So, in her short time alone with him while Orwell was off trying to secure his release from jail, she for the first time allowed him to believe he had some hope of winning her away from Orwell when he was released. And in the meantime, she agreed to let him write secret letters to her at her brother's address.

Finally, on the third evening, everything was set for their escape. Orwell, McNair, and Stafford Cottman, an eighteen-year-old who had served in the hills with Orwell, each went separately to the station to avoid suspicion, with Eileen planning to join them at the last minute on the night train to France. But they were in for a very unwelcome surprise – the train, subverting Spanish tradition, had left ahead of schedule! Thus they were forced to suffer through another uncomfortable night in hiding before safely boarding the next morning's train, on 23 June. However, they couldn't relax yet. Spanish police were randomly, and with evident inefficiency, searching the train's compartments for suspicious passengers. Eileen and the others sat in one corner of the dining car, where they posed as caricatures of British tourists, Orwell holding a collection of Wordsworth's poems, and slouching to conceal his unusual height, while Cottman was convinced to feign reading the poetry of John Masefield, which they propped in his hands. Having a British woman with them on the train added to their chances of avoiding suspicion. As they escaped safely from Catalonia that day, there is no doubt that Eileen was responsible for saving all of their lives.

They were relieved that their ruse had fooled the police, but at the same time they well knew that their friends, whom they'd been forced to abandon in jail, had not been so lucky. As they later learned, some of them were subjected to torture and even death. One friend who had tea with the couple at the border said, 'Orwell was absolutely shocked by the Stalinist actions . . . It was about the only time I saw him really angry.'[80] Orwell and Eileen vowed to spread the truth about Spain when they were safely back in England. They'd escaped into France just in the nick of time. The first newspaper they saw there had a report claiming that McNair – who was reading the article with them – had been arrested the day before for espionage. As Orwell joked, 'Fortunately, "Trotskyism" is not extraditable.'[81] One of Eileen's friends later concluded, 'It was lucky that [Eileen] got there as . . . George could not speak intelligibly for two months, and she was able to bring him home.'[82]

Though they no longer had a great desire for it, Eileen and Orwell spent a couple of days in a French coastal town, as they had long ago planned to do when the timing of leaving Spain had been in their control. Orwell still wanted to relax on 25 June, his thirty-fourth birthday, and do some fishing after all those desperate and disillusioning days and nights on the front lines. But the hoped-for holiday was a dud. The town was now pro-Franco, and as Orwell remembered, the place was 'a bore and a disappointment. It was chilly weather, a persistent wind blew off the sea, the water was dull and choppy, [and] round the harbour's edge a scum of ashes, corks, and fish-guts bobbed against the stones.'[83] Eileen and Orwell both realised that what they now longed for most was the tranquillity of their country cottage.

9

From Overwork to Near Tragedy

The bleeding seems prepared to go on for ever.
Eileen on the phone to Jack Common

When Eileen and Orwell arrived back in England at the end of June 1937, after six months in Spain, they both knew they badly needed a rest. On the train from the coast to London they noticed that the countryside was strangely calm and quietly beautiful, 'the railway-cuttings smothered in wildflowers . . . the green bosoms of the elms, the larkspurs in the cottage gardens . . . all sleeping the deep, deep sleep of England,'[1] as Orwell put it, all symbols of the country they loved. But at the same time, they worried that there was no foreboding about what they feared was the coming nightmare: war with Germany.

They had barely managed to escape arrest in Spain and marvelled at their good luck, but there was no way they could forget what they'd left behind in Barcelona. They were anxious to share everything that had infuriated them during their last weeks there. Orwell told a friend, 'I happened to know . . . that innocent men were being falsely accused,' and to his publisher he wrote, 'I hope I shall get a chance to write the truth about what I've seen. The stuff appearing in the English press is largely the most appalling lies.'[2] Therefore, mental anguish accompanied the more obvious physical effects of those months in Spain. Orwell's neck wound was mostly healed, but he was weak from all the freezing months on the front, his voice was reduced to a near whisper, and lingering blood poisoning in his right hand kept his arm in a sling for weeks to come. Eileen also vividly remembered those anxious last days in Barcelona, with Orwell in hiding while she had to pretend that life in the hotel was mundane so that no one would suspect that he had returned to town. 'I hope your wife is well after her very trying time in Barcelona,'[3] a prominent English socialist ended his letter to Orwell.

Before facing the mess they knew awaited them at the cottage, the couple stopped at Eileen's brother's home, in Greenwich, for some days in comfort. They were happy to indulge in clean sheets and regular meals for a few days, and hoped a local specialist might have a better remedy for Orwell's hand than they'd found in Spain. When they did finally reach Wallington, early in July, the house and the garden were in worse shape than they'd even imagined. Eileen's mother had not been able to stop the mouse invasion after Aunt Nellie had abandoned the cottage months earlier, most of the farm animals had been dispersed, and the vegetables had all gone to seed in the garden. They realised reluctantly that the recuperation they needed was going to prove impossible.

Writing a book that would reveal the truth about Spain was a top priority, but work on that had to be shared with so many other responsibilities: getting their smallholding functioning again, finding a way to support themselves in the next months, and writing letters and articles to expose the lies being printed by the British pro-communist press about the horrors they'd experienced in Spain. As soon as they safely crossed into France, Orwell had sent an idea for an article to the *New Statesman*, a paper he believed would be sympathetic. But when that article idea was rejected on the grounds that it would 'cause trouble'[4] – presumably from the British communists who supported what Russia was doing in Spain – and a later book review was rejected on the grounds that it 'too far controverts the political policy of the paper',[5] Orwell's head began to boil. So instead of resting, Orwell and Eileen began a hectic and exhausting eight months.

An easy early decision was not to reopen the shop in the large front room that they'd once had such hopes for. Its tiny income versus the multiple hours required to keep it supplied and functioning were, the two optimists now conceded, a poor deal. Their licence as a 'Patent Medicine Vendor' – signed just after their marriage a year before, and of doubtful necessity even then in such a tiny village – was not renewed. Deciding to close the shop meant that they could transform that room into a much more comfortable living room. According to one guest during this time, 'All meals . . . were [now] taken at the large round oak table in the living room before the fireplace',[6] a great improvement on the earlier necessity of squeezing guests into the smaller middle room.

The garden and animals required intense energy just to restore the everyday order they once enjoyed, and, having very little money, Eileen and Orwell were again counting on providing their own milk, eggs, and vegetables to partially sustain themselves. They both enjoyed digging their fingers into the soil across the road in the 'common land' they'd claimed for a garden, but it was hard and time-consuming work. As Orwell told a friend after being back over a month, 'We are very busy trying to do something about the garden, which was in a ghastly mess when we got back and is now empty of everything.' At the same time, he mentioned, 'We are going to get some more hens. We have some young ducks but they didn't do well, owing I think to improper feeding in their first week, and we lost several.'[7] And by the end of the year Eileen told a friend, 'We have nineteen hens now – eighteen deliberately and the other by accident because we bought some ducklings and a hen escorted them.' The extra hen was considered unnecessary, so Eileen added, 'We thought we ought to boil her this autumn so we took it in turns to watch the nesting boxes to see whether she laid an egg to justify a longer life, and she did. And she is a good mother, so she is to have children in the spring.'[8] As always, Eileen managed to make a strenuous, dirty chore seem almost fun. These hens laid around fifty eggs a week, in part due to the addition of the rooster 'Henry Ford', a name most likely chosen by Eileen, 'because he had such a brisk businesslike way of going about his job, in fact he trod his first hen literally within 5 seconds of being put into the run,'[9] Orwell explained to a friend.

Although Eileen had professed to hate boiled eggs early on in the marriage, she seemed to come round to them, perhaps by necessity. Norah had given her a gift of two eggcups, and in the process of thanking her, Eileen wrote, 'Since we got back . . . we have eaten boiled eggs almost all the time. Before we had only one eggcup from Woolworths . . . and one that I gave George with an easter egg in it before we were married (that cost threepence with egg). So,' she concluded, 'it was a Happy Thought, dear, and [the eggcups] are such a nice shape and match your mother's butter dish and breadboard, giving tone to the table.'[10] Perhaps we have to accept her use of the word 'tone' as a straightforward appreciation of the gift from her friend, but it's hard not to read it as tongue-in-cheek, since 'tone' might be the last attribute their ancient, barely functioning home would possess. And, of course, Norah had never been there.

Muriel, their favourite goat, had somehow survived and was soon befriended by a second goat, named Kate after Aunt Nellie's middle name[11] – a second supply of the milk that Orwell claimed he preferred and that Eileen claimed she hated. And every evening the couple once again could be seen strolling through the Wallington lanes at twilight, giving these goats their evening exercise, a fond memory passed down by residents of the time to their children and grandchildren. On these walks they would pass by the gates to the huge, productive Manor Farm, after which they styled the eponymous farmstead years later in *Animal Farm*, located in the not-so-fictional town of Willingdon.

To round out their farm family, they of course needed a dog. Their wedding-gift dog, Hector, was never mentioned again. The one they chose now had been promoted as a prized miniature poodle, but Eileen cleared up that misconception in her clever riff to Norah: 'The dog is a French poodle, supposed to be miniature and of prize-winning stock, with silver hair. So far he has black and white hair, greying at the temples, and at four and a half months is rather larger than [his] mother. We think however he may take a prize as the largest miniature.'[12] They named the dog Marx, and as Orwell told a comrade from Spain, 'You could tell something about the visitors who came because when they learned the name of the dog they would perhaps ask was he called Marx because of some association with Marks and Spencer, or with Karl Marx, or with Groucho Marx!'[13] A photograph of this dog reveals a very large, joyous animal with lots of wild multicoloured hair and an almost gleeful grin on his intelligent face, a comical combination of the two Marx men. The playful names they chose for the animals are often attributed to Eileen, and she had a different version for this choice of name. 'We called him Marx to remind us that we had never read Marx and now we have read a little and taken so strong a personal dislike to the man that we can't look the dog in the face when we speak to him,'[14] she said. She was joking for sure, since Orwell had impressed people at a meeting about the Spanish Civil War the year before with his insightful remarks about Marxism. Lydia said Marx's 'movements were as precise and delicate as a cat's when he picked his way through the bric-a-brac on the cottage window sill, where he liked to sit and watch the rare village traffic.'[15] Eileen was very fond of the dog, describing to Norah in more detail what life with him was like: '[Marx] is very appealing and has a remarkable digestion. I am proud of this. He has never been sick, although almost daily he finds in the garden bones that no eye can have seen these twenty years and has eaten several rugs and a number of chairs and stools.' She continued with more exaggerated fantasy, 'We weren't going to clip him, but he has a lot of hairs which are literally dripping mud on the dryest day – he rolls on every cushion in turn and then drips right through my lap – so we thought we would clip him a little,' with unintended results. As she concluded, 'Now we shall never get him symmetrical till we shave him.'[16]

A nother immediate problem was to find a publisher for the book on the Spanish Civil War that Orwell was planning, the book that would become *Homage to Catalonia*. Victor Gollancz, the publisher of all of Orwell's previous books, had rejected this one, 'though not a word of it was written yet'[17] – a fact Orwell repeated bitterly over and over in letters to friends. Gollancz's explanation for his decision – 'I ought never to publish anything which could harm the fight against fascism'[18] – was far from satisfactory to Orwell. He refused to accept the prevalent belief of most people on the left that it was not the right time to criticise the communist strategy – that '[I]f you tell the truth about Spain it will be used as Fascist propaganda.' Orwell saw Gollancz's refusal to publish the book as 'cowardice'.[19]

Happily, an alternative though less prosperous publisher, Secker and Warburg, was quickly found, and Orwell seemed unfazed by promising to complete the book by December, probably trying to fulfil his self-imposed quota of one book a year. But at this exhausted point, with his health still not back to normal and his arm still in a sling, he had foolishly given himself only six months to write a large and complicated book. And this particular project was especially daunting since most of his notes had been confiscated by the Spanish police. Orwell was well aware, however, that he had a prize asset close by: Eileen was so expert that she could type a five-page letter with very few mistakes in utter darkness. And since she had been in Spain practically the whole time he had, and had typed all those now missing notes from the front lines, she was able to recall some precious details needed to present the facts they wished to tell the world.

Eileen even typed some personal letters for Orwell when they first got back from Spain, since his hand was still partially disabled. As he explained to a friend at the end of July, 'I've started my book but of course my fingers are all thumbs at present.'[20] Eileen told Norah some months later that, as she was typing drafts of *Homage to Catalonia*, she was also adding suggestions for revisions: 'I give him typescripts the reverse sides of which are covered with manuscript emendations that he can't read, and he is always having to speak about it,'[21] she joked. Orwell was certainly a man of many drafts, telling his agent, 'I always alter [my books] a good deal in rewriting.'[22] He told Cyril Connolly, 'I suppose it's true what you say about people not revising their stuff nowadays, though it's incomprehensible to me.'[23]

So, Eileen was typing the drafts as he had rewritten them, then 'covering' the backs of the typewritten pages with her handwritten suggestions. And Orwell was reading her 'emendations', and taking them seriously, sometimes having to ask for further interpretation of her thoughts. That he would respect her suggestions should not surprise us since he had trusted her to make any needed changes in *The Road to Wigan Pier* after he had left for Spain, and, of course, he had once told another friend, 'Eileen herself could have been a writer.'[24] Lydia Jackson and some of Eileen's other friends despaired that she wasn't interested in doing her own creative writing during this period. But Eileen was entirely satisfied to be helping Orwell improve this challenging book, which would indeed become a unique and highly respected portrayal of what truly happened in one part of Spain in those early months of 1937, a book still widely read by scholars of the Spanish Civil War.

Unfortunately, they could devote only part of their time to working on this important book. After six months in Spain with no real income opportunity, the couple now couldn't exist on minor royalties from *The Road to Wigan Pier* and what they could scrounge from their large egg crop. As a result, Orwell had to constantly pump out book reviews, managing to read and critique at least twenty-four books between July and the following February. In those eight months, he also composed four long essays related to the war in Spain as well as copious letters to friends and publications. Even though Orwell disagreed with some magazine editors about what was happening in Spain, they respected him enough to keep him extra busy with reviews, and he chose to concentrate mostly on the vast outpouring of books on the Spanish

Civil War. As he told Common, 'It seems only yesterday that nobody would print anything that I wrote . . . and except for the [book] I actually have on hand [*Homage to Catalonia*] I am as empty as a jug.'[25] Tosco Fyvel remarked that around this time Orwell 'had turned himself into an efficient and indeed prolific journalist', but he would not have been able to produce such an output if he hadn't had Eileen's extensive help. This made for two exhausted people pushing themselves way beyond their physical capacities.

The mental anguish they'd brought back from Spain continued to torment them. As Orwell explained to a friend, in anger and exasperation, 'To think we started off as heroic defenders of democracy and only six months later were Trotsky-Fascists sneaking over the border with the police on our heels.'[26] They'd had to abandon Georges Kopp in jail, along with hundreds of others whom Orwell had fought alongside. And it couldn't have escaped their realisation that, if Orwell hadn't been shot when he was, he would still have been in the hills with the other POUM fighters when the orders came down from the communist leaders that they and other assorted left-wing groups had suddenly become enemies in the fight against Franco. Orwell might then have been rounded up and thrown into jail with the others, since Eileen would likely have been unable to warn him. Just before they left Barcelona, Orwell had considered writing to the troops in the hills about what was happening, 'but I dared not, because I thought any such letter would simply draw undesirable attention to the man it was addressed to.'

They could only justify their good fortune by working tirelessly to make sure their version of the war was told at home and help was provided to those left behind. Thus, Orwell was compelled to spend hours and hours of many days broadcasting his anger and disappointment, exposing 'the lies and suppressions in the English press', and even resorting to a threat of libel action if certain extreme falsifications about his own beliefs – some in the often negative reviews of *The Road to Wigan Pier* as well as allegations that he had been 'a coward, a shirker' in the hills of Spain – continued to be published. As he told friends over and over again, 'What I saw in Spain has upset me so badly that I talk and write about it to everybody.'[27] At one point he sent an uncharacteristically rude letter to a society woman who had an idea for a book showing all sides of the war. He demanded of her, 'Will you please stop sending me this bloody rubbish . . . I am not one of your fashionable pansies like Auden and Spender . . . If I did compress what I know and think about the Spanish war into 6 lines you wouldn't print it. You wouldn't have the guts.'[28]

An early visitor to the cottage on their return was the local vicar, who caught Eileen and Orwell by surprise and didn't 'at all approve of our having been on the government side [in Spain]. Of course we had to own up that it was true about the burning of the churches,' Orwell wrote to a friend. But he finished the thought with what sounds like an Eileen flourish: 'But [the vicar] cheered up a lot on hearing they were only Roman Catholic churches.'[29] Eileen later told friends that the vicar's wife had told her that she and her ladies' prayer circle prayed weekly for Orwell.

Late in July Orwell was still putting forth the story that, in Spain, 'Eileen was wonderful, in fact actually seemed to enjoy it.'[30] But by October she had corrected this contention, and Orwell had come to understand that '[M]y wife really had the worst time, being in the middle of that awful nightmare of political intrigue in Barcelona.'[31] In fact, Eileen grew to so detest war that she told a friend she had 'returned to complete pacifism and joined the Peace Pledge Union partly because of [working on the book with Orwell].' She went on to elaborate in her fanciful way, 'War is fun so far as the shooting goes and much less alarming than an aeroplane in a shop window, but it does appalling things to people normally quite sane and intelligent . . . Hardly anyone can stay reasonable, let alone honest.'[32] This Pledge card has survived, with the signature 'E. Blair', a fact that confused Orwell scholars who didn't think he would ever sign such a pledge. An examination of the signature makes it clear that Eileen was the E. Blair who signed it, and not Eric.

In early August, Orwell managed to find the time to attend the Independent Labour Party summer school nearby, where he was reunited with members of his militia unit. And Eileen accompanied him to a November ILP meeting when an organiser suggested that he 'bring Eileen to have a meal with John [McNair, her old ILP boss in Barcelona] here before we go to the meeting'.[33] And with the help of Eileen's brother and his car, again most likely accompanied by Eileen, Orwell also found time to visit Bristol to take part in a rally to help defend Stafford Cottman, the young fighter he and Eileen had escaped with from Spain, who was now being hounded at home by members of the Young Communist League 'as an enemy of the working class'.[34] As Eileen told a friend, 'The difficulty about the Spanish war is that it still dominates our lives in a most unreasonable manner,'[35] implying that she was just as caught up in correcting the distortions as Orwell was.

And then there was Georges Kopp to consider. On 8 July he'd sent a letter to Eileen from prison in their secret way, through her brother, but she didn't receive it until the end of the month. She copied parts of this letter – the only parts that have survived – and sent them to John McNair, while keeping to herself most of Kopp's personal thoughts. In his letter to Eileen, and in another one to the Barcelona chief of police, a copy of which he sent to Eileen, Kopp threatened a hunger strike if his situation wasn't immediately relieved. He needed Eileen to publicise his threat, since without publicity in England his act would be useless. Eileen felt that John McNair would 'be best able to decide the manner of this publicity', although she understood how difficult it would be to find anyone willing to reprint these letters. As she told McNair, 'Judging from Eric's [Orwell's] experiences in attempting to publish the most conservative truth, we shall not find the English press at least enthusiastic.'[36] McNair 'arranged to see the Spanish ambassador and tell him that if something is not done . . . he will spill the beans in

Parliament,' and subsequently two articles were published in the *New Leader* concerning Kopp's plight. But he was not immediately released. Strangely, although he had been in prison a few weeks, he seemed unaware of what was happening to the POUM troops throughout the country, complaining in his letter that he was 'an officer of the Spanish Army . . . mixed up with pickpockets, tramps, thieves, fascists and homosexuals,' and ending with the plea, 'I am needed at the front.' Without knowing whether Kopp was alive or not, Eileen and Orwell were still thinking of him when they visited her brother in Greenwich some months later. In January they sent a package to Kopp in prison, and the Customs Declaration stated the contents as: 'two four-ounce slabs of chocolate, three ounces of tobacco, and a cake of soap.'[37]

It's hard enough to imagine how Eileen and Orwell were able to fit in all these activities while *Homage to Catalonia* was being typed and retyped. But somehow, during these hectic eight months, they also continued to host countless visitors. Almost every letter Orwell sent to a friend during this time ended with an invitation to use their often cold spare bedroom with the early-morning birds chattering under the corrugated-iron roof. Their first guest that July was Jock Branthwaite, a comrade from Spain, who remembered staying at the cottage for a month. 'It was the same old Eric, no different. The same drip off his nose, and I remember him on the lawn in the front of the house, milking the goat. I hadn't seen him since we both escaped from hiding in the cemetery in Barcelona.'[38] Although Branthwaite doesn't mention it, there's no doubt he noticed the tinder lighter that Orwell, the annoyingly heavy smoker, had brought back with him as a souvenir from Spain, and, according to his family, kept with him the rest of his life. Branthwaite found it hard to believe, but 'we always had to dress for dinner at Wallington, always white shirt, black tie, the whole works, *yes sir!*'[39] He was shocked, considering that Orwell appeared to be utterly careless about how he looked, but in fact, as we have seen, his choice of clothes was very important. Certainly, the casual look –

baggy trousers, working man's dark shirt, crumpled handkerchief in jacket pocket – was a carefully planned uniform.

Eileen's mother came to stay for a week or so in the middle of August, presumably after Branthwaite had left. This was a dutiful visit perhaps, as she was never enthusiastic about the cottage. The only hint of her being there, in fact, is an offhand remark in an Orwell letter to a friend: 'During the next week or so . . . my wife's mother will be in our midst.'[40] Humphrey Dakin, Orwell's brother-in-law, referred to the cottage after his visit as 'that comic place where the post office was and what [Orwell] called his farm, with a few moth-eaten hens wandering about on it'.[41] Douglas Moyle, another Orwell comrade from Spain, also stayed in their spare room, and he remembered long walks in the neighbouring countryside as well as Eileen cooking 'a lovely late dinner, with all the trimmings'.[42] On 10 October, Eileen and Orwell set off for Southwold, where they spent two weeks in comfort with his parents, but not before inviting Connolly to make use of their spare room sometime after their return. It appears that room was seldom empty.

During what was indeed a far too busy eight months, Eileen did manage to get breaks away from the cottage occasionally, while Orwell stayed home to care for the crops and creatures. In a letter to Norah, she mentioned a visit to Mary Lovett, another of their Oxford classmates, in Surrey, where she stayed a few days. She had a cheerful memory of that visit, where she also saw the St Hugh's librarian, Winifred Mammatt. At one party that Eileen attended, 'the MAMMETT CAME TO TEA,' she wrote with glee. 'She might just as well have been in Girl Guide uniform but now she organises play-readings, when all the old St Hugh's girls go to her house and read *Julius Caesar*. Mary went once but she thought they would be given something to eat and they weren't, not even a bun or a cup of tea, so she is embittered and not being a good old girl any more.'[43] Eileen sometimes went too far with her teasing.

Eileen also visited Phyllis Guimaraens, another fellow student from

Oxford, whom she hadn't seen for about ten years. She told Norah that Phyllis 'was just the same as she used to be in her most charming moments . . . It seems to me superlatively clever for anyone to keep herself on the Stock Exchange, as she says she does. I wonder about it all the time I'm with her.'44 Although this is an example of Eileen's irony, it has a mean quality. At any rate, she really enjoyed the parties, telling Norah hopefully, 'I think perhaps we might have a proper reunion some day. Couldn't you come and stay with [Mary] and while she is at the office eat potato crisps at the Criterion?'45 – another happy memory from their Oxford days.

Orwell also got breaks from Wallington, while Eileen managed everything alone. He visited his agent and his publisher in London from time to time, and early in December, as he was putting the finishing touches to *Homage to Catalonia*, he felt enough confidence in his health to promise his next book by October 1938, revising his quota to more than one book a year. He stayed with Richard Rees, editor of the literary journal *The Adelphi* and one of Orwell's early admirers and closest friends. While there he was introduced to Stephen Spender, the person whom he admitted he had 'said rude things about' some months earlier, but the two men soon became good friends. Rayner Heppenstall – one of Orwell's roommates before his marriage – and his wife vividly remembered an overnight stay when Orwell shared their one-room flat in London. 'After supper, he and I went out drinking and . . . returned between one and two o'clock in the morning [to go to bed],' he wrote. 'An hour or so later, Orwell, pyjamaless, had to get up for the usual reason. My wife remembers waking to see, in the dim light from a street lamp . . . the tall bony figure of our guest padding, naked but for his little moustache, out of the room and presently back again.'46

The moustache is an interesting subject. It's hard to imagine he could have kept one so trim while suffering months in the hills of Spain. But now, back at the cottage again, he was finding time to fashion what he must have still considered an appealing attribute, all the while telling friends how ugly he thought he was. The fact that women found him attractive had always baffled some of his friends, who saw Orwell variously as having a 'lengthy, hollow-cheeked face', a 'rusty laugh and woebegone expression', and 'a lined face suggest[ing] the grey asceticism of a medieval saint carved in stone and very weathered'. Connolly left a wonderful description of a gathering Orwell attended during this time. 'I remember him coming to a cocktail party we gave. [Among the guests were] rather nice, jolly girls with lots of money who were unpolitical', he wrote. 'And [Orwell] came along, looking gaunt and shaggy, shabby, aloof, and he had this extraordinary magical effect again on these women. They all wanted to meet him and started talking to him, and their fur coats shook with pleasure.' Connolly went on to muse, 'They were totally unprepared for anyone like that and they responded to something . . . this sort of John the Baptist figure coming in from the wilderness and suddenly the women feel it doesn't matter what his political views are, he's a wonderful man.'[47] Even a sixteen-year-old girl at the ILP camp that summer was remembered by others as becoming completely stuck on Orwell, seeming to want him close to her for comfort through the night, though Orwell apparently resisted, as he felt a true gentleman would.

It's doubtful Orwell had time in those strenuous months for an active affair, although Heppenstall claimed to have rescued him from a 'tart' in London one evening when they drank way too much together. And Lydia wrote years later, 'Soon after he came back from Spain [Orwell] began to behave amorously towards me', telling her, 'You have a lovely face, quite different from the English faces. I would regard it as a privilege to see you naked.'[48] He did carry on a seeming flirtation by mail with a supporter, giving her endless political advice in two very long letters, while adding in a postscript, 'I would much like to meet you some time. You sound the kind of person I like to know.'[49] Orwell admitted to a friend later that he'd assumed she was young and single, and he conveniently had never mentioned to her that he himself was married. Orwell and Eileen seem to have agreed on a somewhat open marriage, and they were aware of some of each other's personal letters.

So when this woman revealed later that she was thirty-three, 'had two children, and had left her husband because he struck her so often,'[50] Eileen got a good chuckle from the aborted affair.

Another extremely important issue preoccupied them throughout all these months: Eileen and Orwell were still anxiously hoping for a child and were constantly being disappointed, each one taking the blame. As Heppenstall recalled at the end of an evening of heavy drinking with Orwell, 'My own clearest memory of that night is of confidences at the bar-counter. Orwell had concluded (whether by any systematic means and with medical confirmation, I do not know) that he was biologically sterile. He badly wanted children and was miserable about it.'[51]

And Eileen spilled out her own disappointment, telling Norah about an evening she had spent with a married friend who had a son, which, as Eileen said, 'makes me slightly jealous because I should like a son and we don't have one'. She went on to elaborate with some dark irony on the contradictory hopes of the two women: 'Mary and I summed up human history in a dreadful way when I was there – I was in the throes of pre-plague pains, which had happened so late that I was wondering whether I could persuade myself that I felt as though I were not going to have them and Mary wasn't having any pre-plague pains at all and was in a fever and going to the chemist to try to buy some ergot or other corrective.'[52] Sadly, Eileen longing to be pregnant, was realising her late period was about to start, while her friend, who desperately did not want another child, was worried she was pregnant again and was wondering whether she could find a 'corrective' to stop the pregnancy.

At this time, Eileen and Orwell decided to make what would turn out to be a critical improvement to their home. Sometime in early December – though still persevering with a privy in the backyard, chamber pots that of course had to be emptied, and no electricity or hot water – they had a telephone installed inside their house, only the third one in the village at that time. Perhaps they had some foreboding of what was to come.

A s *Homage to Catalonia* was reaching its final draft, Eileen and Orwell 'spent an incredibly family Christmas with the Blairs',[53] celebrating the holiday with Orwell's parents and his sister Marjorie, her husband, Humphrey, and their three children. Later Eileen related an elaborate memory of that visit, saying, 'Humphrey wanted to tell me a story that wasn't fit for the children. It was a very long story, lasting through every passage & always converging on the larder which was colder than any place I remember.' Then, in true Eileen style she added, 'I never knew what the story was about, though the children explained several bits to me, but it was a good story.'[54]

Happily back at the cottage on New Year's Day, Eileen started one of her typically long and informative letters to Norah that evening, while Orwell was upstairs writing. She began, 'You see I have no pen, no ink, no glasses and the prospect of no light, because the pens, the inks, the glasses and the candles are all in the room where George is working and if I disturb him again it will be for the fifteenth time tonight. But full of determined ingenuity I found a typewriter, and blind people are said to type in their dark.' She went on to say that she and Orwell had built a new henhouse that afternoon and joked, 'There is probably no question on poultry-keeping that I am not able and very ready to answer. Perhaps you would like to have a battery . . . in the bathroom so that you could benefit from my advice. It would be a touching thing to collect an egg just before brushing one's teeth and eat it just after.'

She ended the long letter on a joyful, somewhat Joycean rant, as Orwell came downstairs from his workroom after hours of writing, playfully jabbing at him by emphasising the fact that he had just been 'Working', with a capital W: 'Eric (I mean George) has just come in to say that the light is out (he had the Aladdin lamp because he was Working) and is there any oil (such a question) and I can't type in this light (which may be true, but I can't read it) and he is hungry and wants some cocoa and some biscuits and it is after midnight and Marx is eating a bone and has left pieces in each chair and which shall he sit on now.'[55] This complete letter is reproduced in the Appendix, on page 413.

She was in high good spirits, a perfect companion at that moment for a somewhat grumpy Orwell who had had to stop writing because the oil for his lamp had run out and who didn't seem capable of or at least willing to solve the problem himself, let alone sympathise with the fact that Eileen had been left in the dark for hours. Apparently he even expected her to make his cocoa and clean off the living-room chairs. She was also gently criticising him for not even noticing that she'd been struggling to write a letter while he had deprived her of all the amenities. It couldn't have been easy to deal constantly with this compulsive, rather self-involved man, but, to her credit, Eileen finished typing that long funny sentence before she stopped to help him. Still, she believed completely in his genius as a writer, and, as her old friend Lydia sized it up, 'One of her tasks was to keep George from doing too much.'[56]

Eileen was feeling rested and cheerful after the Christmas break and was ready for a rough two weeks devoted to finishing the book. But she didn't seem to realise that they were both pushing themselves too hard. Eileen wasn't focusing yet on her own health problems, and they were both busily ignoring Orwell's. As she explained to a friend, 'I don't know whether I can get away even for a day because the book is late and the typescript of the final draft is not begun and Eric is writing a book in collaboration with a number of people including a German and I keep getting his manuscript to revise.'[57] No such collaboration with Orwell has been found by other researchers, and a closer reading would suggest that Eileen was referring here to her brother, Eric, who wrote books in collaboration with a German surgeon named Ferdinand Sauerbruch, books that Eileen did indeed edit and revise. This appears to be one case where the two Erics completely confused biographers. Orwell was apparently also preparing some writing for a filmmaker who asked around that time, 'If you can, let's have something to work on soon.'[58] This project never materialised.

Homage to Catalonia was finally finished in the middle of January, uncharacteristically a couple of weeks late, but so nearly on time because of the frantic energy they had both exerted at the end. When Orwell explained that the title was chosen 'because we couldn't think of a better one',[59] he formally credited Eileen's influence on this book, the first he had written in its entirety since their marriage. Her optimism permeated *Homage to Catalonia*, and when thinking back on it, Orwell said, 'The result is not necessarily disillusionment and cynicism. Curiously enough the whole experience has left me with not less but more belief in the decency of human beings.'

With *Homage to Catalonia* finally in the publisher's hands, and the couple exhausted and once again dreaming of some deserved vacation, Orwell suddenly had to consider seriously an offer to be chief leader writer (responsible for writing editorials) for *The Pioneer*, a weekly journal in Lucknow, India. He made it clear that he'd rather not take this on, telling a friend, 'It is a frightful bore and I seldom wanted to do anything less . . . I wish it didn't come at this moment, because I particularly wanted to vegetate for a few months.' But he was also tempted, as long as it could be on his terms. 'I feel that it is an opportunity to see interesting things, and that I should afterwards curse myself if I didn't go,'[60] he wrote, since he wanted 'to try and get a clearer idea of political and social conditions in India.'[61] Eileen's thoughts are nowhere recorded, but it's almost impossible to think she would have supported this idea, either for herself or for him, who she firmly believed should be concentrating on writing novels from then on. Luckily for them both, Orwell's stubborn refusal to bend his convictions to fit into this job frightened the powers that be, who then warned the editor – who had so admired Orwell as the best person for the job – that they deemed him 'probably temperamental, unbusinesslike'.[62] The offer was withdrawn.

By the end of January Orwell was so physically worn down that he felt unable to prepare the garden for the spring planting. As he explained somewhat apologetically to Common, 'I had to have some help with heavy digging and various other things I couldn't do unaided.'[63] He didn't suggest having Eileen do this work, perhaps aware that she was equally exhausted.

Orwell managed to review five more books in the next few weeks and to make a quick visit to London in the middle of February. And he still wanted to entertain Heppenstall and his wife at the cottage. They finally made the voyage there on 15 February, probably the couple's last visitors for over a year, considering the dramatic event about to happen. Heppenstall was not in the least charmed by the place. 'The Stores was not a pretty cottage, and the village seemed a little desolate. There were two goats in a stinking shed at the back, and the Blairs rented a strip of ground, across the road at the front and above road level, in which they grew vegetables and in which Eric and I dug together.' He did, however, notice the happiness of the couple, writing that Orwell and Eileen 'behaved with conspicuous affection, fondling each other and sitting, if not on each other's knees, at any rate in the same armchair.'[64] At last, it seemed, they were able to relax, have some fun, make plans for the future.

But Orwell was never able to rest completely. After pushing himself so hard in the last months, he was down to eleven and a half stone (73 kilos/159 pounds), way too thin for his tall frame, and more frail than usual. Even so, he made plans to spend a day with Common, who lived quite close by. 'How about meeting in Hitchin on Saturday at 3:30 p.m. which will be in comfortable time for tea which might stretch out till pub-opening time and then I can take the late bus home,'[65] he suggested. No doubt they had a pleasant visit, but it was a visit with a drastic outcome.

Shortly after, Eileen and Orwell's over-extended eight months' work caught up with them. During the winter of 1937–38 there was a severe flu epidemic throughout England, and on 8 March, Orwell took to bed with a heavy cold, a common occurrence for him. But this time he suddenly started haemorrhaging from his mouth, something that had happened to him a couple of times before in his life, but never since he'd married Eileen. When the bleeding finally stopped, Eileen called her brother on the newly installed telephone and he recommended having X-rays taken at the Preston Hall Sanatorium, a hospital he was affiliated with in Kent, to the south of London, many miles away. But after that phone call, they inexplicably waited almost a week, with Orwell in bed the whole time. Perhaps they were trying to figure out the logistics of getting him to the hospital, while at the same time hoping that nothing too drastic had really happened. Orwell downplayed the situation in a letter to Connolly, on 14 March, telling him, 'I've been spitting up blood again, it always turns out to be not serious.' But he admitted that Eileen had been 'alarmed.'[66] At that point, he seemed to be planning an overnight visit to the sanatorium, more or less at his leisure, then visiting his friends in London after the X-rays had been taken.

But in the middle of that night, all alone in their isolated cottage, disaster struck. Orwell started haemorrhaging profusely again, and this time it wouldn't stop. Eileen was hysterical. Rather shockingly, after all those months, she didn't have a single neighbour to rush to. So she grabbed the new phone and frantically begged Common to come and help her. It's not hard to imagine her utter panic, since '[T]he bleeding seems prepared to go on for ever,'[67] she told him, and she had absolutely no idea of how to stop it. Common promised to rush right over, but he was six difficult miles away and only had a bike.

Eileen of course also called her brother, who 'agreed that Eric must be taken somewhere where really active steps could be taken if necessary – artificial pneumothorax to stop the blood or transfusion to replace it,'[68] and her brother knew what ambulance to call and what procedures Eileen should take in the meantime. Then somehow, terrified, but with her brother's instructions, and perhaps helped by Orwell's constant belief that 'I've no doubt they'll find as before that I am OK,'[69] Eileen managed to reach the right people who could help her save his life. But without her being there, and without her brother's connections, it's entirely possible that Orwell would have died that night.

A day later, with Orwell in the sanatorium under professional care and the bleeding stopped, Eileen found time to thank Common and describe to him in relatively calm terms the desperate situation of the night before. She explained that her brother 'got on to a specialist who visits a smallish voluntary hospital near here & who's very good at this kind of thing & he also advised removal, so it happened in an ambulance like a very luxurious bedroom on wheels.' Also prone to understatement, she continued, 'The journey had no ill-effects, they found his blood pressure still more or less normal – & they've stopped the bleeding, without the artificial pneumothorax. So it was worth while.' Then she added, thinking perhaps of her own worries, 'Everyone was nervous of being responsible for the immediate risk of the journey, but we supported each other.'

She also apologised for leaving before Common arrived, saying, 'I only hope you didn't get soaked to the skin in discovering it,' probably referring to the rain he had biked through, but possibly also to the house full of blood he encountered when he got there. And she thanked him 'for being so neighbourly from such a distance, and in such weather.' Her only mention of the terror she herself had gone through was the mild explanation, 'One gets hysterical with no one to speak to except the village who are not what you could call soothing.'[70]

Once again Eileen had been abruptly reminded of how much Orwell relied on her. And once again she was to be left all alone at the cottage, no hoped-for holiday in sight. She also had the sad duty of informing Orwell's family of another near disaster. She ended her note to Common, 'I have fearful letters to write to relations.'[71]

10

Abandoned Again

No wonder that by the end of the summer Eileen looked thinner than ever.

Lydia Jackson

When Orwell was first admitted to the sanatorium and the X-rays were examined, the doctors ruled against tuberculosis. They were hopeful that, with the recent bleeding stopped, they'd be able to control any future haemorrhaging. But two days later they completely reversed course and decided that Orwell did indeed have tuberculosis, or 'phthisis', as they called it, and would have to stay in the sanatorium for an indefinite period, completely bedridden for at least two months. Orwell's case record at the sanatorium showed that, besides suffering from pneumonia four times in the past, he had coughed up blood previously in 1929, 1931, and 1934.[1] Although Eileen had been present for just this latest episode, which had so shocked her, Orwell himself must have been well aware of the gravity of his illness. Nevertheless, he kept insisting to friends that his TB diagnosis was 'evidently from a very old lesion and not serious'.[2] Eileen, however, no longer had any doubts about how dangerous his condition was, and her first job was to write those 'fearful letters'.

Orwell's family and close friends had to be told that he was seriously ill again, that this time he had a disease from which no exact recovery time could be promised. Richard Rees was one of his many friends who got the news about his condition from Eileen.[3]

Another person on her early list was Emma Goldman, since Orwell had agreed to attend an anti-fascist literary evening with her that had been arranged by a group of which he was a sponsor. Goldman responded to Eileen's letter on 21 March, saying, 'I am frightfully sorry to learn that Mr. George Orwell is so ill. I hope sincerely that the rest which the physician has imposed on him will bring back his health. Needless to say, my friends of International Anti-Fascist Solidarity will regret very much indeed that your husband will be unable to participate in the literary evening we have in mind.'[4] Eileen had offered to help the group by typing and distributing their 'announcements', and Goldman promised to get back to her with more details. But Eileen left no information about any future contact with Goldman.

Preston Hall Sanatorium, which mainly took care of ex-servicemen, was housed in a majestic Victorian manor house, surrounded by spacious grounds, in the countryside south of London, 'a terrific place looking rather like St Pancras station',[5] according to a friend. (It has now been converted into luxury apartments.) At first Orwell had his own room, which was unusual for a new patient, and it seemed to others that he was getting 'preferential treatment', especially when a new mattress arrived for him.[6] Since Eileen and Orwell couldn't afford to pay large sums for his stay there, the fact that Eileen's brother was a consultant surgeon apparently helped secure Orwell's special care. Although the doctors demanded complete inactivity for Orwell, they did agree, probably at his insistence, to give him pen and paper so he could write occasional letters. However, he was not allowed to use a typewriter until the middle of July, almost four months after his admission. No one doubted the severity of his illness, considering the harsh necessity of keeping him bedridden for so long. Fortunately, Orwell was certified as non-infectious, making it safe for Eileen and

A letter to Eileen from Emma Goldman, when Orwell was
a patient at the Preston Hall Sanatorium in 1938.

other friends to sit close to his bed when they visited. And when, after
a couple of days, it was time for Eileen to leave him alone there, she
promised to make the tedious, as well as costly, five-hour trip between
cottage and sanatorium every two weeks.

Back at the cottage, Eileen's first job was to clean up the bloody
mess left after their abrupt departure by ambulance. When she sat
down that evening, after the worst part of cleaning was over, Eileen
finally had the time to realise that she was all alone once more. For the
second time in less than two years of marriage, Orwell had left her in
sole charge of the cottage and all its problems. She had already begun
to blame his chronic colds and bouts of 'bronchitis' on the difficult
living conditions at Wallington: the constantly smoking chimney, the

flooding kitchen, the freezing bedroom, the outhouse in the backyard, the poisonous gas lanterns, the outdoor chores of chicken feeding, egg gathering, and goat milking that continued no matter what the weather. And now, after this horrific haemorrhaging, Eileen made up her mind that their cottage life in Wallington should end. During the time that Orwell was recovering, she hoped to find a place somewhere in the south of England for their future home.

Orwell, in perhaps too light a tone, told his friend Geoffrey Gorer in mid-April that 'Eileen is battling with the chickens etc. alone but comes down once a fortnight.'[7] She was collecting the eggs and selling them, planting and managing the garden, and 'feeding etc. about 30 fowls and feeding and milking the goats', as Orwell later explained in his list of cottage necessities. And we can be sure that 'etc.' implied even more hard work. Orwell fully understood the problems he'd left Eileen with, worrying later that 'there won't be many vegetables [this summer], as of course Eileen alone couldn't cope with all of the garden.'[8] She did, however, somehow manage to spend quite a bit of time planting vegetables for the future. Eileen was also taking care of Marx, of course, although she clearly loved the dog and he was no doubt more of a companion for her than a chore.

Every two weeks for around four months, Eileen would spend a stressful day or two of travel in order to visit Orwell, as she had promised. She would leave the cottage early in the morning, starting with a three-mile walk to the Baldock train station, since buses to town ran only twice a week and at odd hours. The train ride to London took over an hour, after which she had to go by Underground to a different train station, then jump on another train and another bus, before she finally got to the sanatorium, a total travel time of more than five hours. And among all the essentials she was lugging with her, Eileen would also bring Orwell some homemade buns and bunches of wild flowers that he particularly liked, according to Lydia.[9] Hopefully Eileen would have been able to leave the animals alone for one night and stay with her brother and mother in Greenwich before setting off back to Wallington the next morning, but Lydia thought she often did the whole trip back and forth in one day.

*H*omage to Catalonia hit the bookshops on 25 April, a little more than a month after Orwell had arrived at the sanatorium. A few review copies had been sent out beforehand, arranged through the publisher by Eileen, and at first they heard back nothing but praise. The art historian and literary critic Herbert Read wrote that the book 'moved me deeply . . . by far the best book that I have seen on this Spanish war'.[10] The *Observer* reviewer said Orwell was 'the giant of . . . any other writers on the Spanish War . . . My admiration for him is unqualified'.[11] And Gorer wrote such a rave review that Orwell was uncharacteristically exuberant on reading a draft of it, telling him, in a fairly long handwritten letter, 'I must write to thank you for your marvellous review. I kept pinching myself to make sure I was awake, but I shall also have to pinch myself if T. & T. print it – I'm afraid they'll think it's too long & laudatory'.[12] Orwell's worries were baseless, and Gorer's review was printed in *Time and Tide* shortly after. Cyril Connolly said the book was 'as good as anything you've done . . . I think the mixture of honesty, imagination, and talent is not usually present in writers on Spain'.[13] Although the couple were both aware of Eileen's crucial input for this book, neither she nor Orwell ever made a point of it. Other friends did notice improvements in his writing, but never thought of crediting Eileen. Although Richard Rees realised 'there was a striking change of mood in 1936' in Orwell's work, he remained stubbornly puzzled as he tried to sort out the reason. About *Homage to Catalonia*, he noted, 'This is the first occasion in any of Orwell's books on which one feels that he really looked at, saw, and paid attention to another human being'.[14] Amazingly, he just couldn't seem to make an obvious connection to Eileen, whom Orwell had married in 1936, just at the point Rees noticed the change in Orwell's writing. A few friends and scholars later took note of and praised Eileen's influence, but in her lifetime, Eileen got no official recognition.

In a letter to Orwell's agent at the end of May, Eileen wrote optimistically, 'On the whole the reviews have really been very good don't you think? It's interesting that the C.P. [Communist Party] have decided not to be rude – and extremely clever of them to be reticent in the definitely Communist press and to say their little piece anonymously in the T.L.S. [*Times Literary Supplement*] and the Listener.'[15] But, unsurprisingly, the later reviews in the communist press were mostly dreadful, condemning Orwell for betraying the Republican cause. Stephen Spender, a communist at the time but an exception to many others, liked Orwell's book and refused to condemn it, as the party wanted him to. He was also admirably able to ignore the fact that Orwell had earlier felt fine lumping him in with the 'fashionable pansies' he was then biased against. The two men had since sorted out their disagreements and Spender made visits to him at the sanatorium.

Orwell began to believe that the publisher Victor Gollancz, who'd rejected the book when it was offered to him, was deliberately sabotaging sales by preventing reviews of it, or encouraging only those that condemned it. As Orwell wrote to Common in July, 'Gollancz is such an octopus you can see his tentacles everywhere.' But Orwell was still optimistic about sales, adding, 'I should doubt whether it will sell less than 3,000, but very likely it won't go to 4,000.'[16] As it turned out, a total of only 1,500 books had been printed, and Orwell was utterly devastated when, after six months, only 683 had sold, a flop by any standards. In fact, *Homage to Catalonia* didn't receive its far-reaching acclaim until well after Orwell's death. And he would be gratified to know that today it is still essential reading for anyone who wants to understand the vast intricacies of the Spanish Civil War.

While Eileen was making her trips back and forth to the sanatorium, a very important exchange was taking place, one not acknowledged before now. Although Orwell wasn't allowed to use a typewriter for four months, no one could stop his mind from composing, and during those months he did manage to publish four formal letters rebutting some points made in negative reviews of *Homage to Catalonia*; a long article titled 'Why I Joined the Independent Labour Party'; and nine book reviews, mostly in the *New English Weekly*, which, as Eileen noted, 'will print anything he writes & never presses him', though unfortunately it didn't pay contributors.[17] This sizeable output could never have happened without Eileen's help, especially her excellent stenographic skills. It seems certain that, during the spring and early summer of 1938, Eileen was picking up handwritten articles as well as making shorthand notes, then returning to Wallington and typing them up in whatever breaks she could manage, ready to bring back to Orwell on her fortnightly visits. If necessary, she would wait while he made corrections for a second or third draft by hand, which she would then take back to Wallington to retype. Some shorter pieces could perhaps have been completed when she stayed overnight in Greenwich. Supportive as always, Eileen told Orwell's agent, 'I think it's quite good for him to write short articles when he feels like it.'[18] Eileen also found the time to work with Orwell on an extensive pacifist pamphlet, 'Socialism and War'. As he wrote to his agent in June, 'I suppose it's just conceivable we might find a publisher for it. When [it is] done & typed my wife will send it along.' Eileen did finish typing it and sent it out for publication, but it was eventually rejected by the Publications Committee of the ILP on the grounds that it was 'too long and absolutist'.[19]

We can assume Orwell allowed Eileen to continue to make 'emendations', most likely even more than usual, in order to cut down on rewrites. Peter Davison, the editor of the vast twenty-volume collection of Orwell's complete works, was aware of Orwell's acceptance of editorial assistance in a different instance, noting, with a touch of regret, that '[Orwell's] willingness to rely upon others to correct his text is of importance to an editor of his work.'[20] Eileen was generous in offering these extra services and Orwell accepted them without much fuss. Hopefully, he was privately making Eileen feel appreciated while his public stance seemed blasé. Perhaps he didn't notice that Eileen's health was beginning to deteriorate.

Eileen did complain about one facet of Orwell's writing: blurbs recommending other people's books. She particularly requested that Fredric Warburg, the publisher, not ask Orwell for this favour any more. As she told Orwell's agent, 'I had to write an almost unintelligible letter to Warburg which did convey I hope the idea that he should stop asking Eric to write blurbs.' As she explained further, Warburg 'persists in doing this & Eric hates getting the books but there is some suggestion (to Eric anyway) that if he doesn't write the blurb he is letting someone down.' So it became her job to be the enforcer, since she felt strongly that 'the compulsion [of writing blurbs] is exhausting.'[21] Earlier, when Orwell was less well known, Eileen had teased him about blurbs, telling him that his reviews would 'never be quoted in a blurb because what [he] said about people's books was always too offensive.' But Orwell as usual enjoyed this teasing, concluding that 'though it wasn't meant as such I took this as a compliment.'[22] Now, in the sanatorium and exhausted, Orwell told Common, 'I don't want to become a sort of fixture on the backs of [Warburg's] dust-covers with "Genius – G.O." kept permanently in type.'[23]

Perhaps to help her with some chores, but most likely just to relieve her loneliness, Eileen invited guests to the cottage, continuing the custom of entertaining at Wallington that she'd practised when Orwell was still there. Karl Schnetzler, her old admirer, may have been an occasional guest, since Eileen surprised Orwell one day by having him accompany her on one of her visits to the sanatorium.[24]

Money was a constant problem for the couple. With Orwell now unable to make as much as usual from reviewing books, and with proceeds from *Homage to Catalonia* disappointing, Eileen was also somehow finding time to make a little extra urgently needed cash by taking in outside typing. As she told Orwell's agent on 7 June, 'I am busy . . . typing a novel about the Afghan frontier, complete with a "man-child" being reared to avenge his dead father by a devoted mother & a half-blind grandmother. The grammar is as original as the plot & the punctuation perhaps unique.' She couldn't help adding, 'Does it not surprise you to see what books are completed?'[25] And, possibly without telling Orwell, she borrowed money from their friend Denys King-Farlow as she was waiting for the advance payment for *Homage to Catalonia*.[26] In fact, Eileen was handling all their business problems now, quietly behind the scenes, asking Orwell's agent about what royalties she thought were due,[27] filling him in on Orwell's plans for the future, and informing him of the necessity of extending the proposed date for completion of Orwell's next book from an impossible October, which had earlier been agreed on, to spring of the following year.

Eileen told friends at the end of May, 'Eric is still being extraordinarily amenable and placid about everything, and everyone is delighted with his general condition.'[28] And Orwell told a friend, 'I am quite happy here,'[29] although he also complained mildly, with variations on, 'Of course it's a bore not being able to work and I spend most of my time doing crossword puzzles.'[30] Eventually, reacting to Orwell's constant resistance to the absolute ban on work on his new book, one doctor, possibly Eileen's brother, felt compelled to write in his case record on 21 June, 'I have . . . warned him duly of the risks of literary research!',[31] playfully adding that exclamation point.

On 1 June, Orwell was finally allowed out of bed, but just for one hour a day, then a week later, on 8 June, for three hours a day. Eileen told his agent on 7 June that 'Eric has been allowed up & is very pleased with himself.'[32] There's no mention by either of them of their second wedding anniversary, on 9 June, the second time they had celebrated that event with Orwell in bed in a hospital with a serious ailment. Eileen kept his friends up to date on his condition, and after King-Farlow visited, Eileen wrote to him on 22 June, 'I'm so glad you went to see Eric & took him out. I think it's really more depressing for him to be in this semi-confinement than to be in bed, & he loved having a party.'[33] So at least his thirty-fifth birthday was celebrated, albeit a little early.

Of course, all this stenography, typing, retyping, letter writing, travelling, and Wallington chores were keeping Eileen way too busy. At the end of June she was in bed with the flu, although she told that news as if it were partly a joke, saying her flu attack happened 'incredulously because the time even of this year seems so odd',[34] as if no one should get the flu in June. It took Lydia to notice that circumstances were clearly eating away at Eileen's own health, and to honestly report, 'No wonder that by the end of the summer Eileen looked thinner than ever.'[35] Just like Orwell, Eileen tended to dismiss as minor any signs of ill health, and also like him, sadly, she ended up waiting too long for treatment.

Throughout his months in the sanatorium, Orwell was always looking forward to when he could start working on his next novel, which would become *Coming Up for Air*. At this point he described it as being 'about a man who is having a holiday and trying to make a temporary escape from his responsibilities, public and private',[36] while Eileen told Lydia it was 'about a man with a couple of children and a nagging wife'[37] – and neither description sounded too exciting to their friends. Although Orwell had finished a sketch of the new novel by the end of June,[38] he felt unable to start writing it while he was still at the sanatorium. As Eileen said, 'The book seethes in his head and he is very anxious to get on with it,' but the conditions at the hospital, with staff rushing in and out of his room, were not at all conducive to an author like Orwell, who needed to write on a 'work timetable'.[39]

During this anxious time, Orwell got an attempt at consolation from Henry Miller, who told him, 'Do nothing! You'll find it's very difficult at first – then it becomes marvellous and you get to really know something about yourself – and thru yourself the world.'[40] But it seems highly unlikely that Orwell, or even Eileen, could appreciate such counsel. In fact, as soon as he could manage, Orwell started going for long, often solitary walks in the vast sanatorium grounds. He also sometimes took a bus to a nearby pond, where he could spend the afternoon fishing.[41] As he told Connolly in July, 'I am much better & most of the day out of doors.'[42]

One of his fellow patients remembered Orwell at the sanatorium.

'He never said a lot, but he acknowledged everybody . . . He always seemed to get *you* round to talking about yourself. And when he looked at you he had *penetrating eyes*. I've never seen such eyes, especially if he was questioning you on things.' Once this man ran into Orwell in a hayfield, 'sitting there cross-legged, laughing to himself'. On approaching closer, he discovered Orwell watching two caterpillars 'doing all sorts of funny things'. This is reminiscent of Rosalind's memory of Orwell studying the movements of a caterpillar on his windowsill back in 1935.[43] This patient also recalled that Orwell had many visitors. He met 'his wife Eileen on quite a few occasions . . . She was a very pleasant lady. Very kind.' He noticed that some of Orwell's many other visitors were 'quite important-looking people' with big cars, while others were 'rough working men, probably men who had fought with him in the Spanish war'.[44] Fortunately the sanatorium was close enough to London to allow easy trips there by Londoners.

One quite significant visitor, as it turned out, was Eileen's good friend, Lydia. In fact, when Eileen asked her if she would have time occasionally to visit Orwell, who she worried was too often alone, Eileen unwittingly helped start what developed into an unfortunate liaison between the two. Lydia dutifully paid a visit one afternoon (at least that's all she acknowledged), also bringing Orwell 'some home-made scones and a bunch of cowslips, of which they both were very fond'. She 'found George fully dressed sitting in a deckchair outside'. But, 'on my arrival, he got up and suggested we should go for a walk in the park'. Then, seemingly out of the blue, 'When we were out of sight of the buildings, we sat on the grass and he put his arms around me,' Lydia continued. This came as a complete surprise to her, or so she said, and she later recorded some of her confused thinking: 'It was an awkward situation. He did not attract me as a man and his ill health even aroused in me a slight feeling of revulsion. At the same time, the fact that he was a sick man, starved of intimacy with his wife, made it difficult for me to repulse him. I did not want to behave like a prude or to treat the incident as a serious matter.' After such contradictory speculation, she concluded, 'Why should I push him away if kissing me gave him a few minutes of pleasure? I was convinced that he was very fond of Eileen and that I was in no sense a rival to her.'[45] Many years later, Lydia left a more detailed memory in her personal diary, writing, '[Orwell's] kissing was good and "clean", his mouth firm, but his hands were coarse and clumsy.'[46]

Lydia's reasoning is somewhat peculiar, especially for a woman with a master's in psychology. She knew Eileen visited every two weeks, so Orwell wasn't exactly 'starved of intimacy with his wife'. She could easily have reminded Orwell that Eileen was her close friend and explained, without insulting him, that she wasn't interested in hurting her. Instead, because she perhaps selfishly decided not to resist him, a complex situation developed between the two of them, a situation that was further exacerbated when Eileen and Orwell returned to England from Morocco the following spring.

One day that summer, feeling adventurous and rebellious, Orwell took a bus to nearby Rochester, though he was theoretically not allowed to stray that far away. It has been assumed the attraction there was the cathedral, but in fact Orwell was starting to extend his interest in Charles Dickens and had just checked out the *Collected Works of Charles Dickens* from the sanatorium library.[47] Rochester is the city that Dickens used as the setting for some of his best-known novels, having spent his last thirteen years there, and Gads Hill Place, his last home, as well as the ornate Swiss chalet in which he wrote his novels, are both preserved in Rochester. Orwell was most likely gathering notes for his future essay 'Charles Dickens', which was published shortly after he and Eileen got back to England from Morocco the following spring. The Rochester visit in the summer of 1938 might well have been the seed that flowered into that well-loved work.

When Orwell was finally allowed to use a typewriter in mid-July,[48] he began typing some of his own letters, so possibly he himself typed the letter printed in the *Manchester Guardian* of 1 August about the upcoming trial in Spain of the POUM prisoners that he and Eileen had left behind over a year earlier. Orwell wanted assurance that the men would 'be tried in open court' in the 'absence of faked evidence or extorted confession',[49] believing that they would then be able to clear themselves of any guilt. Obviously, he and Eileen were still feeling guilty themselves.

During all these exhausting months, Eileen continued to make concrete plans for the winter and the future. As she wrote to Orwell's agent at the end of May, 'After [going abroad for the winter] we hope he will be able to come home, though not to this house. We think of trying to find somewhere to live in Dorset.' Eileen was completely convinced that the cottage in Wallington should be 'handed over either to the landlord or to an unfortunate old uncle of Eric's', and that they should move to an area where the general climate would be warmer.[50]

At first they had thought they might spend the winter in southern France, but Eileen's brother insisted on French Morocco, where Orwell would experience warmth and a dry climate, both deemed necessary for a man in his condition. Eric O'Shaughnessy, who was at the time writing what would become an authoritative textbook on tuberculosis,[51] had initially told the couple that Orwell had tuberculosis 'in both lungs which could have been pretty hopeless',[52] as Eileen later told a friend. But at the end of May she discovered that her brother had been lying to them. 'They'd kept him in Preston Hall on a firm and constantly repeated diagnosis of phthisis[53] for two months after they knew he hadn't got it & I discovered in the end that on the very first X-rays the best opinions were against even a provisional diagnosis of phthisis.' It's not clear why Eric O'Shaughnessy would misrepresent his findings, except perhaps as a way to convince Orwell to take his lung condition more seriously. Orwell might have refused to stay in bed for two months with a simple case of 'bronchiectasis',[54] as his condition was eventually diagnosed.

Eileen was furious. At first she had a hard time accepting her brother's advice that Orwell could not risk spending another winter in England and should instead go to North Africa. But, as she told Norah months later, Orwell 'felt that he was under an obligation though he constantly & justly complains that by a quite deliberate campaign of lying he is in debt for the first time in his life & has wasted practically a year out of the very few in which he can expect to function'.[55] This was an extremely drastic prediction for Eileen to make. She was conflicted, torn between understanding that Orwell did not have much chance of a long and productive life, and being furious that her brother had deceived them by forcing Orwell to rest such a long time precisely in order to extend his life. She summed up this conflict in herself by explaining that 'Brother Eric' 'can't help being a Nature's Fascist', though she lovingly added that he 'is upset by this fact which he realises'.[56]

When Orwell and Eileen reluctantly agreed to take her brother's advice and spend the winter in French Morocco, they had no idea how they would cover the expense, since there would be no possibility of income during those six months. They'd managed to fulfil their dream of sustaining themselves away from the society they'd been raised in, but it had taken a toll. Now they had no choice but to take Orwell's illness seriously. And when a friend who had heard of their predicament offered some money anonymously for the trip, they ended up accepting it, but with the important requirement that it be considered a loan. They were extremely reluctant to borrow money, and they remembered this loan through many years until it was eventually repaid.

Eileen was more than ready to find a more suitable place to live than the cottage when they returned, and she believed 'the position has been made clearer to [Orwell]'; she, and probably her brother also, had been working to convince him that he had to seriously consider his health in any future plans.[57] At some point in June, Denys King-Farlow dropped in at the cottage unannounced, and he found Eileen 'apparently packing up, the geese had been sold and the goats and the chickens gone to somebody else and she was really locking up the whole place'.[58] In early July, Orwell seemed willing to go along with her decision, telling Common, 'The doctors say I must live somewhere further south. That means giving up the cottage', but, he added, the move would take place 'when we come back at latest'.[59] Since there didn't seem to be enough time to settle the cottage affairs conclusively before they left for Morocco, and perhaps with some ulterior thoughts in the back of his mind, Orwell devised the idea of asking Jack Common and his family to stay in Wallington rent-free through the winter in return for looking after the animals. He argued that this would be more practical than storing the furniture and paying someone to care for the animals, and Eileen eventually agreed to this plan.

Being a somewhat compulsive cataloguer of sometimes trivial bits of information, Orwell proceeded to give way too much advice to Common as he was trying to make up his mind whether to take the cottage on or not. In a few back-and-forth letters, Orwell, always the honest man, informed Common that the cottage was 'bloody awful', 'the kitchen tends to flood', 'the living room fire . . . smokes', and there was no hot water. But to compensate, he thought to portray its attributes – lots of potatoes, a quart of goats' milk a day, and more eggs than could possibly be eaten – ending one letter with 'I dare say it would be a quiet place to work in'.[60] Some time later, when Common had somehow been able to disregard all the ominous warnings and agree to stay in the cottage over the winter, Orwell went into far-too-detailed goat-milking 'hints', beginning with 'I did tell you to grease your fingers, didn't I?', then on to such particulars as 'Get her up against the wall (if she gives trouble you can steady her with your shoulder) . . . massage the udder a little & then grip the nearest teat pretty firmly at the root . . . Draw the hand down the teat, being careful not to relax the pressure till you reach the end.' Then, after all this, he tried to assure Common that 'the whole operation should take about 5 minutes', and only had to be done twice a day!'[61] Orwell didn't seem to worry that Common could still change his mind.

As a fascinating aside, Jack Common sold many of his letters from Orwell to a London dealer in 1962, and a few of them ended up in the

Berg Collection of the New York Public Library. The dealer agreed to pay Common £40 for one batch and £85 for another, even though, as he complained, 'Like you, I find Orwell's absorption in the minutiae of chicken-rearing well worth reading about but, in terms of hard cash, it does not mean as much as any comment he makes on how and why he wrote his books.'

Eileen too couldn't help herself from listing the cottage's many failings. As she made the arrangements, she told Common that the cottage 'hasn't got a bathroom or any hot water', 'it's 3½ miles from a shop', 'the sitting room chimney is not manageable by me', and it has 'an ill-designed kitchen'. She then also attempted to convince Common of what she saw as advantages. Besides the potatoes, parsnips, and onions she had planted that would see them through the winter, there was 'a good crop of cooking apples . . . & quite a few plums'. But she warned him to bring a wheelbarrow, since the one Orwell had constructed himself 'is permanently in the field as its wheel developed a split personality & I can't persuade it all to go home together'. Her goat information differed a bit from Orwell's. 'The goat still has her kid because I like goats & don't like goat's milk', she informed him, 'but if you don't like killing kids a man will do it'.[62] That, of course, would mean more goats' milk for Common and his family. Eileen at least thought to add at the end of her letter to Common, 'Heaven knows I don't want to put you off . . . I must say I hope you are strong-minded enough to take on Wallington.'[63] While neither she nor Orwell could allow themselves to lie, she desperately needed Common to take the cottage over.

While Eileen was seriously planning to give up the cottage for good the following spring, she didn't realise that Orwell was not completely onboard with this decision. While they were away that winter, and without her knowledge, Orwell started sharing his secret wishes with Common. 'The official theory is that we are to give up the cottage next spring . . . But . . . I'm not so certain . . . It's a great thing to have a roof over your head even if it's a leaky one', he explained. He went on to romanticise their old times there, telling him how he and Eileen had been forced to rely on a diet of spuds and eggs when they were first married.[64] Going even further with his hoped-for plans of returning to the cottage, Orwell told Common, 'I expect we'll get [Muriel, the goat] mated again when we come back from Africa.'

After all, Orwell loved the cottage. He'd spent probably his happiest six months there with Eileen just after their wedding, when they were so much in love. In fact, in *Nineteen Eighty-Four*, the room that Winston and Julia sneak off to, a small bedroom above a cramped shop full of forgotten relics where they make love, was most likely modelled on his and Eileen's cottage bedroom, on the floor above the muddled shop they had run together.

Before all the details for their departure for Morocco were finalised, Eileen took off all alone to spend two weeks in Windermere, in the Lake District. She stayed at Chapel Ridding, quite a fancy guest house in beautiful grounds, and a stark contrast with her usual Wallington life. An advertisement at the time claimed: 'The House is spacious, with large airy reception rooms, has central heating; electric light and ample bathrooms; good catering and comfortable beds are a special consideration.' A recent visit did indeed reveal a large house, now divided into luxurious apartments, 'in 11 acres of garden facing west, overlooking Lake, with beautiful views of the mountains,' as the advertisement went on to say. It would seem impossible for Eileen to have found anywhere to stay so exactly opposite to the beloved cottage. Orwell casually told people she would be away the last two weeks of July, but neither of them left any reason for the visit. Perhaps it was simply that holiday Eileen had been dreaming about for so long, the one she and Orwell had promised themselves, and she decided to go alone when it was clear he was too ill for such a voyage. She was about to spend the winter helping Orwell recuperate and they both felt she deserved a couple of weeks just pleasing herself. Windermere was near the homes of her beloved Lake Poets and far away from the hot London summer she hated, a place remote enough to ensure no intrusions. But Eileen was very frugal, and she certainly wouldn't have been able to afford to stay there with the minuscule income she was living on. There must have been another reason for her visit.

As it turns out, Ernest de Selincourt, her old Oxford tutor and one of her questioners in the final oral examination, was at that time staying at his home, Ladywood, in Grasmere, a village close to Windermere. Throughout the 1930s, he was in the process of editing many volumes of William and Dorothy Wordsworth's collected letters and journals. 'He believed in women and was a vigorous advocate of their higher education,' and 'for a student who really cared about his subject he could not do enough,' a contemporary woman remembered. 'To many of his pupils he became a lifelong friend.' His conversation was described as 'memorable for its mellow charm and its ironic, slightly impish humour,'[65] a sentence that reverberates with Eileen's personality. It would seem a good possibility that he and Eileen had kept in touch, and perhaps she was there to help him. In one volume of his work, de Selincourt thanked F. P. Wilson, another of Eileen's tutors and examiners, for his assistance, but Eileen's name cannot be found in the credits of the published volumes. Windermere, a much larger town than Grasmere, was the last stop on the train from London, with service only twice a week. There were a few smart hotels in town, and Chapel Ridding would have been an obvious place to stay if she were indeed assisting de Selincourt.

A ceremony was held that month at which de Selincourt made a speech commemorating the acquisition of Wordsworth's birthplace, in Cockermouth, by the National Trust,[66] and Eileen would definitely not have wanted to miss that celebration. As an added attraction, Beatrix Potter, the author of *The Tale of Pigling Bland*, the book that Orwell and his childhood companion Jacintha had so enjoyed when they were young, was then living nearby, at her home, Hill Top. With these enticements in and around Windermere, it seems entirely possible that Eileen and Orwell had been planning a holiday there together when

Homage to Catalonia was finished. And they may have both agreed that Eileen should not be denied these pleasures, even though Orwell was too ill to accompany her.

In her letter to Common, making the final arrangements for him and his wife and son to move into the cottage early in August, Eileen magnified the extreme remoteness of Windermere, saying, 'Posts leave here practically never' and warning him not to try to telephone her because 'we can't [even] hear the local exchange.'[67] Whatever her reason for going there, she was clearly savouring being completely out of touch with her normal, exhausting world.

Common and his family agreed to move into the cottage at the beginning of August, a few days after Eileen got back from Windermere. She had hoped he would make up his mind before she left for Windermere so she could have got the place ready for them earlier. 'The difference between packing it up for store & for lending is considerable – e.g. one fills the drawers to store them & empties them to lend – so I couldn't do anything constructive or much destructive'[68] while waiting for his decision, she explained. On her return, she met Common at the cottage, where she found time to 'demonstrate the creatures'. She claimed, 'Goats are not difficult to manage but there are some growing chickens who need special food for a few more weeks,'[69] so perhaps she had memorised Orwell's goat-milking hints.

Eileen's plan was to spend August at her brother's house while she made the final arrangements for their winter trip, and she left Marx, their dog, at the sanatorium. Orwell seemed pleased with this arrangement, and told his mother – still starting his letter 'Darling Mum,' as he had done when a child – that Marx 'sleeps in a shed with . . . a very large golden retriever puppy . . . and last night they fought fiercely at feeding time, but I think they are settling down a bit.'[70]

Orwell started a Domestic Diary on 9 August 1938, while still unable to begin work on his new novel. In it he kept careful track of some incongruous minor events now that he was well enough to wander around the sanatorium grounds all day. Apparently, besides his constant smoking of heavy black tobacco, he also used snuff, since he complained to his diary on 11 August: 'A curious deposit all over my snuff-box, evidently result of moisture acting on lacquer.' Perhaps a little bored in those last three weeks before leaving for Morocco, he made a point of jotting down odd facts in his diary, highlighting such various revelations as the shape of a zebra's front hooves, the large udder size of Sardinian mouflon sheep, and 'Elderberries now ripe & bird-shit everywhere deep purple.'[71]

He and Eileen intended to make a short visit to his parents' house in Southwold before leaving, since they expected to be away for six months and his father was eighty-one and rather frail. Eileen was trying to schedule this visit early enough in August so that she would have time later in the month to visit Norah, whom she hadn't seen for some time. This seemed entirely feasible since Norah lived in Bristol, the same city where Orwell's sister Marjorie and her family had a home, and they had arranged to leave Marx with Marjorie for the winter. Eileen planned to deliver the dog and then have a nice visit with her friend, a small break she was very much looking forward to. But her brother interfered again. He didn't want Orwell to go to his parents' place at all, since the visit would take up too much of his energy reserves. But if he must go, her brother insisted, it should be close to the end of August, not in the middle of the month.

As Eileen told Norah in a letter from Morocco, 'I'd made all the arrangements to come to Bristol, bringing Marx the poodle (who is wintering with Eric's sister there) but staying with you.' She added, in her playful way, 'Of course you hadn't heard but you know how pleased you would have been.' However, as she explained, 'largely because Eric defied brother Eric to the extent of going to see his father,'[72] her brother had arranged things so that they had to leave for Morocco as soon as they got back from Southwold. Thus the Bristol trip had to be cancelled.

And at the end of the summer, in 1938, Eileen and Orwell set off together to another foreign country on yet another unique adventure.

11

Coming Up for Air
in Morocco

*It's a good climate now and I think we sha'n't die
of it, which until recently seemed probable in my
case and certain in Eric's.*

Eileen, writing from Morocco

On 2 September 1938, Eileen and Orwell reluctantly boarded the SS *Stratheden*, docked on the Thames near London, on their way to Morocco for the winter. Eileen felt that they had been 'hurled out of the country [since] Brother Eric was unable to think of any more lies about the disease'. She was not at all convinced that this trip would be beneficial for Orwell. But, in the end, as she told her friend Norah, 'I found it impossible to refuse.'[1]

They were equipped with Moroccan maps, an Arabic phrase book, proofs to correct of the French translation of *Homage to Catalonia*, one typewriter to share, and £300 to finance their planned six months in a warm climate, an anonymous gift from a friend. They also brought along another important acquisition, a concoction called Vasano, a German invention to prevent seasickness. Orwell had been seriously distressed by that ailment on his long ocean voyages back and forth from Burma, and he was excited to test the new medication's effectiveness. Eileen didn't mention in her letter to Orwell's mother whether she herself had experimented with Vasano, but she delighted in its success for Orwell, writing that '[He] walked round the boat with a seraphic smile watching people being sick & insisted on my going into the "Ladies' Cabin" to report on the disasters there.'[2]

Unfortunately, Eileen, who had been in charge of all their travel plans, did not have a great understanding of the geography of the region, and as they set out, determined to put the best face on the trip, they had no idea what a horrendous voyage was ahead of them. They had expected a comfortable four-day cruise to Casablanca, but instead, the trip ended up stretching into twelve often stressful days. As Eileen admitted later, 'We went to Gib[raltar] by mistake & then got held up at Tangier because the boats to Casablanca were full.'[3] Apparently the 'mistake' she had made was to book a boat to the wrong city. So she was apparently as absent-minded as Orwell on occasion.

With no available boat from Tangier to Casablanca, they were forced to take a tiring trip by train down the Moroccan coast, including an unplanned couple of days in Casablanca, before they finally reached Marrakech, the city where they intended to spend the winter. Eileen explained that, after having 'fled across the station [in Tangier] surrounded by hordes of Arab porters', who she claimed were 'aged 10–70', she and Orwell 'went through endless agonies to satisfy police & customs authorities of all nations before getting into the train at all'. She concluded, 'The French were in custom, absolutely refusing to believe that we were not coming to Morocco to break the law. However', she joked, in the end 'they agreed to let the Morocco police do the arresting.'[4]

Orwell later elaborated on their tortuous journey, complaining to a friend, 'Coming down we lost most of our luggage', since 'at every station there is an enormous horde of Arabs all literally fighting for the job of porter', and 'they grab all luggage they can see, carry it off & store it away in any other trains that happen to be in the station, after which [the train] steams away into various parts of Africa.'[5] As a result of this, they had been forced to waste some precious days in Casablanca waiting to retrieve the missing luggage.

When they finally arrived in Marrakech, they went straight to the recommended Hotel Continental, which had been a first-class hotel earlier in the decade when Marrakech was called 'the red city of spices and souks', a favourite destination for European artists and writers. But, unbeknownst to the travel agents in London that Eileen had consulted – and not even noticed upon arrival by the micro-observant Orwell, who was too busy entering into his new Moroccan Diary the multiple local variations of birds, insects, and fruits – the hotel had recently been drastically downgraded. In a letter the next day, Eileen explained her discomfort to Mrs Blair: 'I haven't much direct knowledge of brothels but as they offer a special service they can probably all afford to be dirty & without any other conveniences.' Also, as she informed her mother-in-law, 'My additional achievement was some kind of fever.' She was so exhausted after the long journey that 'I only wanted to lie down . . . & to get drinks, which were brought me by a limitless variety of street Arabs who looked murderous but were very kind.'[6]

It turned out that Eileen was much sicker than she had divulged to Orwell's mother. When they arrived in Marrakech, she had a high fever, 'going up about one degree an hour', which stayed with her for three days, an ill omen for the rest of her stay. Orwell sent postcards home saying Eileen had been 'upset', but he was obviously understating her situation. Eileen assumed her high fever was a reaction to the vast colonies of mosquitoes that had welcomed them, since 'Eric has eaten the same things [as I have] but hasn't been bitten to any extent whereas I look as though I were made of brioches.' After a night recuperating in the 'brothel', they immediately changed hotels, and when Eileen continued her letter to Mrs Blair a few days later, she added, 'Eric made me go to bed at that point.'[7] Eileen's lively, informative letter is full of the kind of detail one might send a good friend, and it was saved by Orwell's mother, while she apparently threw away most of her son's postcards.

It seemed at first that the planned desert cure would turn out to be a complete disaster. Eileen confessed to Orwell's mother, 'Eric was so depressed that I thought we should have to come home' right away.[8] To begin with, it was way too hot for both of them, with the temperature 'touch[ing] about 90 or 95 [32° or 35° Celsius] in the daytime.'[9] Eileen told a friend, 'I protested a lot about coming here at the beginning of September & I like to be right but I did feel too right [this time]. The weather was practically intolerable.'[10] She told Mrs Blair, 'We could both be said to have been upset [as Orwell had described Eileen's condition to his mother], partly I expect by the climate & partly by the horror we conceived for this country.'[11] They might have enjoyed Marrakech as weekend visitors, but 'We loathed it . . . largely because we were sentenced to live in it for six months.'[12]

Fortunately, Orwell discovered the Villa Simont, an attractive house they could rent about three miles outside of town. His new novel was to be the main Moroccan activity, and within a few days, they had found somewhere conducive to writing it. Orwell was 'now quite excited . . . & I think will be happy there', according to Eileen. As she explained it to a friend, 'We [were] both choosing our shrouds (the Arabs favour bright green & don't have coffins) . . . but we have now chosen instead a villa.'[13] Unfortunately, it wouldn't be available until 15 October, so they had about a month to distract themselves in the middle of a city they both hated.

On the day of their arrival, before they had any chance to explore the city, Orwell had already noted in his diary, 'Mendicancy so bad as to make it intolerable to walk through the streets . . . Children beg for bread and when given it eat it greedily.'[14] And as the days passed they found more and more incidents that upset them. Eileen told Marjorie, Orwell's sister, 'There are beautiful arches with vile smells coming out of them & adorable children covered in ringworm & flies,'[15] while a friend was informed, 'The markets are fascinating if you smoke (preferably a cigar) all the time & never look down.'[16] They were constantly distressed by the severe poverty. 'People sleep in the streets by hundreds and thousands, and beggars, especially children, swarm everywhere,' Orwell recorded in his diary. And Eileen corroborated his view, telling a friend, 'Marrakech crawls with disease of every kind, the ringworm group, the tuberculosis group, the dysentery group.'[17] Describing the Jewish quarter in his essay 'Marrakech', Orwell wrote, 'Many of the streets are a good deal less than six feet wide, the houses are completely windowless, and sore-eyed children cluster everywhere in unbelievable numbers, like clouds of flies.' And, to top it off, 'Down the centre of the street there is generally running a little river of urine.'[18] Orwell summed up their feelings about their adopted city to his old school friend Cyril Connolly, telling him that the people were 'utterly debauched by the tourist racket and their poverty combined, which turn them into a race of beggars and curio-sellers.'[19] According to Eileen, it took some time before they were 'hardened to the general frightfulness of the country.'[20]

During the month of waiting for the villa to be ready, they tried to find activities they could enjoy, but each attempt deteriorated. Eileen explained to Marjorie that she was excited to find 'an open space to watch the sunset from & too late realised that part of the ground to the west of us was a graveyard.' Orwell couldn't resist teasing her about that, and she concluded, 'I really couldn't bear Eric's conversation about the [sunset] view as dominated by invisible worms & we had to go away.'[21]

Another time, they were sitting at a café, trying to enjoy a snack, when a funeral went by, a fairly common occurrence, with the deceased person simply wrapped in a bright shroud. Eileen deplored what happened next, telling Norah, 'If you lunch in a restaurant the flies only show themselves as flies as distinct from black masses when they hurry out for a moment to taste a corpse on its way to the cemetery.'[22] They must have discussed this peculiarity at the time, and Orwell described it himself later in the opening of 'Marrakech': 'As the corpse went past the flies left the restaurant table in a cloud and rushed after it, but they came back a few minutes later.'[23] As one of Orwell's biographers, without knowledge at the time of Eileen's letter to Norah, wrote, 'Some of [Eileen's] descriptions of the place are almost as good as Orwell's.'[24] Other readers may judge that her version of this particular scene was indeed superior.

On yet another day of wandering through the city, Eileen and Orwell discovered the 'Arab drug kiff, said to have some kind of intoxicating effect, smoked in long bamboo pipe with earthenware head about the size of a cigarette holder,' as Orwell recorded in one of his diaries. 'The drug resembles chopped grass. Unpleasant taste & – so far as I am concerned – no effect.'[25] Presumably Eileen also tried this version of marijuana, being a very heavy smoker herself, but she recorded no information one way or the other.

Throughout these months in Morocco, Orwell kept two diaries, though unfortunately neither of them was used for any personal thoughts. His Moroccan Diary, which he started on the ship as they left England, was for his Moroccan discoveries, and his Domestic Diary was mostly for mundane day-to-day facts. He managed to jot down short entries even when he was ill, recording for six consecutive days in mid-November, after they had acquired some chickens, simply 'One egg' or 'Two eggs'.[26] 'I am as usual taking careful notes of everything I see,'[27] he told Jack Common back in Wallington. Orwell kept meticulous track of all his vast variety of interests. Among his copious diary entries were: 'Caught a water-tortoise . . . It smelt abominable';[28] 'Found the decayed head of what . . . I think is a jackal. Have put it up on a stick for the insects to get it clean';[29] and, when examining a grave site, 'Stole one of the charms, a sort of little leather purse. Inside it a bunch of wool and a paper with writing.'[30]

These diaries, with their minute discoveries all precisely recorded in exacting detail, have survived, parts being carefully typed for preservation.

Orwell's diary-writing habit continued through the years back in England, and reflected a side of his personality that Eileen must have appreciated and shared. She didn't keep a diary herself, but fortunately her letters to friends and family were chock-full of the kinds of information another person might have reserved for a diary. Her letters were so revealing and so detailed and often hilarious that many of them were saved and have survived. Her lengthy insights are often necessary for keeping track of just what was happening from day to day in their lives.

Buying furnishings for the villa was a necessary activity that first month, and one that was fun for them both. While Orwell filled six pages of a tiny, separate 'Marrakech Notebook' with lists of comparative prices of local products, from 'camel' to 'common wine' to 'second-hand axe-head' to 'Canadian apples,'[31] Eileen concentrated on 'grass & willow chairs,' 'a bed & several camel-hair couvertures,' and 'essential crockery & some chessmen.'[32] Apparently, on quiet evenings after dinner at the villa, they planned to play chess, though neither of them mentioned their comparative skills. Eileen also shopped for some 'exquisite white clay mugs with a very simple black design inside'[33] and 'some decent rugs as we want them to take home.'[34]

One acquisition they disagreed about was one of the three massive copper trays on Orwell's shopping list. As Eileen complained to Marjorie, Orwell was so excited by their move to the villa that he was 'even buying things for the house, including a copper tray four feet across that will dominate us for the rest of our lives.'[35] There is no mention of whether this tray made it to the villa, let alone back to England. Another somewhat peculiar shopping choice was recorded by Orwell on 25 September: 'Bought two turtle doves this morning.'[36] Eileen approved of this acquisition, telling Norah, with apparent enjoyment, when they were finally settled in the villa, 'We also have two doves. They don't lay eggs but if they think of it will doubtless nest in our pillows as they spend most of the day walking about the house – one behind the other.'[37]

The couple clearly were hoping to recreate their beloved Wallington cottage right there in the desert of Morocco, since, as Orwell explained to Common, 'I simply have to have a bit of garden and a few animals.'[38] Eileen added, 'We shall also have goats who will be physically as well as emotionally important.'[39] And before they even moved into the villa, Eileen joked to their friend Geoffrey Gorer, '[Eric] is also carpentering – there is a box for the goats to eat out of & a hutch for the chickens though we have no goat yet & no chickens.'[40] When they later acquired some animals to make use of the goat box and the chicken hutch, Orwell told his diary lovingly, 'The goats are gentle with each other & do not quarrel over food. Were taken to the house in paniers one on each side of a donkey,'[41] while the dozen chickens were 'crammed together in two small baskets, then sent on donkey back'.[42]

Finally, on 15 October, it was time to move into the villa. Eileen described the house as having 'a large living room, two bedrooms, a bathroom & a kitchen', so it somewhat resembled their cottage back in England, but there was also 'a sort of observatory on its roof which will be good to work in.'[43] And of course that extra bedroom invited the idea of visitors, as was their constant custom back home. Eileen told a friend, while urging him to visit, 'We have a spare bedroom (quite spare I should say, not even furniture in it).'[44] Orwell's sister Avril was their first hoped-for guest. But the villa was even more inconvenient to reach than their out-of-the-way English cottage, and, as it turned out, no one managed to make the trip. In fact, as Eileen told Mrs Blair, 'It's entirely isolated except for a few Arabs who live in the outbuildings to tend the orange grove that surrounds it.'[45] So once again they had chosen a secluded refuge without some of the refined amenities others would have needed.

Looking after the villa was not easy for Eileen, though she did have a Moroccan servant, Mahjroub, who 'arrives here about seven with fresh bread and milk for breakfast', and 'does the shopping & pumps the water & washes the floors'. At first he was hired to stay until after dinner, but 'There is nothing for him to do in the evening except wash up the supper things'. So he would 'sit on the kitchen step' all day until there were some dirty dishes to wash, 'often in tears, getting up every ten minutes or so to tidy the kitchen and put away (generally in the cellar) the things I was just about to use for the cooking,'[46] Eileen told Mary Common. She decided she would rather do some of the villa chores herself without worrying about hurting Mahjroub's feelings, and she arranged for him to go home after lunch, while she cooked all the meals. Eileen also did all their washing because the laundries were very expensive. She assumed this was because 'probably no one uses them except me so they have to engage a staff every time I send anything.'[47]

No matter how hard they tried, they never managed to create a substitute for their beloved home. The hoped-for garden was an almost total failure, and of the twelve chickens they started out with, four died immediately. Orwell was quite disappointed that it took till 26 October, eleven days after moving into the villa,[48] for the first egg to be laid. Even Eileen got caught up in the egg output, telling Mary Common on 5 December that the hens 'have become very productive – they've laid ten eggs in four days'.[49] But this didn't match their Wallington output. As Orwell told Common, 'The hens in this country are miserable little things.'[50]

The goats were also disappointing, and apparently even more difficult to milk than the ones at home. Orwell described in his diary the new milking method he had devised, which was to take 'hold of the whole quarter & squeeze as if squeezing out a sponge.'[51] Eileen had a more comical view, describing the scene 'with Mahjroub holding head and hind leg, Eric milking and me responding to cries of agony while some good cows' milk boiled over' – the milk she much preferred. She concluded her description with the information that 'the total yield of the two [goats] per day was well under half a pint,' joking that 'the two goats are more satisfactory now because they went right out of milk and that saves trouble.'[52]

Now that they were installed at the Villa Simont, Orwell could finally get down to work on the novel, and the typewriter was busy in that room on the roof – at least when he was well enough to write. Judging by their many letters home and Orwell's dutiful diaries, the hope that a winter in Morocco would be the answer to Orwell's lung problems proved drastically wrong. According to a diary entry on 21 October, less than a week after moving into the villa, they both suffered with 'the almost continuous belly ache we have had since coming here', caused, they thought, by the 'almost undrinkable' water at the villa.[53] But this turned out to be a minor setback since, in a letter to Orwell's old book-dealer friend at the end of December, Eileen said, 'Eric hasn't properly recovered from the first six or eight weeks – indeed no one has,'[54] a typically self-effacing remark. And she told Norah, just before Christmas, 'Eric . . . lost 9lbs in the first month & coughed all day & particularly all night so that we didn't get thirty minutes' consecutive rest until November.'[55] By this calculation, Orwell was in poor shape from 14 September, when they arrived in Marrakech, until at least the end of October. That would imply that November had been a healthy month. But Orwell noted in his Domestic Diary, 23 November, 'Have been ill (chest) since 16th,' so that seemingly took a chunk out of November. On 5 December, Eileen corroborated the bad week in November, telling Mary Common, 'Eric was ill and in bed for more than a week and as soon as he was better I had an illness I'd actually started before his but had necessarily postponed,' a rather sad joke. Then she continued, in her customary downplaying of any hardship, 'I enjoyed [my] illness: I had to do all the cooking as usual but I did it in a dressing-gown and firmly carried my tray back to bed.'[56] So, although in the old, unmarried days Orwell enjoyed cooking for his occasional dinner guests, now, with a wife, it seemed natural to him, and also to Eileen, that she should take over that task, even when she was sick in bed the rest of the day.

After almost two weeks of relative good health in early December, Eileen told Norah she had 'suddenly got violent neuralgia and a fever,'[57] her old and continuing affliction from her time at Oxford, forcing her to stay in bed for many days. On 12 December, Orwell noted the beginning of her illness rather casually in his Domestic Diary, writing, 'Eileen has neuralgia, probably owing to going out in the rain yesterday.'[58] Eventually, with no improvement, and too sick to ride her bicycle to town, Eileen took a taxi to Marrakech for an X-ray. By then she and Orwell thought 'it seemed obvious that I had another cyst – indeed I even packed a bag in case I had to go into hospital again.'[59] Her casual mention of 'another cyst' – most likely an ovarian cyst – and the use of 'again', with the implication that she had had at least one cyst removed in the past, is the first indication of such a possibility. But considering her later health problems, it does seem likely that she had been suffering for some time with this problem. Fortunately, in this case, the X-rays were negative, and they ended up just waiting patiently for her fever to recede.

Then, as Orwell informed Common one day after Christmas, 'Eileen was ill on Xmas day and I actually forgot till the evening what day it was.'[60] This was apparently a different occasion from the cyst possibility. Orwell certainly had a casual way of revealing Eileen's problems, perhaps as a way to keep himself from worrying too much. But Eileen wrote to a friend a few days later, 'Unfortunately, [Orwell] is ill . . . It's really my fault because I collected a cold somehow & then of course Eric caught it.' She added, 'Indeed we have been ill in turns for the last month.'[61] So now she was saying that December had also been a difficult time for them.

Eileen summed up the trip so far in her Christmas letter to Norah, telling her, with heavy irony, that Orwell 'doesn't cough much (though still more than in England) so I think he may not be much worse at the end of the winter abroad than he was at the beginning.' Then she added a sombre thought: 'I expect his life has been shortened by another year or two but all the totalitarians [Stalin, Hitler, and Mussolini] make that irrelevant.'[62] She was constantly worrying that Orwell had only a few years left in his life, and always assuming that he would be the first to go. Another friend was told, 'It's a good climate now and I think we sha'n't die of it, which until recently seemed probable in my case and certain in Eric's . . . He has been worse here than I've ever seen him.'[63]

Orwell did not have much good to say about Morocco either, reflecting, in mid-December, 'I have been in this place about three months, as it is supposed to do my lungs good to spend the winter here. I have less than no belief in theories about certain climates being "good for" you, on enquiry they always turn out to be a racket run by tourist agencies and local doctors.'[64]

Neither of them mentioned how they were fitting in the writing and rewriting of *Coming Up for Air*. Yet somehow, perhaps even when they were both ill in bed, besides transcribing into his journal all his copious notes about Morocco, Orwell was also using his 'very retentive memory'[65] to look back to his happy youth in the peaceful English countryside, and writing a disturbing novel about what that gentle world was turning into. It was 'a book that pleases both of us very much,'[66] Eileen told Norah. So, as they talked together about the plot, and as Eileen typed the chapters as they were finished, it is evident that she was involved in the novel's progress, probably writing her 'emendations' on the back of the typed pages, as she had with *Homage to Catalonia*. 'Key ideas in [Orwell's] later work may have emerged from mutual observations and discussion with the poetic Eileen,'[67] one of Orwell's biographers surmised. In this novel, Lydia's summation of Eileen's impact on Orwell's writing began to ring true. 'He was on the defensive against [Eileen's] psychological knowledge, and she was wise enough to keep it in the background,' Lydia believed. 'But as time went on, he allowed some of this knowledge to penetrate his defences, and it is clear from his later writings that he had accepted much of what he at first tended to ignore, or brush aside, in modern psychological theory and practice.'[68] In her view, '[Eileen's] logic, her feeling for accuracy in the use of words influenced him, perhaps without his being aware of it, in improving his style of writing, which in earlier years had a certain crudity and calculated exaggeration, detracting from its power to carry conviction.'[69] Another of Eileen's friends believed, 'There was a noticeable increase of light and colour in his writing,' after meeting Eileen.[70] Richard Rees thought this book was an example of Orwell's 'most light-hearted work',[71] showing a 'hopeful and humorous' approach.[72] He wrote, 'There are indications in *Coming Up for Air* and elsewhere that he was capable of a more contemplative and psychological approach.' However, Rees again failed to recognise Eileen's influence. 'I can't understand it or explain exactly what happened; I just don't know. But I quite agree there was an enormous change.'[73]

During those six months in Morocco, Orwell somehow managed to fit in many letters to friends, including nine very long and intricately detailed ones to Jack Common. Throughout these letters, among such niceties as 'We forgot to warn you not to use thick paper in the WC',[74] Orwell often fixated on the mating of Muriel, their favourite goat. He started worrying at the end of December about how this might be arranged for the coming February, the propitious time. 'Whatever happens don't let her go to that broken-down old wreck of Mr Nicholls's [a Wallington neighbour], who is simply worn out by about twenty years of fucking his own sisters, daughters, grand-daughters and great-grand-daughters,'[75] Orwell warned. This important subject came up again on 12 January, with Orwell suggesting this time that Common contact a woman who 'has a very superior breed of goats . . . Her billy is a beauty', and again on 23 February[76] and 5 March.[77] Finally, still wondering whether Common had made the proper arrangements, Orwell wrote in the middle of March, 'I hope Muriel's mating went through. It is a most unedifying spectacle, by the way, if you happened to watch it.'[78]

Although the mating of Muriel was top of his list of cottage concerns, Orwell was also a bit obsessed with the obscurities of goat feeding. 'If there are any run-to-seed cabbages etc. about,' he wrote, 'I used to hang them on a meat-hook you'll find in the shed . . . They should never have more than a little cabbage as it gives them diarrhea [*sic*].' And then 'Once or twice in very cold weather I've given a hot bran mash, & sometimes in bad weather when a goat is confined all day & bored, a good idea is to bulk out the hard food with chaff.'[79] As he spent his time worrying about the possible boredom of goats, he always included infinitely more minute detail than Common could possibly use. He was a very fast typist and just allowed his letters to run on and on, seemingly typing every idle thought. Curiously, he was never accused of being a non-stop talker. It would seem that, in order for Eileen to be able to endure such fastidiousness, she must have had those tendencies herself. But when it was her turn to count the chickens' eggs, she seemed able to step back from the chore a bit and see the humorous side of the compulsion.

Every diary entry and many of Orwell's detailed letters make it emphatically clear how difficult a man he must have been to live with day to day. But Eileen somehow managed to overlook his sometimes annoying traits, concentrating instead on her belief in his greatness. Her obvious dedication must have been an enormous asset and comfort to Orwell as he worked. His first official biographer described Eileen as 'a cool but loving voice beside him'.[80]

By early November, missing the cottage dreadfully, Orwell was already developing grand plans for the future, telling Common, 'Our idea when we get up to a respectable number of fowl, say 200,' is to invest in more goats. 'When we go in for [goats] properly,' Orwell continued, we will keep 'good ones not scrubs like M[uriel].' It's doubtful Eileen shared this enthusiasm, what he called 'our idea', especially when he continued, 'Then if goats' milk ever gets onto the map, as I hope it may some day, you could start in as a dairy at any given moment.'[81] Not surprisingly, Orwell was way ahead of his time in predicting the popularity of goats' milk and its products, but it's odd to hear him fantasising about such a large business plan instead of just concentrating on his writing, as Eileen wanted.

All of this focused dedication as to how the cottage was faring back home strongly signalled Orwell's desire to settle in Wallington once again on their return to England. At the end of February, contradicting what were clearly his preferred wishes, he dutifully wrote that 'Eileen as soon as possible is going to look for a new house' when they got back, since that was what he had promised her. Then, he continued, 'Either Eileen or I will have to come down to Wallington to superintend moving the stuff. We shall take the hens . . . but shall probably dump the fowl houses and buy new ones, which would not be dearer than transporting and less fag.'[82] He was letting himself be hopeful about the future, writing, 'I wonder if we can possibly get 5 years of respite before the next war.'[83] However, as he assured both Common and himself, if war did indeed break out, 'I don't want to be caught with my pants down and shall keep the cottage.'[84]

After confessing all these hopes to Common, Orwell once again began trying to convince Eileen that it would be a good idea to just stay in Wallington when they got back. And by 5 March, he was able to tell Common, 'After much thought we've decided to go on living in the cottage for the rest of the summer and not move till the autumn.'[85] Eileen left no record of her agreement to this arrangement, but Orwell's careful words, 'after much thought', imply long discussions with her. By agreeing to stay in the cottage only until the autumn, Eileen must have felt she was still being true to her original strong belief that another winter in Wallington would be a threat to Orwell's life. And that September, the outbreak of war upset everything.

Throughout their time in Morocco, the worry that war might suddenly start back home was a constant concern. As Eileen wrote to her sister-in-law Marjorie at the end of September 1938, shortly after they arrived, 'Yesterday we were rather hysterically writing semi-business letters in the hope that they'd be delivered before war broke out.'[86] With newspapers reaching them '4 to 8 days late & those at the moment might as well be years late,' they had a difficult time keeping up with the war news. 'We keep seeing & being exasperated by pictures of London crowds "demonstrating" when we don't know what they're demonstrating for.'[87] Just at that moment, Prime Minister Neville

Chamberlain had famously compromised with Hitler and wishfully proclaimed, 'It is peace for our time', causing both widespread anger and relief.

Eileen at first worried that Orwell would insist on returning to England if war did break out, but 'to my surprise he does intend to stay here whatever happens'. Then, she explained, 'In theory this seems too reasonable & even comfortable to be in character; in practice perhaps it wouldn't be so comfortable.'[88] So, from time to time, Eileen managed to slip in some gentle teasing of her husband. She was glad Orwell wanted to remain in Morocco, because she believed that 'So long as we're allowed to stay here . . . we probably have a better chance than most of keeping alive.' But then she added, in uncharacteristic dejection, 'Though what we should be keeping alive for God knows. It seems very unlikely that Eric will publish another book after the outbreak of war.'[89] For once, Eileen's ability to keep a humorous perspective on serious events had abandoned her. She was now equating her own reason for living entirely with her husband's literary output.

Throughout their ten years together, Orwell was certainly aware of Eileen's sacrifices, even though he was rarely able openly to acknowledge them. His use, throughout his letters and diaries, of the words 'Eileen and I' was a constant recognition of their deep partnership, and he often ended his letters with 'Eileen sends love.' He was capable of appreciating her, as when he noticed in his diary, 'Eileen compares the sound of the starlings' twittering to the rustle of a silk dress.'[90] And later, he recorded with approval her sharp awareness of the misery of Moroccan life: 'Eileen remarks that Arab children have no toys whatever. This seems to be the case', since 'in the Arab quarters no toys of any sort are on sale, no dolls, kites, tops or what-not.'[91]

As he watched events develop at home, Orwell became strongly anti-war, signing, along with 148 others, a manifesto titled 'If War Comes, We Shall Resist' that was published on 30 September 1938.[92] He told a friend at the end of November that he hoped there was still time 'to provoke a real popular anti-war movement in England, in

France and above all in the Fascist countries. [Then] I think Hitler is done for.'[93] He was also encouraging friends back in England to gather together 'some body of people who are both anti-war and anti-fascist.' After that, he believed, 'If we laid in printing presses etc. in some discreet place we could then cautiously go to work.'[94]

Eileen felt Orwell was being naïve. She confided in a letter to Marjorie, 'Eric, who retains an extraordinary political simplicity in spite of everything, wants to hear what he calls the voice of the people. He thinks this might stop a war, but I'm sure that the voice would only say that it didn't want a war but of course would have to fight if the Government declared war.'[95] She clearly was more cynical about human nature. She had a practical viewpoint about what had happened so far, telling a friend, 'I am determined to be pleased with Chamberlain because I want a rest,' by which she no doubt meant a rest from having to listen to Orwell worry about what he should do when war came. She went on, 'Anyway Czecho-Slovakia ought to be pleased with [Chamberlain]; it seems geographically certain that that country would be ravaged at the beginning of any war fought in its defence.' Referring to the criticism of Chamberlain's 'appeasement', she added, 'Of course the English Left is always Spartan; they're fighting Franco to the last Spaniard too.'[96]

When Marjorie wrote in early October that 'I took the children down to get their gas-masks the other day,'[97] as the government required, and 'All the parks and gardens have been dug up into shelters [in Bristol],'[98] she was responding seriously to Eileen's teasing in a previous letter about Orwell's plans to build his own air-raid shelter back home. As Eileen had explained, 'The plans received rather a check after he did construct one in Spain & it fell down on his & his companions' heads two days later, not under any kind of bombardment but just from the force of gravity.' As Eileen made fun of Orwell's construction abilities, she assured Marjorie that the idea of building an air-raid shelter had 'generally been by way of light relief; [Orwell's] specialties are concentration camps & the famine.'[99] And he was indeed obsessed with these possibilities. As early as the end of September he told a friend, 'I personally do see a lot of things that I want to do and to continue doing for another thirty years or so, and the idea that I've got to abandon them and either be bumped off or depart to some filthy concentration camp just infuriates me.' Revealing his strong bond with his wife, he added, 'Eileen and I have decided that if war does come the best thing will be to just stay alive and thus add to the number of sane people.'[100]

Towards the end of November, continuing this compulsion, Orwell wrote, 'The concentration camp looms ahead,'[101] and he told another friend – after being 'bitten with the desire to write a Saga . . . an enormous novel in three parts'[102] – 'I hope war won't break out, because I don't think I could write a Saga in the middle of a war, certainly not in the concentration camp.'[103] By mid-January, adding some morbid humour to this phobia, he declared, 'We may get home just in time to go straight into the concentration camp if we haven't been sunk by a German submarine on the way.' He ended this letter with, 'I trust when we next meet it won't be behind the barbed wire.'[104]

Eileen smiled through Orwell's constant repetitions, but she shared his fears, telling Marjorie, with a wry slant as usual, 'Anyway I am thankful we got here. If we'd been in England I suppose [Orwell] must have been in jail by now & I've had the most solemn warnings against this from all the doctors.' Then, showing her understanding of her inability to control her husband, she added, 'though they don't tell me how I could prevent it'. As for his fears of famine, she joked, 'He buried some potatoes against the famine & they might have been very useful if they hadn't gone mouldy at once.'[105]

A ll of these shared and anxious bouts of illness, along with war worries and personal concerns, had delayed their Christmas shopping, an activity that Eileen genuinely enjoyed every year. But this time the pleasure was badly compromised. After a tiring day in town on 5 December, Eileen complained to Mary Common, 'We just got back from a Christmas shopping. It began by my bicycle having a puncture. The next stage was my arrival in Marrakech, entirely penniless, two minutes after the bank had shut.' She somehow 'succeeded in cashing a cheque and in collecting a retinue of guides, porters etc., all of whom had most charmingly waited for money so long that they might be said to have earned it.' She met Orwell for lunch, and then '[W]e began to shop and we went on for two and a half hours, surrounded by as many as twenty men and boys, all shouting and many of them weeping.' She described her system of sending many gifts to one person, who would then distribute them. 'You are a key recipient,' she told Mary Common, 'and you ought to get a dish for Mrs. Hatchett, a brass tray for Mrs. Anderson [two Wallington neighbours], and a "couverture" for yourself (and Jack).' But, she added, 'You may of course get something quite different, or nothing at all,' because of the way the shopping in Marrakech was haphazardly organised. 'A porter is engaged if he succeeds in laying hands on any piece of property, and as I put each thing on its appropriate pile it was instantly seized by one to four helpers and put somewhere else,'[106] she explained.

When they finally got home from shopping, Eileen tried to make light of the day's problems, saying, 'This evening we are literally swaying on our feet and the menu for supper, which once included things like a mushroom sauce and a souffle, has been revised to read: Boiled eggs, bread, butter, cheese; bread, jam, cream; raw fruit.'[107] While it must have been impossible to make a soufflé on her makeshift stove, she managed to joke about her exhaustion and not expect any sympathy. Nonetheless, for the most part, they were experiencing Marrakech as privileged tourists.

There were other activities at the villa that took time away from the novel. For instance, there were the eight books that Orwell claimed to enjoy reviewing,[108] plus two long articles he managed to fit in, one on his 'reflections' about the coming war[109] and another looking back on Spain.[110] He and Eileen also miraculously found time to read books for pleasure, and on 29 December, she wrote to their book-dealer friend in

London, 'We are desperate for something to read, something long . . . So we wonder whether you would . . . send us *Martin Chuzzlewit* & *Barnaby Rudge*.' They liked to read books together, and they were having trouble agreeing on what to read next. 'If either of us has an inspiration the other has either read the book very recently or doesn't want to read it at all,' she explained. They had read the books they brought with them extremely carefully, perhaps more than once, because, as Eileen informed him, 'We had *Our Mutual Friend* with us but are now competent to pass the most searching examination on it.'[111] The Dickens books were also necessary research for the essay Orwell would write shortly after they got back to England. But they had time for even more reading, with Orwell requesting, on 15 January, 'Thackeray's *Pendennis*, Trollope's *Eustace Diamonds*, H. James' *Turn of the Screw*, and J. S. Mill's *Autobiography*.'[112] What a list! And they planned to leave Morocco two months later.

A round 20 January, with the first draft of the novel somehow finished, Eileen and Orwell took off on a long-planned trip to the nearby Atlas Mountains, which were strikingly visible on the horizon, tempting them ever since they had arrived in Marrakech. Orwell was excited about the week-long break, and he jotted down his usual exhaustingly detailed observations in his diary as the bus wound up the mountain for three hours on a spectacular switchback road.

In Taddert, the town where they stayed for the week, the local Berber villagers caught Orwell's attention immediately. 'The women are exceedingly striking . . . with black hair and remarkable eyes . . . with tattooing on their chins and sometimes down each cheek,'[113] he noted in his diary. In a long, handwritten letter to Gorer on the day of their arrival in Taddert, Orwell added more detail, telling him, 'What fascinates me most of all is that [the women] are so dirty. You will see exquisitely beautiful women walking about with their necks almost invisible under dirt.'[114]

Apparently, their 'remarkable eyes' won out over the dirt because, after a few days there, Orwell begged Eileen to allow him to visit a local prostitute. And, according to the accounts of two friends, she finally acquiesced. One remembered Orwell enthusing that 'He had seldom tasted such bliss as with certain Moroccan girls, whose complete naturalness and grace and candid sexuality he described in language so simple and direct that one could visualise their slender flanks and small pointed breasts and almost sniff the odour of spices that clung to their satiny skins.'[115] Perhaps Orwell was bragging when he used the plural 'girls', because another friend remembered Orwell confiding to his wife that 'he found himself increasingly attracted by the young Arab girls and the moment came when he told Eileen that he had to have one of these girls on just one occasion.' According to this account, 'Eileen agreed and so he had his Arab girl.'[116]

As far as we know, Eileen never mentioned this incident to anyone, but we do know that over and over again she would give in to Orwell, even when she found some of his requests unreasonable or hurtful. In this case, she surely felt personally maligned and frightened as she sat alone in the tawdry Auberge Les Noyers, in a foreign and not particularly friendly town, waiting for Orwell to get back from his bragged-about adventure. There's no evidence that Orwell noticed or even considered how Eileen might feel. Perhaps he believed it was such an incidental request that she would accept it casually, just as he had seemingly made light of her relationship with Kopp. Orwell admitted that he had not always been faithful to Eileen, and probably, considering her own past, she was able to accept his affairs along with his other eccentricities. As another friend summed up their relationship, 'I don't think George was the kind of person who likes being married all the time.'[117] But this time was different since there was no way to keep his wishes secret from Eileen. First he had to confess how obsessed he was with this temptation and get Eileen to go along with it, and then his decision would mean leaving her all alone in a strange town, waiting for his return. However difficult those few hours were for Eileen, she soon rejoined Orwell for their mountain walks and put a brave face on the whole incident.

There are very few other details of their week in the mountains, since no letters from Eileen survived, and Orwell's long diary entry dealt mostly with local vegetation and housing. They did take hikes through the mountain trails, sometimes accompanied, Orwell noted, by local children who 'beg as soon as they can walk and will follow for miles over mountain tracks in hopes of a sou'.[118] A number of times they met 'with a German in the Foreign Legion, who is there on some job I could not understand . . . He cannot go back [to Germany] as he is wanted for desertion'.[119] And, of course, they had lots of spare time to read the many new books they'd ordered.

For whatever reason, however fascinating and sexually arousing this week's holiday had been, Orwell fell sick immediately after returning to the villa on 27 January. His illness was not identified, but he made no new diary entries for three weeks, until 18 February, and wrote no letters that have survived until 23 February, almost a month later. On that day, Orwell told Common that the novel 'has been set back because I have been ill and was in bed a fortnight'.[120]

Just trying to envision what must have been the constant activity in those five months at the villa is exhausting. Two often frail human beings were in continuous motion, writing, typing, reading, cooking, milking goats, gathering eggs, and tending the failing garden, often struggling to keep up this pace from their sickbeds. Since they had only one typewriter to share, things occasionally got complicated. Eileen added near the end of a handwritten letter to Orwell's sister, 'I expect you can't read a word of this. We only have one table & Eric is typing diary notes on it'.[121] Another time, Orwell explained to a friend, 'I am handwriting this as Eileen has the typewriter'.[122] And a note on the handwritten version of his Moroccan Diary for 12–28 March says, 'To be typed into the diary when machine is available'.[123] He neglected to mention that, in both cases when he was without the typewriter, Eileen was using it to type versions of *his* novel and *his* book reviews, since all but one of her extant letters from Morocco are handwritten.

Eileen's Aunt Margaret, Mother Mary John O'Shaughnessy, CCVI, Superioress General (1918–1930), Assistant General Superior (1930–1938), in San Antonio, Texas, 1920s.

3 Park Terrace, South Shields, where Eileen was born.

Eileen (left) at Sunderland Church High School, age fourteen.

Front door of Westgate House, with name in glass window.

Westgate House, 2½ Wellington Terrace, now 35 Beach Road, South Shields, where Eileen grew up.

Mary O'Shaughnessy, Eileen's mother.

Eric O'Shaughnessy, Eileen's brother.

Gwen O'Shaughnessy,
Eric's wife.

24 Crooms Hill, Eileen's brother's home.

Eileen's St Hugh's class photo, with eclectic mixture of the women at Oxford that year. No one is identified in this photo but, by a consensus of identification specialists, Eileen is in the third row, second from left, and Norah is next to her, third from left.

Detail of Eileen's St Hugh's 1927 class photo, with Eileen (centre) in glasses, second row, and Norah on her right (as is clearly identified on back of photo). It is hard to recognise this as Eileen, but perhaps she and Norah had just been to the hairdresser for popular hairdos. This is the only photo of Eileen wearing glasses, although friends said she was near-sighted.

Norah Symes Myles, Eileen's best friend at St Hugh's.

Four masked Oxford students, staff of *The Fritillary*, promoting the magazine. The woman second from left could be Eileen.

Matriculation Day at St Hugh's, Oxford, 1924. The student second from left appears to be Eileen.

Lydia Jackson (Elisaveta Fen), Eileen's friend from her psychology class at University College, London.

The inside staircase to Orwell's top-floor flat at 50 Lawford Road.

50 Lawford Road, where Orwell moved in the summer of 1935, for more privacy with Eileen.

Eileen in 1937.

Orwell in 1937.

The menu inset reads:

M E N U.

LUNCHEON.

Minestrone Soup.

Fried Fillet of Sole.   Tartare Sauce.

Roast Aylesbury Duckling.
Sage & Onion Stuffing. Orange Salad.

New Potatoes.
Garden Peas.

Sherry Cream Trifle.
Fruit Salad & Cream.

Biscuits & Cheese.

Coffee.

9th June, 1936.

The cover of Eileen and Orwell's wedding invitation, with menu inset. The menu has often been reprinted, but the complete invitation, in full colour and tied together with a pink ribbon, has just recently been discovered. The choice of illustration, most likely by Eileen, is curious.

The cottage in Wallington, as it looked when Eileen and Orwell lived there.

Orwell in the Wallington churchyard, dated 1939, but possibly a wedding photo.

The back garden at the cottage, with someone at the window.

The Plough, the pub next door to the Wallington cottage.

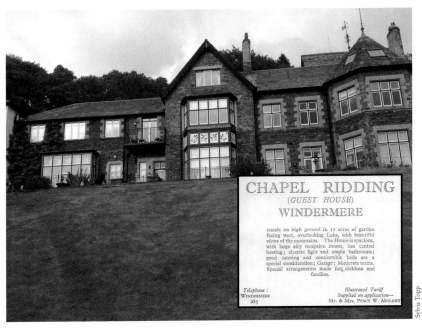

Georges Kopp in Spain, 1937.

Orwell and Eileen at the front in the Spanish Civil War, 1937.

Orwell Archive

Orwell Archive

CHAPEL RIDDING
(GUEST HOUSE)
WINDERMERE

stands on high ground in 11 acres of garden facing west, overlooking Lake, with beautiful views of the mountains. The House is spacious, with large airy reception rooms, has central heating; electric light and ample bathrooms; good catering and comfortable beds are a special consideration; Garage; Moderate terms. Special arrangements made for children and families.

Telephone :
WINDERMERE
285

Illustrated Tariff
Supplied on application—
Mr. & Mrs. Percy W. Molony.

Sylvia Topp

Chapel Ridding, Windermere, today, with an advertisement from the 1930s.

Marx, Eileen and Orwell's dog, with Gwen O'Shaughnessy and her son, Laurence.

Marx, a cross between Karl and Groucho.

Eileen, with nephew Laurence, in spring 1939.

Orwell feeding the goat, Muriel, at the Wallington cottage.

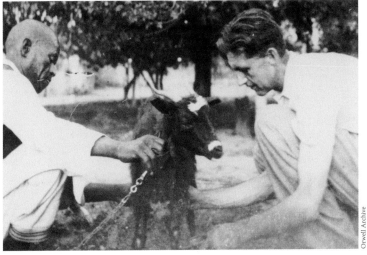

Orwell milking the goat he and Eileen had in Morocco.

Detail; Dorset Chambers, 39 Chagford Street. Eileen and Orwell's first London flat, in 1940, was at the back, on the top floor.

The Senate Building, where the Ministry of Information was located when Eileen worked there from 1939 to 1941.

Eileen in a pub with a wineglass, around 1941, during the terrible year after her brother died.

Langford Court, where Eileen and Orwell moved in 1941. Their flat was the corner one, on the top floor.

LANGFORD COURT	
FLOOR	FLATS
GROUND	1 - 14
FIRST	15 - 30
SECOND	31 - 46
THIRD	47 - 62
FOURTH	63 - 78
FIFTH	79 - 94
SIXTH	95 - 110
SEVEN	111 - 126

The floor list at Langford Court, showing that flat 111 was on the top floor.

Lettice Cooper, Eileen's friend from the Ministry of Food.

6 Mortimer Crescent, right half of building, today. This building is similar to 10 Mortimer Crescent, where Eileen and Orwell moved into the ground and first floors, in 1942. That building was destroyed by a bomb in 1944.

Greystone, 35 miles south of Newcastle, where Eileen was living with baby Richard in 1945, while Orwell was on the continent.

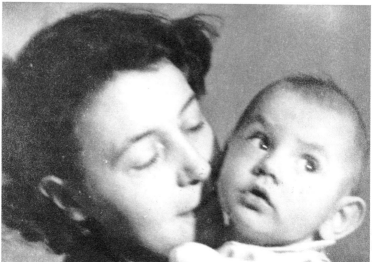

Eileen with baby Richard, 1944.

The doorway, and doorbell (inset), from the back garden to 27B Canonbury Square, where Eileen and Orwell moved in 1944, another top-floor flat. Today a locked gate blocks entry to the back garden.

Orwell with baby Richard, 1946.

Barnhill, Jura, when Orwell was living there, in the late 1940s. His extensive garden is in view, as well as a tent for the overflow of guests. Orwell's room was at the far left on the upper floor, Richard's was the middle room, and Orwell's sister, Avril's, was to the right.

Richard Blair, inside the bathroom at Barnhill recently, for the first time since he was a child.

Fernwood House, a small hospital in Newcastle, where Eileen died during an operation, on 29 March 1945. Her room was on the ground floor, with her windows facing the front garden.

Eileen's gravestone, in 2012. The area in front has since been planted with flowers. Eileen's inscription is straightforward, as Orwell ordered it, while the gravestone to the left shows a more typical inscription for a deceased wife.

Orwell once told Common that it 'generally takes me about two months' to rewrite a novel,[124] but presumably the second draft of this one was somehow completed between 23 February, when Orwell had finally recovered from his almost month-long illness, and mid-March, when they were back in a Marrakech hotel trying to find a ship to take them home. In the midst of the rewrite, Orwell had told Common, 'I think I shall just finish my novel before we board the boat, but it will probably have to be typed on the sea.'[125] But, on 19 March, in yet another letter to Common, Orwell said, 'My novel's finished, which is why I'm writing in pen, as it is being typed.'[126] Despite the passive tense, we know that – as Orwell was worrying in this letter about such luxuries as who would 'look after the creatures [at the cottage] till we arrive' and 'Did my rhubarb come up, I wonder?' – Eileen was close by, typing the final draft. Perhaps she opted for finishing the typing while still on land, so that she could better enjoy the boat trip home.

The new novel's progress was also curtailed by the reappearance of two old friends – the very two who had been involved in their marital transgressions. The first was Georges Kopp. In December they got the good news that Georges had finally been released from a Spanish jail after eighteen months in captivity, during which time he had 'lost seven stone [44 kilos/100 pounds] in weight'[127] and was 'thin, feeble and bent, walking slowly with the aid of a cane'.[128] Eileen spelled out their conflicted reaction to the news, telling Norah that at first, when they got the cable that Kopp was free, Orwell had said, 'George must stay with us.' However, later, when they heard that Kopp was indeed planning to do just that, Orwell revised his position, saying, 'He must *not* stay with us.' The resulting solution, thankfully, was simple: 'George won't find anyone to lend him the necessary money' for the trip, Eileen realised.[129]

Nevertheless, they did feel responsible for Kopp's care, and they managed to convince Eileen's brother and sister-in-law to put him up for a while in their Greenwich home, even though they had never met

Kopp and were the parents of a newborn son. Earlier, Eileen and Orwell had contacted her brother, assuming he would handle all the difficulties that had arisen at the cottage, including disconnecting the telephone,[130] if the Common family decided to abandon the place. Apparently Eileen had by then forgiven her brother for being a 'Nature's Fascist',[131] as she had earlier called him. And now, once again, Eileen and Orwell turned to her family, apparently feeling comfortable asking for somewhat outrageous favours. And, once again, this family yielded to the wayward couple's wishes and took Kopp in. During this visit, Kopp met Gwen's half-sister Doreen, and a romantic relationship began between the two. However, by 5 March, after less than three months, and just as Eileen and Orwell were getting ready to return to England, Kopp's welcome in Greenwich was wearing thin, and Eileen and Orwell decided that it was now Jack Common's turn to take over his care. In all these favours asked, their attitude was some combination of the conviction that their requests were justified, along with the belief that they themselves would have come through if the situation were reversed.

Their new scheme, no doubt masterminded by Eileen, was that Common would find a room in Wallington where Kopp could sleep, which would be paid for by the O'Shaughnessy family, and then Mary Common would prepare his meals in the cottage. As Orwell carefully detailed to Jack the complicated arrangement they were trying to set up, 'Gwen O'Shaughnessy . . . will see about the money for his grub, etc . . . and perhaps it wouldn't be so much trouble for Mary to have one extra person at meals?'[132] They seemed to realise this time that they were asking a big favour, and Eileen added a long handwritten postscript full of intricate plotting that was far from straightforward. As she explained, Gwen herself couldn't 'suggest that George should go somewhere else', so it was important 'that he should be allowed to think that you're inviting him spontaneously'. Then, in an attempt to have the Commons feel lucky to have such a house guest, she added, 'I think you might find George Kopp quite an asset', because 'he is quite handy in the house & <u>adores</u> cooking'. In addition, she assured them, 'He's the sort of man who's happy anywhere if people are pleased to see him & you'd find him interesting to talk to.[133] All these enthusiastic details revealed clearly that Eileen still remembered fondly those exhilarating evenings in long-ago Barcelona.

As it turned out, Common did send the desired invitation, if perhaps reluctantly, but Kopp rejected it.[134] Instead, no doubt being concerned that war preparations were heating up on the Continent, and perhaps because he started to get the picture that his visit in Greenwich had lasted long enough, Kopp decided to join the French anti-fascist forces. He told Common that Eileen had written to him from Morocco saying when she would be back in England. But we have no record of whether they actually met before he headed back to the Continent to fight in the war.

The second friend to reappear was Lydia Jackson. Although she had been careful to downplay the one kiss she admitted sharing with Orwell at the sanatorium, he clearly believed something more serious had happened between them. Once he and Eileen had booked passage home on a ship from Casablanca, and he knew for sure when their boat would arrive back in England, Orwell secretly wrote to Lydia, first giving her the travel information and informing her that 'I don't believe in the alleged marvellous qualities of this climate which I think is neither better nor worse than any other.' Then, after telling her, 'So looking forward to seeing you! So try & keep a date or two open a few days after the 1st of April,' Orwell turned romantic: 'I have thought of you so often – have you thought about me, I wonder?' Then, quickly realising he wouldn't want Eileen to know what he had written, he added, 'I know it's indiscreet to write such things in letters, but you'll be clever & burn this, won't you?'[135] Orwell was so anxious to renew whatever he believed had transpired with Lydia that he sent three more notes to her after he got back to London.

Needless to say, Lydia thought it was more 'clever' to hold on to his letters. In fact she saved twenty-four of Orwell's letters sent to her throughout the next ten years. She was the exact opposite of Eileen and Orwell, who both threw away almost all the letters they received from friends. In her book, Lydia reflected on getting that first letter from Orwell: 'I read that letter with mixed feelings . . . The tone of his letter suggested a renewal of the amorous behaviour I had been too soft-hearted to repel . . . His masculine conceit annoyed me.'[136]

As they waited a couple of days in Casablanca for their ship to arrive, Orwell allowed an unexpectedly peevish tone to intrude in one letter: 'The boat we were to have sailed on on the 23rd has been delayed at sea in some way. Of course if something like that didn't happen on any journey I take this wouldn't be my life.'[137] They quickly ruled out a repeat of the horrendous trip down the coast by train and instead booked passage on a Japanese ship, the SS *Yasukunimaru*, which in a few days would 'stop off at Casablanca to drop a cargo of tea.'[138] Although this boat was capable of accommodating around 500 passengers, on this voyage it was almost empty. It was now the end of March, in 1939, and, as Orwell told his diary, 'English people from the far east will not travel on the Japanese boats.'[139]

This delay meant a week in Casablanca, a city that was already gearing up for war. They 'went to the pictures, & saw films making it virtually certain that the French Gov.t expects war,' as Orwell noted in his diary. Earlier, as he had watched a long line of Senegalese soldiers marching past, he had an epiphany. The typical black soldier, he realised, 'has been taught that the white race are his masters, and he still believes it.' But, he wondered, prophetically, 'How much longer can we go on kidding these people? How long before they turn their guns in the other direction?'[140]

Unsuspected by Eileen and Orwell at the time, the Vichy government would take over French Morocco the following year, and the German officers, so prominent in the magnificent film *Casablanca*, would arrive shortly after that. Perhaps while waiting there for their ship they even visited a 'gin joint' that might later have turned into Rick's Place. When the Allies recaptured French Morocco two years later, Casablanca gained a prominence in the war that they could not have imagined.

Eileen and Orwell finally set sail on 26 March. The trip back to England took a miraculous four days, and Eileen and Orwell arrived in London on 30 March. The novel, all typed by Eileen, was immediately delivered directly to Orwell's agent, with apparently no question that it would be accepted.

Even though Orwell occasionally tried to sound upbeat about the improvement of his health abroad, the Moroccan experiment was probably a failure from the point of view of slowing his future decline. As Lydia wrote, 'It was not too good a choice: the dry, hot climate with much sand dust in the air acted as an irritant on George's lungs. Nor did it suit Eileen . . . Neither of them was stronger or better in health when they returned.'[141]

On the other hand, the time away from England had given Orwell enough mental space and enough physical distance from war fears and war preparation to write, in a remarkably short and complicated few months, what is often considered his best novel: *Coming Up for Air*. Delivering the book to the publisher exactly on time, Eileen and Orwell moved on to a precarious future, starting with only a couple of short months together at the cottage before what they had feared for so long finally happened: war with Germany.

12

War Ends the Wallington Experiment

Eileen would send love if she were here.
Orwell to friends when Eileen was working in London

On 30 March 1939, the day they arrived back from Morocco, Orwell went directly to his agent's office to drop off *Coming Up for Air*, his seventh book in seven years, while Eileen went to Greenwich to spend time with her mother, her brother Eric, and his wife and newborn son. Thus she was not aware of what else Orwell did on that very first day back. It would probably have shocked her, since she believed they had arrived home on particularly good terms with each other. That afternoon, without telling Eileen, Orwell deliberately found time to drop by Lydia's home, assuming she would be happily awaiting him, since he had written secretly, telling her when to expect him. But there was no answer at Lydia's door. He left her a handwritten postcard saying he was 'very disappointed not to find you at home', but 'if clever I <u>may</u> be able to look in for an hour tomorrow morning, so try & stay at home in the morning will you?'[1] As it turned out, he *was* 'clever' enough to get away from Eileen the next morning. But again Lydia was not at home.

At this point, Orwell went to Southwold to visit his parents, and Eileen arranged to join him after picking up Marx in Bristol,[2] not even suspecting until months later that he was secretly making plans for an affair, let alone with her best friend. She had just helped him through many months of illness, interspersed with bouts of feverish work on his latest novel, and she believed he was looking forward to some peaceful weeks at the cottage, as was she. Meanwhile, Orwell was irked that Lydia had not been there to greet him on either of his attempts to see her. 'You were mean not to stay at home this morning like I asked you,' he wrote from Southwold. 'I rang up 3 times. Are you angry with me?'[3] Lydia wrote later in her memoir that she had purposely not been home when Orwell asked her to be. She had mixed feelings about him and his suggestion of renewing something she wasn't willing to admit had happened, and 'I was annoyed by his assuming that I would conceal our meetings from Eileen.' Then she added, rather confusingly, 'I wanted to avoid meeting him when I was in that hostile mood, capable of pushing him away if he tried to embrace me.'[4] Was she implying that she intended to accept his embrace at some later point, but just not immediately on his return?

In his letter from Southwold, Orwell told Lydia that he would call her when he was back alone in London the following week. But then suddenly, forcing a pause in his amorous pursuits, Orwell cancelled all appointments, telling his agent on 6 April, 'I am in bed again.'[5] A few days later he wrote to Jack Common, who was expecting Eileen and Orwell to reclaim the cottage, that he had 'spent a week in bed', though 'it's nothing serious, mainly due to the change of temperature no doubt.'[6]

Back from Bristol with Marx, Eileen heard that Orwell's parents were both ill, so she hurried to Southwold to help care for them. She told a friend, 'I came down all in a rush as they say to do a bit of filial-by-law nursing,' knowing that 'E's father is permanently & very ill [and] his mother got ill with phlebitis.' She was quite surprised to be 'met on the doorstep by Eric with a temperature of about 102'. She had always doubted the efficacy of the winter in Morocco that her brother had insisted on, and now she felt she was at last proved right. She added, in her charming and self-deprecating way, 'Since then all have been in bed & I have spent the whole day creating confusion in one sickroom after another.'[7] She didn't tell her friend that she herself had what Orwell told someone was 'a cold,'[8] although his description of any severity of illness can't be trusted, and it could very well have been more serious.

Although Orwell was too sick to get back to London for another attempt at a secret visit with Lydia, he did find time for a third letter to her, explaining, 'I started being ill almost immediately after I got [to Southwold] & have spent most of this week in bed.'[9] He assured her, though, that he would be back in London soon and they would get together then. One hopes he felt at least a little guilty that Eileen – with absolutely no suspicion that her husband and her best friend were involved in what he at least believed was an amorous affair – was overextending herself looking after him as well as his parents, even as she herself was suffering with a 'cold'. But Orwell's ability to obsessively concentrate on minutiae didn't always translate to being aware of the feelings of other human beings. As one friend summed it up, 'I don't think George ever knew what makes other people tick, because what made him tick was very different from what made most other people tick.'[10]

Eileen and Orwell had planned to get back to the cottage by 5 April and were obviously going to be delayed for many days. Thus Mary and Jack Common were expected 'to look after the beasts,'[11] as Orwell put it, a week longer than had been arranged, and he and Eileen each wrote a letter apologising for the delay. Orwell dutifully repeated the plan Eileen had convinced him to accept – 'to stay the summer, then move' – while at the same time fantasising again about the day when he would have a 'stud' billy goat, who would 'no doubt pay his keep with stud fees . . . later when we go in for goats properly.'[12] Giving up the cottage was clearly something Orwell was continuing to resist.

At this point, yet again, a family member stepped in to give the assistance the couple rarely acknowledged needing. Eileen's mother, unhappy about the marriage at first but now part of the support team, agreed to leave the comfort of Greenwich 'to go & open the house & take the several tons of stuff we have parked in London so that we can go straight from [Southwold]',¹³ as Eileen explained to Mary Common. And arrive at the cottage they finally did, around midnight on Tuesday, 11 April.

Immediately, on 12 April, Orwell made an exceptionally long entry in his Domestic Diary, with many details about how poorly the garden had fared since he himself had left in an ambulance over a year before. Eileen had done her best during the spring and summer of 1938, trying to manage the vegetables and animals alone interspersed with those long trips to visit Orwell in the sanatorium, but he made no mention in his diary of her efforts to keep things going while he was ill. 'Everything greatly neglected, full of weeds, etc.,' except for 'a few leeks & parsnips,' he recorded. They now had twenty-six hens, and Orwell continued his fascination with the number of eggs laid each day. Eileen was excited to discover that the flowers around the cottage were blooming fabulously and a few trees were ripe with fruit. And Marx was thrilled to be back after a winter in Bristol. Orwell was curious how he would behave with 'a live baby mouse. He smelt & licked it but made no move to eat it.'¹⁴

Eileen and Orwell began right away on an extremely busy schedule, attempting to quickly get the vegetables planted and ready to eat. They spent one whole day cleaning out the strawberries, which were covered with weeds but still looked strong. On another day they felt it necessary to move the henhouses. And, besides keeping careful watch on all the movements of birds and the blossoming of wild flowers and the ripening of fruit, they sowed lettuce, broad beans, peas, broccoli, savoys, leeks, sprouts, carrots, onions, radishes, and potatoes. As a fascinating break, on 19 April, a week after their return, they had the great excitement of watching an eclipse of the sun. 'At the time of the greatest eclipse, 7:15 p.m. when nearly half the sun was covered, it became somewhat dark & cold,' Orwell recorded, 'but not enough so for any reactions to be noticeable in birds etc. The hens did not go into the houses.'[15]

Orwell continued his routine diary entries for two weeks, but then suddenly, with no mention of why, Eileen took over the task, making the entries herself for two weeks, from 25 April until 9 May. Orwell had written to his agent on 25 April, 'I am very well again and have been putting in some strenuous gardening to make up for lost time.'[16] So it seems likely he had once again suddenly fallen ill. Denys King-Farlow verified this possibility when he recalled hearing from Eileen around this time that, 'after having recovered apparently pretty thoroughly, [Orwell] had had a sudden relapse and was again in a sanatorium,' where King-Farlow remembered visiting him once.[17] Ruth Pitter, a friend of Orwell's from years earlier, said that Eileen had once told her about Orwell's 'recent illness . . . the sudden severe haemorrhage' that had terrified her, adding a poignant footnote: 'The last straw was that when he had been got off to hospital, she looked for the cat to hold in her arms for a little consolation, but it had disappeared, and she never saw it again.'[18] Eileen had gone with Orwell in the ambulance that first time, in 1938, so there would have been no sad scene with a cat. With these two accounts, there is a distinct possibility that Orwell spent the end of April, at least, back in the sanatorium.

In her first three diary entries, Eileen carefully followed Orwell's form, starting with a mention of the weather, then adding some interesting facts of the day, and ending with the egg count.

25.4.39: Raining most of the day, & cold. 14 eggs.
26.4.39: Sharp frost in the night. Raining. Short fall of snow in the morning. The doubtful hen sat the eggs [sic] during the night but was finally found not to be broody. Shall still put the eggs under a hen if obtainable, & watch results.
Fifteen eggs (highest). 1/10 score [one shilling, ten pence, for 20, the price for which Eileen was selling eggs].
27.4.39: Sharp frost during night & hens' water frozen. Snow &

sleet during most of the day. Short sunny intervals. Blossom seems
undamaged. Perennial alyssum coming into flower. Scyllas & grape
hyacinths coming to an end. Starlings very busy obtaining straw for
nests. Mrs. Anderson [a neighbour] heard cuckoo at 5:45. Caught a
thrush in the kitchen unhurt; a full-grown bird, very yellow inside
beak.
Sixteen eggs (highest).

Clearly, besides filling out the diary, she was handling all the difficult jobs by herself, including selling some of the eggs she collected to the butcher. For the next three days, she reported what she knew was most important, writing simply:

28.4.39: 9 eggs.
29.4.39: 12 eggs.
30.4.39: 14 eggs. Came to Greenwich.[19]

It's not clear exactly how long Orwell might have spent in the sanatorium, if this theory is correct. Eileen could have looked after him at the cottage for a while after his sudden relapse, or he could have gone immediately by ambulance to Preston Hall while she remained to sort out things at the cottage. But on 3 May, three days after Eileen left the cottage, her entry in Orwell's diary noted the wildlife 'Outside Miller Hospital'. It is of course possible that the ambulance took Orwell directly to the hospital rather than to the sanatorium first. Orwell was a patient in the Miller Hospital at some point, and not in the London Chest Hospital, which has been suggested. Miller General Hospital was on Greenwich Road, near the O'Shaughnessy home, and one theory has been that Eric O'Shaughnessy referred Orwell to the hospital for a routine checkup. However, Orwell didn't make it back to Wallington until 24 May, according to his diary entries, over a month after Eileen wrote her first entry on 25 April, so that would seem to rule out any routine hospital visit. The Miller General Hospital patient records of the period between 23 March 1938 and 17 August 1939 are missing,[20] so it's impossible to check the length of Orwell's stay there. Patient records from Preston Hall during that period are not available.

Herbert Victor Morlock, Orwell's doctor at the Miller General Hospital and an expert in chest diseases, confirmed O'Shaughnessy's diagnosis of 'bronchiectatis', which he said would explain Orwell's 'chronic cough'. Known for giving his patients confidence, he went so far as to tell Orwell 'not to worry about coughing up blood; it might even be good for him'.[21] Morlock was described as 'an extrovert' who was regarded as an 'enfant terrible' by his colleagues,[22] so it's easy to imagine him as a friend of Eric O'Shaughnessy's and that he would be recommended as Orwell's doctor.

On 5 May, Eileen made a three-day visit to Wallington alone. In a long summation of that visit, she noted in Orwell's diary the success of some of their newly planted vegetables. The peas, beans, and rhubarb were starting to grow, and 'in three days main crop potatoes, onions, carrots, turnips, second peas & radishes sown,' she somewhat casually wrote. She also found time to sow grass seed in bare patches and scatter lawn sand. The garden was being started later than usual that year, and Eileen knew she had to catch up even though Orwell wasn't able to help her. But throughout her entries there is never any sign of complaint. She ended the 8 May entry with: 'Hens have laid 92 eggs in 8 days,'[23] something of which they both were apparently very proud.

On 9 May she was back in Greenwich, with a one-sentence entry: 'Young pigeons in nest outside hospital window.'[24] So Orwell was still in the hospital over two weeks after Eileen had abruptly taken over writing the diary. There are no further Domestic Diary entries until 16 May, when Orwell, now resting at the O'Shaughnessy home, resumed the task himself. Presumably throughout those weeks Eileen visited Wallington alone a few more times. But she left the diary with Orwell, who continued to stay in Greenwich until 24 May, making detailed entries about the flowers in Greenwich Park and the animals at the zoo.

They arrived together back at Wallington on 24 May, about a

month after Orwell's sudden illness. And on 25 May, Orwell noted proudly that, between 11 April, when they had got back there from Morocco, and the current date, they had collected a grand total of 550 eggs from their twenty-six hens.[25] During most of that time, Eileen had single-handedly kept the cottage running, competently completing the many tasks that were required. She was relieved to have Orwell finally healthy enough to start helping her again. But this overwork, which she was enjoying less and less, was exhausting her and contributing to what would soon become her own serious health problems. She had agreed to another summer in Wallington, and she was committed to making everything work as well as possible, but the primitive difficulties of life there no longer charmed her.

They continued to constantly share a hectic flurry of garden work, and Orwell often singled out Eileen in his diary entries. On 3 June, he noted that she, on her own, 'planted 7 dahlias,' and the next day, 'E. saw a white owl again last night.'[26] On 7 June, 'Eileen cut the lawn with shears & then with the mower,' and on 9 June, 'E. put six broodies in a sort of cage of wire netting, which may perhaps cure them,' evidently trying out a technique learned from other villagers, whose helpful opinions turned up often in the diary. This trick with the hens worked, and on 14 June Orwell wrote, 'The broodies E. put in the cage, released yesterday, have all (seven) gone back to normal.'[27] They even bought eight new pullets, a strange decision if this was indeed their last summer in Wallington.

Towards the end of April, a month after Orwell had delivered *Coming Up for Air*, Victor Gollancz had still not announced its acceptance. Orwell was annoyed and considered switching publishers. Just before his sudden illness, he told his agent about his financial worries: 'I have earned little or no money since last spring and am infernally hard up and in debt.'[28] Money was a constant nagging problem for the couple, who were then partially relying on income from the eggs they could sell, since the shop was no longer open. Orwell ended this letter, as he did most of the ones to his agent, with the line, 'My wife sends all the best.' So, in a quiet way, and despite acting like a schoolboy as he pursued a reluctant Lydia, he was reinforcing his solid partnership with Eileen.

Coming Up for Air was finally accepted and actually went into print so quickly that by 11 June Orwell was asking for extra copies for his friends. He was also anxious to send copies to certain magazines where he would 'be sure of sympathetic reviews'.[29] And, indeed, *Coming Up for Air* was received very favourably. As a friend noted later, 'For the first time . . . one of his novels enjoyed a moderate popular success.'[30] And, also for the first time, Eileen's influence on his work was noted, albeit indirectly. The reviews all describe a well-rounded hero, a very complicated man with deep emotions beneath his ordinary exterior, a man much more subtle and self-aware than Orwell's usual creations. One reviewer wrote, 'Mr. Orwell writes with hard, honest clarity and unswerving precision of feeling . . . an unsentimental artistry in which tact and tenderness are beautifully combined . . . It is the most heartfelt of cautionary tales, with neither display nor self-righteousness in the telling, only an impassioned and ruthless honesty of imagination.'[31] This was the first of Orwell's novels where Eileen had been present throughout the whole process of creation, and her sense of fun in contemplating human nature is evident all through the book, beginning on the first page, with the immediate mention of the 'new false teeth', and then the immediate goal for the narrator of getting to the bathroom 'just in time to shut the kids out'. These are touches that, as the reviewers noted, were not particularly evident in Orwell's other works.

Barely a week after its publication, and in quick recognition of its literary success, A. P. Watt & Son – a literary agency that represented many famous authors, including Kipling, Maugham, and H. G. Wells – informed Orwell that they would like to act as his agent. But Orwell loyally turned them down, writing, in a very brief reply, 'Many thanks for the offer, but Messrs. Christy and Moore have been my agents for a good many years.'[32]

Towards the end of June, barely a month after returning from his long stay in London with an undisclosed illness, Orwell was called anxiously by his family for an emergency visit to Southwold. His father, then eighty-two, who had been in ill health for some time, was finally dying. Orwell had struggled throughout his life with the worry that he hadn't lived up to his father's expectations, and his greatest wish had been to convince his father that he had made a life choice worthy of his respect.[33] And on this visit, very touchingly, the two men had a moment of reconciliation just before the old man's death.

On 25 June, Orwell's thirty-sixth birthday, the *Sunday Times* had printed a strongly enthusiastic review of *Coming Up for Air*. Ralph Straus wrote, 'Blessedly, there is published, perhaps once or twice in the year, a book which . . . has a point of view that is peculiarly its own, because it is about "common" people who are flesh and blood and not unusual puppets brought together for the mere making of a story . . . And so it is with Mr. Orwell's quite exceptionally good *Coming Up for Air* . . . I do not hesitate to say that from first page to last George Bowling's narrative is engrossing . . . Most readers will share my enthusiasm for a novel which may legitimately be called brilliant.'[34]

When Orwell's father asked to see the review, Orwell's sister Avril 'took it in [to his bedroom] and read it to him, and a little later he lost consciousness for the last time'. Orwell was proud to tell his agent that, after hearing the review, his father 'had not been so disappointed in me as before'.[35] Orwell poignantly revealed to a friend that he himself 'had closed his father's eyes in the traditional way by placing pennies upon the eyelids'. But, afterward, he 'had been embarrassed to know what to do with the pennies', since that part of the tradition was not clear. 'In the end,' he said, 'I walked down to the sea and threw them in,' not sure whether 'some people would have put them back in their pocket'.[36]

It was not possible to leave the garden and animals unattended for a week, so Orwell once again left the Domestic Diary, along with the cottage chores, in Eileen's competent hands. Her sometimes extensive daily entries, a few of them reprinted below, show how incredibly busy she had to be while he was once again absent.

26.6.39: Warm sunny morning. Threats of thunderstorms in afternoon but no thunder & little rain. Potatoes earthed up. Gaps filled in French bean rows with extras sown in a box in the frame when the original rows were found to have germinated badly – i.e. after an interval of ten days or so. There is very little difference in development. Blackfly have already settled on about a quarter of the broad beans, though not in great numbers; pinched out growing points. The strings for the runner beans were tangled & stretched by rain & wind. Apparently four or five stakes are necessary for one of our rows. Weeded & hoed onions which are now three or four inches tall but with many gaps in the rows. Beans & peas have grown very rapidly, some runner bean tendrils lengthening by a couple of inches since Saturday.
12 eggs.

27.6.39: Very hot & sunny. Thinned carrots & hoed peas etc. Planted out 48 larkspurs, removing some poor sweet williams. Apparently sweet williams sometimes 'shoot up' for several years but cannot be made to do so.
15 eggs + 8 found in a nest.

28.6.39: Much cooler & occasional showers. Mr H. [Hatchett, a neighbour] finished cutting the hay & collected it today. Sowed turnips & planted out a row of mixed greens from the seed bed. Both broody hens with chickens laid today, & one (the youngest) had three other eggs hidden at the back of the coop.
14 eggs + 3 in coop.

29.6.39: Hot & sunny most of the day. One duck had hatched this morning. Later moved the hen to new coop & left the more backward eggs with another broody . . . Made an awning with adjustable sacking

cover & put flat dish of water in coop. Rehoed onions which are
growing at last. Marrows also growing, one strongly. White rose out.
15 eggs.[37]

Eileen made no mention in the diary of Orwell's birthday or of his father's death, but no doubt they were in touch the whole time.

Orwell arrived back in Wallington on 30 June, after his father's funeral, and took over writing the Domestic Diary on 1 July. It is a matter of conjecture whether by this time Eileen had caught Orwell's fascination with recording the minutiae of their days or whether she had always shared this compulsion. She might have been more thorough this time because she wanted to please Orwell when he came back from the sad week with his family. Or perhaps Orwell had scolded her for writing such skimpy reports the month before, when he was ill in London. At any rate, there is no question that they were both seemingly obsessed with the idea that their farm garden must be successful. We get some clue from Lydia to the reason for this almost desperate pace. Eileen told her friend that her concern in 'keeping chickens and growing vegetables [was] to provide George with adequate food when hard times came'.[38]

After the initial joy of embarking on this life adventure, they must have both had some doubts by this time. Through the years, the cottage had persisted in a drastic enough state to make living there a constant hassle. The hardships of cottage life that were clear those first months only magnified as the years went by. The inconveniences that Eileen had been well aware of before moving in, but had tried to romanticise, now presented themselves in all their true clarity. However, although Eileen and Orwell always knew of the problems, they either didn't care enough to get them fixed or just never managed to find the time to solve them. That extremely low front door, rather charming in appearance at first, became a daily annoyance since Eileen as well as Orwell had to duck each time they entered the house. And, as one friend remembered, 'When it rained heavily, water tended to trickle down the steps [onto] the coconut matting on the floor'[39] of the living room. The ugly corrugated-iron roof magnified even the drip of light raindrops, and it provided no insulation on cold nights.[40] Heating cold water drawn from a tap in the yard outside the kitchen and keeping a supply of candles and paraffin for the evening lamps were no longer quaint nuisances, while having to go outside to reach the ramshackle lean-to that housed the toilet – where too thick toilet paper could easily back up the cesspool, a disaster that led to one of the most horrendous cottage chores[41] – quickly became a nightmare. It was never possible to get everything perfect.

Although they eventually did get running water, electric lights, a better stove, and even a telephone, they never managed to modernise the cottage in any grand way. So there were some negative reports about living conditions there, which Eileen enjoyed elaborating on, telling a friend that the kitchen was overrun by 'battalions of mice, shoulder to shoulder on the shelves, pushing the china off'.[42] A few years later, when Eileen's friend Lettice Cooper stayed there overnight, she reported, 'Nothing in it worked. The sink would be blocked. The primus stove wouldn't work. The lavatory plug wouldn't pull. The stairs were very dark, because there were never any bulbs in the lights, and they'd put piles of books on the staircase at odd places, so there were lots of traps, and the place was rather dusty. But,' she added, as a kind friend would, 'it was a nice cottage, in a lovely part of the country.'[43]

The cottage did eventually have a major facelift, and in the summer of 2011 – complete with a heritage plaque honouring Orwell's years there, but with no mention of Eileen – it went on sale for £450,000.

With war now approaching, their main goal apparently had become preserving and storing away enough supplies to survive the coming winter. Also, at some other points during the day or night, to make a little extra income, Orwell was reading books at his voracious pace in preparation for detailed reviews, as well as writing in-depth articles on the morality of war and collecting notes for his essay on Dickens. And Eileen was finding moments of free time to continue to type and retype his revisions. So any ideas she had of finding that perfect home in the warmer south of England had to be postponed. They both must have been jumping from typewriter to garden to dinner to bed, if indeed they could ever fit much sleep in. Eileen believed that Orwell must survive so that his brilliant insights could help humanity survive. But she was dooming herself.

Sometime during those spring and summer months, Orwell also found time to contact Lydia again. And, although she claimed she did not 'want to disturb [Orwell's] relationship with Eileen, or have anything to conceal from her', she agreed to see him. And not just once but many times. For a psychology graduate, Lydia appeared astoundingly confused when she tried to justify her own motives. At first, she said, 'I felt sorry . . . about him falling ill so soon after he had spent several months in Africa, at considerable expense, for the sake of his health.' So, as she explained, her 'annoyance with him was extinguished by compassion.' Then she speculated that Orwell was 'a sick man, losing confidence in his attractiveness to women, needing reassurance, needing comforting.' She did feel guilty about deceiving Eileen, and had trouble explaining her own behaviour. While claiming that Orwell 'was not merely failing to attract me as a man, but the fact of his being a *sick* man vaguely repelled me,' she continued to welcome his visits. She related in some detail one of Orwell's letters about their plans to meet, where he revealed 'with some amusement how he had "slipped up" by almost blurting out to Eileen that he was going to meet me in London.' Then she went on to complain, 'The unwelcome, the positively repellent role of an accomplice in deceit was thrust upon me,' because somehow she 'could not be unpleasant to him.' She came to the conclusion that, although she allowed Orwell 'to think that I let him kiss me because I liked it. I did not.'[44] It was, apparently, all Orwell's fault for not noticing her repulsion as he kissed her. Lydia didn't disclose how many times she took part in what she saw as 'an amorous affair', not 'a love affair', but it's hard to believe that Orwell could misread her behaviour so poorly. It seems unlikely that he would write those suggestive letters to her after receiving just a few kisses. Towards the end of her life, Lydia added more details in her private diary. 'My main memories of [Orwell] are tactile,' she wrote, 'the sensation of bristly short hair at the back of his head, the touch of his lips on mine, a slight whiff of a faint sweetish smell from his mouth (his damaged lung?).' And, with all her insistence that she didn't find him 'physically attractive', Lydia concluded, 'I think I could have married Eric Blair if at a certain stage I had decided that I wanted to.'[45]

When Lydia wrote to Bernard Crick, Orwell's first biographer, years later about her relationship with Orwell, he was shocked. 'I had heard it said, in a gossipy way, that he continued to have some affairs and some brief encounters even after marrying Eileen. But I had not heard you spoken of as other than a friend of Eileen who became a friend of his,' he told her. Another friend of Orwell's had told him 'that sometimes he made things difficult for his friends by sexual advances "too serious for play, but not serious enough to make one want to change the course of a life, and other peoples".'[46] Lydia implied to Crick that she had indeed had an affair with Orwell, although she did not want this fact to be published. 'I am sorry I still feel [that her letters from Orwell] should not be read by anyone except myself . . . My showing them could only appear to be a claim on my part to have had a "special relationship" with a "great man",' she told him, while still insisting that 'the relationship was not of my seeking and was resisted by me.'[47] Crick, believing he completely understood her reluctance, replied, 'Knowing what you have told me, or rather implied so honestly and delicately, let me say straight away that I wouldn't want to divulge what you have said, nor to hint at it.'[48] So this exchange was excluded from his biography of Orwell and remained hidden in his archives until just related here.

Orwell was never an advocate of monogamy. The couple discussed these beliefs, and Eileen understood that Orwell hadn't promised to be faithful. He told friends that he himself did not suffer from sexual jealousy. Eileen had felt guilty about her own affair with Georges Kopp in Barcelona, but Orwell had not reacted badly when he heard about it. In fact, he'd stayed friends with Kopp for years. And he knew Eileen was still writing to Kopp because he got a letter from him in August, when Kopp was still in France. In it he wrote, 'Eileen gave some news of your goats and cats and hens,' before adding, 'Give my love to Eileen.'[49] So Orwell might have truly believed that Eileen would be able to handle his adventures outside the marriage as easily as he had handled hers. And she had probably assured him that she could, since she wouldn't want to appear emotionally weaker than he was. Eileen's friends and family never reported any details of her feelings on the subject. Of course, Lydia would never have agreed to participate in an open affair with her best friend's husband, so she insisted on secrecy. But it's confusing to contemplate why Orwell seemed so titillated with the idea of keeping this affair secret in a way that suggested he enjoyed deceiving Eileen.

Lydia continued to conceal their meetings from Eileen, with the feeble reasoning that, if Eileen discovered them, '[S]he might not have believed that I was an unwilling accomplice.'[50] And she was right in assuming that this attempt at a defence of her actions was unconvincing. Of course Eileen wouldn't have believed her. While Lydia continued to justify her behaviour as a favour to Orwell, she was also flattered that he seemed so obsessed with her. And he might have been complaining, as men having affairs often do, that his wife was not satisfying his sexual desires. However, this line conflicts drastically with Orwell's summation of sex and women shortly before he died, where he complained that wives are usually 'quite insatiable.'[51]

Lydia did eventually end the affair, but only after Eileen arrived at her London door one day 'in a state of great frustration and anger against her husband'. She told Lydia that 'after their return from Morocco their relationship had been unusually harmonious.'[52] These are Lydia's words, though. Eileen never told people that she and Orwell were 'usually' at odds with each other, as this would imply. Mabel Fierz believed they were not 'idyllically happy,'[53] but neither of them would have tolerated sharing the cottage so intimately for years if the marriage had been so lacking in 'harmony'. However, Eileen suspected that Orwell was having a secret affair, and she was furious. At first Lydia assumed with dread that Eileen had found out about her own meetings with Orwell. So she was mightily relieved when she realised that Eileen was accusing another woman of distracting him. Apparently Wallington neighbours had seen Orwell in the woods with Brenda Salkeld while Eileen was visiting London. (A year later, in a letter to Brenda, Orwell himself mentioned 'that beautiful walk we had last summer just before the war began').[54] Orwell was still pursuing Brenda after all these years, at this point assuring her that 'he and Eileen enjoyed an open marriage and neither was at all jealous and possessive of the other',[55] – a line he probably also used with Lydia and many other women.

Eileen knew all about the very long and unconsummated relationship between Brenda and Orwell. And she had a clever understanding of why Orwell's pursuit of his old girlfriend continued, explaining to Lydia, 'This affair goes on because she wouldn't sleep with him. If she had, it would have been finished long ago'.[56] This seems to imply that it was the secrecy rather than the actual affairs that upset Eileen, and also the pursuit rather than the consummation that motivated Orwell. Lydia quickly saw the wisdom of this interpretation, and wrote in her book that she then understood that it might also be 'the reason for [Orwell's] being so persistent' with her. Although she had later seemed to admit to having an affair with Orwell, she clearly was a reluctant lover, and might have teased him more often than she gave in. However, it became clear to Lydia at that moment that Orwell's persistence and seeming desperation were just part of a game he played with women and that she was not as special to him as she had believed. Lydia also then understood that perhaps it was she who needed 'some reassurance and comfort from the fact that I was still attractive to men'.[57]

Eileen's visit, along with Lydia's new understanding of the nature of her relationship with Orwell, caused her to break things off completely. After writing seventeen letters to Lydia throughout the affair, Orwell stopped at that point and didn't write a personal letter to her again until 1 April 1945, just after Eileen had so suddenly and tragically died. And in the following few years before Orwell himself passed away, he and Lydia stayed in touch, but the affair never resumed.[58] However, as it turned out, Lydia was just the first of Orwell's wartime women.

Because of the debilitating course of events so far that spring, with his own long illness and his father's death, Orwell reported to his agent on 14 July that he was 'terribly behind' with his next book, *Inside the Whale*, which, he informed him, would contain three long essays on the subjects: 'Charles Dickens, boys' weekly papers (the Gem, Magnet etc.), and Henry Miller, the American novelist'. He was 'finishing the rough draft of the Dickens one now, but the others probably won't take so long,' he wrote, adding, 'these infernal illnesses have of course wasted months of time'.[59] Eileen was at the cottage almost full time until late August, and she helped with the Dickens essay. The other two, which were to be written by Orwell without as much help from Eileen, ended up taking about two months longer than the October date he had optimistically predicted. On 12 August, adding further delay to the new book, Orwell and Eileen were surprised at the cottage by a police visit. Orwell's mail had been opened at the local post office and officials were aware that he was illegally importing some books. As Orwell reported, 'All my books from the Obelisk Press this morning seized by police, with warning from Public Prosecutor that I am liable to be prosecuted if importing such things again.'[60] Among the books taken from their home were ones by Henry Miller, the subject of one of the as yet unwritten essays for *Inside the Whale*.

Orwell told his agent in July that he also had great hopes for what he now described as 'a long novel, really the first part of an enormous novel, a sort of saga(!) which will have to be published in three parts.' Eileen had been pressing him to forget book reviewing and get back to writing a new novel, and her persistence was now having an effect. This novel he expected would take a long time to write, 'and even barring wars, illnesses etc. isn't like[ly] to be finished before the summer of 1940'.[61] Even if the war had started a year later, as he was supposing it would, this projection of just over a year to complete the book of essays as well as the first novel of a three-part 'saga' was hugely over-optimistic. Orwell also believed there was still a chance to form 'a real mass party whose first pledges are to refuse war and to right imperial justice'.[62] Eileen, however, saw him as rather naïve in some of his assumptions about human nature. She did not share his faith in any underlying common sense that would energise a majority of ordinary human beings to resist the orders of their leaders.

On 24 August, they both left Wallington, fearing by then that war was imminent. Eileen went straight to her brother's house in Greenwich while Orwell spent the last week of August into early September with L. H. Myers, at Ringwood, Hampshire, before joining Eileen in Greenwich sometime before 3 September. Myers, a great admirer of Orwell's and a prominent communist, was the person who had made the secret loan to allow Orwell and Eileen to winter in Morocco, but Orwell didn't discover this until 1946.[63] While he was at Ringwood, Eileen was Orwell's informant on how the citizens of London were handling the news of probable war: 'Main buildings in London being sandbagged . . . Practice evacuation of school children said to have gone off successfully . . . No mass-exodus from the railway stations, but immense quantities of luggage waiting to leave, by the look of it the luggage of fairly well-to-do people,'[64] and 'E's report of speeches in Hyde Park suggest that Communist Party are taking more left wing line but not anxious to thrash out question of Russo-German pact.'[65] Eileen also informed Orwell that, after visiting the War Office, she had the 'impression that war is almost certain.'[66]

Eileen and Orwell were together in Greenwich at 11:15 a.m. on 3 September 1939, when Neville Chamberlain announced that Britain and France had declared war on Germany, after Germany had refused to withdraw its troops from Poland. But by 5 September, Orwell was back in Wallington, ready to take up the cottage chores alone. Orwell hadn't quite accepted until then that Eileen was tiring of her intensive participation in this hectic life, and was not intending to spend another winter with him at the cottage, which he was insisting on. For the first time Orwell would be doing without Eileen's constant help with typing and emendations. Eileen had spent virtually every hour of three years at Orwell's side, but a whole new life for each of them was about to start.

When Eileen decided to stay in London, she was acting on a variety of impulses. First of all, she had tired herself out doing her share of preserving the garden produce so that Orwell could spend the coming winter alone at the cottage. She had surely argued strongly against this. But Orwell cherished life at the cottage far too much to be uprooted at that point. However, he had been making very little money with his writing throughout the spring, and Eileen would now 'become a bread-winner in London', as Lydia remembered. Somewhat surprisingly, Lydia had no idea what kind of job Eileen eventually got, calling it 'a minor post at the post office';[67] after ending her sexual involvement with Orwell, Lydia became much less of a presence in Eileen's life also. Perhaps Eileen had become aware of her betrayal. Only one letter from Eileen to Lydia has survived, probably because she didn't write many to her, since Lydia would have saved Eileen's letters as she did Orwell's. Eileen's later friends didn't much like Lydia, and this could have been a result of how Eileen portrayed her.

Another serious consideration for Eileen was her brother's enlistment in the Royal Army Medical Corps. He had been a strong advocate of resisting Hitler since becoming friends with Karl Schnetzler, who had left Germany for London when Hitler was rising to power. As a surgeon, Eric O'Shaughnessy insisted on being assigned to the Continent rather than staying in London, as most doctors did, because 'he felt that the good results on wounds of the chest depended to a large extent on their immediate treatment.'[68] Lydia visited Greenwich 'just in time . . . to see [Eric] in his smart uniform . . . a few days before he left for France.[69] This meant that Gwen would now be alone with their infant son, Laurence. At one point Lydia asked Gwen why Eric had made this decision. 'I remember her smile when she replied in her soft, barely audible voice that Eric had decided "the front" was the place for him, and that she had no right, or wish, to stop him.'[70] While making these arrangements, Eric had made Eileen promise that she would help comfort his wife while he was away.[71] This was an agreeable assignment for Eileen, and some of her most endearing photographs show her laughing as she lifts young Laurence high in the air in the garden of the Greenwich home. Eileen believed she had ample excuses for abandoning the cottage chores for a comfortable house with clean sheets and servants. And Orwell stubbornly stuck to his belief that he could manage in Wallington alone.

But beyond all the justifiable reasons Eileen had for moving to Greenwich and leaving Orwell alone at the cottage, Lydia thought that Eileen felt 'On a deeper level . . . that it would be wrong for her to stay in a safe place while the rest of her family were exposed to the danger of air-raids.'[72] She believed also that 'Eileen seemed almost to welcome the dislocation the war brought into her life: for her it was a new, dramatic experience.'[73] One side of Eileen did seem to interpret discomfort and danger as a kind of proof that she was living a life with purpose. But Lydia went even further. She feared that Eileen 'probably even [had] an unconscious *wish* to risk her own life',[74] an ominous and haunting suggestion.

Eileen's job – which, according to Orwell, she got 'as usual . . . by knowing somebody who knew somebody, etc., etc.'[75] – was in the Press and Censorship Bureau of the Ministry of Information, the central government department responsible for publicity and propaganda in the Second World War.[76] One of the people in that department was Cyril Radcliffe, the brother of Ralph Radcliffe, who had been at Oxford with Eileen, so perhaps he was one of her connections. The first gathering of the Censorship Division was on 25 August, which would explain why Eileen left the cottage for London on 24 August. Why exactly she chose to work there was never mentioned, and perhaps her choice was as casual as Orwell made it seem. But perhaps she also had learned from Karl how dangerous Hitler was, and how important it was to work decisively against him. Her interest in psychology could also have been a motivation, as it was believed the country was entering into 'a war of nerves' with the Nazis.[77] Whatever her reasons, knowledge she gained while working there for almost two years certainly helped form some of Orwell's fears that he later expressed in his final novel, *Nineteen Eighty-Four*. One of the first curious titbits Eileen passed on to him was, 'It appears from reliable information that Sir O. Mosley [leader of England's fascists] is a masochist of the extreme type in his sexual life.'[78]

Although Eileen had spent many of her recent years isolated in Wallington, encouraging and assisting Orwell in his dedication to becoming a great writer, she did not present herself at the Ministry of Information as simply a typist and housekeeper. With her excellent skills and connections, she was now ready to display and be rewarded for her capabilities. She knew she had an extremely accomplished experience to offer – her good Oxford degree, years of running her own business, important assistance to her distinguished brother, study for an MA in psychology – a background of which she was very proud. After three years of country life, Eileen could still fairly easily slide back into the elite company of her Oxford colleagues.

She worked in the imposing Senate House, a nineteen-storey prison-like stone block that Orwell used as a model for the Ministry of Truth in *Nineteen Eighty-Four*, describing it in his book as 'an enormous pyramidal structure of glittering white concrete, soaring up, terrace after terrace, three hundred metres into the air'.[79] To today's viewer, it could also be compared to a giant stone wedding cake. But exactly what kind of job did Eileen have? Neither she nor Orwell left any specific information regarding just what she was doing there, and she would have been sworn to secrecy because of the nature of her work, perhaps even lying to Lydia when she asked for details. A study of the Ministry of Information files at the National Archives in Kew revealed the following possibilities.

During the first few months of the war, the Press and Censorship Bureau was being rather urgently reorganised to face the new duties required, and an extensive report was produced by N. D. Bosworth Smith, with many suggestions for changes to avoid contradictory decisions being made. At the beginning of October 1939, Sir Walter Monckton became Director-General of the Bureau and served until the summer of 1941. In his report, Bosworth Smith wanted to replace the civil servant who was then employed as Monckton's Private Secretary, at quite a high salary, with 'one of the shorthand writers who is fully qualified for Private Secretary duties and would be acceptable to the Director-General'. He went on to elaborate: 'At present the Director-General has two personal shorthand-typists. One of these is a lady with a good Oxford Honours degree who has been drawing a relatively high salary for some years past in respect of various private secretarial and political posts which she has held. She is the lady who I propose should be appointed Private Secretary.'[80]

Could this have been Eileen? Most of the shorthand typists were young girls who had been hired to do traditional secretarial work. But Eileen was thirty-four, with over ten years of experience in the field, first with a large London firm, then running her own business, which had been quite successful, and later working on her brother's important medical books and journal articles. And then there was her work with Orwell, which could be described as political, as well as the books she was typing for publishers on the side. And, of course, she had a 'good Oxford Honours' degree. And then, as Orwell said, Eileen had her connections. Monckton was forty-eight at the time and estranged from his wife. 'With his dark and still handsome appearance, sharp intelligence and warm impulsive charm, he was extremely attractive to women . . . and responded to the discovery with almost adolescent delight,' one of his biographers wrote.[81] So it's not hard to accept that he would have eagerly approved of the promotion of an attractive woman such as Eileen for one of his private secretaries, to replace the boring civil servant who then had the job. Shorthand typists were earning £130 to £208 a year and Bosworth Smith suggested that this new private secretary receive £350. However, he added, in an assumption sadly still prevalent today, 'If and when she is replaced by a man Private Secretary a suitable salary + allowance should be fixed.'[82]

A review of Monckton's archives at the Bodleian Library in Oxford revealed no mention of Eileen. However, after an examination of the many letters preserved there that were typed by his three Private Secretaries, one series does have a similar form to Eileen's personal letters that have been preserved. In a letter dated 12 January 1940, there is another mention of this secretary, which again suggests it could possibly be Eileen, since she had friends at the BBC: 'The Director of the Censorship Division . . . had the assistance of a lady secretary who, so far as the Press and Censorship Bureau was concerned, was paid only as a shorthand-typist. This lady performed the full duties of a highly trained secretary, and her emoluments were made up by the B. B. C. from whom she was seconded.' That letter also references another, perhaps more likely, possibility for Eileen: 'One Deputy Director has had the assistance of a private secretary who is similarly paid as a shorthand-typist by the Bureau, but who in fact performs secretarial work and moreover assists in the examination of books which are sent in for Censorship.' When Orwell took over one of Eileen's notebooks years later, he left two full pages of data in her handwriting under the heading: 'Register of Items Received, Censorship Department, Whitehall, 31 August 1940 – 6 September 1940.'[83] Evidently Eileen was doing important work there on a fairly high level. No doubt her discussions with Orwell of her work in this department helped inform the duties of Winston in *Nineteen Eighty-Four*.

One further argument for the possibility that Eileen was an important assistant to Sir Walter Monckton is that she continued at the Bureau until June 1941,[84] exactly the time that Monckton himself finally left the job.

DIPLOMATIC			STAMPS		
Day	Bags	Packets	Day	Censorable	Uncensorable
Saturday 31.8	7 8	6	Monday 2.9.40	3	62
Monday	3 4 1	3 5	Tuesday	5	6 5
Tuesday	1 2 2	1 9	Wednesday	4	6 5
Wednesday	2 2 8	2 8	Thursday	4	4 4
Thursday	8 7	2 4	Friday	3	5 3
Friday	3 4 9	2 9		19	289
	1192	151			

	FOREIGN		IRISH		TOTAL	
	Bags	Packets	Bags	Packets	Bags	Packets
Friday Sep 3L						
Saturday	59	3352	28	1090	87	4442
Sunday	18	911	1	7	19	918
Monday	62	3058	45	1483	107	4521
Tuesday	77	3315	33	1274	110	4589
Wednesday	114	6870	42	1449	156	8319
Thursday	93	12294	35	1356	128	13650
Friday	78	4865	32	1284	110	6149
TOTAL	501	34645	216	7943	717	42588

Some work-related notes by Eileen as part of her job at the Ministry of Information.

Back at the cottage alone, with Eileen now living in London, Orwell was having a dreadful time. He noted the disasters in his Domestic Diary: 'Weeds are terrible', 'the last lot of peas did not come to much', 'lettuces have all gone to seed', 'early potatoes . . . very poor'.[85] During the autumn, he bagged up about 300 pounds of potatoes, and added them to the over twenty-five pounds of fruit jellies he recorded making, as well as the apples he was storing away,[86] all part of the grand plan to stock food for his survival through the winter months. Bit by bit, Eileen had become convinced by a very persuasive husband that one more spring in Wallington was a desirable goal. They 'decided after all not to get rid of the older hens', and Orwell revealed a new spring fantasy: 'If actually here we might go in for rabbits & bees,' he wrote, explaining that a neighbour had 'made a lot of money out of rabbits at the end of the last war'.[87]

Eileen's love and admiration for Orwell convinced her not to abandon him completely to his foolishness. So she agreed to make the trip to Wallington every second weekend or so. As Orwell explained to Connolly, 'My wife can only come down here alternate weekends at present as she works on a late shift one week and an early one the next.'[88] When she was at the cottage, Eileen helped by giving the young broccoli superphosphate, planting spring cabbages, and picking four and a half pounds of blackberries, to add to their jam reserves.

Somehow Orwell also found time to finish the last two essays for *Inside the Whale* by 8 December, a mere two months late, as well as to write four long book reviews. And Eileen, even while working at the Ministry of Information, interspersed with the tough physical toil the garden occasionally demanded, was continuing to help with some of Orwell's typing. He informed his agent that he himself had 'typed most of [his new book] but my wife is typing another portion in London'.[89] Orwell was self-aware enough to realise he found it almost impossible to take even a moment to relax and, as he confessed near the end of his life: 'Even at the periods when I was working 10 hours a day on a book, or turning out 4 or 5 articles a week, I have never been able to get away from this neurotic feeling that I was wasting time.'[90] At least by then, after years of Eileen's training, he was casually using the term 'neurotic'.

With another book finished, Orwell spent a happy two weeks in Greenwich with Eileen at Christmas, just before they set off for another Wallington weekend together. Unfortunately, the winter of 1939–40 turned out to be one of record cold. On 15 January Orwell wrote in his diary: 'The indoor water pipes are frozen again. Dishes of water left in the kitchen sink now freeze almost solid. This must be the longest cold snap since 1916–17,[91] and on 17 January: 'Last night seemingly the hardest frost of all, as even the village pump was frozen. Snow very dry and crunchy. Dung in the hen houses frozen quite hard, so broke this up & scattered on another strip [of the garden], which will do for beans or peas.'[92] Yet somehow, stubbornly struggling through this bitter month, as he tried to make do without running water and occasionally without even a working toilet, Orwell managed to correct the proofs for *Inside the Whale*.

But eventually conditions proved to be so appalling that Eileen had to rush up to the cottage to help Orwell escape, and on 30 January they set out for London together. Orwell later recalled their struggles getting to the train station: 'The day we left, the roads were so completely snowed up that of the 3½ miles to Baldock we were only able to do about ½ mile on the road. For the rest we had to strike across the fields, where the snow was frozen hard & there were not so many drifts. In the road they were at least 6' deep in places. It was sometimes impossible to see where the road lay, as the snow covered the tops of the banks on either side. Flocks of hares, sometimes about 20 together, were wandering over the fields.'[93]

After a six-week absence 'due to 'flu etc.,'[94] as Orwell seriously understated it, he returned to the cottage alone in mid-March. But, once again he pushed himself too far. 'I am busy getting our garden dug & am going to try & raise ½ ton of potatoes this year, as it wouldn't surprise me to see a food shortage next winter,'[95] he told a friend. But it was obvious to Jack Common on a visit that Orwell was damaging his health: 'He was standing with a hoe, looking very frail, deep-furrowed cheeks and pitifully feeble chest. His strong cord trousers gave a massivity to his legs oddly in contrast to his emaciated torso.'[96]

Orwell was also getting increasingly lonely, telling friends, 'Eileen would send love if she were here.'[97] By early April he was complaining, 'Eileen is still working in a Gov.t department but if we can possibly afford it when our affairs are settled I want to get her out of it, as they are simply working her to death besides its making it impossible for us to be together.'[98] His vague reference to 'affairs' being settled, as well as his insistence that he was being 'kept very busy doing reviews which help to keep the wolf a few paces from the backdoor,'[99] underline his conviction that it was somehow in both their best interests for him to suffer through the winter at the cottage, where he was stockpiling supplies for the future, instead of just joining Eileen in London, as she would have preferred. She was making a pretty good salary but Orwell still needed to believe that his minor income from writing reviews – and he managed to pump out thirty between January and May – was necessary to keep them from starving. When asked to write a short autobiography that spring, he ended a list of preferences with 'My wife's tastes fit in almost perfectly with my own,' another clear sign that Eileen was constantly in his thoughts.[100]

Meanwhile, Eileen was leading an interesting life of her own in London, according to her friend Margaret Branch.[101] And when Tosco Fyvel, a recent friend of the couple's and a fellow writer, met Eileen one day, he felt she was clearly enjoying the bustle of the big city and not complaining about being overworked. Although looking a little tired, she 'talked wittily about all the weird characters collected in this as yet amateurish wartime institution [the Press and Censorship Bureau].' She echoed Orwell, Fyvel thought, while 'remaining a personality in her own right with a nice feminine vivacity', even 'recalling humorous incidents during her and Orwell's traumatic experience' in Spain.[102] Eileen found an outlet in conversations, as well as in letters to friends, for her charming descriptions and exaggerations, but after marrying Orwell she had not attempted to bring that infectious voice to any creative work of her own. She had chosen instead to help introduce a lighter, more upbeat tone into Orwell's latest novel and perhaps into some of his longer essays as well.

As spring arrived, Orwell finally decided it was time to move to London with Eileen, though he was still not willing to admit fully that he couldn't get along without her. Instead, he made a new job offer his rationale, informing his agent, 'I am likely to be in London for some time to come, as I am going to do some theatre criticism for *Time and Tide*, and possibly some film criticism as well.'[103] This was an area in which he had little experience, but he was anxious to get some kind of work and not rely entirely on Eileen. So a whole new phase of the marriage began in May 1940. The novelist Lettice Cooper was an associate editor of *Time and Tide* when Orwell began his job there. She later became one of Eileen's best friends when they worked together at the Ministry of Food, but she met Orwell well over a year before she met Eileen. As Lettice remembered, 'I don't think he liked going to the theatre much, especially to "any bloody play". He was apt to be suddenly indisposed before a first night, and I had to nip in and do it for him.'[104] But perhaps she wasn't aware of Orwell's constant illnesses when she seemed to assume he was just shirking work.

Orwell continued to appreciate any information Eileen passed on about events at the Ministry of Information: 'E. says the people in the Censorship Department where she works lump all "red" papers together and look on the *Tribune* [a socialist weekly] as being in exactly the same class as the *Daily Worker* [the Communist Party's newspaper].' And he thoroughly enjoyed another piece of humour she passed on: 'Recently, when the *Daily Worker* and *Action* [the journal of the British Union of Fascists] were prohibited from export, one of her fellow-workers asked her, "Do you know this paper, the *Daily Worker and Action*?"'[105] (not realising that they were two separate journals).

Within a short time Orwell and Eileen had rented a small furnished flat at 18 Dorset Chambers on Chagford Street. Friends remembered it as 'the most miserable two-room fourth-floor flat, above shops, backing on to garages in a mews, with no lift, little light, cheap second-hand furniture, gas water-heater and shared bathroom.'[106] However, a photograph of the building when they lived there – which later became 39 Chagford Street, and existed until at least 1985, but has since been torn down – shows a three-storey structure with no shop on the ground floor.[107] A 1914 plan for renovations to this building depicts a front portion, two side wings, and a back structure, with six small flats on each floor. A central hallway and staircase gave access to all four sections of the building.[108] Eileen and Orwell rented No. 18, which would have been in the back building, and on the top floor, as their friends remembered. A 1975 photograph of the house, presented in a book as depicting the building when they lived there,[109] is inaccurate. This photo was taken after a new fourth floor had been added, and the two existing side wings have been cropped off in the picture. During the year that they rented this tiny flat, Eileen spent many nights in her brother's splendid Greenwich home, and no doubt Orwell himself enjoyed comfortable weekends there as well.

In the spring of 1940, the majority of Londoners were still feeling invulnerable, calling that period the 'phoney war', even though Hitler's forces were quickly taking over Europe. The evening blackouts were not taken too seriously, although one newspaper insisted 'Black-Out Zero Hour To-Night until 4.21 A.M.', with the added helpful information: 'Moon Rises 2.22 A.M.'[110] However, Eileen was very concerned, since as far as she knew her brother was still in Europe caring for injured troops. Orwell recorded on 28 May, 'Last night, E. and I went to the pub to hear the 9 o'c news. The barmaid was not going to have turned it on if we had not asked her, and to all appearances nobody listened.'[111] Eileen went to the pub alone the following evening and Orwell added her comments to his diary: 'Last night a talk on the radio by a colonel who had come back from Belgium, which unfortunately I did not hear, but which from E's account of it contained interpolations put in by the broadcaster himself to let the public know the army had been let down (a) by the French (not counterattacking), and (b) by the military authorities at home, by equipping them badly.'[112] It was clear by then that the Allied troops were retreating westward towards the coastline. Orwell and Eileen believed with many that 'the invasion of England may be attempted within a few days'.[113] This was clearly the end of the 'phoney war'.

13

The Worst Years of Her Life

Eileen cried, incredulously, 'No, no – not again!'
Mark Benney, recalling the time
a bomb hit during their dinner together

ileen and Orwell believed Eileen's brother, Eric O'Shaughnessy, to be one of those stranded at Dunkirk. They kept expecting him to arrive with the other refugees. Miraculously, between 29 May and 4 June 1940, some 350,000 troops and civilians were rescued from the beaches of Dunkirk, although 68,000 died during the evacuation. A huge fleet of 850 vessels – tiny tugs, barges, lifeboats, and navy destroyers – took part in the rescue. 'Ships of All Sizes Dare the German Guns' in 'history's strangest armada', a contemporary newspaper described the scene.[1] On 1 June, Orwell wrote, 'Last night to Waterloo and Victoria to see whether I could get any news of [Eric]. Quite impossible, of course. The men who have been repatriated have orders not to speak to civilians and are in any case removed from the railway stations as promptly as possible. Actually I saw very few British soldiers.'[2] But Eric never arrived.

Lydia was with Eileen when the radio was full of news about Dunkirk. 'She had just made tea, but neither of us was drinking it,' as

Lydia remembered. 'Eileen paced up and down the room, smoking one cigarette after another. "I just don't know what we shall do with Mother", she was saying, "I'm sure Eric is dead."'[3] And Gwen told a nurse who worked with her that she also had a premonition that Eric wouldn't come back alive.[4] They were both correct. They found out later that Eric had died on 27 May, before the evacuation had even begun.

Neither Eileen nor Orwell left word of how they finally learned about Eric's death, and Orwell's diary made no mention of the event. The newspapers reported Eric O'Shaughnessy's death as that of a hero who had been killed while treating wounded soldiers, greeting 'the dive bomber standing up and with a borrowed Bren gun roaring', as one person imagined. But there was quite another story to tell.

For most of his months on the Continent, from September 1939 to mid-May 1940, Eric O'Shaughnessy had a rather leisurely time. He was assigned to No. 5 Casualty Clearing Station, and he and the other doctors spent their days attending to the ailments of those in the communities where they were stationed. But when Germany invaded Belgium and France, on 10 May, everything changed, as advancing German soldiers pushed everyone to retreat towards the Channel ports.

George McNab, a doctor who served with Eric, wrote a diary covering the last days of this retreat, revealing a much darker version of events.[5] His son, Richard McNab, after reading this diary, realised that Dunkirk 'evoked terrible memories' for his father, who had become Eric's friend, calling him 'Shaugh' (which he pronounced 'Shock', Eric's preferred pronunciation of the first part of O'Shaughnessy). Richard came to believe that 'O'Shaughnessy's death at Dunkirk was almost certainly the main reason for George McNab's diary'[6] – which covers the retreat to Dunkirk from 17–28 May. At that point, McNab and other doctors were pulled onto a British destroyer and rescued. But without Eric O'Shaughnessy.

During those final days, as the doctors in their group struggled to reach Dunkirk, German bombs were constantly destroying convoys of refugees and sometimes entire villages. One typical diary entry says, 'German planes came over and AA [anti-aircraft] guns opened up all around us and plastered the sky with shells. A patrol of Spitfires [British fighter planes] arrived and toured round and round in a wide circle.'[7]

On 27 May, while searching for cellars in Dunkirk for civilians and troops to shelter in, as bombs were dropping all around them, McNab came across Eric in a café, making no attempt to take cover, explaining that he was waiting for other officers to arrive. '[Eric] repeatedly refused my father's instructions to go down into the cellar for shelter as the bombs began to fall,' his son said.[8] Just at that moment there was a direct hit on the café, and, as McNab fell into the basement, he saw right away that Eric had been seriously injured, a splinter of a bomb entering his chest. 'I went up and found [poor old Shaugh] obviously *in extremis* [at the point of death], demanding morphia and water, which I gave him,' McNab wrote. 'We carried him to one of the other cellars, and I went off to find an ambulance . . . I went down to bring Shaugh up, but . . . Shaugh was moribund.'[9] Then, to McNab's lifelong regret, as the buildings around them began to collapse in flames, 'We had to leave Shaugh's body and the wounded. There was no way of getting them away.'[10] Eric O'Shaughnessy's body was never found. 'I'm sorry to say that some surgeons later suggested that he had caused his own death by his stubbornness,' McNab's son said.

What had motivated Eric O'Shaughnessy not to take cover? Was it foolish bravado that killed him while the other doctors survived? Did he feel invulnerable somehow? Could he have had a wish to die, as Lydia believed Eileen did? Or could he have simply suffered from claustrophobia?

Eileen never heard this story, as it has only recently been told. But it didn't matter to her that her brother was considered a hero. It didn't help her to read obituaries praising his brilliant career, including his 'treatment of grafting onto hearts of elderly persons tissue which strengthened them and gave them a longer life'. She was devastated. Her poor health deteriorated further, compounded by watching her mother slowly fade away after her son's death, as she had expected would happen. Eileen never properly recovered from this loss. Lydia thought that 'Eileen's own grip on life, which had never been very firm, loosened considerably after her brother's death.'[11] Her remarkable brother, only thirty-nine years old, her closest friend in the world, the one person she could always count on, was no longer able to help her.

Eileen was profoundly depressed for well over a year. People tried, but it was impossible to console her. Adding to her misery, she also had to endure the horrifying months of the Blitz – constant nights of sirens and indiscriminate bombing throughout the city – the worst year of the war for those living in London. And, beyond all that, Eileen continued to work day after day at the job she had begun to hate, still their main source of income. Orwell tried to comfort and distract her, but that wasn't something he was very good at. He admitted this inability months later, telling the wife of a friend who had recently died, 'You know how it is, the seeming uselessness of trying to offer any consolation when somebody is dead.'[12]

Throughout the summer of 1940, Eileen and Orwell often spent weekends at Scarlett's Farm, a house just outside London shared by some of their friends. 'We all noticed a profound change in [Eileen],' Tosco Fyvel remembered. 'She seemed to sit in the garden sunk in unmoving silence while we talked. Mary, my wife, observed that Eileen not only looked tired and drawn but was drably and untidily dressed.' When they tried to involve her in conversation, she seemed 'completely withdrawn.'[13] And Eileen's friend Margaret Branch, later a Jungian psychotherapist, said that for a time Eileen 'became almost mute. One saw in her visible signs of depression. Her hair was unbrushed, her face and body thin. Reality was so awful for her that she withdrew – the effects lasted perhaps eighteen months.' She believed Eileen 'was facing the dark night of the soul. Nobody could get through to her.' Eric's death had 'shattered Eileen's dream of life'.[14] No wonder Orwell told his diary shortly after Eric died, 'Now I feel so saddened . . . Everything is disintegrating.'[15]

During those devastating first weeks, as Eileen struggled to find a way to focus on daily necessities, she and Orwell walked the London streets together, surveying the still quiet neighbourhoods that they believed would soon be invaded by Hitler. Two days after Italy had declared war, on 10 June, there were rumours that Italian shops in Soho had been ransacked, and one evening they explored those streets, investigating the reports. 'We did see, I think, 3 shops which had had their windows smashed,' Orwell recorded, but 'the majority had hurriedly labelled themselves "British".'[16]

They also continued to go to bars to hear the nine o'clock evening news, and they watched the working-men customers carefully as they listened to Churchill's speeches. Eileen told Orwell that she believed that 'uneducated people are often moved by a speech in solemn language which they don't actually understand but feel to be impressive,' and Orwell felt there was 'some truth' to her conjecture.[17] Indeed, when Churchill proclaimed on the radio, 'The whole fury and might of the enemy must very soon be turned on us. Hitler knows that he will have to break us in this island or lose the war. If we can stand up to him, all Europe may be freed and the life of the world may move forward into broad, sunlit uplands,'[18] he easily gained the support of the British people with his noble rhetoric.

The expectation of imminent invasion was shattering everyone's nerves, causing many cases of confused behaviour. Although engulfed in Eileen's depression, Orwell somehow decided that 25 June, his thirty-seventh birthday, was a good time to send another pleading love letter to his old girlfriend. 'Dearest Brenda,' he began, 'I've tried so often to forget you but somehow didn't succeed . . . It's a pity though we never made love properly. We could have been so happy.' He went on to tell her, 'Today is my birthday & Eileen said I was to give myself a birthday treat,' since 'I've been longing for months to write to you & compelling myself not to.' At that point in her depression Eileen would have agreed to anything. She was completely alone with her loss, and nothing could make it worse. Brenda had continued to refuse an intimate relationship with Orwell, even though he had claimed before, as he did once again in this letter, that 'Eileen said she wished I could sleep with you abt twice a year, just to keep me happy.' The fact that Orwell was able to think of Brenda during this bleak month proved Eileen's earlier acceptance that only her brother would have 'come at once' if she had been in a desperate condition. She had been able to dismiss Orwell's fascination with Brenda because she never expected to count on him when she really needed someone. In his letter to Brenda – referring to Eileen's depression, as well as to the general infusion of anxiety into his world – Orwell added, 'If things just break up & go to pieces as I fear they may, I must try & see you once again.'[19] This sort of thinking reflected a common sentiment throughout the years of the war. Love affairs were started precipitously since it was not irrational to believe that there might truly be no future.

Eileen was also loved from a distance, and in September she got a six-page, tightly spaced letter from Georges Kopp. They had kept in contact, though how often is unclear. In this letter, he reminded her, 'You remember you wished me a "good war" – well I got it.' He told her in great detail how, while fighting with the French Foreign Legion, he had been badly injured and captured in Europe. After two months of treatment in primitive German hospital centres, he had managed to escape, minus a thumb, in such elaborate disguises and with so many French civilians risking their lives to help him that the details of his story are almost impossible to fully believe.

Eileen saved this letter, a rare occurrence for her. She would have treasured all the romantic references to their past love in Spain: 'The country is splendid, hills with parasol-pines like in Catalonia on the road between Monserrat and Barcelona on which we sped in this coach back from Lerida . . . I would love to come here some day with you . . . They make little pies, fluffy and stuffed with anchovies which you would like and [chocolate rolls] I am sure you would be crazy about.' He was hoping to get to England soon and it might have cheered her, as she struggled with the loss of her brother, to read: 'Must I tell you what joy it will be for me to see and hear you . . . You know all that. You even know what sort of *pensées choisies* I am sending you.' It was signed, 'With love, Georges.'

Kopp didn't know of Eric O'Shaughnessy's death, but even so he added, in one of six handwritten PSs to the letter, 'How <u>you</u> must have suffered through this war, Eileen dear!'[20] Perhaps this was the perfect letter for her to cherish, with Orwell unable to find the right words to comfort her. However, it seems Eileen didn't answer it, perhaps because of her great depression. Or possibly her return letter was lost in the uncertainties of wartime mail. Because a year later Kopp, without any news from England, was desperately writing to other acquaintances trying to find out what had happened to her.

Gwen also was not behaving in her usual competent, unflappable way. Perhaps she managed a smile when she read her husband's rather ornate will, written in 1929, just before his father died. Among other details, it said, 'I bequeath free of duty to my said Wife all my carriages, horses, stables, furniture and effects, plate, plated articles, linen, china, glass, books, pictures, prints, furniture, jewellery and articles of household or personal use or ornament, wines, liquors and consumable stores.' In her quiet yet extreme distress at losing her husband, Gwen somehow decided just weeks after his death, and rather surprisingly, that it was the right thing to send their young son to Canada.[21] Ships with hundreds of children aboard began leaving for safe countries in the middle of July and continued to do so until one was sunk by a German submarine in mid-September. Laurence O'Shaughnessy Jr., nineteen months old, accompanied by his nursemaid, left on one of these ships to stay with Dr Gordon, in Montreal.[22] It is unsurprising that these childhood separations often deeply disturbed the children whom the parents were trying to save. Harold Pinter called his separation from his parents at that time 'traumatic'. He believed 'one became . . .

nastier . . . We were all a bunch of horrid little boys because of the loss of security.'[23] Laurence did not return until he was five years old, a separation from his family that scarred him for life.

In June, when the first bombs started falling on England, sirens rang in such a general way throughout the day and night that people were confused. Once, hearing an alarm at 1 a.m., Eileen and Orwell got up and dressed, but then they stood around talking with neighbours when there was no sign of any bombs falling. 'In the absence of gunfire or other excitement one is ashamed to go to the shelter,'[24] Orwell wrote. They somehow turned into an advantage the fact that their small apartment was on the top floor of Dorset Chambers, arguing that 'the beauty' of it was that 'One could more easily get out onto the roof to put out fire bombs if one lived on the top floor.'[25] And before bedtime, 'Whenever the sirens let out their warning wail, Eileen would put out the lights in the top floor flat, open the window and watch the happenings in the street,' Lydia remembered.[26] One night when she was with Lydia during a raid, Eileen 'remained cool and calm prepared to go on drinking tea and talking through the noise', while 'the roar of anti-aircraft guns struck a primitive terror' into Lydia.[27] Eileen claimed to friends that staying alive no longer mattered to her.

In the middle of August, hoping to escape the racket, Eileen and Orwell managed to spend 'two glorious days at Wallington', in Orwell's upbeat wording, visiting their dog Marx and their potato crop. Throughout their time in London, various friends were making use of the cottage for various emergencies, but they tried to spend time there at least once a month.[28] Back in London a few days later, when they were staying the night with Gwen in Greenwich, 'We were watching at the front door when the East India docks were hit,' Orwell wrote, seemingly as an interested spectator,[29] mirroring Eileen's casual attitude to the danger all around her. By the end of August, reacting with false bravado, he noted, 'Air-raid warnings, of which there are now half a dozen or thereabouts every 24 hours, becoming a great bore.' And, later that night, 'Woken up by a tremendous crash, said to be caused by a bomb in Maida Vale [about a mile from where they were living]. Eileen and I merely remarked on the loudness and fell asleep again.'[30]

For the first three months after Dunkirk, Hitler's goal had been to destroy British airfields and ships, in preparation for a land invasion, so civilian homes were rarely hit. But early in September, Germany concluded that an invasion at that point might be repelled, and the tactic changed. The goal then became to destroy homes and lives in London and other large cities, thereby demoralising the citizens and forcing Britain to surrender. On the evening of 7 September, a devastating barrage of attacks began what became known as the Blitz. Hundreds of German bombers dropped hundreds of tons of bombs on the London docks,[31] and four more consecutive nights were filled with continuous, intense raids, causing families to line up at shelter doors with their bedding. On the night of 10 September, Orwell had to suddenly stop writing his diary entry about general damage to London and rush to a shelter with Eileen for the first time. They spent the night with frightened neighbours, 'having been driven there by recurrent whistle and crash of bombs not very far away at intervals of about a quarter of an hour'. Finally being shocked into accepting the actual danger, Orwell was forced to reflect that '3 months of continuous raids at the same intensity as the last 4 nights would break down everyone's morale.'[32] Yet, even after that fright, Eileen and Orwell often tried to sleep through the sirens. 'Many bombs last night . . . The whole house shakes, enough to rattle objects on the table,'[33] Orwell noted just two weeks later. But that night they again just went back to sleep.

From 27 September until mid-November London was continuously bombed, every single night. There was a hope on some evenings that a bright moon might scare the planes away, but nothing deterred them through those mind-numbing autumn nights. Orwell worried about the ability of people to retain their sanity if they were subjected to months of sirens and random explosions and midnight trudges to shelters. And, true to his prophecy, after weeks of constant attacks, many people were close to madness. Throughout the daytime, the London streets were filled with groups of homeless people, wandering disconsolately, carrying suitcases and bundles, their houses destroyed. The only choice for many was to line up at the Underground stations each night, even though inside was the 'heavy sickening stench . . . where one picked one's way through lines of corpse-like figures asleep among their household goods'.[34] These dejected people might have been unaware of the alternative available to some rich citizens, such as Lady Diana Cooper, who could afford to spend their time in the Dorchester Hotel. 'Each night she descended, carrying her treasured diamond dolphins, trembling diamond spray, £200 in cash, her passport and make-up essentials, to a cubicle in the subterranean Turkish bath and slept there (with the aid of a sleeping-pill) until the all-clear came at dawn.'[35] A perhaps not uncommon war trauma was passed on by a personal friend: 'We had a Flying Bomb on us, destroying the house. My mother and I were buried for over five hours before we were rescued,' she recalled, adding, with regret, 'It has had the effect of making it impossible for me to use the underground rail system anywhere! Such a nuisance but I have to use transport above ground!!'[36]

The amazing nightly scene was never forgotten. 'Imagine yourself standing in a darkened street and whichever way you looked the sky is aglow with the light of many furnace-like fires and every building around you is floodlit with the white glare of parachute flares. Also, the many coloured tracer shells which look like giant strings of beads,' one person remembered. 'The whole scene has a kind of terrible beauty.'[37] Even Orwell was 'struck by the size and beauty of the flames' after one major attack.[38] Walking on an empty Oxford Street one day, Orwell noticed 'a pile of plaster dress models, very pink and realistic, like a pile of corpses,'[39] outside a bombed department store. Just the discovery each morning of new 'Blitz grime' covering furniture and dishes was disheartening. They didn't record this, but he and Eileen must have also seen, as others did, 'bits of bodies that had come to rest in the branches of trees' or 'piles of brick rubble, perhaps with an arm sticking out or a leg'.[40] Even for those who survived unhurt, that year caused nightmares. 'After a bad night of Blitz you either sleep too late for breakfast or you can't eat it,' as one of Eileen's friends remembered.[41]

On 15 October, again escaping London's horrors, they spent a whole week at the cottage, but this time it was because Orwell was 'more or less ill for about a fortnight with a poisoned arm,'[42] the cause of which was not explained. Eileen spent the week there with him, as always putting his needs above anything else. As she later boasted to Norah, 'My department head is almost as frightened of me as he is of taking any decision on his own & I can get Time off.'[43] Most likely it was during this week that Lydia and Patricia Donahue, another friend, decided on the spur of the moment to visit Wallington. They had been forbidden to stay in their London home because an unexploded parachute landmine was 'hanging by its cords from an iron staircase' outside.[44] 'We had to walk the last three miles from Baldock . . . We arrived at the cottage and knocked on the door. We weren't expected, of course,' Donahue remembered. 'George came to the door and we went in and they were in the middle of supper. They were very welcoming. We shared their supper and had some of Eileen's very nice apple meringue pie.'[45] The Wallington neighbours would complain to the air-raid warden when the couple were at the cottage because they ignored the blackout regulations requiring them to block the windows after dark.[46] But at that point no one expected the German planes would bother with a village so far away from London.

Although there was a temporary lull towards the end of 1940, bombs were regularly dropped on London until May 1941, and the blackouts continued for months after that. More than 20,000 civilians died in London from air raids through 1941 and another 16,500 died throughout Britain.[47] And maps with colour-coded dots for buildings damaged throughout the city suggest that every neighbourhood, and almost every street, was hit. Yet no mention was ever made of surrendering to Hitler.

Through the year of the Blitz, Eileen had many worries. She continued at her 'daily work of inconceivable dullness,'[48] struggling home at night through the dark streets, climbing over unfortunate individuals sleeping in the tube stations. Sometimes large families were spotted, 'father, mother and several children all laid out in a row like rabbits on a slab,'[49] as Orwell remembered. Walking the last blocks, they often found 'so many streets . . . roped off because of unexploded bombs that to get home . . . is like trying to find your way to the heart of a maze.'[50] Eileen might have stayed at her job at the Ministry of Information out of some kind of loyalty to her boss, but she couldn't really quit anyway because her income was still their main support. They now had to pay rent for their flat in London as well as the cost of food and daily transport – the kinds of expenses they had been able to avoid for years. But Orwell agreed with Eileen that they had to stay in London as an example for others who had no possibility of leaving, even though they both hated it there, and even though they were continually risking death. 'You've got to stay here while the war's on,' Orwell told a friend. 'You can't leave when people are being bombed to hell.'[51]

Orwell realised Eileen was slowly wearing herself down, but he had no immediate solution, and she wasn't complaining enough for him to act. 'Eileen's chief concern remained, as before, George's health,' Lydia complained, as she watched Eileen struggling with 'the strain of too much work and not enough sleep'. 'Whenever I pleaded with her for wisdom of taking reasonable care of herself, she replied that it was George's health, not hers, that was valuable.'[52] After suffering with him through some debilitating bleeding eruptions, she eventually realised just how precarious his health was. And these days, if she possibly could, she would spend her lunch hour rushing back to prepare a good meal for Orwell whenever he was at home sick, 'so that he had fresh vegetables,' as a friend put it. One time, when Eileen knew she would be at Greenwich for a few days, she left 'some quite nice fish [she'd cooked] for him, and she boiled some eel for the cat,' the friend continued. 'Well, George apparently absent-mindedly ate the eel, and I suppose the cat had the other stuff!'⁵³ The couple were also known for sharing their rations with people who, they felt, needed them more, and some friends were sure this contributed to their constant ill health. However, another friend was doubtful that Eileen and Orwell 'starved during the war by giving away all their rations'.⁵⁴

Although she defiantly ignored her own increasing ailments, by November, just five months after losing her brother, Eileen's health had deteriorated so badly that she had to take over a month off work. 'I have been ILL. Ever so ill. Bedridden for 4 weeks & still weak,' she wrote to Norah in early December. Her doctors were unable to discover exactly what her illness was, and Eileen went off on a playful rant against them: 'They diagnosed cystitis and then they diagnosed nephrolithiasis & then they diagnosed Malta fever with ovarian complications & then they went all hush-hush while they diagnosed a tuberculous infection . . . They haven't yet diagnosed cancer or G.P.I. [general paralysis of the insane], but I expect they will shortly.' She summed up the whole experience: 'So now I hear I'll be cured when I weigh 9 stone [57 kg]. As my present weight is 7st 12 [50 kg] with my clothes on I think perhaps they'll lose interest before the cure is complete.'⁵⁵ As always, she was able to joke about serious matters. Although it can't be proved at this late date, it's quite possible Eileen was suffering from endometriosis, a disease with symptoms similar to hers, which could have explained her inability to get pregnant. Very little was known about endometriosis in 1945, though it's now estimated that perhaps one in ten women suffer from it, and many have been successfully treated in recent years.

Eileen mentioned to Norah that 'I may give up this job for a bit anyway & perhaps see for myself after all,' which is a bit confusing. However, that was at the beginning of December, and she ended up staying at that job until the following summer. Eileen never admitted to herself that overwork, combined with her desolation after losing her brother, could be contributing to her own deteriorating health. It's possible she wasn't aware of the deadly gene in her family history that had killed her father's father as well as his newspaperman brother, her talented uncle, both at a young age. And she might never have been told that her mother's mother had died in childbirth, if indeed her mother even knew this. But she had never forgotten her own narrow escape from death when she suffered as a teenager from the deadly Spanish flu pandemic at the end of the First World War. She never considered any of these things as relevant to her current illnesses, and perhaps she was right.

After two weeks of convalescence with her mother's family in Norfolk, Eileen once again planned to visit Norah in Bristol, after previous attempts had been thwarted by Orwell's bouts of 'bronchitis'. But this time she had to cancel because of her own illness. 'I had arranged a long weekend (which I was going to spend with <u>you</u>) because the pain was worse but then it got a lot worse & the long weekend was merged in sick leave,'[56] she told Norah. However, since it was December, Eileen was looking forward with some of her usual delight to shopping for Christmas presents. 'I am now allowed to go shopping on medical grounds though the financial ones aren't so good,' she joked. Unfortunately, after 'having walked twelve or fourteen miles to find mother <u>soft</u> slippers with heels, I had to buy everyone else hcfs [handkerchiefs] in a horrible shop,'[57] she complained, nostalgic for the years when she had carefully sought out splendid gifts for all her friends. Christmas was very important to Eileen, and even when she was ill in Morocco, she had chosen to spend a harrowing afternoon trying to find the perfect gifts for everyone. One aged relative still remembers the gorgeous silk scarf of different shades of blue that she got one Christmas from Eileen – whom she remembered as 'very thin, neatly dressed, with very dark hair, and jolly good company'.[58]

Another constant occupation during the Blitz was taking care of friends who were bombed out of their homes or just caught away from home during a blackout. Visitors often ended up sleeping on sofas or carpets in their friends' homes after dinner. Eileen and Orwell had always welcomed overnight company, and they had a camp bed for anyone who was stranded and gladly shared whatever dinner Eileen had prepared that evening. One friend recalled that they were 'always hard up, always bombed out, always in difficulties, but always helping somebody else, and never really ruffled by their difficulties'.[59] This casual and often impulsive behaviour was accepted by their friends, but often these 'difficulties' were caused by their sometimes whimsical choices, as well as by their total lack of concern for the risky outcomes that might result. Occasionally they themselves were forced to spend the night with friends when it was too dangerous after dinner to find their way home in the dark. Lydia remembered that Eileen had once arrived at her flat 'with a large bruise on her forehead' after 'she had walked into a lamp-post in the black-out'.[60] On a visit to Gwen in Greenwich, an unusual incident impressed Orwell so much that he described it at considerable length in his diary. When they discovered that a mouse had fallen into a deep sink and couldn't manage to climb up the slippery side, they went to 'great pains to make a sort of staircase of boxes of soap flakes, etc., by which it could climb out', he wrote, but to no avail. Finally, Eileen took control of the situation – as she often had to – and 'gently took [the mouse] out with her fingers and let it go'.[61]

For well over a year in London, Orwell was unable to get a well-paying job. He continued to review films and plays, but he also managed to write a copious number of essays and to review a massive number of books, receiving some compensation for this. During those months, however, with Eileen no longer able to type and retype all his work, he was forced to change his routine. 'Nowadays when I write a review, I sit down at the typewriter and type it straight out', he noted in his diary. 'Till recently, indeed till six months ago . . . virtually all that I write was written at least twice, and my books as a whole three times – individual passages as many as five or ten times.' He concluded, 'It is a deterioration directly due to the war.'[62] Although he blamed this change of routine on 'the war', the explicit difference was that Eileen was no longer free to be his constant assistant. After some months, while she continued to help with all his rewrites, they must have agreed that the reviews would be just fine as first drafts. However, during those months Orwell also wrote some of his most significant essays, including 'The Lion and the Unicorn', which Eileen described ironically as 'A little book . . . explaining how to be a Socialist though Tory.'[63] These long essays needed revisions, and Eileen certainly found time for this important work.

Eileen did not feel she was 'sacrificing' herself for Orwell, and he didn't think he was overworking her. When he told friends that Eileen could have been a writer herself, he was acknowledging that she had given up a possible writing career to help strengthen his, as well as acknowledging her astuteness and way with words. They now shared the understanding that Orwell's writing was their most important occupation. 'Both Eileen and Gwen insistent that I should go to Canada if the worst comes to the worst, in order to stay alive and keep up propaganda,'[64] Orwell wrote at the end of June 1940. But he was not interested in saving his life 'as a refugee'. 'Better to die if necessary, and maybe even as propaganda one's death might achieve more than going abroad,' he wrote, adding, 'Not that I want to die; I have so much to live for, in spite of poor health and having no children.'[65] A year earlier he had told Jack Common, 'If I was biologically a good specimen and capable of founding a new dynasty, I would devote all my energies during the war to keeping alive and keeping out of sight.'[66] But he was now convinced that this fantasy future was futile. Although Orwell did not directly mention Eileen here, he was well aware of how important her dedication was and of how much he relied on her being close by for his development as a positive voice during those years of fear and confusion. And still in the back of his mind was the hope that Eileen would eventually get pregnant.

Eileen also had her mother to worry about. She told Lydia, 'No one knows what illness Mother has. She isn't really ill, she's just fading away.' Her mother was so saddened by Eric's death that 'she just appeared to grow more frail with every week that passed', Lydia remembered.[67] When Eric died, Eileen's mother was living at 65 Pevensey Road, possibly a retirement home, in St Leonards-on-Sea, on the south coast. And in her letter to Norah in December, Eileen said, 'Mother is still away of course.'[68] Her use of the phrase 'of course' is confusing. Perhaps she didn't quite understand why her mother wasn't with her in London, considering how ill she was herself. Or at least close by so that they could share each other's sorrow.

By 20 March, her mother was in a Greenwich hospital, and Eileen was staying with Gwen, as she still often did. Orwell telephoned her there, after a night of heavy raids, and he recorded the unusual phone call in his diary: 'A lot of bombs at Greenwich, one of them while I was talking to Eileen over the 'phone. A sudden pause in the conversation and a tinkling sound: I. "What's that?" E. "Only the windows falling in."'[69] A bomb had just hit in Greenwich Park, across from the house, and soon the nearby church was on fire, with the crypt full of families who had sheltered there. But Eileen, with her mother now near death, had refused to react with panic. A few days later, after scoffing to Norah at the possibility of dying herself, she wrote with black humour, 'NOTHING EVER HAPPENS TO Pig.'[70] And again Orwell confided to his diary, 'The feeling of helplessness is growing in everyone.'[71]

Sometime near the end of March, Eileen told Norah, 'The difficulty is that I'm too profoundly depressed to write a letter.' Mary O'Shaughnessy had died, on 21 March, of 'Coronary Thrombosis, Cerebral Arteriosclerosis, Heart Failure,' and this letter must have been written shortly after. Eileen had badly wanted to visit Norah, and in her depression about her mother, she allowed herself to complain honestly about how Orwell's illnesses had often restricted her personal freedom. She told Norah, 'It is literally years since a weekend belonged to me & George would have a haemorrhage.'[72] This was a rare admission. Unable to visit her good friend yet again, she was blunt for once. She never suggested that Orwell embellished his illnesses just to keep her at home, but some of her friends were suspicious that was the case.

Mary O'Shaughnessy was a patient at Miller Hospital in Greenwich, the same hospital where Orwell had been treated in March 1939, and her doctor is listed as J. S. Morlock. However, no such doctor is listed as working at that hospital then, so perhaps Orwell's doctor, Herbert Victor Morlock, attended her. Her age is recorded as seventy, but she would really have been seventy-five. Orwell was the 'Informant' on the death certificate, relieving Eileen of that depressing task. In her will, written on 15 August 1930, shortly after her husband died, Eileen's mother left everything to Eileen, even though her son, Eric, was still alive at the time. Eileen inherited £895 and the Harefield house, her parents' home that she had shared with her mother just after her father died. Since the net value of her inheritance was only £94, it can be assumed the house came with a mortgage. For the next four years, Eileen received rent from this house as she confronted its burdensome upkeep, but she never got around to selling it. After her own death, Orwell had some difficulty finally dealing with this property, which he no longer wanted to own.[73]

In her March letter to Norah, Eileen told her friend that she and Orwell were planning to move to an unfurnished flat, a slightly larger one, and that she hoped they might actually share their lives completely once again. Her mother had just died, Gwen had sent her son to Canada and didn't need her presence as much any more, and Eileen was now ready to dedicate all her energy to Orwell once again. But she was pessimistic about life in general, and distraught at the endless air raids and blackout dangers, telling Norah that their plans would probably 'be frustrated by continued lack of five shillings to spend & increasing scarcity of undemolished flats & perhaps by our ceasing to live anywhere.'[74] She didn't mention any bomb damage to the Dorset Chambers flat, but friends hinted there had been enough disruption to hasten the idea of moving. One friend said, 'They were bombed in real earnest, and they came and stayed with us for the few days that it took Eileen to find and furnish a new place.'[75] But Dorset Chambers, later called Chagford House, was still standing, with many improvements, in

1985.[76] Some friends believed that Orwell was concerned about Eileen's safety, and thought the new building was more solidly constructed. Whatever the actual circumstances, on 1 April 1941, Eileen and Orwell did move to 111 Langford Court – on the corner of Abbey Road, about two blocks from what would become the Beatles' Abbey Road studio – an eight-storey building with an occasionally working lift and, as it turned out, more room for extra beds for visitors caught in the blackouts.

Although it has been reported that their flat, No. 111, was on the fifth floor of this building, it was in fact another top-floor flat, with noticeably lower ceilings, on inspection from inside and out, than on the floors below, yet another handicap for the tall Orwell. The doorman said recently that he was not aware that this flat had been occupied by Orwell at one time, and there is no plaque commemorating him. This is almost certainly the building that Orwell referenced as Victory Mansions in *Nineteen Eighty-Four*. Some have suggested that their flat on Canonbury Square, where they moved in 1944, was his model, but that building is only four storeys tall and had no lift. Orwell wrote in his novel that the hallway smelled of boiled cabbage, and that Winston Smith had to climb seven flights to get to his flat, because the lift seldom worked. The flats in their new building were rented almost entirely by 1930s European refugees, hence the cabbage reference, which seems a little out of place at the time portrayed in the novel. A friend remembered that Eileen was shocked enough one day to phone her with 'the sensational news' that she had actually met *another* Englishwoman in the lift and 'they had fallen on each other's necks'.[77] The structure of this building was indeed sound, and it survived the war, though they had many close calls while they were living there.

Two weeks after they'd moved in, they went to a pub to listen to the nine o'clock news, the best way to keep up with the progress of the war. They arrived a bit late and asked the landlady what news they had missed. 'Oh, we never turn it on,' she told them. 'Nobody listens to it, you see. And they've got the piano playing in the other bar, and they won't turn it off just for the news.'[78] As Orwell commented, 'You have all the time the sensation of kicking against an impenetrable wall of stupidity.' But then he added proudly, 'Any European nation situated as we are would have been squealing for peace long ago.'[79] Somehow the London citizens, living in fear every day, had agreed to 'Keep Calm and Carry On,' as the Ministry of Information hoped they would.

The next night, there was a very heavy raid, 'probably the heaviest in many months' in London. We know Eileen and Orwell slept closely in bed because, as he poignantly told her, 'Sometimes I know when [a bomb] is getting nearer in the night because I feel your heart beating faster against me.'[80] That evening, 'The guns kept up their racket nearly all night,' Orwell recorded, and 'Today I can find no one who admits to having slept last night, and Eileen says the same. The formula is: "I never closed my eyes for an instant."' But, he added, 'I believe this is all nonsense.' Eileen and Orwell were getting used to the constant barrage, and they assumed their friends were also, even though they were refusing to admit it. Orwell concluded, 'Certainly it is hard to sleep in such a din, but Eileen and I must have slept quite half the night.'[81] Nevertheless, the continuation of the random but intense bombing, compounded by her serious physical ailments, was rattling Eileen's nerves. In a letter to a friend, she tried to joke about the stress, but it's impossible to laugh when you read her words: 'Physical condition – much improved by air raids, possibly because I now sleep several hours a night longer than ever in my life; Mental condition – temporarily improved by air raids which were a change, degenerating again now that air raids threaten to become monotonous.'[82]

A few days after that intense night they went to Wallington again. As Orwell mused on one of their monthly visits, 'Now and again in this war, at intervals of months, you get your nose above water for a few moments and notice that the earth is still going round the sun.'[83] On this visit, they expected to escape the noise, but 'Saturday night's blitz could easily be heard there – 45 miles distant.'[84] During these raids, Marx was 'subdued and uneasy', but Eileen wasn't surprised because, whenever she visited Greenwich, 'All the dogs in the park now bolt for home when they hear the siren.'[85] While at the cottage, they sowed '40 or 50 lb of potatoes, which might give 200 to 600 lbs according to the season, etc.'[86] There was already a scarcity of some foods, and Orwell noted that 'The onion shortage has made everyone intensely sensitive to the smell of onions . . . Eileen the other day knew as soon as I kissed her that I had eaten onions some 6 hours earlier.'[87] They believed, rightly so, that in the future there would be a period of serious rationing of food, and Orwell mused, 'Those potatoes [might] seem a more important achievement than all the articles, broadcasts, etc. I shall have done this year.'[88] However, as it turned out, their crop was far from magnificent, and England soon had so many potatoes, combined with so few other goods, that it became necessary to promote the food value of the lowly potato to sceptical citizens.

While at the cottage, Orwell was also making and acquiring different types of artillery and bombs. One friend remembered that 'Eileen used to get fed up with all the weapons around,' and once told her, 'I can put up with bombs on the mantelpiece, but I will not have a machine gun under the bed.'[89] Orwell had joined the Home Guard in June, right after moving back to London, when he was rejected for any other military service because of his recurring 'bronchitis'. As he phrased it, he reluctantly held 'what half the men in this country would give their balls for'[90]– an exemption. But he believed that '[T]he Home Guard would become the revolutionary militia of the impending insurrection,'[91] and that belief strengthened his enthusiasm for the outfit. When his nephew Henry Dakin stayed with them for a few weeks in London, he remembered that 'At the weekend, Uncle Eric would appear in full regalia as a sergeant in the Home Guard, boots shining and rifle at the ready.'[92] Fredric Warburg, who served with Orwell, remembered 'the zeal which inflamed his tall skinny body. His uniform was crumpled, but it had been cut to fit him by a good tailor.'[93] On one cottage visit, there was an unexpected knock at the door, and by this time their reaction to strangers was no longer automatically welcoming. Eileen told a friend that 'George immediately picked up his gun, stood behind the door at the ready, tense,' then asked her to open the door. The plan was that 'if it was an unwelcome visitor he could be shot forthwith!'[94]

Back sleeping in their new London flat, on 10 May, barely six weeks after they had moved in, there was 'a devastating crash, which woke us up but did not break the windows or noticeably shake the room,' Orwell noted in his diary. 'The first time this has happened to any house I have been in.' One of Hitler's most furious attacks on London occurred that night, just as he was being forced to realise that Britain might never surrender. 'Eileen got up and went to the window, where she heard someone shouting that it was this house that had been hit,' Orwell wrote. One might assume they would leave the building at that point, but, instead, 'Going up on the roof, saw enormous fires at most points of the compass . . . with huge leaping flames . . . Smoke was drifting over the roof . . . By this time the smoke was thick enough to make it difficult to see down the passage.' So, finally, 'We slipped on some clothes, grabbed up a few things and went out.' Summing up later, as Orwell so casually phrased it, 'Actually all that had happened was that the bomb had set fire to the garage and burned out the cars that were in it.' When they were back in their own flat, Orwell 'remarked on Eileen's blackened face, and she said "What do you think your own is like?"'[95]

This was most likely the raid that a friend remembered Eileen telling her about. As Eileen was going down the smoke-filled stairs to the street, 'There was an elderly woman . . . crouching down in the hall trembling.'[96] Eileen saw Orwell next to the woman, 'kneeling on the floor by her, looking, [Eileen] said, like Christ and putting his hand on her head and his arms round her shoulders and comforting her.'[97] The friend concluded that Orwell 'was compassionate, though more so to strangers than to people in his immediate entourage, including his wife.'[98] But Eileen was impressed that, in the midst of all this turmoil, Orwell was able to hug and comfort a stranger. Although he might not have been able to find the right words to console Eileen through this debilitating year, he knew how important a hug could be.

They definitely had their share of close calls, and one of the final London bombings in May affected them deeply. Their friend Mark Benney was also not healthy enough for the army, and he and Orwell shared the shame of 'walking the streets, obviously of military age and without apparent disability, in civilian clothes'.[99] Benney's wife and Eileen lunched together frequently and the men 'were drawn into the kind of spurious companionship that befalls husbands when their energetic wives decide to see more of each other'. Shortly after the garage of their own building had been hit, Eileen and Orwell were having dinner at the Benneys' flat – 'quite a spread to console them for their ill-luck', including 'a rare bottle of claret' – when 'a bomb fell some fifty yards away and we were lifted out of our seats by the blast', their dinner host remembered. Orwell's comment was simply, 'If we'd been in one of those working-class hovels round the corner we'd be dead as mutton now!' But 'Eileen cried, incredulously, "No, no – not *again!*"' She had clearly had enough. 'When we picked ourselves up the room was covered with the fine splinters from the shattered window, and the only light came from the incendiary bombs burning in the street outside', Benney added, 'but none of us was hurt'.[100] At that point, after many months of serious bombing of Britain, Hitler changed plans again, deciding to attack Russia instead, and for about three years German soldiers were busy elsewhere.

Orwell could see that all this chaos was interfering with Eileen's recovery from her losses. In fact, at this point her health was deteriorating enough that he began to seriously worry. Lydia noticed that Eileen 'seemed to have less energy. Less sparkle. She seemed to me always tired. She neglected her health.' In fact, Lydia was pessimistic about Eileen's ever recovering, adding, perhaps prophetically, 'I think there was a death wish there as well'.[101] Finally, towards the end of June, Eileen agreed to quit her much-hated Ministry of Information job. 'For more than a year Eileen was working in the Censorship Department, but I have induced her to drop it for a while,' Orwell told a friend at that point, somehow underestimating her almost two years at the hated job. The fact that Sir Walter Monckton decided to leave the Ministry at about this point could have been another factor in Eileen's departure. In Monckton's diary of that time, he noted, enigmatically, what looks like 'Lunch E. B.,' but this is impossible to interpret. Eileen 'is going to have a good rest and then perhaps get some less futile and exasperating work to do,'[102] Orwell said. He blamed the job for 'upsetting her health', but he surely knew the other devastating factors involved.

From July 1941 until early in 1942, Eileen had no paying job. She slowly started to get her light-hearted sense of humour back, helped by the fact that Hitler had turned his attention to Russia. But her physical ailments were intruding more often. Near the end of 1941, when a friend 'met Orwell and Eileen a few times in pubs . . . I was glad to see her recovered from the blow of her brother's death, outwardly anyway,' he recalled, adding, 'I had a strong feeling, however, that she did not really like pubs but she loyally sat alongside Orwell, sipping her beer. I thought him lucky to have a wife who looked after him so well.'[103] In the only existing photo of Eileen at that time, sitting in a pub with a glass of wine, she looks patient but exhausted.

Along with his other odd jobs after moving to London, Orwell had been preparing successful and respected radio programmes on literary themes for the BBC.[104] By the summer of 1941, criticism of the BBC's regular broadcasts to India had increased, and Orwell's programmes were considered a better competition for Indian listeners, who were then enjoying 'the racy style' of German propaganda.[105] Consequently, in August 1941, shortly after Eileen quit her job, Orwell was hired full-time as a Talks Assistant for the BBC's Eastern Service. He earned a salary of £640 a year,[106] at last a well-paying job, and, as usual, he threw himself compulsively into his work. Although he described the 'atmosphere' of the BBC as 'something half way between a girls' school and a lunatic asylum,'[107] Orwell proved excellent at compiling stimulating radio programmes to broadcast to India, featuring famous British authors such as T. S. Eliot, Rebecca West, and E. M. Forster, among many others. This series of programmes had challenging topics – 'Books That Changed the World' and 'Emancipation of Women', for example – and he even created a 'Magazine Programme' on the air, with participants commenting on poems as they were broadcast. Might Eileen have been helping him with these programmes? Desmond Avery, the author of *Orwell at the BBC in 1942*, said that while researching his book he 'was often puzzled by how academically thorough [Orwell] seemed to be . . . Some of the subjects he wrote about would have come up in conversation' with Eileen. He noticed 'how much deeper [Orwell's] critical intelligence and wider his knowledge became after their marriage'. He added, 'Looking at the wide range of well-informed writings Orwell published during his time at the BBC, I felt sure Eileen must have helped with at least some of them.' He believed that 'Orwell always conspicuously needed help,' including from, among others, Richard Rees, Mabel Fierz, and his sister Avril, but 'probably [from] Eileen most of all.'[108]

As part of this job, Orwell also wrote throughout the two years over 200 weekly newsletters, having now acquired a couple of secretaries to type his work-related letters and scripts. But that didn't stop him from writing outside the job, managing to prepare a long 'London Letter' every two months for the American *Partisan Review* as well as many extensive essays and the occasional book review. Eileen began once again devoting much of her time to his creative work, as well as cooking for their many dinner and overnight guests. She hated the fact that Orwell was forced to take this job and waste what turned out to be over two years of the limited time she knew he had left. But they needed the money and she was too ill to work herself.

One day, shortly after Orwell started at his new job, he approached a fellow BBC worker, saying, 'Come along to tea on Sunday. My wife isn't a bad old stick.'[109] The new acquaintance found this description of Eileen 'extraordinary'. Others also remember Orwell describing Eileen as 'a good old stick'. But this could be interpreted as a sign that Orwell considered Eileen a close and trusted friend, and someone he knew would welcome unexpected strangers arriving at odd times. The fellow worker did accept the invitation to tea, and he remembered Eileen as 'a very nice, very tired-looking person'.[110]

Being at home through those first months of his new job, Eileen was also there to care for Orwell during his increasingly frequent illnesses. He was at home sick for two weeks in October, just over a month after he had started the job, and again for three weeks in December,[111] as well as for a few days in February.[112] The wife of another fellow worker at the BBC said that Eileen talked with her 'quite frankly' about the smell of Orwell's 'rotting lungs', and what she called 'a sweetish smell of decay' that was most intense in a confined room.[113] Eileen was now Orwell's primary carer. How she must have missed her brother, the one person with the skills and stubborn opinions who might have known how to prolong Orwell's life, since he had been experimenting, just before the war, with ways 'to develop and further the surgical methods in the treatment of pulmonary tuberculosis'.[114]

For over two years, Orwell devoted his vast creative intensity to preparing these impressive programmes for educated listeners in India. Yet, he was never sure how many people actually heard them. He complained in his diary the next spring about 'the ultimate futility of what we are doing',[115] though he did hear later that Indians had always looked forward to his programmes. However, the work consumed so much of his creative energy that he came to believe he had indeed wasted two years there. Orwell participated in countless variations of these radio broadcasts, but no recordings have survived. So, amazingly, there is no existing record of Orwell's actual voice, and thus no way to form an opinion on how 'unfortunate' a voice he really had.

On 18 December 1941, conscription for women was imposed, requiring all women without young children to help in the war effort. Eileen was beginning to recover some of her old vitality, and to feel well enough to take on something new, so she explored the idea of working again.

14

Coming into Her
Own at Last

*When Eileen was going out for the evening, she
would dress up to the point where she looked
'quite dazzling.'*

Henry Dakin

Early in 1942, Eileen began working in the Public Relations
Department of the Ministry of Food, a job she truly enjoyed.
Lord Woolton had been appointed Minister of Food in April
1940, and when rationing later became necessary, his Ministry was
responsible for distributing fairly whatever produce was available, while
also helping housewives adapt to these shortages. 'It was necessary
for us to devise publicity that would appeal to every individual
woman in the country,' he believed, and 'to sell an idea . . . requires
an understanding not only of the technique of publicity but of the
psychology of the individual.'[1]

The Kitchen Front, a five-minute radio programme broadcast by the
BBC at 8:15 in the morning, right after the 8 a.m. news, was one of his
creations. Beginning on 11 June 1940, the programme presented recipes

for housewives that had been tested in the Ministry of Food kitchens, using the limited ingredients that were available during the war. On some days presenters would give general cooking and nutritional advice. At first, these five minutes were scheduled irregularly every week, with broadcaster Freddie Grisewood interviewing special guests, but in May 1941, the programme was extended to six mornings a week and included three regular speakers in addition to Grisewood.[2] When a survey in September found that housewives were, in general, 'quite satisfied' with the programme,[3] discussions were held on how to use these five minutes a day, six days a week, most effectively.

By early 1942, when *The Kitchen Front* had become increasingly important for housewives, Lord Woolton decided to increase the staff. Howard Marshall, one of the most skilful broadcasters in the country at that time, became the Director of Public Relations, and Eileen, with her background in psychology as well as her skills as a cook, was hired to work along with Robert Westerby as a second officer in the Public Relations Department. Since Orwell was working at the BBC at the time and knew Westerby from the days before the war, he might have helped set this up. Also, Harman Grisewood, Freddie Grisewood's cousin and a BBC employee, had been Eileen's fellow student at Oxford. Whichever way she got the job, there's no doubt that once again Eileen knew 'somebody who knew somebody, etc., etc.,'[4] in Orwell's words. The earliest surviving work letter by Eileen is dated 28 February 1942, but it is clear from its content that she had already been in the job for some time.

Eileen was hired as a liaison between the Ministry of Food, where the recipes were tested and the scripts edited and approved, and the BBC, where the programmes were broadcast. 'People invited to broadcast on *The Kitchen Front* submitted scripts and recipes and Eileen had to see that the final version was in a form that satisfied both the BBC and the Ministry of Food,' according to a woman who was a Ministry of Food official. 'It was not an easy job but she did it with great skill and tact.'[5] After the new recipes were approved, Eileen would make sure the scripts were appropriate for a five-minute presentation. The ingredients had to be recited at just the right speed, and with just the right amount of repetition, to give the listeners time to copy them down. The BBC staff needed to check the broadcasting quality of all the new speakers, and Eileen also oversaw that process. 'Inevitably there were sometimes differences of opinion between the Ministry, the script writer and the BBC,' the Ministry official remembered. 'Mrs. Blair had to see a reasonable compromise was reached and an approved script produced.'⁶ It quickly became a popular programme for housewives, and many complimentary articles were written about the series. However, from the very beginning, serious conflicts arose between the two departments, and they were never completely resolved.

With her new, more rewarding job at the Ministry of Food, and Orwell almost completely entangled in his time-consuming work at the BBC, Eileen began to enjoy a much more independent phase of her life. And with her new income added to Orwell's, the couple were at last free from their years of skimping. Lettice Cooper, who later became the president of PEN, was one of the first people Eileen met at her new job, and they quickly became close friends. 'She walked into my room at the ministry forty years ago, and I can see her as clearly as if it had been this morning,' Lettice wrote in 1984. 'She was very pretty, and had what George called "a cat's face", blue eyes and near black hair.'⁷ Lettice remembered Eileen as 'very thoughtful and philosophical, and very much interested in everything.'⁸ The two women worked side by side for over two years, and together they interviewed 'would-be speakers, of whom there were a large circle who used to visit us weekly in the hope of getting jobs, and who vigorously tried to impress us with their personalities,'⁹ Lettice remembered. These women, prominent in their various fields, appeared on Eileen's *Kitchen Front* programmes, reciting scripts she often wrote for them,¹⁰ as well as at Food Meetings that Lettice scheduled throughout the city. Some of them were so anxious to have their five minutes on the air that

Eileen would groan, 'Oh, I hope I don't have to see any more women of great vitality this week!'[11] Another part of Lettice's job was to see 'that all the people who wrote personal letters to Lord Woolton got individual answers'.[12] He later acknowledged that his responses to listeners 'were largely conducted for me by a lady novelist, Miss Lettice Cooper'.[13]

Eileen had a secretary to type her letters as well as to put the scripts she had worked on into the proper form, and she and her new friend 'had a lot of spare time while our work was being typed', Lettice said. 'We spent a good deal of it across the road in Selfridge's coffee bar' talking about books and food as well as confiding their work problems to each other.[14] Spending so much time away from the office was 'frowned on by our bosses', according to Lettice, 'but we did it anyway'.[15] With their increased income, Eileen and Orwell often ate at restaurants, able to avoid some of the food shortages that affected many others in London. They certainly were not starving themselves, as some have suggested, even as they continued to be generous with their rations. 'Eileen and I had lunch together each day', Lettice remembered, 'and we lurched around fairly energetically and humorously to find what was the best cheap buy, whose corn beef, fritters or shepherds' pie was the best that week.'[16]

One of the first programmes developed for the expanded *Kitchen Front* series was based on *The Buggins Family*, a series of comic radio skits that Mabel Constanduros had written and performed in for years. These early shows included the characters Grandma, her daughter Mrs Buggins, and her grandchildren Emma and Alfie, as well as, occasionally, Mr Buggins. Several of those recordings have survived. In them, Grandma and Mrs Buggins are portrayed as somewhat mean-spirited and petty, and both are acted in a sometimes aggressive and sarcastic voice, with a rather broad sense of humour. When Lord Woolton decided that '[T]he public was either going to laugh or to cry about food rationing, and that it was better for them that they should laugh,'[17] an adaptation of Constanduros's skits was suggested for use on *The Kitchen Front*.

On 7 October 1941, Jean Rowntree, a producer at the BBC, asked Constanduros whether she would be interested in doing a series of four talks for *The Kitchen Front*, 'in the form of a family discussion', on Tuesday mornings, starting on 28 October. 'The object of these talks would be to lighten the series and attract a new audience, and at the same time to get across some useful information on wartime food questions,'[18] she explained. Constanduros answered immediately that she was interested, but she requested the favour of recording them at home in Evesham to avoid travel and hotel costs. 'I'd like to give them a useful food hint or recipe every time', she wrote, adding, 'It can be wrapped up in comedy dialogue.'

A series of pre-recorded trial talks were broadcast between 28 October 1941 and 3 February 1942. The Ministry of Food would send her recipes to use, and she would write comedic scripts that included reciting the recipe ingredients. On these shows, which included Grandma, her daughter, and two grandchildren, Constanduros said that she played Mrs Buggins and used Gladys Young – an actress who later had a successful film career – for one of the other characters. Mrs Buggins, who presented the recipes for the most part, often teased and criticised Grandma, who had a smaller part. And the recipes were often too complicated to be easily copied down by a listener, as they crammed in a dessert recipe along with the main meal. However, these programmes were 'very much appreciated by the listeners', and the series formally began on 10 February, continuing on a fortnightly basis.

When Eileen started her job, it can be assumed that one of her early assignments was to work with Constanduros preparing the scripts. The shows for 10 and 24 February and 10 March, which were broadcast live in London, have only two characters, Mrs Buggins and Grandma. In the shows recorded in Evesham, the Mrs Buggins character, played by Constanduros, was the primary voice, but on the 10 February live show, Grandma dominated, using a heavy Cockney accent and getting the best jokes, while Mrs Buggins became more polite and secondary. It seems likely that at this point Constanduros began playing the

Grandma role, while someone else played Mrs Buggins. The tone of the first live London shows was also significantly changed from the *Buggins Family* days as well as from the trial shows that were recorded in Evesham. For the most part, the *Kitchen Front* scripts from 10 February onwards were more joyful, with a gentler humour. Each skit began with some comedic repartee between Mrs Buggins and Grandma, after which the characters go on to recite the recipe, but now they repeat the ingredients more slowly, so the listeners have time to jot them down.

Eileen's influence on the scripts seems likely when certain lines are read. For example, in one script, a bit of old-fashioned class critique was displayed, in a way that's reminiscent of Eileen's wit. In that show, Grandma had the line: '[My marge] was took from me by a woman in the bus . . . I know I 'ad that marge when I got in the bus, and I see this woman ogglin' my basket, and I remember 'er brushin' against me when I got out . . . A woman in a fur coat, too . . . But a fur coat don't always cover a honest 'eart, I know that.' Other shows attempted to convince wives that there were still ways to please their husbands with delicious dinners even as they were forced to use the awkward combination of rations available to them. Considering that Eileen's role by then was as cook for a sometimes cranky husband, these shows have a touch of Eileen's playful approach, teasing the characters while always allowing them to be very likeable. For example, in one show, Grandma said, 'If you want to be 'appy when you're married, you got to learn to cook. A man don't think of 'is wife's face when 'e comes 'ome, you know. 'E thinks of 'is dinner.' In another one, Grandma had the line, 'If ever you meet a man you can't cook into a good 'umour don't 'ave nothink to do with 'im.' However, as another show warned, 'It don't do to cook too well' for your husband, because then you 'shan't never git rid of 'im.' Other examples of Eileen's possible contributions include the complaint in one show about a friend's husband who 'won't do without 'is cup o' tea at nights. You never saw such a chap for tea. Wants it three or four times a day,' a possible reference to Orwell, who always had a large pot of tea nearby. In another show, the two women bemoaned the shortage of eggs. Mrs Buggins was upset when, in a movie she had seen, 'They sat down and started to fry eggs and bacon at a picnic. Egg after egg they chucked into that frying pan till I could 'ave screamed.' However, Constanduros had a similar sense of humour to Eileen's, so it's almost impossible to separate their contributions to the dialogue. By the end of 1942, this show, described as 'Cockney back-chat with recipes,' was the most popular *Kitchen Front* programme.[19] Eileen didn't like taking credit for her work, and never mentioned helping with these skits, but a case can be made that she did.

Eileen liked nicknames, calling herself 'Pig' with her Oxford friends, as we know, and she may very well have had another nickname at the Ministry of Information. Perhaps she even had one with Orwell. At this point, she had been known for six years as Eileen Blair, or Mrs Orwell, the wife of a man sought out for his prolific energy and brilliant insights. But now, at the Ministry of Food, with a job she liked, a job where her skills at organisation and cooking, as well as her competence as a mediator, were appreciated, Eileen chose yet another identity: Emily Blair. That's the name she signed all her work letters with. And Lettice and her other co-workers called her Emily. Nell Heaton, another fellow worker, wrote in the Foreword to one of her books, 'I owe a debt of gratitude . . . to George Orwell and Emily Blair, to whose sympathy and encouragement I owe so much,'[20] using the name Eileen was known by at work. Lettice couldn't remember why, but even forty years later she said, 'I find it difficult now to remember her as Eileen.'[21] And, indeed, Eileen's last letter to Lettice, in March 1945, is signed 'Emily.'

Taking her own individual name was a choice similar to the decision by some women today to keep their maiden name after marriage. And because Eileen called herself Emily Blair, some people she worked with had no idea she was the wife of the well-known writer George Orwell. They sought her friendship based on what she offered as a competent worker who could charm them with her ease at shooting off humorous quips. It must have been exhilarating for her. After interviewing people who had worked at the Ministry of Food, Bernard Crick, Orwell's first biographer, wrote, 'Eileen's friends of the Ministry days are all very firm that she was a remarkable person in her own right, who supported George completely, but did not allow her personality to be submerged by his, and kept her affection towards him while standing up to him, bringing him down to earth on small matters of fact.'[22] As Lettice summed it up, Eileen 'had a group of affectionate and admiring friends. I think no picture of her is complete which leaves that out.'[23]

But why did she pick the name 'Emily'? This mystery is perhaps solved when we discover that Mrs Buggins's first name was Emily. It seems entirely possible that Eileen – who enjoyed performing in school plays and was certainly theatrical in her personal life – convinced Constanduros to let her play the part of Emily Buggins in at least some of the first live *Kitchen Front* programmes that they worked on together. Constanduros had used Gladys Young for some of the parts when she recorded the original shows in Evesham, and the idea of playing Emily on the first live show would have immediately appealed to Eileen. Perhaps, if she agreed to let Eileen play Emily Buggins, Constanduros decided to make that character a kind of sane sidekick to the flamboyant Grandma, who began to dominate the programmes. The date of the first Buggins programme to be broadcast formally as part of *The Kitchen Front* was 10 February, which coincides with the first days of Eileen's work at the Ministry of Food. Emily Buggins was written as a delightful character with a lilting, on-and-off cockney accent who approached each new recipe and difficulty with all the good humour Eileen was once again enjoying. The only tape that survived from this long series was the beginning lines of one recorded on 27 May and broadcast on 16 June. There is no consensus as to whether Eileen was playing Emily Buggins on that tape, but there is still a slim chance that we actually have a recording of Eileen's voice.

In a curious footnote to this, the 1854 book *Lalla Rookh*, by

T. Moore – inscribed 'Emily Blair, January 28, 1857' – was in Orwell's collection when he died. That Emily Blair, born in 1838, was a distant relative of Orwell's,[24] and this had been offered as a wild guess as to why Eileen chose the name Emily. But that premise seems highly unlikely. Characteristic of her mischievous spirit, the name Eileen settled on was a playful choice, and such a subtle one that no one could remember why she had chosen it.

Yours sincerely,

Emily Blair
Public Relations Division.

Eileen's signature as Emily Blair, the name she used while working at the Ministry of Food.

Eileen's regular signature as Eileen Blair, for comparison.

A large collection of correspondence between the principals at the Ministry of Food and the BBC has survived. Eileen appears first in a letter she sent to Jean Rowntree of the BBC on 28 February 1942, a letter signed 'Emily Blair.'[25] To dispel any doubt that this letter was indeed written by Eileen, the word 'Blair' matches her existing signatures as 'Eileen Blair', while the E in Emily appears exactly like the E in Eileen. This first extant letter began, 'I am returning the two scripts from Mr. Hopkin. Mrs. Horton will not hear of them so I am afraid that is that.' Clearly she had already been at that job for some time. 'I am also enclosing two sets of recipes from a Miss Pamela Pain,' the letter continued. 'I think she cooks very attractively but our people feel that she is altogether too fancy. She may have some interesting ideas because she has apparently quite a collection of old cookery books that she uses – and, in spite of the Kitchen's qualms, she is, in fact, a practical housekeeper cooking with ordinary rations.' Following that, there are a few letters from Jean Rowntree enclosing recipes for Eileen to consider using on *The Kitchen Front*. If Eileen thought a recipe would be appropriate for one of the presenters, she would have it tested in the Ministry of Food kitchens. At one point, Eileen addressed the issue of the 'sheep's head script': 'I am nervous of arranging a broadcast on a rare commodity (though this may seem an odd description of a sheep's head) much in advance,' she wrote. 'These things have a habit of disappearing from the shops for no apparent reason.' But, she added, 'I do think it a good recipe.' Eileen's playful, easy-going sense of humour shines through in the more than thirty letters written by her – as well as many more to her and concerning her – that have survived. She started out in her new job gung-ho and full of spirited advice and creative solutions. But she later turned out to be a bit of a troublemaker.

Part of her job involved finding solutions to problems that were constantly arising. In a letter to Rowntree on 8 April, concerning the confusion between two separate food broadcasts, Eileen joked, 'The great public, of course, are quite unable to distinguish between Ministry of Food and B.B.C. talks on food – this is probably a bitter pill for you but has to be swallowed!' And in a footnote, she apologised for what she called 'the gin and cocoa contretemps'. 'As you know I couldn't help it,' she insisted. And soon afterwards, there was a double scheduling of speakers to be resolved. 'I have written to Mrs. Webb cancelling her broadcast for April 27th and Mr. Westerby has done the same for Mrs. Buggins on the 20th,' Eileen wrote. The only problem here is that Eileen had the dates wrong. These programmes were scheduled for 21 and 28 April. This confusion of dates also appeared in some of her later letters, suggesting that, with all her praised efficiency, Eileen was sometimes vague about exact details. 'The only thing that is still disturbing me about the business is your end of it. I mean your sufferings,' she told Rowntree, in this letter of apology. 'Anyway, by one means or another I hope the crises will become less frequent.'

But the 'crises' never stopped. The BBC staff felt the need 'to safeguard us against the Ministry's habit of making overtures to speakers before we have had a chance of checking their broadcasting records,' since apparently Eileen and Westerby would occasionally break this rule. In a detailed letter on 13 April, Eileen tried to get the process straight once and for all, but she ended her letter with, 'I'm not sure whether this would simplify or complicate our lives. I am in fact just beginning to see how this combined programme doesn't work' at all. And she was basically right, no matter how many attempts were made to sort things out. At one point Eileen asked Jean Rowntree, 'Could you have lunch with me one day next week? There is a pub called Shelley's in Albemarle Street which has large English meals and large tables on which we could spread the documentation and so clarify my mind.' This elegant pub still serves good food and has preserved those large, polished tables, and a visitor can easily visualise Eileen's ghost bending over her 'documentation' as she savours her meal. At another point, Eileen and Rowntree compiled a list of possible speakers who could quickly fill in, after someone had cancelled at the last minute, providing 'a safeguard against a repetition of last week's difficulty'. 'From my point of view, the more we have to pick from the better. I am particularly glad to see another man' on the list, Eileen said. She suggested they also include 'a small collection of woman writers' since, 'Women who write, like women who act, often make rather a cult of cooking.' Unfortunately, one woman whom Eileen particularly liked had been deemed 'difficult to handle', and at any rate could not be considered 'until her most unfortunate broadcast the other night . . . has been forgotten'. At another point, Eileen informed Rowntree that Ethel Mannin, a prominent left-wing writer, had written to the Ministry offering to help in some way. 'She has a remarkable personal popularity among women and I think would be a draw for us. On the other hand she has told Lettice Cooper that she does not wish to speak.' Eileen knew Mannin personally, and she added, 'I might be able to persuade her.' She then got Orwell to tell Mannin's husband that she was 'very anxious for Ethel Mannin to broadcast in *The Kitchen Front*',[26] and this request did the trick. After their many discussions, Rowntree reported, 'I find [Mrs Blair] very easy to co-operate with, and I think she sees the problems on both sides.'

Eileen and Rowntree continued to cooperate. After some new recipes had been tested, Eileen returned them to Rowntree, saying, 'Here are your two scripts. I am sorry they have been held up, but we have had that kind of week.' Commenting on one recipe that contained sardines, Eileen decided that, since 'there aren't enough sardines for the people who already wish to buy them,' they should not be used in a recipe. She then added as a droll aside, 'The Kitchen made some of the recipes (the flapjacks were delicious) and were a bit free with their fat apparently. You'll find it on the paper.' She concluded her letter, 'I do apologise for the unmannerly treatment of your script.'

By the spring of 1942, with their new well-paying jobs, and both of them in a stretch of good health, Eileen and Orwell felt they could at last afford a more spacious and more cheerful place to live. There was a break in the letters between Eileen and Rowntree at the beginning of May, so perhaps Eileen took a week or two off to move. Also, after being cancelled on 21 April, the Buggins show skipped the next scheduled time and did not appear again until 19 May, another clue pointing to the possibility that Eileen was playing Emily Buggins.

After a year in a small, low-ceilinged flat on the top floor at Langford Court, they moved to 10A Mortimer Crescent, a semi-detached, four-storey Victorian building, again just up from Abbey Road, where they rented the lower two floors and had the use of a large back garden. There were six similar pairs of attractive houses on that block when they moved in, but only one pair survived the war, numbers 6 and 7.[27] Their building resembled 6 Mortimer Crescent, the house on the right side of the remaining pair. This new flat, with its two spacious floors, gave them more room for their books, furnishings, and dinner gatherings, and the ground-level area doubled as a more private guest room for their constant visitors. Anthony Powell, not much impressed by his friends' lifestyle, recalled that 'the sitting room, with a general background of furniture dating from more prosperous generations of bygone Blairs, had two or three eighteenth-century family portraits hanging on the walls',[28] and Tosco Fyvel thought it was a 'remarkably dreary flat'.[29] But David Astor, who had recently met the couple, had a more pleasant memory: 'Their living rooms were very simple and agreeable; nothing very striking one way or the other, but I'd say just a touch of elegance.'[30] However, the new flat was also 'desperately cold and draughty' and often without hot water. One night, when a guest was wakened at 4 a.m. by the deafening blast from a local anti-aircraft battery, he heard his host come blundering downstairs to restoke the boiler. 'I'm rather glad to have been woken up', Orwell explained. 'It means we shall get some hot water in the morning.'[31]

Orwell's nephew, Henry Dakin, stayed here for a few weeks in 1942, when he was around sixteen.[32] He was hoping to land a job with Orwell's help, and he went out on a few interviews, though without any success. He remembers well the easy companionship between Eileen and Orwell. 'She obviously cared a great deal for Eric, as he did for her', Dakin believes. 'I do not remember any great show of affection, but then that was much the way of the Blairs.'[33] At a recent lunch with Henry, his wife Marjorie, and his two sisters, Jane Morgan and Lucy Bestley, Henry provided a written sheet of his fond memories of his aunt. 'Eileen was one of the nicest and least dressy women that I have ever known. A great deal of the time she wore her black overcoat – it was rather chilly in the flat – and chain-smoked cigarettes, letting the ash fall off the end of her cigarette and down her coat', he wrote. Eileen knew she and Orwell smoked too much, but she saw that as yet another thing to joke about. 'If George and I didn't smoke so much', she told a friend, 'we'd be able to afford a better flat.'[34] If only she'd also known that, if they didn't smoke so much, they might both have managed to live a little longer. Dakin's memories continued: 'Her hair, whilst rather curly, seemed in perpetual need of a comb, but through it all came the

Irish charm – she was originally an O'Shaughnessy – her delightful smile and her apparent interest in whatever subject was the topic. In the evening, after a 'quickly prepared but excellent supper', Orwell 'retired to his room and you could hear the typewriter clack clacking away whilst Eileen and myself talked or read or listened to the radio.'[35] When asked what he and Eileen had chatted about, he shrugged his shoulders as if their conversation was too insignificant to remember. He felt Orwell 'didn't notice Eileen's good cooking' or 'make the most of her', but she didn't complain. And Dakin did take note, as a young man would, that – although he was surprised Eileen 'didn't usually make the most of herself' around the house – when she was going out for the evening she would sometimes dress up to the point where she became 'quite dazzling.'[36] Jane Morgan saw Eileen in Bristol, when she picked up Marx after just returning from Morocco, and 'once or twice during the war'. She remembered her as an attractive woman who 'smoked a lot' and was 'laid-back, more a professional than a housewife'. With Eileen, 'Luxury and show didn't come into it.' Recently, as Morgan was preparing to move, she was surprised to discover that she owned a copy of Samuel Butler's *The Way of All Flesh*, with the signature 'Eileen O'Shaughnessy' inside, presumably from the time before she was married. This book was in Orwell's collection when he died, and must have gone to his sister Avril and then on to Jane.[37] Lucy Bestley was too young to remember Eileen, but she recalls being very fond of Marx.

Orwell and Eileen set out immediately to create a replica of their beloved cottage – which they had little spare time to visit any more – with flowers in the garden and a lathe downstairs, where Orwell could fool around with his carpentry. Even after his early attempt at bookshelves, which collapsed easily when a bomb dropped streets away, he loved working with wood. Unfortunately, with their full-time jobs, they were not able to care for the lovable Marx. So he stayed at Greenwich with Gwen, and then was taken to Norfolk, where Gwen moved her practice after the war. Catherine, Gwen O'Shaughnessy's adopted daughter, remembered Marx clearly. She was haunted for a long time after his tail got infected and the vet 'discovered that an elastic band had been wrapped tightly around it and was biting into his flesh'. She had kept it secret that she was the one who had applied the rubber band. 'I don't remember when he died but I was convinced for years that I had caused his death with this rubber band,' she said. 'I felt so guilty that I eventually confided in my mother and she told me he had died a natural death.'[38]

Lydia and a friend had taken over care of the cottage during the Blitz, and it's likely they sold off the chickens and goats. But now, with their large garden in London, Eileen and Orwell restored one element of cottage life they both missed – hens. One friend's chief memory, after spending a night at their new flat, was 'being woken by the clang of buckets as George fed his chickens at sunrise.'[39] He also never forgot Orwell's wise advice: 'It's not a good idea to give the chickens names,' he said, 'because then you can't eat them.'[40] It's not clear how many they purchased while living there, but one of Orwell's handiworks was building a new home for them. 'Busy at every odd moment making a hen-house,' he recorded in his diary that summer. 'This kind of thing now needs great ingenuity owing to the extreme difficulty of getting hold of timber.' Then he thought to add, 'No sense of guilt or time-wasting when I do anything of this type – on the contrary, a vague feeling that any sane occupation must be useful, or at any rate justifiable.'[41] Orwell once joked, as Astor remembered, that '[H]e liked solid objects and useless information.'[42] With the henhouse ready, he told a friend, 'I should be very glad to buy another pullet if you come across one,'[43] adding later, 'You may be interested to hear the black hen is now beginning to lay, as well, and lays a very nice light brown egg.'[44] As this correspondence continued months later, Orwell asked, 'How are [your] hens doing? Ours didn't do so badly. Those two you sold me laid about 25 eggs between them during January. Now only one is laying but we get about two a week from her.'[46] So, perhaps no surprise, they were still counting the eggs. These memories of a joyful, energetic Orwell reveal the odd, playful man whom Eileen still loved, and was still willing to put up with.

When Crick interviewed David Astor, who had become friends with the couple around the time they moved to Mortimer Crescent, Crick noted: '[Astor] talked a good deal about Eileen O'Shaughnessy, what a remarkable woman she was. Plain and unfashionable compared to Sonia, but a great character, matching Orwell very much in face and mannerism – occasionally uncanny how much they seemed alike and how much they spoke alike.' But, he added, 'They had their quarrels, two distinct personalities despite her very great respect for him.'[46] By then Eileen had become the ideal editor of Orwell's work, allowed to make minor changes that Orwell readily accepted. It's apparent from some of his letters that his spelling and grammar skills were not always excellent. Also, his rage against semicolons at one point was most likely a rejection of an Eileen suggestion for a solution to run-on sentences. Astor later remembered Eileen as 'very lively and energetic . . . and I think her attitude to George was a very good one. They were like partners.' He concluded, 'There was a good bit of harmony on general things as well as their marital relationship.'[47] Even their handwriting had become similar, as is apparent in two examples from 1943.[48]

For a while, after moving to their new flat, Eileen's and Orwell's personal lives settled into a basic busy routine, but one quite unlike the earlier years of their marriage. They were both taking their new jobs seriously, enjoying the challenges, and pleased to be appreciated by their colleagues. During the days, Eileen almost always had lunch with the women at work and didn't arrive back home till at least seven. Each evening she would prepare dinner for Orwell and whoever else might be camping with them that night, often not serving the meal until around nine and not cleaning up until after eleven. 'Eileen made delicious meals in a nonchalant way, mixing pastry while joining in the conversation in the sitting room, smoking constantly,'[49] their niece remembered. Apparently Orwell especially enjoyed puddings and fruit pies, and he made 'a highly satisfied sort of squeaky whine, rather like a puppy', when he ate them, according to her.[50] Orwell had long ago given up doing any of the cooking, but he did keep the huge pot of strong tea overflowing, and he sometimes made after-dinner coffee.

In one of his London Letters, which he wrote every two months for the American magazine *Partisan Review*, Orwell said, 'It is becoming a common practice when you dine at anybody else's house to sleep there,'[51] since the blackouts were still in effect. And he and Eileen were certainly part of that crowd. Orwell invited T. S. Eliot to take part in a number of BBC programmes that he was organising, and he and Eileen tried a few times to have Eliot to dinner and overnight. Once, Orwell told him he could 'Come to my place in the evening [and] we could always put you up for the night as we have spare rooms,'[52] and, another time, 'I wonder if you could come to my place for dinner on Tuesday . . . It would be much better if you stayed the night and we can make you quite comfortable.'[53] There is no record of how often Eliot came to dinner, or if he ever stayed overnight, but years later this invitation was returned, with Eliot writing, 'I should like you and Mrs. Orwell to lunch with me this time.'[54] Many other guests came for dinner and overnight, and for some of them, including David Astor, Orwell 'insisted on putting the bread knife and board, that was always on the table, well away out of sight', Eileen teasingly told a friend.[55] So Orwell had retained the genteel manners from his 'marmalade dish' days of their early marriage.

Lettice believed, as did other friends, that Eileen 'liked the kind of gypsy way they lived' and was 'never really ruffled by their difficulties'.[56] Yet, in a letter to Orwell a few years later, Eileen went on a rant about how much she hated the way they lived. 'I don't think you understand what a nightmare the London life is to me. I know it is to you, but you often talk as though I liked it,' she wrote. 'I don't like even the things that you do. I can't stand having people all over the place, every meal makes me feel sick because every food has been handled by twenty dirty hands and I practically can't bear to eat anything that hasn't been boiled to clean it.'[57] Was Eileen just in a grumbling mood as she waited to have the operation which she hoped would make her well again? Or had everyone, including Orwell, mistaken her willingness to quietly handle difficulties to mean that she actually enjoyed taking care of others? Certainly Eileen was not a constant complainer.

It was in this flat that Eileen told Michael Meyer, in intricate and exuberant detail, the story of the conciliatory H. G. Wells dinner, held at Langford Court, that had gone so horribly wrong. Meyer, a young poet, was impressed by Orwell and Eileen, remembering her as 'delightful – Irish and pretty. A good cook and great fun. She was an ideal wife for Orwell, without being cloying or boring.'[58] She was also 'an interesting woman . . . very much a person in her own right.'[59] Meyer quickly became a close friend and dinner guest, and one evening Eileen regaled him with a rather wild version of the final rift between the two men.

As Meyer remembered the story in 1984, at some point earlier Wells had invited Eileen and Orwell to stay for a while in a flat over his garage. But then, probably after reading Orwell's article 'Wells, Hitler and the World State,' Wells sent a note saying, 'I've heard what you've been saying about me, you ungrateful swine. Leave my flat by Monday morning.' Reflecting later on Orwell's regret at upsetting Wells, a writer he had admired when he was younger, Eileen told Meyer she decided to try to heal the rift. 'It's ludicrous you shouldn't be on good terms with H. G.,' she said. 'Why don't I ask him to dinner and see if he's forgotten the whole thing.' Wells seemed pleased to hear from Eileen and replied, 'Yes, of course, I shall be delighted to come to dinner,' after first telling her, 'I thought it was extraordinarily ungrateful of you to leave that flat I gave you above the garage without any notice.'[60]

When Wells arrived at the appointed time, he announced, 'Now you know I'm suffering very badly from an ulcer. I have to be very careful what I eat.' Eileen told him, apologetically, 'I've cooked a curry, an Indian curry,' and she couldn't think of anything else to offer him. After hesitating, Wells said, 'Oh well, never mind, I'll eat it.' He then proceeded to indulge in enormous amounts of curry along with many glasses of wine, as Meyer remembered Eileen recounting the evening. When another guest arrived after dinner, Eileen offered him some plum cake she had made, and Wells, who was diabetic, apparently ate two large slices of that plus a bit of brandy. Eventually, he left the flat, 'rather drunk and in the best of humour'. All seemed fine until five days later, when Eileen got a note from Wells saying, 'You deliberately tried to poison me . . . You deliberately cooked me food that you knew would make me ill . . . And I never want to see you again.'[61]

Unfortunately, this delightful version is complicated by Inez Holden's memory. A friend of the Orwells', she herself lived in the flat above Wells's garage for some time, and when she heard this story thirty years later, in 1972, she insisted that Eileen and Orwell had never lived there.[62] However, Rebecca West, another close friend of Wells's, was equally sure they had.[63] In Inez's recollection of events, she had arrived at the flat on this fateful evening to find Orwell and Wells arguing loudly in what she called a 'God-awful row'.[64] Eileen was sitting on the sofa 'mute and stunned', and she remained there until the argument suddenly stopped. Inez also insisted there was no 'reconciliation party' and no note from Wells accusing Eileen of trying to poison him. However, it was well known that Wells could 'fire off these hysterical letters',[65] and Inez acknowledged that Orwell did receive a nasty pencilled note from him. Eileen had quoted 'a few 'snappy extracts' to her on the telephone.[66]

Confusing the matter even further, Inez had made a contradictory entry in her diary on 28 April 1942, just after the argument occurred. At that time, she wrote that Eileen had asked her, 'Did you know that H. G. wrote to George forbidding him the house?' Eileen then quoted to her from the note Orwell had received. 'Why do you attack me in this way? Is it some perverted jealousy or some insane political machinations. Read my early works, you shit.' Then he added, according to Inez's diary entry, 'I shall be glad if you will never again visit my garage, as I never want to see you again.'[67] Orwell was very upset when he received this, noting in his diary, 'Abusive letter from H. G. Wells, who addresses me as "You shit," among other things.'[68] There's a tantalising footnote to all of this. According to one of Orwell's nieces, 'There is a family story that,' when meeting Wells, Orwell 'tried to hide his huge feet under his chair, while Wells was doing the same thing with his extra-small pair.' Then some time later Wells called Orwell 'a Trotskyist with big feet,'[69] a description which 'Eileen related with relish' to a friend.[70]

As late as 1986, Meyer was still insisting that his version was exactly as he had heard it from Eileen, and Inez's own words in her diary seem to verify much of what Eileen told Meyer. However, Meyer did concede that, although 'I would not have thought George would have embroidered . . . I suppose Eileen might possibly have, and George not have bothered to correct an amusing tale.'[71] Eileen left no record of making another attempt at reconciliation.

Eileen was back at work by 22 May, after the move to Mortimer Crescent and the break in the Buggins shows on *Kitchen Front*. Jean Rowntree sent a script for her approval on that day, along with the suggestion that *The Kitchen Front* might be 'rather overdoing the recipes'. '[W]hat is wanted is more general advice about planning food, and perhaps rather less about preparing it.' She continued, 'If you think this point of view is worth discussing would it be possible for me to come round to the Ministry?' But, she added, 'Of course, you may disagree with the whole suggestion, in which case it would hardly be worth having the meeting.' By then Eileen apparently had enough authority to reject Rowntree's suggestion, and, although no response from her has survived, there was no obvious reduction in the number of recipes used. As the *Kitchen Front* programme grew in scope, a wide variety of approaches to food preparation and rations developed, and Eileen worked with Rowntree on improving the presentation. When it was announced, in June, that Rowntree would be replaced by Winifred Holmes, in August, as the BBC producer of *Kitchen Front*, Rowntree told her department head, 'It seems to me very important that [Holmes] should get our relations with the Ministry [of Food] absolutely clear from the first broadcast she handles.' She wanted Holmes to take immediate control of the problems she saw brewing. Then she wrote a last letter to Eileen, saying, 'I hope we shall continue to meet from time to time.' Before that transition took place, Eileen went on holiday with Orwell from 27 June to 13 July. They stayed on a farm at Callow End, in Worcestershire, and Orwell spent most of the time fishing. While there, he continued to keep up his Wartime Diary, even as he detailed a day-by-day record of his catch of fish, along with complaints about the shortage of beer in the village pubs.[72]

When she got back to work, Eileen had to develop a relationship with the new BBC producer. At first Holmes seemed less friendly than Rowntree had been, complaining immediately about some recipes by one *Kitchen Front* speaker that used 'edible fungi'. Two people had gone to the hospital after being 'poisoned by eating the fungi he recommended', she wrote, so Holmes insisted that Eileen be careful about using any recipes that didn't contain illustrations. And Holmes and Westerby began quarrelling immediately. She was convinced that part of her job was to forward to Westerby and Eileen all the letters she received containing recipes for possible use by *The Kitchen Front*, and apparently their number kept increasing. After a few weeks, Westerby was pleading, 'To stop me going insane, can you put a check on the flood of manuscripts, suggestions and recipes which are pouring into the Ministry from the Corporation? . . . When I look at the huge pile of suggestions on my desk I want to run away and cry.' In a long reply next day, Holmes teased Westerby about his complaints, which she didn't take seriously. But he was not amused. He answered her the same day – at Eileen's request, he said. He wanted Holmes to follow the procedure that had been in practice before her arrival. He asked her not to send anything at all for a while, and he ended that letter with, 'I hope you agree. But if you don't, a glimpse at the harassed and inundated Mrs. Blair would soften your stony heart – even if the prospect of the same emotions in myself might not do so.' Holmes answered, 'I shall not be deterred from putting forward to you any speakers or ideas which seem to me worth considering.' However, she suggested having their superiors clarify once again the division of work between them. 'Certainly, I should be moved to tears if I saw Mrs. Blair snowed under with material – I will do my best to prevent that happening,' she added. 'She looked far from well when we lunched together on Monday.'

Meanwhile, Eileen and Holmes were carrying on their business in a friendly fashion. Holmes's letters are always full of humour and curious detail, and it's easy to see why she and Eileen began to get along so well. In one letter, Eileen wrote, 'So far as Mr. Barratt is concerned, I think you have dealt with him very nicely. Of course we couldn't ever use this script or, I should say, any from him because he always finds the answer in a tin can. As for Mrs. Thorne,' she continued, 'she may of course be the answer to all our prayers – but I have no confidence in people who feel sure that we should find them useful. Do you want to follow her up?' At another time, they discussed the pros and cons of a 'very persistent' woman whose recipes Eileen liked, but whose personality and skill as a broadcaster were double negatives for Holmes. 'She has virtues,' Eileen wrote. Her recipes were 'economical and practical and . . . the jelly was made here with apple and I think would be very popular with children.' However, she gave Holmes the final decision on whether to use her, and Holmes concluded that 'her faults are ineradicable' as a speaker. Days later, Eileen wanted another possible presenter to be rejected because she was 'emboldened by ignorance. From her point of view, the fact that she knows exactly nothing about either M.O.F. propaganda or about food is a reason for her to give authoritative judgments on both. About a third of her statements are repetitions of what we – and all the kindred organisations – have been saying for years, though I think she believes she is being startlingly original. The other two-thirds are just plain misstatements.'

Before she left her job, Rowntree scheduled a full week of *Kitchen Front* with just one speaker, in order to make the transition to

Holmes as smooth as possible. Eileen prepared all the scripts, recipes, and shopping lists used in those programmes, and the series produced an enormous number of favourable letters. Rowntree concluded to Eileen, 'That sort of thing is what people want.' However, weeks later, one angry official, a Miss M. J. Michael, wrote a scathing review of that week of programmes Eileen had managed. She claimed that it contained many 'inaccuracies' and 'the impression given was that the talks were completely out of touch with the practical side of housekeeping'. Eileen took the time to refute in great detail all twelve points of criticism. In her reply, she said that all the material used had been carefully checked by the *Kitchen Front* staff, and '[W]e have had more than 750 requests for the shopping and menu chart.'

Eileen's rebuttal was calmly worded, but she was furious. As she explained to Holmes early in September, in a scrawled, handwritten letter, 'I hope you got my long long letter written at Miss Michael. I generally would like comment, but in this case the criticisms were really frivolous. I could see no motive in making them except a very natural desire to be rude now and then.' She went on to say, 'It depressed me. But doubtless there will be some more depressing necessities before we serve the last potato with a pre-war Christmas tree ornament on top to make a Victory Dinner.' She ended this letter with what seems like a joke: 'I am now starting my sick leave. Such is the power of suggestion that I feel ill!' But Miss Michael was not at all consoled. She sent a long reply in answer to Eileen's defence of the week-long programme, saying, 'I am grateful for all the trouble that has been taken, but in self-defence regret that I must return to the attack. One gets the impression on reading Mrs. Blair's replies to my criticisms that she bases them on the Ministry of Food leaflet, and not on the actual talks as broadcast.' She then proceeded to elaborate on all her petty complaints about what was by then a long-past broadcast. Eileen felt free to express her annoyance, writing in one letter, 'My trouble today is that I definitely don't like any part of anything whatever!'

After about seven months on the job, Eileen was feeling exasperated. She realised at this point that it might not be possible to please everyone on both sides of the shaky coalition between the Ministry of Food and the BBC. It's not entirely clear whether she just needed a break from the tensions and criticism at work, or whether her recurring illness, including ovarian cysts and bouts of vaginal bleeding, had struck again. But that September she disappeared from the job for a few months.

When Eileen left on 'sick leave' in early September, Holmes wrote, 'I am so sorry not to have been able to see you before you went into hospital, but I didn't know until yesterday that you had gone. I am sure you will be glad to relax for a bit, and hope you will feel very much better after the first discomfort is over.' This presents quite a mystery, since neither Eileen nor Orwell left any record of her being in hospital that autumn, and during those months Orwell never mentioned Eileen's health. One personal theory, that Eileen had become pregnant and then suffered a miscarriage, was explored, but ended with no conclusion one way or the other. No records were found of Eileen being admitted to hospital during that time. Holmes ended this letter, 'May I now thank you very much indeed for your cooperation. We have been so pleased to get the scripts in good time lately, and it is very kind of you to have taken the trouble to do this.' There are no further work letters from her until November.

Holmes might have been wrong about Eileen's being in hospital, since she and Eileen didn't know each other well yet. Ruth Pitter, a friend of Orwell's from years earlier, said that sometime during the autumn Eileen met her at the BBC and invited her to their 'damp basement flat' for supper. Eileen looked tired, and as she prepared an apple pie for dessert, 'She was nervously anxious not to leave a scrap of core in the apples, as she said [Orwell] disliked it so,' Pitter remembered. When he arrived home for his dinner, he looked 'like a ghost'.[73] Pitter also left a compassionate description of Orwell. 'How he did adore life!' she recalled. 'His nature was divided. There was something like a high wall right across the middle of it. A high wall with flowers and fruit and running water on one side, and the desert on the other.' [74]

During these autumn months, Orwell was overextending himself at the BBC, producing brilliant programmes. Eileen was at home with him for a few months, and it's possible she had decided to take some time off work in order to help him. However, it's more likely she was on sick leave. Even so, she would have continued to help her husband. At one point that autumn, Orwell told his agent that his diary from 1940 to 1941 'is being typed' in the hope that a publisher might be interested in it, and should be finished 'in about 10 days'.[75] Orwell was keeping up a detailed Wartime Diary during those months, and Eileen could have been typing that as well as a letter Orwell sent to *The Times* on 12 October. Orwell ended this diary with a short entry on 15 November, just the day after Eileen went back to work.

Eileen was often home sick from work, as Lettice remembered. Doctors were never able to come up with the cause of her frailty, although she was constantly being tested for TB, a logical worry since she lived with Orwell. Eileen's friends had no faith that Orwell was even conscious of the severity of her periodic relapses. Lettice disapproved of his behaviour towards her, saying 'Eileen needed a good deal of care and George was incapable of giving it'.[76] Orwell should certainly be criticised for seeming oblivious to the gravity of Eileen's health problems, but Eileen, like Orwell, was intent on denying any weakness in herself. She deflected any concern he might show by hiding anything serious from him. She knew that he needed her to be strong, and she had promised him she would be, so he might be forgiven a little for not realising that her constant illnesses were more serious than she revealed to him. Lydia thought Eileen was struggling through those months with 'an illness which left her seriously devitalised'. Lydia worried that her recovery had been compromised by the couple's 'icily cold flat'.[77] As the years went on, Eileen increasingly understood how important Orwell's work was, and she came to believe that it was even more important than her own health.

15

But Smooth Sailing Was
Never an Option

*I came in to drop my 'unfit to follow her
occupation' chit and have been following
my occupation since then without drawing
breath.*

Eileen, when considering whether to resign in protest

While Eileen was away from work that autumn, the squabbles
between *The Kitchen Front* and the BBC grew increasingly
intense. Winifred Holmes continued to criticise Robert
Westerby, Eileen's colleague in the Public Relations Department,
for ignoring the rules as she understood them, believing that 'dual
control' was impossible since he had 'stated publicly that he runs *The
Kitchen Front*.'[1] Her angry, sarcastic letter to her superior mentioned
the 'constant friction' between them, and her boss complained to
others of 'the consistently difficult attitude of the Ministry of Food
[which] is constantly invading our province and inviting speakers
direct'. One of those speakers, he said, 'could not read English or make
himself intelligible'. Others at the BBC complained about what they

believed was 'a growing dissatisfaction among the housewives' with the presentation of the recipes, saying that the comedic style used by Constanduros and Grisewood was insulting. After a few months, it was suggested that 'Mrs. Blair' be consulted. And on 14 November, Eileen was suddenly back at work, writing her routine programme considerations to Holmes, with no mention of any illness.

Holmes was definitely glad Eileen was back. She sent long, chatty letters, asking her opinion on future speakers, and was very appreciative of her promptness with the scripts. They worked together in early December on a calendar for the *Kitchen Front* programmes for the last two weeks of December, including some major changes they had agreed on after analysing mail from listeners. Problems still arose, but together they resolved them. In one letter Eileen wrote, 'Mrs. Buggins has just come in, and I find rather to my horror that one of her recipes is very like one of Ruth Drew's. Apple and Potato.' However, after considering some possible fixes, she decided they were differently presented and hoped no one would notice. '[Mrs Drew's] are most excellent recipes from our point of view – we have no other speaker (except Mabel Constanduros perhaps) who has this sort of instinctive feeling for the nuances of our policy.'

Eileen and Holmes were meeting weekly, and 'our new arrangement with the Ministry of Food is working quite well and no bad blood seems to have been roused by it,' Holmes told her boss. However, she warned, 'I have to remember to bark at Westerby if he tries to slip up on our agreed working arrangement.' As she explained, 'The speakers I have now are definitely realising that they work with us chiefly, but there are some old ones like Freddie Grisewood and Mabel Constanduros who still think they work for the Ministry [of Food].'

A few days later, as the two women prepared the Christmas schedule, Eileen wrote, 'We postponed Mary Ferguson partly so that she should not coincide with the Bruce Blunt series, but that will have been forgotten, I should think and rather hope, by the 28th.' Then she asked, 'Are there any points at issue? I am now rather hopelessly busy.' This she explained to Holmes was because her secretary 'Mrs. Search's flu has turned into nervous debility, which I suppose may last for weeks, and my own flu has turned into a daily low fever and a nightly high one which I suppose will last as long.' Although this is presented in a joking manner, Eileen added, 'It makes me slow and single-minded – I think very hard about how to copy the recipe for Christmas pudding,' which she was doing in order to make it easy for listeners to jot down the ingredients when they were read on *The Kitchen Front*. 'So if more adult thinking can be postponed I shall be rather glad,' she concluded. In another short but confusing letter, Eileen wrote, 'I hope I understand correctly that you are now doing the typing in quintuplet,' adding, 'This is the only really comforting news I have had since Mrs. Search got 'flu.' In answer to Eileen's plea, Holmes wrote, 'I am so sorry about Mrs. Search and know how awful it is to be left without a secretary who knows all one's work. Let's postpone "adult thinking" for today; I myself am slightly bewildered by work here and trying to arrange a family Christmas.'

For months, the *Kitchen Front* programmes had been stressing the shortage of fuel and the need to advise housewives to bake less bread. One speaker was inspired to write a programme called 'Bread Waste' 'after his small son was given a rabbit to be fed on toast!' Eileen explained. During this time, housewives were encouraged to substitute potatoes, and Eileen had suggested recipes for potato scones and potato and cheese pastry. But by 6 January, the situation became 'of such extreme urgency and far-reaching importance' that Lord Woolton declared, 'Every day for a month' *The Kitchen Front* must 'introduce the phrase, "Eat potatoes instead of bread" into every programme.' And, in order to avoid such awkward phrasing as, 'This is *The Kitchen Front*, eat potatoes instead of bread, here is Mrs. Buggins,' the suggestion was made by the BBC 'to dress up your five-word slogan' appropriately. 'No doubt your Mrs. Blair and my Mrs. Holmes will find means of doing this idea.'

Perhaps part of Eileen's being 'hopelessly busy' was the new work she took on for Venu Chitale, one of Orwell's assistants at the BBC.

Towards the end of 1942, Orwell had suggested another innovative BBC series, *In Your Kitchen*, as part of his Eastern Service broadcasts to India. These programmes, based on Eileen's *Kitchen Front* programmes, were planned with recipes that would appeal to Indian housewives. In introducing the new programme on 22 December, Chitale raved about her first impressions of Eileen, saying, 'Mrs. Blair has a reservoir of quiet humour, and again and again some of it seems to come out in between an amused smile and a penetrating remark.' She was charmed by Eileen's connection between war and diet: 'Many battles have surely been lost because the Field-Marshal concerned had not had the proper allocation of vitamins and calories,' Eileen had claimed. And when Chitale asked her how she had drifted to food from psychology, she was impressed by Eileen's 'clever' response: 'Perhaps it is the psychological reactions to food and cooking that interest me more than food for its own sake.'[2]

On 23 December, when Eileen introduced the new series on the air, she explained first how the *Kitchen Front* programme had developed since its inception:[3]

Every morning for 2½ years now there has been a broadcast from London called The Kitchen Front. *It's part of the ordinary B.B.C. programme, but the idea behind it is that for 5 minutes the Ministry of Food shall try to help British women to do a very difficult job. And that is to give their families the food they need – and food they'll like – in spite of wartime restrictions. We haven't really any hardship to complain about. There is enough food for everyone, extra allowances for children and invalids and so on. But on the other hand, two things have combined to convert catering from a habit into a research. Many women here, of course, have always cooked for their families – but now they have to cook without foodstuffs that they always relied on and to make up for their absence by using new foods, like dried eggs and dried milk, or foods that always existed but were not as important in peacetime. The other change is that many women are now cooking for the first time – they may know how to write a book or do a complicated surgical operation or teach philosophy, but they don't know how to make a vegetable stew and pre-war cookery books aren't much use to them. Obviously it's more than ever important that meals should be well cooked and well balanced, and* The Kitchen Front *tries to show how they can be both.*

We have all kinds of speakers. Once a week the radio doctor explains the essential food values, the function of vitamins, proteins and calories in the diet, and particularly the importance of child-feeding. And the other talks are generally recipe talks – interpreting the results of scientific experiment in terms of actual dishes. Often the recipes come from the Ministry of Food's kitchens, where new dishes are tried out every day. Then once a week a foreign housewife tells us something about cooking in her country – at least not always a housewife exactly – one of our speakers was the High Commissioner for India who gave us a very good lesson on how to make Indian curries. Then once a week we broadcast recipes that have been sent in to us by ordinary housewives up and down the country – sometimes recipes for special dishes that their mothers and grandmothers made, sometimes recipes that they themselves have invented on the very day they write to us. But wherever they come from they're fighting recipes – they're very economical in rationed food, they don't need any of the foods that are scarce, they're good sound nourishment, and they're attractive too. We are ambitious. We hope that the good result of this war may be that many more people will recognise that cooking is both an art and a science, worth all the intelligence and originality that anyone can put into it.

Well this programme has been going on, as I said, for 2½ years. That's a lot of recipes, and looking back it seems extraordinary that they haven't come to an end yet. But on the contrary, we haven't time to broadcast nearly all we'd like to. The shortage of food we used to have in abundance has inspired all the good cooks in the country to get the same effect from something else or to find new ways of cooking the foods we have got.

Especially vegetables. We can grow vegetables in England, vegetables of some kind all the year round, but many of us never appreciated them till now. For instance, before the war nearly everyone in England ate potatoes every day. And very nearly every day they ate boiled *potatoes. Now we have over 100 ways of cooking potatoes, plain and savoury and sweet, and we've learnt how to preserve their very important food values too. Our foreign speakers help us a lot with vegetable recipes. People in Central Europe particularly have always lived mainly on vegetables (potatoes and cabbage, many of them) and now they're telling us how they ate them. The cabbage has come to England as an ambassador, and a very good internationalising influence it is, full of Vitamin C. That's the story of the* Kitchen Front *broadcast.*

Then Eileen explained how the new programme, *In Your Kitchen*, would work for Indian housewives: 'And now once a week, you're going to hear one or two of our recipes.' But even in this serious endeavour, Eileen's sense of playfulness shone through, and, since Orwell had told her how unreliable the Eastern Service could sometimes be, she couldn't resist adding, 'At least I hope you're going to hear them. Miss Panthaki is going to broadcast them anyway.' Then she went on:

Some of them will be new to you I expect, as they are to us. Some of them may seem pretty odd to you – a lot of them seemed very odd to us until we cooked them and found that they were good. And some of our traditional English and Scottish and Welsh dishes may be new to you too, but perhaps you may like them, even adapted as they have had to be for wartime. If you do, if you share our excitement in this adventuring after new experiences in eating, you might like to tell us something about your food. We have lentils, we have some rice and spices too, as well as fresh vegetables, and if we were to broadcast a recipe sent specially from India millions of English listeners would appreciate it and thousands of them would be cooking it the same day. That would be another internationalising influence.

Eileen's idea of introducing Indian food to the British public no doubt contributed to its vast appreciation throughout England today.

Eileen did several talks for the Indian Section of the Eastern Service early in 1943, usually with Dr Gangulee, but none of her scripts has been found.[4] The *In Your Kitchen* programme continued almost weekly until 8 July, when Orwell announced the series would end for a time,[5] and apparently it was never reinstated.

Perhaps naturally – as they were both in their late thirties and exposed to so many new people, especially with the war still causing havoc in everyone's lives – Orwell, and quite possibly Eileen as well, began to look for new lovers. They'd each had affairs before, but now, being apart most of the day, they were constantly running into opportunities. Orwell no longer had to plot to meet women in secret, as in the days when he resorted to romancing Brenda in the Wallington woods. His reputation was now at the point where literary figures of the time were curious enough to seek him out and eager to take part in the vast array of visionary programmes he was creating for his BBC broadcasts to India. He had the opportunity for long lunch hours where he could socialise with the new friends he was gathering as his celebrity grew. With numerous magazines begging for contributions, his already almost impossible level of creative energy exploded to new heights as he managed to write important, well-crafted essays even as he was dreaming up his remarkable BBC projects. He had what one person described as 'a certain kind of luminosity',[6] reminiscent of the days in the late thirties when Connolly recalled 'the extraordinary magical effect' that Orwell's presence had on the 'jolly girls with lots of money' at a cocktail party.[7]

This new lifestyle was made easier because neither Eileen nor Orwell suffered from traditional jealousy. 'I don't much care who sleeps with whom,' Orwell later wrote, claiming that physical jealousy had never been a problem for him. 'It seems to me what matters is being faithful in an emotional and intellectual sense.'[8] Eileen also was 'as free from [jealousy and rancour] as anybody I have ever known,'[9] her friend Lettice Cooper believed. Orwell told friends later that both he and Eileen had been unfaithful during their marriage, and this wasn't as big a problem between them as it would have been for some other couples. Orwell had accepted rather calmly Eileen's affair with Kopp while he was fighting in the hills in Spain, and 'George could hardly have had anyone more suited for him,' one friend believed. Eileen 'had a sort of tolerance, and humour, too, which helped her put up with things some women probably wouldn't have been prepared to put up with.'[10] Lettice thought Eileen 'had an affectionate, amused, somewhat sceptical love of [Orwell],'[11] which didn't seem to be based on any sexual commitment. He had never promised her monogamy, and now, six years after their wedding, he was experiencing an active 'seven-year itch'.

Many women were intrigued by Orwell's bashful, flirtatious, sometimes over-insistent attempts at intimacy. One described 'his mild amourous [sic] approaches' as 'those of a very sex-shy adolescent'.[12] Inez Holden, a lively novelist and journalist around Orwell's age, was an early attraction. Being an accomplished mimic and amusing storyteller, she was another version of a playful, witty Eileen. Orwell would take Inez to lunch and then back to the flat, while Eileen was at work, where he regaled her with his past adventures. One day, after a few such meetings, he suddenly 'pounced' on her with an 'intensity and urgency' that astonished her. The very next evening the couple took Inez out to dinner, perhaps a conscious attempt, on Orwell's part, to prove that he had told the truth about the openness of his and Eileen's marriage. 'There was rather an atmosphere of submerged strain,' Inez remembered years later. It wasn't entirely clear to her whether Eileen was part of the reassurance party or whether Orwell was just using her in his pursuit of Inez without her direct knowledge. Whatever version Inez ended up believing, she continued to be in contact with Eileen as a friend even as she claimed to be seeing Orwell 'several times a week' for many years.[13] However, it's possible that she was more a friend of the family than Orwell's lover. 'Inez was very fond of George and he of her,' a friend remembered, but she 'very much doubted' that they were lovers.[14] And, according to Sonia Orwell, Inez 'wanted George very much indeed but George didn't want her as much.'[15]

Stevie Smith, another writer in Orwell's new crowd, was also at least a very close friend. 'She dropped allusions to an affair between herself and Orwell,'[16] and another friend thought 'Stevie had a sort of *amitié amoureuse* for George who was awfully boyish in his attentions to women . . . She liked the jokey side but . . . when it got more sexually orientated she fled.' This friend remembered that Orwell 'liked taking ladies to the cinema and rather shyly holding their hand, his hand around the thumb which had, [Stevie] told me intensely, some erotic significance.'[17] Rumour had it that Stevie was the woman Orwell boasted about 'having in a park'.[18] But a friend claimed later that the attempt at sex had failed because Orwell was 'too well endowed'.[19]

Then there were the secretaries at the BBC and, later, at *Tribune*, when he was literary editor, some of whom resisted Orwell's approaches while others did not. '[Orwell] seemed to think that he was obliged to have an affair with [Nancy Parratt, one of his secretaries] out of compassion and duty,' Sonia Orwell said. 'He wasn't used to having a secretary at all and didn't know how to behave towards her.'[20] When Orwell confided in Lydia about an affair with one of his secretaries, she felt 'he spoke dismissively, almost contemptuously, in a way I did not like.'[21] And Lydia remembered what she claimed was a stressful weekend visit by Orwell around this time. 'Once, after a row with [Eileen] in London, [Orwell] declared [to Eileen] that he was going to me at Wallington cottage,' she wrote in her diary years later. And when he arrived, 'to my great annoyance, George came to my room and got into bed with me . . . I had to spend the next half hour wrestling to ward him off from forcing himself on me.'[22]

Lettice had her own opinion about Orwell's possible affairs. 'He was in many ways a very ingenuous and almost stupid man,' she told Crick.

(He chose to leave out the words 'almost stupid' in his biography.) But she thought Orwell had 'an immense charm that was very difficult to define', which caused him to be 'surrounded by adorers, male and female'.[23] And he angered these admirers at times when he seemed indifferent to their approaches to him. When that happened, Eileen, with her 'inexhaustible capacity for being interested in other people's affairs', was often turned to for sympathy by these ignored admirers. Eileen complained to Lettice that 'somebody was always ringing up and saying, "Have I annoyed George? . . . George wouldn't speak to me," when George had just not happened to be thinking about them at all.'[24] Lettice believed that 'Stevie Smith and Inez Holden both fell in love with him and sobbed out their troubles to Eileen when he would take no notice of them.'[25]

There's only one account of Eileen showing any jealousy during this period, and that was over an affair Orwell had with Sally McEwan, his secretary at *Tribune*. According to one friend, this affair caused Eileen so much distress that she made a 'fiendish row' over it, convincing Orwell to break it off.[26] But, even so, a letter he sent Sally from Paris in March 1945, when he was writing about the retreat of the German troops, began, 'I hope you are getting on O.K. I won't say without me but in my absence.'[27] So he retained his romantic feelings for her.

Only one of all these women whom Orwell was tempted by claimed he had suggested leaving Eileen. Hetta Crouse – a vivacious fellow BBC worker – believed that Orwell was so jealous when she chose to marry William Empson that he refused to go to her wedding.[28] Did Orwell really abandon his 'Eileen doesn't mind' line and suggest he might divorce her for Hetta? Or was this a misinterpretation by a very self-confident woman of Orwell's sometimes over-zealous approach? Any famous person will be aware of claims by rejected lovers who rewrite the actual history with their wished-for results. In Orwell's case, he believed so strongly in his marriage to Eileen that he would be highly unlikely to give it up for a romance, even with a very enticing woman. According to Susan Watson, the woman Orwell hired about three years later to look after their adopted son Richard, 'George once said [he and Eileen] weren't quite happy at all times but wouldn't ever have dreamt of getting a divorce.'²⁹ At any rate, it's hard to believe that Orwell could have possibly fitted in so many serious affairs, considering his time-consuming job and his well-documented days and weeks sick in bed, as he fought to control his worsening health.

Eileen's possible affairs during these years are harder to track down. Karl Schnetzler, her brother's German friend whom Eileen had met in 1935, reappeared in her life after being released from internment in 1943. Lydia believed strongly that Karl was in love with Eileen, but he refused to admit any truth to this, and Eileen left no real clue.

As we know, Georges Kopp had not forgotten those blissful months with Eileen in Barcelona, as he detailed in his 1940 letter to her. He was disappointed when he didn't receive any answer, still hoping to have retained her love. Over a year later, he reached out in a long letter to Dr George Mason and his wife Evelyn – friends of Eric and Gwen O'Shaughnessy – who had taken him in 'for a few days' in 1939. He asked them for information on his British friends. He recounted some details about his injuries, then explained, 'I am speaking of these trifles because of Eileen who sort of wrote that she was wishing me to get some medals in the war.' He ended on a sad note: 'I am more sorry than I can tell you to be nearly 2 years without any news.'³⁰ When that letter also failed to elicit any reply from Eileen, Kopp wrote to her again on 18 August 1942, a letter that Orwell determined was in code. Although Kopp appeared to be informing them about a supposed job he was considering taking, Orwell believed he was actually telling them, 'I am afraid France is going into full alliance with Germany. If the Second Front is not opened soon I shall do my best to escape to England.'³¹ Whatever sentiments he might have been sending in those letters, Kopp remained on the Continent as a British spy for another year. In July 1943, he wrote Eileen and Orwell an informative letter about his exploits, with no intimate particulars for Eileen alone,³² and

351

then, after being betrayed to the Gestapo and flown out of France by the British,[33] Kopp reappeared in Eileen's life in September, just when she was experiencing a decisive moment at her job. Being an overtly passionate man, quite the opposite of Orwell, he no doubt approached Eileen again with his deep and insistent love. Although she was glad he was safe, it must have been distressing for her to have him back so directly in her life, forcing her to tell him once again that she was not going to leave Orwell. She was still very fond of Kopp, but by then she was even more dedicated to Orwell than she had been in Barcelona, and she couldn't allow Kopp back in her life the way he wanted.

Although he did finally accept Eileen's rejection, Kopp nevertheless managed to keep very close to her for the rest of her life. Back in England, he stayed once again with Gwen in Greenwich, and reunited there with Gwen's half-sister Doreen, who preferred him over her other suitors. Doreen and Kopp soon married and had three children, all well aware as adults of the stories of their father's early infatuation with Eileen. Could Gwen have worried that he had married Doreen in order to stay close to Eileen? According to Quentin Kopp, one of Georges and Doreen's children, Gwen never mentioned any such fear to anyone, and Doreen never talked about this.[34] 'I have absolutely no way of knowing what Gwen felt about either my Father, or the marriage. Gwen took people as she found them . . . I do not think that they had a 'coup de foudre,' because I know that my Mother considered marriage proposals from at least one other person while George was away during the War.'[35] However, according to Catherine, Gwen's adopted daughter, Kopp was one of the few people of whom Gwen was *not* fond: 'She saw right through him.'[36] Doreen and Kopp lived a few doors away from Eileen and Orwell after they moved to their last flat, in 1944, and the two couples often shared childcare duties and favours.

In her new life at the Ministry of Food, Eileen was in constant contact with the two Grisewood cousins and was rumoured to have had an affair with one of them.[37] Freddie worked closely with her on the *Kitchen Front* programmes, but he was married and a little older.

Harman had been at Oxford with her, where he had had leading parts in *Henry IV* and *King Lear*, plays Eileen might have had minor roles in. He had an announcer's job at the BBC at this time, and he's the most likely cousin for this role. Whether Eileen had any other possible affairs has been speculated on but is unknown. She was working more than full-time, and her own health was precarious, so finding time for any serious romance would seem unlikely. No personal letters from Eileen during this period have been discovered.

As Orwell later summed up their infidelities: 'I was sometimes unfaithful to Eileen, and I also treated her very badly, and I think she treated me badly too at times, but it was a real marriage in the sense that we had been through awful struggles together and she understood all about my work, etc.'[38] Although they each knew that the other might be having affairs, in the end they agreed that staying together was the best choice for them both.

Early in 1943, Orwell took his turn being at home sick, this time for three weeks. Although not completely recovered herself, Eileen again spent her lunch hours rushing back and forth to the flat, making sure Orwell was being properly cared for. She could see that his lifelong affliction with 'bronchitis' was not improving, and all she could do was make sure he was as comfortable as possible when an episode came on, even as that dedication was wearing her out. 'Eileen did everything she could in a practical way to keep him well,' a friend remembered. 'Though [she was] not a motherly type, mind, even a "faintly detached" observer watching the scene [could see she had] to put up a lot with unpredictable behaviour.'[39] In February, Holmes contracted pneumonia, and was away from work until the beginning of April. Her secretary sent out an apology for any delays, explaining that the Ministry of Food was also 'short-staffed at the moment, owing to illness'. So probably Eileen took some time off during that period to look after Orwell. Orwell's mother and his sister Avril must have known Eileen needed more help than she was asking for, since they had moved to a flat nearby in the summer of 1942, and they most certainly shared in Orwell's care during the autumn and winter months. But Mrs Blair died on 19 March 1943, of heart failure, at the age of sixty-seven. Two secondary causes of her death were listed as 'acute bronchitis and emphysema of the lungs,'[40] suggesting her son's lifelong problems were hereditary. Orwell was present at the time of her death, as he had been with his father in 1939.[41] 'He was obviously affected by the fact that she was dying and even more so by the fact that on her bed there was a copy of *Homage to Catalonia*,'[42] his sister Avril remembered.

When she first started working with Holmes, Eileen began her letters 'Dear Mrs. Holmes' and signed them 'Emily Blair', but by January, as they began working more closely together, she had changed to 'Dear Winifred', while signing them simply 'Emily'. By mid-April, 'Emily' and 'Winifred' were dealing with an annoying problem Eileen thought had been solved the year before: Holmes told her superior, 'I have consulted with Mrs. Blair about the Ministry of Food's attitude towards these announcements [on fruit preservation] and she is definitely against putting them in the *Kitchen Front* period.' She added, 'Mrs. Blair herself would be very pleased if we said we could not use them,' and shortly afterwards it was formally announced that there was no time for them. Emily and Winifred also discussed a new programme, 'Men in the Kitchen', which would 'bring to the microphone various men cooks, from an Army mess officer to the manager of the Dorchester' hotel, as well as a shop steward at a tanks-parts factory. In March, another *Kitchen Front* speaker was told that Mrs Blair was very pleased with the idea and wanted to use it. But, while Eileen and Holmes continued to try to settle problems civilly, their superiors were arguing behind their backs, and the whole arrangement between the BBC and the Ministry of Food began to fall apart.

A 'crisis' was reported on in great detail by Holmes on 28 April. A script that had been completed and approved for an 8:15 show one Wednesday was suddenly rejected late on Tuesday afternoon, and Holmes was furious with Westerby, who had made the decision. It turned out that one of his superiors, who never ate breakfast, was upset at the suggestion that the 'efficiency' of people like him 'was below par until lunch time'. A new script had been written overnight, but Holmes and Westerby kept up their battle. In what appears to be barely hidden sarcasm, she wrote, 'I am so sorry that I was stupid enough to misunderstand about who should make the preliminary enquiries' for a future talk.

Shortly afterwards, when Westerby proposed 'a great many "starry" names' as guests on *The Kitchen Front*, including John Gielgud, Clark Gable, and even the Queen, Holmes told her superiors, 'I am afraid the irrepressible Westerby will be doing some private inviting on his own if I don't take care.' And she reported on another meeting where Westerby 'moaned that they have no space in which they can tell people to eat more carrots at a moment's notice – or something like that.' This might have been at the time when eating carrots was being promoted as an aid to better eyesight. Near the end of June, Westerby had had enough. He informed his superior that it had been a year since Ministry of Food employees had met with the officers of the BBC, including Holmes, and that 'such meetings are valuable'. There is no record of what was said at the meeting, at which both Westerby and Eileen were present, but shortly afterwards it was announced that Holmes would be replaced by Anne Harris at the beginning of September.

This infuriated Eileen, and, after a rage-filled weekend deciding how to react, she told Holmes she was considering quitting. When she arrived at work some days later, 'Winifred' wrote to 'Dear Emily', 'I'm so glad you have sheathed the hatpin . . . I hope you won't resign, and certainly not on my account.' Then, showing what good friends they had become, Holmes added, 'What a joke if you had been staying with us for the week-end when your rage came upon you!' Taking the situation more calmly than Eileen did, Holmes told her that she had informed her boss 'some time ago that I should have to give up this work, as family and domestic difficulties caused by my continual absences from home are too much to cope with and I am afraid the children are suffering in consequence.' Then she added, 'I have really enjoyed working with you and am very sorry to hear that you have been hiding up all kinds of grievances.' Eileen would of course have kept Orwell informed daily about her 'grievances' at work, and about her attempts to save her friend's job. And she explained her appearance at work as temporary. 'I came in to drop my "unfit to follow her occupation" chit and have been following my occupation since then without drawing breath,' she told Holmes. 'I can't really take in the news about your leaving – my head is very peculiar and I am doing an odd sort of day by day thinking.' However, she added, 'I know I do think it's a) a pity and b) a good thing because you have looked too tired . . . since your pneumonia.' Eileen was still too angry to make any definite decision, so she told Holmes, 'I think I'm going to take two weeks, so I'll see you on Monday the 17th.' Once again, with all her seeming attention to detail, she had misread the calendar, since 17 July 1943 would have been a Saturday. She told Winifred that she had arranged some speakers for her time away, and that Westerby would follow up on her work. 'There's a chance that [the scheduled speakers] may be very good, but you may need some of my new strychnine medicine nevertheless,' she warned. Although Eileen had said she'd be gone for two weeks in early July, she continued to be 'on leave' from the office throughout most of the summer. As becomes clear when we consider Lettice Cooper's novel *Black Bethlehem*, Eileen had attempted to organise a rebellion against the bureaucracy of the BBC and the Ministry of Food, in order to save Winifred Holmes's job. These efforts surely make Eileen the perfect model for Orwell's creation of Julia as a rebellious woman in his final novel, *Nineteen Eighty-Four.*

Lettice Cooper's novel *Black Bethlehem* was published in 1947. In it she lovingly created a character named Ann who, she proudly acknowledged, was her best attempt at portraying her friend Eileen, a person she truly admired. However, 'Ann's husband was never intended to be like George,'[43] Lettice claimed later, perhaps partially as self-protection, since Ann's husband was not an entirely sympathetic character. Ann and the narrator work together at the Ministry of Food during the war, with jobs parallel to the ones Eileen and Lettice actually had. As a novelist, Lettice probably made notes about the conversations and conflicts surrounding her at work, making her book a believable portrayal of what actually happened during those years. Eileen's work letters give a few enticing details of the upheavals happening at *The Kitchen Front*, and Lettice elaborated on those conflicts in *Black Bethlehem* a short time after they had happened. With this novel, she left a poignant record of her impressions of Eileen through the three years of their close friendship, a portrait of Eileen as a very devoted and complicated woman.

In the person of Ann, Lettice introduced many facets of Eileen's personality that hadn't been widely known before, but which have been verified by the newly discovered letters and in documents from her sometimes tumultuous time at the Ministry of Food. Ann, like Eileen, is pretty but not at all vain, more interested in ideas than appearances. While the other women are constantly adjusting their hair and makeup as they peer into the long mirrors throughout the workplace, Ann rarely does, sometimes absentmindedly pushing back her 'thick mop' of hair with one hand, 'a cigarette stuck out of one corner of her mouth'.[44] Lettice described her friend Eileen in real life as someone who 'always looked as if she was drifting into a room with no particular purpose there', and yet, although 'diffident and unassuming in manner, she had a quiet integrity that I never saw shaken'.[45] And the fictitious Ann mirrors that personality perfectly. The men in the department are charmed by her because 'she looks a dear little thing', but beneath her charm is someone who always stands up for fellow workers. When Ann sees any injustice, she is often the only one brave enough to interfere. In fact she and her fictional husband, Christopher, are 'two of the bravest people' the narrator knows. However, Ann's 'passion for justice does not exclude justice to herself'.

Just as in Eileen's real work experience years earlier – when she staged a walkout from the secretarial agency where she worked in protest over the treatment of her fellow typists – when Ann becomes aware that one of their favourite co-workers is about to be fired, she warns him and tries in vain to get him to stand up for himself. In the novel, the bosses at the Ministry of Food are afraid of Ann, just as Eileen had bragged earlier that the bosses at the Ministry of Information had been afraid of her. 'Ann is a firm believer in protests and in joint action,' and she suggests that her fellow workers 'should all resign in a body'. But, as it turns out, she can't convince anyone to even sign a petition, and the person is indeed fired. In an attempt to explain this end result, Ann wisely sums up human nature: 'Honest men are always a menace to dishonest men. They shake their nerves'.

Lettice writes in the novel that Ann and her husband are the 'real citizens of the new world', since they are not concerned about physical comfort and 'live by a burning morality'. They believe in 'the people on the march', and have faith that eventually common sense and love will win out over evil. In the novel, Ann mimics Orwell's belief 'that we all ought to be much more trained for street fighting', an idea that will, Ann believes, be rejected by the powers that be, who are 'afraid, of course, of getting a trained people's army'.

While Ann appears to be rather absent-minded, constantly missing breakfast and forgetting to shop for necessary food 'because she had not finished what she was saying at lunch', she does manage to prepare a good dinner every night for her husband as well as for all of the many friends who camp out at their apartment. Lettice was aware that Eileen often acted as mediator in her friends' as well as Orwell's friends' personal problems, and this role impressed Lettice enough that she made use of it in *Black Bethlehem*, presenting Ann as a woman who 'attracts crises. Her own friends are constantly ringing up to say that they wish to be divorced, are going to have babies or nervous breakdowns, or have quarrelled with their husbands or lovers.' As with Eileen and Orwell, Ann's husband's friends also 'have crises. They are . . . unable to stop drinking or unable to get drink . . . bitterly wounded by each other or betrayed by their wives. They all come to tell Ann about it.' Lettice gave Ann almost superhuman skills, which she must have believed Eileen herself had, portraying Ann as adept psychologically and able to look at people 'as though their faces and manners were glass. What she sees are their feelings.' When Ann is asked a question, 'She generally looks at you for a minute before answering . . . as though anything you said to her needed careful consideration.' Then, when she does finally respond, her thoughts on any subject are 'generally worth hearing'. It appeared that 'everything was important to her because her sense of life was so intense.'

In her novel, Lettice was not sympathetic to Ann's husband's constant illnesses. When Ann doesn't appear for work one morning, everyone is 'frantically worried' until her husband calls to say that 'Ann had been sick all night, but was now asleep and would be all right when she woke up.' Apparently he always minimises Ann's illnesses, and the narrator can't resist the comparison: 'If there is anything the matter with him he is a stretcher case at once.' Perhaps Eileen had helped lead Lettice to this conclusion by always downplaying her own illnesses while rushing home to make Orwell lunch whenever he was the least bit indisposed.

Lettice ends the section about Ann by having her die when a bomb destroys their flat while she is cooking dinner for her husband. As the narrator thinks back about her friend, she reflects, 'I felt her spirit near me, with its wide and sympathetic delight in the whole flow of human lives, its deep instinctive experience, its gentle wisdom. I felt her saying to me that life was short, and the people who loved were most of it that mattered.'

This novel helps us gain a greater appreciation of the unusual and admirable woman Eileen was – knowledge that is hard to gather considering the few letters from her that survived, as well as her own reluctance to ask for praise of any kind. As Lettice summed up her re-creation of Eileen: 'People like Ann, whose love moves out in a widening circle, are rare. Under what star was she born? Why is it that so few of us are like her?'

In the summer of 1943, the whole future of the *Kitchen Front* programme was in peril. Holmes had agreed to take a holiday from 5 to 17 August, then stay in the job until the end of August, when Anne Harris would take over. Just before she left on holiday, she wrote a long letter to 'Emily', who was in contact while still 'on leave'. She had some last-minute thoughts of possible speakers 'as a final burst'. She might have been joking about one idea for the 'Men in the Kitchen' slot, 'Gipsy Petulengro, who is a splendid cook, especially of hedgehogs, nettles, field-mice, etc. etc.' She added, 'I think this is grand – do you, or am I being too flippant?' But as they joked, Holmes's boss was preparing a letter to one of Eileen's superiors 'about the proposed change in "The Kitchen Front" which has now been approved by the Board' of the BBC: they had decided to cut the *Kitchen Front* broadcasts to three instead of six mornings a week, and to fill the other three morning slots with various other types of housewife information. The BBC official believed the Ministry of Food had been acting as 'would-be dictators', and he wanted the BBC to regain control. But, in his letter, he tried to soften his decision, claiming that '8:15 a.m. has proved to be a very good listening time for the housewife, and that food . . . is by no means the most urgent or difficult.' He ended his letter rather slickly: 'I hope very much that you will see the force of this argument and that when we meet . . . to discuss the future of "The Kitchen Front" and the change of producer, we shall be able to decide . . . the most important features in "The Kitchen Front" to retain in the reduced time available.' Eileen's superiors were caught completely off-guard. One responded, 'I was deeply shocked by your letter of 7 August, a real "block buster," even if wrapped in cotton wool!' He went on to explain, 'We think for several reasons . . . that the demand for the "Kitchen Front" is greater than ever and the listening figures appear to support that opinion . . . Perhaps our secretaries could fix a day [for us to meet].'

In her last two weeks at work at the end of August, Holmes was busy correcting a scheduling mishap that had happened when Harris was covering for her on holiday. 'I got to Miss Harris and then to Mrs. Blair about this,' she explained. 'The confusion seems to have been caused by Mrs. Blair asking over the telephone for various dates to be changed, to fit in with her absence on leave.' After a detailed rescheduling of the speakers involved, Holmes ended the note with, 'These arrangements have been confirmed with Mrs. Blair, by telephone.' Using Lettice's novel as a guide, Eileen quite likely was purposefully causing confusion. Harris was covering for Holmes when she was on holiday, and Eileen called her with conflicting information, which would have caused trouble for Harris. Eileen also phoned Holmes on 20 August with information about a Westerby decision that once again defied the new agreement. He had been given Eileen's work to follow up on while she was away, and he had made a script change on his own without discussing it with Holmes. Holmes reported him yet again to her superiors, perhaps hoping along with Eileen that he would be seen as the problem rather than Holmes herself.

In addition, possibly acting in solidarity with Eileen, Mabel Constanduros told Holmes that she was feeling 'seedy' and extremely overworked and would have to cancel her 3 August show. She presented two recordings for them to use, then told Holmes, 'After that, I shall probably stop altogether.' Holmes reported that 'Mrs. Constanduros is not well, needs a rest and is also busy with her play.'

An important meeting was called on 30 August to work out the future of the *Kitchen Front* programme. All the principals were present, the BBC staff along with Eileen and Westerby and other officers from the Ministry of Food. An official memo was then distributed on 10 September, formally cutting the *Kitchen Front* programme to three mornings a week instead of six, beginning on 4 October, and giving the

BBC control of almost every part of the process except 'food policy', whatever that meant. The Ministry of Food was adamantly against the reduction of time for the *Kitchen Front* programme. Lord Woolton believed, 'There is a greater need than ever before for advice on food . . . We have abundant evidence of its usefulness to the housewife.' They argued strongly against this decision while realising they had no choice but to accept it. The main concession they won was to have the name *The Kitchen Front* retained as a subtitle for the three food programmes that would remain during the week, since Lord Woolton 'attaches great value to the title'. At that point, Woolton himself decided it was time to resign, which he did in November. As a final attempt to sweeten the poison pill, the BBC prepared an official statement, saying, 'It is obviously a compliment to the Ministry of Food that they have handled the rationing situation so well and kept the public so well informed and advised on every new regulation, that the need for guidance on this subject is not now so keenly felt.'

From October on, the food programmes were produced on Tuesdays, Thursdays, and Fridays, while the talks on the other days dealt with 'a variety of problems not concerned with food'. Westerby's name is mentioned most often in letters about the reduced *Kitchen Front* programmes, and there are no further letters between Eileen and Harris in the files. Meanwhile, after six weeks without a show, Mrs Buggins resumed again on 12 October, and continued until the end of the war. For months there were no letters from, or references to, Eileen, suggesting that she had either quit the job entirely or moved on to other tasks. However, on 6 December, one of the *Kitchen Front* speakers told Anne Harris that she had given her script to 'Mrs. Blair'. And when Harris decided to leave her job later that month, after only a few months, it was suggested that 'Miss Harris take an early opportunity of introducing [her replacement] to Westerby and Mrs. Blair.'

The last letter from Eileen that is in the files is dated 17 February 1944. She wrote, cheerfully, 'Dear Miss Quigley, I'm sorry the vegetabull [a large poster of a bull made out of vegetables] has been so slow-moving, but here he is. If you've ever seen the Ministry's other posters you'll understand that there is considerable competition for these. Yours sincerely, Emily Blair.' However, Eileen continued at the Ministry of Food until October 1944, with many letters in the files referring to her and her involvement in decisions. However, none are personally written by Eileen.

Eileen clearly preferred her job at *The Kitchen Front* to the one at the Ministry of Information, but friends said she sometimes treated her official work 'with much irony'.[46] One purpose of the recipes they broadcast was to steer housewives away from fats, eggs, and sugar and encourage them to substitute instead grains, potatoes, and vegetables. But 'Eileen didn't like the potato, salad and vitamin dishes we had to try and put over', Lettice said. 'She liked meat, eggs, cheese, wine.'[47] Another friend remembered that Eileen was 'always making fun of the Ministry of Food. She had a spoof pamphlet about what to do with a bone: first, scrape all the meat off it, the first soup, then the second soup, then give it to the dog, then wash it, then take it to salvage.' This was a reference to the use of bones as 'essential for making munitions of war', as Holmes explained to Constanduros, when asking her at one point to 'include a reference in your next talk to the importance of separating bones for salvage'. And then there was the suggestion that eating carrots would improve your eyesight, which Eileen certainly would have scoffed at. But, although she felt she had the right to talk 'about the comedy of her life at the Ministry of Food', she would snap at Orwell if he was 'a little contemptuous of it'.[48] And, behind Eileen's frivolous and joking exterior still lurked the loss of her brother. Years after Eric had died, Eileen continued to tell Lettice privately, 'Don't mind if I am alive or dead nowadays.'[49] And she didn't just say that occasionally; 'She said that all the time.'[50]

Years later, one old friend of Eileen's was upset that Orwell's first biographer, Bernard Crick, might present a too favourable portrayal of

Eileen. 'Nor was Eileen a self-sacrificing angel incarnate,' Lydia wrote to him. 'She could be vindictive and could lash with her tongue. I have known her turn against people for a relatively trivial cause and then have nothing good to say for them.' According to Lydia, Eileen could also be bitter in her feelings about Orwell. She remembered her 'angry' remark that 'the deep folds at the corners of his mouth which made him look like a suffering Christ were merely due to the loss of a few teeth.' Of course it's possible Eileen did make that remark, but perhaps in humour rather than in anger. Lydia also told Crick that Eileen had complained to her 'half-ruefully, half-resentfully on [Orwell's] having no idea of the size of war-time rations.' Apparently he wasn't always able to concentrate on the intricacies of ration allotments. However, when he once absentmindedly ate both their shares of butter, Lydia was upset that Eileen too easily managed to smile and accept this behaviour. 'It was most important for his health to have all the fat he could eat,'[51] Eileen explained. One wonders whether Eileen at some point had a falling out with Lydia herself. Her new friendship with Lettice had perhaps cut into her time with Lydia, and the two women were far from friends – 'plainly with no love lost on either side', as Crick noticed, although he was clearly more impressed with Lydia than with Lettice. For her part, Lettice thought Lydia concentrated on 'the externals of their married life,'[52] and thus had a superficial understanding of Eileen and Orwell's relationship. But perhaps neither of them completely grasped its complexity.

In the summer of 1943, while Eileen's troubles were intensifying at work, Orwell decided that it was time to put an end to his 'two wasted years' at the BBC. In the process of creating many innovative literary programmes for an audience in India that he was never sure actually existed, Orwell had worn himself down to the point where he realised he was curtailing his creative future. No doubt, Eileen's travails at work were brought home to share, and during those months they talked about what other changes they might make in their future lives.

Although they both hated London, and seemed stuck there for a while, they were constantly considering country alternatives. It must have been an extremely taxing period for them both. They went on holiday from 3 to 20 September, while Eileen was still protesting about the changes at *The Kitchen Front*. Then, after a few days in October when he was too ill to even go into the office, Orwell finally resigned on 24 November. As he told a friend, 'At present I'm just an orange that's been trodden on by a very dirty boot.'[53] He also left the Home Guard at that point, with a medical discharge, after three years of service.

For years Eileen had been urging him to slow down his output of reviews and essays and to concentrate on writing another novel. 'I think it's essential that you should write some book again,' she constantly implored.[54] However, Orwell wasn't yet ready to tackle any serious creative writing and, instead, he took a part-time job as literary editor of *Tribune*. This gave him more free days in the week to write about what really interested him. But he wasn't a very decisive editor, and when he left that job, his successor found a drawer full of manuscripts Orwell had accepted and paid for but never used. 'As you know, I thought *Tribune* better than the BBC and I still do,' Eileen wrote to him over a year later. 'Indeed I should think a municipal dustman's work more dignified and better for your future as a writer.' But she reiterated her annoyance that he seemed to be avoiding any serious writing, adding, 'And of course you must do much less reviewing and nothing but specialised reviewing if any.'[55] But Orwell was not a man who enjoyed a leisurely life.

However, perhaps because of Eileen's persistence, after leaving the BBC he immediately started work on *Animal Farm*. It was a quick interim book for him, and apparently didn't count as a new novel, since he wrote in 1946, 'It is 6 years or so since I wrote [a novel],'[56] referring back to *Coming Up for Air*, which had been published in 1939. During the three months it took to finish this important book, Orwell still somehow managed to review twenty-two books as well as write sixteen scripts of a new *Tribune* column called 'As I Please'. Perhaps this kind of writing on the side, which he now knocked out without rewrites, was a sort of breather for him from the serious work of the new book. But he confessed later that he didn't know why he had been 'such a fool as to let myself in for' taking on some 'ghastly' and 'rubbishy' writing in the past.[57] Although he continued to claim in letters that he was 'overwhelmed with work', he was well aware that no one, especially not Eileen, was forcing him to review so many books. Yet somehow, with amazing speed, *Animal Farm* was perfected, and on 9 March Orwell told his agent that it was 'being typed now'.[58]

A perfectly typed version of *Animal Farm* is preserved in the Orwell archives. One copy at least was damaged when a bomb hit their flat in June 1944, and when Orwell delivered a copy to T. S. Eliot for possible publication by Faber, he apologised for its 'blitzed' and 'slightly crumpled condition'.[59] The copy in the archives is an extremely clean manuscript that only required very minor pencilled instructions by an editor at that time – the kind of manuscript every publishing house would dream of receiving. Eileen typed the final versions of most of Orwell's work, including some adaptations that he prepared for the BBC,[60] and it can be assumed that all the manuscripts Orwell delivered to publishers were in the same excellent shape.

Orwell explained his inspiration for *Animal Farm* in a later preface: 'I saw a little boy . . . driving a huge cart-horse along a narrow path . . . It struck me that if only such animals became aware of their strength we should have no power over them.'[61] Orwell had always been terrible at describing his books ahead of time, and he told one friend that this new one was 'a little squib which might amuse you',[62] and another that it was 'about a farm run by people, where the animals take over and make just as bad a job of it'.[63] Perhaps he really had no idea how significant a work it really was.

*A*nimal Farm was written quickly, in an elegant style that seems to flow almost effortlessly. Eileen was delighted that Orwell was at last finding the time to devote to this new book and she was encouraging him to speed through what she immediately realised was an important work. She loved what he was producing each day even though he himself was downplaying its importance to friends. When she got home from work in the evening, Orwell would read the parts he'd written out loud to her and they would laugh together in bed – the warmest place in the flat – as she came up with enthusiastic suggestions. Other couples may relate to this way of sharing creative comic ideas. Each morning at work Eileen would tell her friends about the book's progress, making them laugh as she recreated some of the scenes for them. 'She saw at once that it was a winner . . . And she would quote bits out of it when we were having our coffee,' Lettice remembered. 'It was very exciting.'[64] Lettice believed Eileen 'was keenly alive to George's work and seemed to me a very good critic of it.'[65]

When Lydia first read *Animal Farm*, she 'could recognise touches of Eileen's humour in some of the episodes. Whether she had directly suggested them, or George had unconsciously assimilated some of his wife's whimsical ways of talking and viewing things . . . I have little doubt that . . . Eileen had collaborated in the creation of *Animal Farm*.'[66] Indeed, some parts do resemble the gentle humour Eileen was contributing to scripts for *The Kitchen Front*. Tosco Fyvel agreed that Eileen 'had a very positive influence on Orwell's writings, especially on *Animal Farm*.'[67] He continued, 'It has so often been remarked that, unlike Orwell's other works, *Animal Farm* is a supremely well-written little satire . . . And if *Animal Farm* is a tale so perfect in its light touch and restraint (almost 'unOrwellian'), I think some credit is due to the conversational influence of Eileen and the light touch of her bright, humorous intelligence.'[68] Lettice wrote, 'Some people who knew Eileen feel that the simplicity and elegance of *Animal Farm* may be due in part to her influence.'[69] Ian Angus said, 'I'm sure that she influenced her husband's style of writing very much.'[70] And Peter Davison believed that '*Animal Farm* is a last, and worthy, tribute to Eileen's beneficial influence on Orwell.'[71] Others noticed that this new book was filled with more humour than was typical in Orwell's other books – a humour that is light-hearted and not at all bitter or despairing, reminiscent of the wry and gentle whimsy that filled Eileen's letters. Fredric Warburg wrote, 'The writer of rather grey novels . . . had suddenly taken wings and become – a poet . . . There was, after all, little in Orwell's previous work to indicate that he was capable of this supreme effort.'[72] However, Warburg, like Rees, wasn't able to imagine that Eileen's influence could have brought about the changes he noticed. Even Sonia Orwell said that Orwell 'probably did talk to [Eileen] fully about his works', since she was 'such a nice woman' and had been 'a great help to George'.[73]

Eileen was not interested in claiming credit for any help she gave Orwell, so it's no surprise that she didn't emphasise any input of her own to Lettice or her other friends. She did, however, tell her family, including Gwen O'Shaughnessy and Doreen Kopp, about how involved she had been in this book. According to current members of Eileen's family, Orwell had originally written a more traditional essay criticising Stalin and totalitarianism, an unpopular subject at that moment, since Stalin was helping the Allies defeat Hitler. Doreen told her son Quentin that 'Eileen had suggested rewriting the work as an allegory when the issue of Stalin as an ally made it difficult for his publisher in the original format'. As he went on to explain, 'My mother lived in a neighbouring house in Canonbury Square [and] she was close to the Blair household. In consequence that is probably how she was able to say that to me.'[74] Catherine Moncure, Gwen's adopted daughter, remembers that 'there was always a murmur in the background of my youth that [Eileen had a hand in the creation of *Animal Farm*]'.[75] In fact, as he was looking for a publisher, Orwell expected to include a long, explanatory essay, 'The Freedom of the Press', as a Preface, but this idea was later rejected. That essay was perhaps the original one that had been changed to an allegory. And Orwell himself later told a friend, 'It was a terrible shame that Eileen didn't live to see the publication of "Animal Farm", which she was particularly fond of and even helped in the planning of.'[76]

When Eileen's letters to Norah were discovered in 2005 it became clear that Eileen had been contributing 'emendations' to Orwell's typescripts for years. And it is not just her suggestions, but also her memories (particularly in *Homage to Catalonia*) and her playful spirit that often surface in his work. It should now be clear that, although *Animal Farm* is the first of Orwell's books where Eileen's contributions have been widely acknowledged, she was a constant influence on his richness of voice and sometimes whimsical tone throughout her time with him.

Which parts of *Animal Farm* might Eileen have contributed? Of course, the name Willingdon clearly refers to Wallington, the village where they lived for many years, but it might also reference Hillingdon, the section of London where Eileen shared a home with her parents for a while after graduation. The choice of pigs as the animals which become corrupted is a curious one. Although Beatrix Potter's *Pigling Bland* – the story of two pigs who escape the clutches of an evil farmer – was one of Orwell's favourite books as a child, he told a friend that pigs 'are most annoying destructive animals, and hard to keep out of anywhere because they are so strong and cunning'.[77] Also, since 'Pig' was Eileen's nickname among her Oxford friends, she might have playfully contributed to this decision.

Eileen, with her knowledge of psychology, might have helped with the creation of various personalities for the different types of farm animals. Some characters in Orwell's novels seem a bit superficial at times, and he was noted for his lack of character insight, causing him to accept some people as friends in an uncritical way. The study of personality traits, such as a tendency to agree with 'the one who was speaking at the moment' and not trusting the truth of one's own memory, are part of psychological training, and Eileen would have been very helpful in developing these tendencies in the various animals. Also, Eileen is credited with naming their dog Marx, as well as with giving their goats personal names. Muriel, their first goat, named by Eileen and a favourite of the couple's for years, was of course the inspiration for the sympathetic goat named Muriel in the book. Benjamin, with his stubborn but winning personality, sounds like a tolerant wife's depiction of a beloved but occasionally cranky mate. Benjamin could also have been a flashback to her brother, Eric O'Shaughnessy, a very stubborn and stern man. Perhaps the line 'Asked why [he never laughed], he would say that he saw nothing to laugh at' was a remembrance of him. Both Erics could have used Benjamin's perfect projection: 'Life would go on as it had always gone on – that is badly', a sentiment that also reflects Eileen's occasional pessimism. A more poignant scene that definitely shows Eileen's influence is when Boxer dies: 'A thin stream of blood had trickled out of his mouth . . . "It is my lung," said Boxer in a weak voice.' How many times had Eileen herself suffered through that moment? Mollie, the 'pretty white mare' who reluctantly gives up the ribbons she had worn in her mane, and who is discovered 'admiring herself in [a mirror] in a very foolish manner in front of Mrs. Jones's dressing table', would seem to be the inspiration of an observant woman, as would the description of Clover, 'who had never quite got her figure back after her fourth foal'.

Many other sections of the book resonate with Eileen's rhythm and sense of mischief. She was definitely teasing her brother – whose name Eric was short for Frederick, his middle name – when the owner of one of the adjacent farms, Pinchfield, was named Mr Frederick. This character represents Hitler, and Eileen had famously called her brother 'a Nature's Fascist', although in a bemused way. And the section when 'it was discovered that the greater part of the potato crop had been frosted in the claps, which had not been covered thickly enough. The potatoes had become soft and discoloured, and only a few were edible' must also have been a teasing reference to the time Orwell had failed to store extra potatoes properly when he worried about future rationing. The names of the committees Snowball is forming – Clean Tails League for the cows and Wild Comrades Re-education Committee 'to tame the rats and rabbits' – also mimic Eileen's spirit. And, although it's blasphemous to suggest, it seems at least possible that Eileen could have come up with one of the best-remembered concepts in the book:

'All animals are equal. But some animals are more equal than others.' This is definitely a complaint most women have had from time to time.

With this book finished, and ideas for new novels piling up, life for the couple seemed headed towards a smooth successful future. After a setback the year before, Eileen was once again enjoying her job. She chose the title 'Old Friends with New Flavours' for one show and was busy altering scripts in ways that pleased her and her superiors. Orwell was full of creative energy, which was just what Eileen had been encouraging, while she was again enjoying her social life with friends from work, making them laugh with her exaggerations about some of the food restrictions and the characters she had to deal with at work. But then, just at that positive point, Orwell presented Eileen with two startling new ideas: perhaps they should move to Jura, a far-distant island off the west coast of Scotland; and perhaps they should adopt a son. With these sudden suggestions, is it possible that Orwell was attempting to draw Eileen away from her new independent life?

16

Nearly a Happy Ending

*Eileen had bathed the baby and was giving
him his bottle. George was kneeling before her,
watching, entranced, rather in the manner of an
adoring shepherd in a Nativity painting.*

Lydia Jackson

There were two immediate problems with Orwell's newest
dreams for the future. Eileen was worried that Jura might be
even worse for Orwell's health than Wallington had been. And,
more important, she wasn't at all sure she wanted to adopt a baby. But,
at that moment, the first and most compelling step for them was to
find a publisher for *Animal Farm*. Even as Eileen was typing the final
manuscript – with at least three carbon copies – Orwell was already
making suggestions to his agent of possible publishers. And at first they
were optimistic that someone would be found quickly.

Orwell was worried that Gollancz, who had the rights to his next
two novels, would not properly promote the book because of his
political beliefs. And, to his relief, Gollancz rejected it immediately
because it was perceived as critical of Stalin. The couple had high
hopes that a few other prominent publishing houses would be

interested, even though Orwell was aware that 'this book is murder from the Communist point of view, though no names are mentioned'.[1] However, to their dismay, months went by as publisher after publisher got cold feet, worrying among other things that Russian leaders, at that point allies of Britain, would be angry at being compared to pigs. And Orwell was furious at the 'imbecile suggestion that some other animal than the pigs might be made to represent the Bolsheviks'.[2] A firm that had published some Ministry of Food books that Eileen must have had a connection with was approached to no avail, and T. S. Eliot again rejected an Orwell future best-seller by misinterpreting it, even as he continued to ask the couple to join him for dinner. Dial Press in the US was anxious to see a copy, but it eventually came back with the absurd excuse that 'it was impossible to sell animal stories in the USA'.[3]

Orwell and Eileen commiserated together about the early rejections. He told an American friend, 'I am having hell and all to find a publisher for it here though normally I have no difficulty in publishing my stuff.'[4] They even toyed with the idea of printing the book themselves, vowing to do whatever it took to get it into bookshops quickly. As Orwell told his agent, 'I think what it says wants saying, unfashionable though it is nowadays.'[5] Sometime later, he explained his intention in writing the book. 'I meant the moral to be that revolutions only effect a radical improvement when the masses are alert and know how to chuck out their leaders as soon as the latter have done their job . . . People . . . assume there is no alternative except dictatorship or *laissez-faire* capitalism . . . What I was trying to say was, "You can't have a revolution unless you make it for yourself; there is no such thing as a benevolent dictatorship."'[6] Margaret Branch remembered Eileen expressing her indignation against the successive publishers who rejected *Animal Farm*.[7] She was proud of Orwell for being willing to brave the harsh criticism directed against him as he refused to soften its message.[8]

After all the possible large publishers had turned the book down,

Orwell finally approached Fredric Warburg, a man who he had initially assumed would not be interested, both for political reasons and because his small publishing house had been affected by the dire paper shortage. But by then it was mid-July, four months since the book had been finished, and Orwell was running out of options. He astonished Warburg by thrusting a copy of *Animal Farm* into his hands as he was finishing lunch in a pub. 'I don't suppose you'll like it,' Orwell cautioned. 'Much too anti-Russian for you, I'm afraid.' But Warburg was excited to be offered the book, and after reading it that evening, he 'never doubted that it was a masterpiece . . . We told Orwell immediately.' However, Warburg still had to deal with his wife, who, as it turned out, disliked *Animal Farm* so vehemently that she threatened, 'If you publish that book I'll leave you.'[9] In the end Warburg decided to brave her ire. He managed to find a printer with enough paper for 4,500 copies, and Eileen and Orwell were checking the proofs by the following February. However, with many perhaps unavoidable delays, *Animal Farm* was not officially published until 17 August 1945, well over a year after Warburg had accepted it, and seventeen months after Eileen had typed the final version. By then VE day had passed and the concerns about Russian leaders being offended had receded. *Animal Farm* was immediately successful, with the first copies quickly selling out. Orwell was at last on his way to world fame and more money than he'd ever expected to earn from his writing. But the delay in publication meant that Eileen would not live to enjoy the book's triumph.

During the long search for a publisher, Eileen and Orwell had many discussions about adopting a child. He had always longed for a son, and with the extra freedom at his new job, the new book finished, and the war believed to be nearing its end, this seemed to him to be the perfect time. By then they had accepted that Eileen wasn't going to get pregnant, although whether Orwell was sterile, as he himself believed, or Eileen had problems – though she assured Lettice it had nothing to do with her[10] – was never clear. This uncertainty could have been resolved if Orwell had been willing to be examined, but he had refused 'because it is so disgusting'.[11] They could also have clarified the situation if Orwell had accepted the poet Paul Potts's suggestion that Eileen try to be impregnated by someone else, but Orwell was repulsed by that idea too.

It was an easy time to find a baby to adopt. From 1942 to 1944, some two million American and Canadian troops filled the British cities. The young soldiers exuded an easy-going sexual energy, and the women on the home front were charmed by these gregarious men who doled out nylons and invited them to lavish parties, overwhelming them with luxuries and delicacies they hadn't seen for years. A young American soldier who spent a night with Eileen and Orwell at Mortimer Crescent told them what was possibly a representative story. A British girl, the soldier said, 'had come up to him on the pavement and seized hold of his penis with the words, "Hullo Yank!"'[12] Orwell wrote in May that 'no less than 20,000 English girls had already married American soldiers and sailors, and many more would'.[13] However, some of the lonely wives, whose husbands had been absent for years on the front lines, were also charmed and wooed by the soldiers. And of course these affairs often produced unwanted babies. Gwen O'Shaughnessy, as a gynaecologist, had constant access to babies whose mothers were anxious to give them up. She herself had recently adopted her daughter, Catherine, a six-month-old baby girl she'd been particularly drawn to when the baby's mother informed her that she had reluctantly decided she couldn't keep the child.

The real problem was that Eileen continued to resist the idea of adopting a child. She was happy at her busy, creative job that gave her time to help Orwell with his major writing as well as to look after their constant houseguests. She had told Lydia years before that '[S]he could not imagine anything more boring than playing with children,'[14] and forced now to examine her reluctance, she told a friend that '[She] was nervous for fear that she might not be able to give to an adopted child the love and empathy that she felt she could have given to one of her own.'[15] She also knew, without admitting it to anyone, that she probably had enough, if not a little too much, to deal with already, and adding the care of a baby might be overwhelming for her. One friend felt sure that this added responsibility would cause Eileen's health to deteriorate even more rapidly.[16]

But Orwell was extremely persuasive. He told someone later that '[O]ne of the reasons for adopting [a child] was to stop Eileen from working so hard.'[17] He 'passionately wanted a son, who was to have a cream-coloured perambulator with gold lines on and to be put down for Eton,'[18] Lettice remembered. His only requirement was that the new baby had to be a boy. For Eileen, her friend said, adopting a child would mean 'giving up her own work in the Ministry of Food where she was very happy and where she had a life of her own, not as George's wife.'[19] But Eileen was eventually worn down by the intensity of Orwell's desire for a son, and once again she agreed to bend her will to his.

While they were still discussing how exactly they would care for a new baby, given their extremely busy lives, Gwen was told by her doctor partner that a child was available. On 14 May, Nancy Robertson, a married woman living nearby in Greenwich, whose husband was a soldier at the front, had just given birth to an unwanted baby boy. So there was no turning back. The preliminary adoption proceedings took three weeks, during which time Eileen and Orwell did their best to prepare, buying various baby clothes and other essentials, including a basket to carry the child in. Then, early in June, Eileen arrived at the hospital with a little suitcase containing a nightgown and shawl to dress the baby in, after which she somehow got him back to Mortimer Crescent, apparently without Orwell's assistance. The child's original name was Richard Robertson, but Orwell took the tip of a burning cigarette to the birth certificate, attempting to obliterate that surname. Their new boy was named Richard Horatio, with the last name Blair. Neither Eileen nor Richard ever used the surname Orwell. According to friends, they were both immediately thrilled with their new baby, and

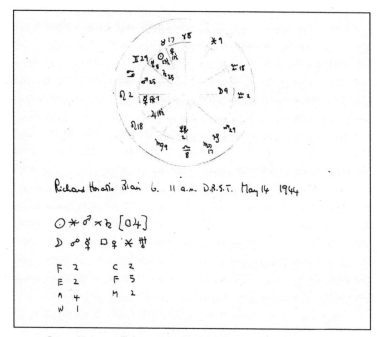

Rayner Heppenstall's horoscope of Richard Blair as a baby, October 1944.

Orwell didn't waste a minute before asking Heppenstall 'to draw little Richard's horoscope'. Heppenstall's letter back to Orwell contained the chart in the illustration plus a one-page sketch of Richard's horoscope, beginning, 'At first glance there seems to be a strong child who will be a bossy boy and run rather to intellect and height [but] the Moon is in opposition.'[20]

Just after Eileen brought Richard home from the hospital, just at the moment when she and Orwell were expecting some peaceful months as they reshaped their lives around their new child, London was bombarded by a new threat from Germany. D-Day had begun on the morning of 6 June, and Hitler was retaliating. The first V-1 buzz bombs, or doodlebugs as they were called, hit London on 13 June. These tiny, pilotless bombs were particularly terrorising because, just as the noise of their engines stopped rattling, the bombs would dive downwards, giving no time to take cover. Later, the V-2 rocket bombs added their even more serious destruction, with Orwell complaining once that his whole house was 'rocking from a recent explosion.'[21] On another evening, he noted in a column, baby Richard, who was in the next room, 'woke up and let out a yell or two' when a not-too-distant explosion shook the house again, causing the windows to 'rattle in their sockets.'[22]

On 28 June, just a few weeks after they had adopted Richard, a doodlebug landed across the street from 10A Mortimer Crescent, completely collapsing the roof and ceilings of their building and burying all their books and furniture in dust and debris. By their good luck, Eileen and Orwell and the baby were in Greenwich that night, so their lives were saved. But many of their belongings were damaged or destroyed. They each took a week off work[23] to sort through what was salvageable, finding among other things a damaged copy of the manuscript of *Animal Farm*. For many days afterwards, Orwell would go to the ruined building with a wheelbarrow and collect any books and papers as well as furniture and family portraits that had survived. After that attack, Lydia thought that Eileen 'seemed at the end of her tether . . . It was the first – and only – occasion on which I saw Eileen lose her poise on account of an air-raid.'[24] She now had a baby to care for, and during another raid Lettice saw her lay Richard on the floor and cover him with her own body.[25]

It's hard to completely track the family's movements during the summer as they looked for a new flat. Inez Holden told people thirty years later that they had all stayed with her at 106 George Street until early October. However, in a diary entry on 30 June 1944, Inez wrote that, although she had suggested they could all stay in her flat, 'it is no longer necessary as they are staying in George's brother's flat [in Bristol]. George is going to rent a room [in London] to write in.'[26] The flat she referred to in Bristol would have belonged to Orwell's sister Marjorie and her husband. This diary entry apparently negates the belief, claimed by

Inez years later, that they all immediately moved to her flat. But Bristol was too far away to be convenient for long. Probably Eileen stayed there for the week she took off work while Orwell sorted through their books and furniture, but she wasn't ready yet to give up her job.

An obvious safe home for Richard was the cottage in Wallington. Lydia and another friend had taken it over in 1940 when an unexploded land mine prevented them from using their London flat, and they continued to stay there off and on until 1947. After Orwell moved to London in the spring of 1940, he and Eileen visited the cottage only occasionally. But for a short time that summer, when bombs were again falling on London, a nurse and Florrie Taylor, Catherine's nanny, brought Richard and Catherine there, along with Gwen's son Laurence, who had recently returned from Canada. Eileen and Orwell expected the cottage to be shared when others were in need, and it was also used off and on for perhaps a year to house refugees, and possibly for a short while by Orwell's sister Marjorie and her family.[27]

The only letter from Eileen to Lydia – or at least the only one Lydia presented to researchers – was written that August while Eileen was still working at the Ministry of Food. In it, she was dealing mostly with cottage problems, trying to manoeuvre enough clean linen for several groups of possible cottage residents, including *two* babies . . . one with a mother and father the other with a mother', and she needed Lydia's cooperation. Eileen hoped to 'come down there for an hour or two while you're there and pack away some of our oddments – papers chiefly',[28] she wrote. She and Orwell were planning to accompany Gwen a few days later on a trip to Greystone, the home in County Durham that Gwen had recently inherited, as they decided how to care for Richard until they found a new flat to move into.

In this letter to Lydia, Eileen also made what she called a 'confession': 'Lettice Cooper and her sister went down to the cottage for the week-end,' she wrote. 'Barbara the sister is in the act of recovering from a nervous breakdown and this life is not good for her. She won't go away without Lettice and Lettice couldn't free herself for the week-end until just before it came . . . Anyway I hope you don't mind.'[29] It's somewhat distressing to realise that Eileen felt the need to apologise to Lydia for letting another friend make use of her own cottage. Although this letter mentioned only one weekend, as it turned out Lettice and her sister used the cottage for two or three weekends, which Lydia referred to as 'quite a long spell'.[30] And, as Lettice recalled, their stay 'was ruined by [Lydia], who . . . kept on popping into the cottage'.[31] Eileen's two close friends clearly didn't have any affection for each other.

Although Lydia was constantly getting book-review assignments from Orwell and continuing to visit Eileen for another year, this letter to Lydia feels a little distant. Lydia did, however, continue to be a presence in Gwen's life: 'She stuck to Mummy like glue and spent almost every Christmas with us,' Catherine recalled.[32] Another relative repeated Gwen's recurring lament: 'I wish I could choose my friends instead of my friends choosing me,'[33] partly in reference to these visits. Gwen rarely complained about anyone, but she did find Lydia 'trying'. 'I wouldn't call Lydia her friend and I didn't get the impression that Mummy admired her. She simply tolerated her,' Catherine believed. 'Lydia wanted Mummy to retire and share a cottage with her and Mummy was very opposed to that.' As for the children, 'Everyone in our house groaned when we knew Lydia was coming to stay . . . There was something about her demeanour that put us off. My brother hated her and didn't make any bones about it.' Looking back on her mostly negative memories of Lydia, Catherine was astonished 'when I found out she was a child psychologist since children didn't warm to her at all. I was even more astonished when I read her books and found out that there was a real person there at one time.'[34] Kopp's son Quentin, however, remembered that Lydia 'conducted some intelligence tests on me, which she said showed that I had an IQ of 150 . . . which left me with good memories of her.'[35]

At that point, with one of Orwell's dreams fulfilled by baby Richard, the idea of eventually moving to a remote Scottish island as the perfect get-away resurfaced. Ever since he'd mentioned in his diary at the beginning of the war, 'Thinking always of my island in the Hebrides, which I suppose I shall never possess or see,'[36] this thought had been percolating. Now, with the war clearly coming to an end, he shared his dream with Eileen. She understood that Orwell needed a place where it would be much harder to be pestered by those now clamouring for his work, but she wanted to be sure they made a careful choice. David Astor suggested that Orwell stay for a few days with a family he knew on Jura, as he believed that island might appeal to him for a summer home, and Orwell went there alone for two weeks at the end of September, looking for a suitable house for them to rent.[37] At the north end of the mostly uninhabited island, he discovered Barnhill, a large empty farmhouse with no telephone and mail delivered to a neighbour's home only twice a week. However, those definite benefits had to be weighed against the fact that the house was so completely isolated that it was twenty-five miles from the nearest shop and took most of two days to reach from London, including two separate ferry rides for a seasick-prone Orwell. Or, in Orwell's optimistic wording, as he later tried to encourage his friends to visit him, 'It's quite an easy journey really, except that you have to walk the last eight miles.'[38]

Orwell came back so hugely impressed that Eileen got in touch with the owner, with the prospect that she, Orwell, and Richard might spend the summer of 1945 there. Her main priority was to find somewhere that was a major improvement over the Wallington cottage, which, as she repeated in one of her last letters to Orwell, 'makes you ill – it's the damp and the smoke I think'. Eileen asked the owner many logistical questions about the functioning of the house and how supplies could be obtained, all sensible considerations before making such a big move, even for just the summer. 'I liked her instantly from the letter, a very good letter,'[39] the owner recalled.

Eileen was not immediately won over. She assured Orwell that she was 'not actually frightened . . . of living a primitive life again,' so she was definitely open to the remoteness, which Orwell loved. But she reminded him practically that a primitive life 'does waste a lot of time'.[40] They had been considering the idea of spending the following summer at the Wallington cottage, 'but it would be better to find somewhere with more space because you and Richard would be too much for the cottage very soon,' she wrote, adding, rather surprisingly, 'and I don't know where his sister would go.'[41] Apparently they were now so thrilled with one child that they were ready to take on another. Thinking of Richard as he grew into his 'difficult second year', when he would need space to run around in, Eileen told Orwell that their son would be much more likely to keep his positive outlook 'if he has the country and you have the kind of life that satisfies you – and me'.[42] At least in this sentence, although loosely added at the end, Eileen was also looking out for herself.

Finally, after being somewhat reassured by the owner of Barnhill, besides listening to many persuasive arguments from Orwell, Eileen agreed to the Jura experiment. She became convinced that the house was indeed 'quite grand – 5 bedrooms, bathroom, W.C., H & C and all, large sitting room, kitchen, various pantries, dairies etc. and a whole village of "buildings",' as she wrote to Orwell, concluding rather surprisingly, 'In fact just what we want to live in twelve months of the year.'[43] Eileen was ready for another extreme adventure in living, a requirement as Orwell's wife.

In the summer of 1944, Orwell and Eileen found a new London flat. 'We shall have [a flat in Canonbury Square] unless the bombs beat us to the post which is rather likely,' Eileen told a friend. She was excited about the new flat, pointing out one particular detail that pleased her: 'The outlook is charming and we have a flat roof about three yards by two which seems full of possibilities.' But she was already wary of the problems the new top-floor flat would present. 'To get to it you climb an uncountable number of stone stairs . . . I don't know how Richard will be managed,' Eileen worried, before joking, 'I thought we might have a crane and sling and transport him the way they do elephants in the films but George thinks this unsuitable.'[44]

By September they had signed a lease for 27B Canonbury Square, but they didn't take over the flat completely until October. They probably brought Richard home from Greystone just before 6 October, since Orwell complained in an article that day about the extreme discomfort of long train rides where some passengers are required to stand for many hours.[45] He told a friend some days later, 'It is no joke travelling with a child now,' though, he added, 'We had good luck about porters etc. and [Richard] was very good all through the journey.'[46]

The new flat was remembered by one friend as having five rooms, including a long sitting room with a fireplace at one end, where they sometimes enjoyed a peat fire, and a dining table at the other end, with two other small adjoining rooms. However, the woman who rented the flat from Orwell in 1946 and 1947 had a different memory. 'The flat was a conversion ranging across the attics of two nineteenth-century houses . . . with a long climb to the top floor' through an entrance door opening from the garden at the rear of the building. The plaque indicating that Orwell lived there is displayed on the front, or Canonbury Square, side of the building. However, a visit to this flat years ago required entry through the back garden, as this renter remembered. Today the back garden is enclosed by a wall with a locked entrance. 'The front door opened into a long, narrow [linoleum-covered] passage, with doors to two large rooms on one side and four small rooms on the other.'[47] The walls were decorated as usual with Orwell's Burmese swords and family portraits,[48] and also contained 'a Victorian draught screen . . . embellished with coloured cut-outs depicting angel children, carol singers, Newfoundland dogs, [and] Persian kittens', a scene that 'might have been lifted straight out of an old-fashioned ladies' journal.'[49] This screen, which appears in photographs of Orwell, might have been designed and created by Eileen, in an effort to protect Orwell's work chair from the constant draughts in that flat. In the back garden two goats were installed, since Orwell believed their milk was superior for Richard.[50]

As mentioned earlier, many have assumed that this apartment was the prototype for Winston Smith's apartment building in *Nineteen Eighty-Four*. However, their eighth-floor flat at Langford Court seems a much more likely comparison.

As usual, friends had quite different impressions of this new flat. Tosco Fyvel, a frequent visitor, remembered 'the utter cheerlessness of the awkwardly built flat', no doubt because it had been fashioned to connect the attics of two adjoining buildings. 'It looked as if every door had a slice of the bottom sawn off so that cold draughts could whistle through.'[51] George Woodcock found it 'a dark and almost dingy place', cluttered with crammed bookshelves and various inherited portraits and knickknacks.[52] And yet another friend said it consisted of 'a very large but ordinary, messy room' with 'books and papers scattered around', adjoined to 'a small bedroom and a little room where he did his carpentry'.[53] But Orwell's future rental tenant was a little more complimentary, saying the flat 'was provided with everything necessary and it was indeed luxurious' compared with other places she had rented. She remembered bookshelves 'weighed down with long lines of volumes [with] piles of literary and political journals' scattered around.[54] Orwell himself acknowledged some of its problems, complaining that they hadn't been able to get carpets installed right away. Later on, he was upset that they had no water for three days because the pipes were frozen, and that plaster kept falling from the ceiling because of melting drifts of snow on the roof.[55]

But their friend Paul Potts loved it there. 'Nothing could be more pleasant than the sight of his living room in Canonbury Square early on a winter's evening at high-tea-time. A huge fire, the table crowded with marvellous things, Gentleman's Relish and various jams, kippers, crumpets and toast.' He also raved about 'the conversation and the company; his wife, some members of his family or hers, a refugee radical or an English writer'.[56] For their part, Orwell and Eileen were clearly pleased to have a new home large enough to welcome all the visitors they loved. The discomforts that worried their friends were often invisible to them.

Although Orwell was immediately ready to show off the new flat and child, even to near strangers, Eileen told him she needed more time 'to get quite used to looking after the baby' by herself before visitors started arriving in the usual numbers. She had continued working at the Ministry of Food throughout 1944, even after the adoption, with many work letters mentioning her and asking her advice during the spring and summer. But she finally resigned after they brought Richard back from Greystone, so 'she can be at home all day and we don't have to make use of the day nursery,' Orwell told a friend. And when he first suggested that Lydia visit them at the new flat, he told her, 'You'll find us at home almost any evening . . . We can't go out at night much because of the baby.'[57] A final Ministry of Food note on 30 October informed Eileen's former co-workers that 'Miss Gordon' would be 'deputizing for Mrs. Blair' at the next meeting.

As the months went by, Richard's parents became even happier with their child. Lettice was pleased to notice that Eileen immediately stopped saying she didn't care whether she lived or died. She now overwhelmingly wanted to live. Eileen studied her son carefully, comparing him favourably with the other children he was often with. 'Richard really has a natural tendency to be sort of satisfied, balanced in fact,' she thought. 'Faced with any new situation he is sure that it will be an exciting and desirable situation for him.'[58] She also believed that he 'had great charm' and was 'a hard worker.'[59] She understood that Orwell relished any details about his new son, and she agreed when he told friends that Richard was 'a very thoughtful little boy' and a beautiful baby. She had reluctantly agreed to adopt a child, but she was soon fully content with her decision, and even more so as she constantly saw the joy Richard was bringing Orwell.

However, Eileen also suffered with some of the same silly worries that new mothers often have. She described the Kopp baby as having 'the hair and hands of a talented musician,' and she worried that Richard was somehow inferior. 'I expected to be jealous,' she told Lettice, 'but found that I didn't prefer him to Richard, preferable though he is.'[60] Was it possible, as some have wondered, that Eileen had a well-hidden regret that she had rejected Kopp's offer of a more traditional marriage, a marriage where she might have had her own child with him? She was certainly always glad to have Kopp nearby as a friend.

After a short time, Orwell was quite pleased to report that Richard 'has settled down nicely in his new home', adding, 'I'm no judge but I think he is a very nice child and quite forward for his age, especially as he was very tiny at first.'[61] When Lettice visited Eileen at the new flat, the two women would shop for supper ingredients, wheeling Richard in his borrowed dark-blue pram, a practical substitute for the dreamed of cream-coloured one with the gold lines. Back at the flat, 'Richard instead of going into his cot generally slept on George's knee while Eileen cooked.'[62] When Lydia first saw the child, 'Eileen was at Greenwich, being instructed in yet another skill – that of looking after a young baby – by the nurse of her 6-year-old nephew just returned from Canada.' Lydia was impressed as she watched the scene unfold. Eileen 'had bathed the baby and was giving him his bottle. George was kneeling before her, watching, entranced, rather in the manner of an adoring shepherd in a Nativity painting.'[63] Lettice also noticed that, after the adoption, Orwell 'was transfigured with gentleness'. She said later that the photographs of him with Richard 'show such an open loving feeling in George's face that it was moving to look at them.'[64] Orwell's niece recalled that he 'quite liked' children, and Gwen's daughter, Catherine, remembers Orwell walking at her side and holding her by the hand, a gentle uncle. Their friend David Astor believed that the couple 'were renewing their marriage round their new child'.[65]

At this point the future promised more for them than it ever had. They were as happy again as they had been in those first six blissful months of marriage. Orwell had at last finished another book, one they were both very proud of. And, although it wasn't yet published, in December they received an advance royalty cheque of £45. They were making plans to live in the country again, as they both much preferred, with gardens and fruit trees and even more goats and chickens. Orwell was getting almost everything he wrote published and they now had enough income to allow Eileen to spend as much time as she wanted with Richard. They were even dreaming of a daughter to join the family. On one visit, Lydia remembered, 'As we drank tea in front of the fire . . . and Richard lay on his back on the couch, cooing happily and playing with his toes, his adoptive parents looked more serene, more relaxed and happier than they had done for some time past.'[66] They now also had more time to travel, and at one point that autumn the three Blairs took the train to Wales to visit Arthur Koestler and his wife, who had become their good friends. Eileen liked the custom in Wales for allowing babies in a pub. Apparently there was a shelf under the bar counter where a child could be placed in a basket while the parents drank nearby.[67]

Looking back at how blissful Eileen and Orwell were with the new baby makes it doubly sad that Richard had these loving parents for such a very short time. He didn't realise he'd been adopted until he'd been living for a few years with his Aunt Avril, after both his parents had died, and she surprised him with that news. When Lettice saw him as a young man in his thirties, she remembered Richard confiding to her that he'd never felt sure whether either of his parents had loved him. Lettice had sadly assured him that they had both loved him very much.[68] Richard doesn't remember this conversation, but he realises now, 'There is no doubt they did indeed love me. I think that goes without saying.'[69]

Unfortunately, even with all these new pleasures, Orwell couldn't stop his compulsive acceptance of virtually every assignment offered him, managing to write 110 reviews and short articles for major publications during 1944,[70] along with some more extensive essays. Although he already had the retreat to Jura in mind, the realisation that he might soon escape from this compulsion didn't seem to slow him down. Some of his old friends 'saw something terrible in the pace at which he drove himself'.[71] Managing to read all the books he listed, as well as review them, was a feat hardly anyone else could have accomplished. And, in fact, this prodigious output would not have been possible without quite a bit of help from his professional-typist wife. Although she took a bit of time off from typing at the beginning of the summer, Eileen was busy helping him with his work again by the end of August.[72] As Koestler summed it up, 'She was the ideal wife for him, matter of fact, practical, brave, warm but not sentimental. She combined the qualities of a hospital nurse and a literary companion.'[73] Although she realised she would never recover completely from whatever her illness was if she kept pushing herself that hard, Eileen, like Orwell, didn't really know how to stop.

While attempting to keep up with their typical but much too busy schedule through the autumn and winter, they each grew noticeably weaker. Eileen continued to suffer from excessive vaginal bleeding that drained her energy. She told a friend that she was 'in bed more than half the time' during those months.[74] When Lydia visited one day, Eileen 'was in the back garden trying to wheel the pram with Richard asleep in it into the entrance hall by the stairs.' She complained to her friend, 'He's got to be carried upstairs, but the creature's put on so much weight lately that I just can't manage it.'[75] As Orwell's niece remembered, 'It was most inconvenient, as there was no lift,' and they 'had to haul [Richard's] pram up and down endless stairs.'[76] Eileen explained to Orwell later that she felt 'suicidal every time I walk as far as the bread shop' near the flat.[77] Following the advice of Gwen and George Mason, a doctor friend, Eileen had begun a course of injections in an attempt to increase her strength. But instead she continued to weaken.

Orwell continued to pretend that nothing too serious was wrong with either of them. Avril was sure that he 'did not neglect [Eileen] intentionally. He was really pretty vague about other people's conditions of health and ailments, although closely observing their habits.' And 'Eileen certainly did not neglect him,' Avril added. 'I well remember her doing her best to give him things to eat that he liked – she was an excellent cook. She herself seemed to live on weak China tea & nothing else'.[78] Once during this time, Orwell agreed to accompany Michael Meyer on an all-day theatre adventure, which included seven hours watching Laurence Olivier and Ralph Richardson in *Henry IV*, with dinner afterwards. Afraid of being late for the opening curtain, the two men had rushed through the London streets. As Meyer said later, 'I remember the dreadful whistling heaviness of his breathing for fully five minutes after we had taken our seats, and my shame at having forgotten the state of his lungs'.[79]

Early in 1945, Orwell still somehow managed to get an assignment from the *Observer* as a war correspondent in Europe for two months. As Astor, the magazine's editor, remembered it, 'He'd never been in a country that was under a dictatorship [and] he wanted to go and breathe the atmosphere'.[80] Eileen revealed no objection to his going, but she decided to take Gwen's advice and spend those months at Greystone, where she hoped to have complete rest while Richard was cared for by the staff already there looking after Gwen's two children. As Eileen explained later, it was, at least on her part, 'a ridiculous attempt to avoid an operation'.[81]

The family stayed together in London until just before Orwell took off for Paris, on 15 February, with Richard sleeping in the next room as Orwell wrote his 'As I Please' column for 2 February.[82] Then, on 9 February, he wrote a complicated 'As I Please' piece complaining about housework, starting 'Every time I wash up a batch of crockery', and going on to call that kind of work 'sordid time-wasting drudgery' and 'of its nature an uncreative and life-wasting job'.[83] Parts of the downside of family life were clearly getting to him, although to give him credit he understood it was his duty to share this tedious work with Eileen. Shortly before, or possibly just after, that column was finished, Orwell accompanied Eileen and Richard up to Greystone, where he left them for what he believed would be about two months. As he poignantly confessed to a friend years later, he knew he needed a woman to care for him, and at this point, he somehow took it for granted that Eileen would always be there.

On 15 February, after a flurry of last-minute letters, complaining to friends about being 'snowed under with work', Orwell took off for France. He settled at the Hotel Scribe in Paris where, with his name now recognised, he met many of the renowned French authors who shared his political views. He also had a few Scotches with Hemingway, who thought he looked 'very gaunt and . . . in bad shape'. Orwell divulged that he was afraid he might still be an assassination target of the communists who had hunted him in Spain, and Hemingway lent him a pistol to use for protection while he was there.[84]

Attached to the end of a very long letter from Eileen to Orwell dated Wednesday, 21 March, as printed in the *Complete Works*, is a separate letter, simply headed 'Wednesday'. It has always been assumed that second letter was an addition to the longer one, even though it included many baffling facts that were hard for scholars to explain. Close examination now shows that the 'Wednesday' letter was really written on 14 February, the Wednesday before Orwell left for Paris, and perhaps a week after Orwell said goodbye to Eileen and Richard at Greystone. Many parts of the letter lead conclusively to the accuracy of changing its date from 21 March to 14 February.

First, Eileen mentioned in the letter that she had recently received from Orwell books, oranges, 'fats', and a playpen for the children, and these items could only have been sent before he left for France. Second, Eileen told Orwell in the letter that she was going to Newcastle – over an hour away by bus – the next day, Thursday, and would stay there until Friday, in order to fit in a number of chores relating to rations for Richard – an exhausting two-day trip she would not have undertaken less than a week before the operation she had by then been convinced was essential. Third, Eileen mentioned that she had recently bought some extra blankets and didn't need him to send any, even as she worried that Orwell himself had enough blankets 'at home' in order not to be forced to economise 'by leaving out the underblanket because without that you'll be cold if you have a dozen on top of you'. This is kind, wifely advice to a husband who rarely concentrated on such practicalities without her reminding him. However, keeping warm with enough blankets would not have been a problem in Paris, where he informed her in a later letter that he was enjoying 'central heating'. Fourth, Eileen mentioned that Richard might have a couple more teeth 'by the 21st', which she would not say if she were writing the letter on the 21st. Indeed, she must have been referring to 21 February. After a lot of joyful details about Richard – 'in whom Eric is passionately interested', as she told Orwell's agent – Eileen wrote, 'I've been dressed every day since you went away', which must mean since he left them at Greystone about a week earlier. This remark would make no sense to write on 21 March, six weeks after he had gone, especially with the knowledge that Eileen had made a few visits to London during those weeks. Orwell had been with her when she had a debilitating pain the day before they left for the North, so she probably spent a day or so in bed.

If it's still not obvious that Eileen wrote this letter before Orwell left for Paris, the last section of her letter leaves no doubt. She finished writing it on Thursday, on the train to Newcastle, and she told Orwell, 'I got your wire last night (Wed). I hope you'll be able to do the Court [be at the hearing to finalise Richard's adoption] but of course you mustn't mess up the French trip. Could you ring me up on Friday or Saturday evening? . . . Unless of course you're coming up this weekend which would be nice.' The court hearing was scheduled for 21 February, but for whatever logistical reasons Orwell rushed through his last-minute tasks on 15 February, then took off abruptly for Paris, leaving her to handle the adoption hearing by herself. So he didn't make a final visit to his family that weekend, as Eileen had hoped, and thus could not have seen this letter from Eileen until he went back to England, which explains why it survived. Eileen only found out after mailing it to London that Orwell had suddenly decided to leave for Paris that very Thursday. We know they continued a lively interaction while he was overseas because a few extremely informative letters from Eileen survived, probably because they were written near the end of March, and no doubt arrived in Paris after he had left. Later, Orwell told Potts that 'The last time he saw Eileen he wanted to tell her that he loved her much more now since they'd had Richard, and he didn't tell her, and he regretted it immensely.'[85] Orwell never saw Eileen again.

As she settled down up north, Eileen believed she had done everything Orwell asked. She had quit the job she loved, giving up her independence and creative activities. She had agreed to adopt a baby, even as she feared she wasn't strong enough to undertake the care that would involve. And she had consented to isolate herself with him once again, so that he would be forced to free himself from city affairs and concentrate full-time on his writing. She had chosen to abandon her own personal pleasures and, instead, to renew, as her prime purpose, the goal of helping Orwell fulfil his destiny.

And what did Orwell suddenly decide at that very moment? Once again, just as he had interrupted his joyful marriage after six months to fight in Spain, he abruptly left alone at home the son he loved and the wife who had newly dedicated herself to him, while he followed the retreating German troops, an activity he knew to be extremely dangerous. Personal happiness was clearly secondary to the importance of his 'work'. Orwell must have realised on some level how extremely ill Eileen was. He knew she often spent days in bed and was getting weaker. But she continued to refuse to admit to herself, let alone tell him, that she needed him at home. Perhaps she was afraid he would reject her wishes even if she did ask him to stay. She was already considering having an operation. 'I knew I had a "growth",' she wrote to him, saying she wished she'd talked it over with him more before he left, 'but I wanted you to go away peacefully.'[86]

Alone for what she expected to be two months, Eileen discovered that 'complete rest' was a bit of a dream. All of a sudden there were a million things she had to take care of. 'It's odd – we have had nothing to discuss for months but the moment you leave the country there are dozens of things,'[87] she wrote to Orwell, in one of a series of last letters to him that he most likely didn't read until after her death. In fact, Eileen was heading into a hectic six weeks of exertion. Orwell had told his agent and others that Eileen 'has full powers to make decisions for me on any questions that may come up'[88] while he was away, and she did her best. He had received two sets of page proofs for *Animal Farm* on 31 January, and most likely she took one copy up north with her to correct. Orwell also assigned Eileen to handle proofs of the Wodehouse essay he'd just completed, even as he continued to offer her typing and editing services to friends. And she was happy to take on this extra work as a way to help with their expenses. One of her last large jobs was editing and typing a final version of Evelyn Anderson's book *Hammer or Anvil: The Story of the German Working-Class Movement*. But she also helped other friends, some of whom we will never be aware of.

Gwen's son and daughter were also being cared for at Greystone and, besides all the literary work, Eileen was spending a lot of time helping to look after all three children. She was accompanying them for whooping-cough injections, reading to them at night, making strings of beads and other inventive toys, getting hot-water bottles ready at bedtime, trying – with little success – to get the two youngest toilet trained. One day 'Richard did a <u>terrible</u> thing . . . He had done what Mary [Catherine's original name] calls tick-tocks for the third time, got his hands in it & <u>put his hands in his mouth</u>.'[89] She tried in vain to wash his mouth out and later just hoped for the best.

On 21 February, a week after Orwell had left for France, Eileen took Richard to London for an important meeting with a judge before the adoption could be finalised. Since she was apprehensive that 'the judge might make some enquiry about our health as we're old for parenthood,' she wrote in one letter to Orwell, she had postponed her own serious discussions with doctors in case she was diagnosed with cancer. 'It would have been an uneasy sort of thing to be producing oneself as an ideal parent a fortnight after being told that one couldn't live more than six months or something,'[90] as she explained, rather too off-handedly.

She arrived at the court with 'a neat coat and skirt on – she wasn't generally very neat,'[91] as Lettice remembered. And 'for the first time in her life [she had] bought a hat, a honey-coloured felt hat which she thought might impress the judge with her suitability as a parent,' her friend added. 'She came into the Ministry [of Food] afterwards to show us the baby, and to tell us proudly that although he had held onto her tightly, he had not cried at all, and had even given the judge a smile.'[92] But shortly after the hearing with the judge, Eileen collapsed once again, which forced her to stay in London somewhat longer than she'd planned.[93]

Lydia last saw Eileen on her February visit to London. 'She was serene and talked of "the children" . . . She seemed much better,' Lydia thought. 'I hate writing 1945,' she had surprised Lydia by blurting out. And 'I should hate even more writing 1946, and as for 1947, I just couldn't bear it.'[94] They laughed together, unable to foretell the sad irony of this whimsical remark. Just as Eileen parted from Lydia, 'With sudden intensity of feeling she spoke of her brother Eric.'[95] Perhaps Eileen was thinking that if he were alive he would be there with her, as Orwell was not. Eric had died at thirty-nine, and she might also have been worrying about her own possible death at exactly the same age. With Lydia, it was another unforeseen but final goodbye.

Around 9 March, Eileen visited London again, but alone this time. The main purpose was to see her dentist, she told Lettice.[96] As she arrived at the Canonbury Square flat, she discovered a huge pile of Orwell's important mail that she had asked Georges Kopp, who lived nearby, to forward to Paris. Because of his failure to handle this mail, Eileen inherited three weeks' worth of problems and letters to reply to, including shut-off notices from the electric company and miscellaneous requests to Orwell that needed responses, which she detailed in her last letters to Orwell's agent. While she was at the flat, Inez called and they had a long conversation,[97] during which Eileen told Inez of her health concerns and the likelihood of an operation.

On that March visit to London, Eileen also found time to have dinner one night with their doctor friend George Mason. She had complained to Orwell that she found eating in restaurants 'the most barbarous habit and only tolerable very occasionally when one drinks enough to enjoy barbarity'. And Mason had obliged, giving her 'to drink just what I would have drunk in peacetime – four glasses of sherry, half a bottle of claret and some brandy – and it did cheer me up I admit,'[98] she told Orwell.

She had arranged to deliver the book manuscript by Evelyn Anderson the next day, but she 'was taken with a pain just like the one I had the day before coming North, only rather worse,' she explained to Orwell. 'I tried to have a drink in Selfridges' but couldn't and all sorts of extraordinary things then happened, but after a bit I got myself into the Ministry.' Her bleeding was so extensive and her condition so fragile that her friends there had to call for help. In fact, they were so concerned that they wanted to get in touch with Orwell. As Eileen wrote to him, in another letter that he probably read only much later, her friends offered 'to get you home [from Paris]. I was horrified.'[99] A visit she'd expected to last a couple of days instead kept her in London for a week, as she recovered in bed from her breakdown. She told Lettice – leaving the disastrous details to her imagination – that she had 'finished with all kinds of dramas' while looking for her friend at the Ministry, and was sorry not to have found her.[100] But she must have forgiven Kopp for his failure to forward the mail since she went back north at night-time 'so George Kopp could see me off at King's X which was very nice'.[101] They also had no idea they would never see one another again.

On that last trip to London in March, Eileen made a stop in Newcastle on the way. She had an appointment with Harvey Evers, a local surgeon Gwen had recommended. Henry Harvey Evers was a flamboyant doctor who had known Eric O'Shaughnessy back in their college days. He had a reputation as an outstanding clinician with the ability to put his patients completely at ease. 'His elegant style – always well turned out with a rose or carnation in his buttonhole and driving an immaculate Rolls or Bentley – became part of medical folklore in Newcastle,'[102] one obituary declared. In 1945 Evers was spending most of his time at Fernwood House, his own private nursing home with only twenty beds.

Eileen was finally ready to 'deal with the grwoth (no one could object to a grwoth) I knew I had,' she wrote to Lettice, using her typo for yet another stab at levity in the midst of gravity. She understood that there was 'hardly any chance that the tumours can come out without more or less everything else removable,'[103] meaning a hysterectomy. Lettice and Gwen were perhaps the only two who really understood what a serious operation Eileen was about to undergo. The truth had been hidden from everyone else. They all, including Orwell, continued to believe, even after the dire results were known, that Eileen had been in the hospital for only a minor operation. The London doctors whom Eileen also consulted had insisted that she have a 'preparatory month of blood transfusions' before she would be strong enough to be operated on, but Eileen immediately rejected that approach as over-cautious. 'London surgeons love preparing their patients as an insurance against unknown consequences,'[104] she joked prophetically, while Evers 'will finish me off as quickly as anyone in England,'[105] a line almost impossible to read without tears.

After examining Eileen and discussing the results with Gwen, Dr Evers recommended that Eileen be operated on as soon as possible. She was glad to hear there would be 'none of the fattening up in hospital before the operation that I was to have in London,'[106] Eileen told Lettice. On the other hand, Dr Evers thought 'the indications are urgent enough to offset the disadvantages of operating on a bloodless patient; indeed he is quite clear that no treatment at all can prevent me from becoming considerably more bloodless every month,'[107] she wrote to Orwell in her mock cheerful tone. If Orwell had received this letter before the operation, he would have known how serious Eileen's illness was. And perhaps he would have come back in time to be with her. Dr Evers was a well-respected surgeon, but in this case his judgement was badly flawed. Gwen said later that she had grave misgivings about

Eileen's ability to survive the operation, but she apparently agreed with the decision not to take more time in London to prepare her.

Orwell had been completely against the idea of Eileen's having any operation at all, perhaps because he was afraid it would guarantee she could never have a child of her own. But with Gwen and Dr Evers warning her of the dangers of postponing it any longer, Eileen decided she should send Orwell a telegram asking his permission. 'I had a phase of thinking that it was really outrageous to spend all your money on an operation of which I know you disapprove,' she wrote, and she wanted his 'ruling', since 'I really don't think I'm worth the money.'[108] Her use of the phrase 'your money' was an outrageous worry that Eileen repeated many times in the long letter, which Orwell probably didn't read until much later. She reminded him that his own hospital stays had cost nothing, partly because they were poorer then, but mostly because her brother Eric had taken care of everything. Although almost impossible to believe, one of the main reasons Eileen gave Orwell for the quick operation in Newcastle was that it would save them money. Eileen even promised to try to find some work afterwards to help cover the expense. Of course, if their roles were reversed, she would have agreed to pay whatever it cost to improve Orwell's health, and he would have been concerned, as she was, that they couldn't afford it. It is hard not to reflect that if only *Animal Farm* had found a publisher more quickly these silly worries would not have intruded so drastically.

In the midst of all her bouts of extensive pain and bleeding, and her concerns regarding how to best prepare herself for a healthier future, Eileen remained optimistic. This very extensive letter, mostly written through one afternoon and evening, was like a stream of consciousness deluge of emotions made possible by someone who could type as fast as she could think. Perhaps many of her letters to Orwell were like this one. But at this point Eileen wanted to settle every important detail that might possibly arise before she could subject herself to the operation. And one of her chief concerns was that Orwell was wasting his time at *Tribune*. She told him once again that he should stop editing soon, and do much less reviewing. 'It's quite essential that you should write some book again,'[109] she urged, even resorting to saying this 'would be much better for Richard too, so you need have no conflicts about it. Richard sends you this message. He has no conflicts.' She was glad Orwell would miss 'the hospital nightmare you would so much dislike'.[110] As she told Lettice, 'George visiting the sick is a sight infinitely sadder than any disease-ridden wretch in the world'.[111] She was looking ahead to April when Orwell would get back, hoping he would take a week's leave and stay with her at Greystone. At that point, she told him, she would be in 'the picturesque stage of convalescence'.[112] And in a letter to a friend, she wrote, 'I'm going to have my dear operation next week & hope to be back again exceedingly healthy in a month or two'.[113] She displayed no regret that she hadn't asked Orwell to be with her at this obviously extremely distressing time.

Throughout this letter it becomes abundantly clear that Eileen cannot be described as a feminist. Although she often revealed her strong will, she had accepted the role of a wife as secondary to the husband, something Orwell needed since he believed his writing was more important than anything or anyone. Although they both knew her income was essential for his life as a writer, they agreed that in some way he controlled how it was spent. And of course neither of them knew that *Animal Farm* was about to resolve all future money problems.

There was one other very important bit of information Eileen needed to tell Orwell, and she wrote to him again four days later. She had decided to make her will. As she explained in a matter-of-fact way, 'I thought I must cover the possibility that you might be killed within the next few days & I might die on the table on Thursday'.[114] She had decided to leave everything to Gwen in that case, with the provision that she would take care of Richard. She had ruled out a few other possible foster parents, and ironically concluded, 'Avril I think & hope would not take him on anyway. That I couldn't bear'. As it turned out, Orwell's sister Avril did indeed end up looking after Richard, and he was very happy growing up with her. At the end of this letter, to soften the dire possibilities she had raised and focus instead on his favourite subject, Eileen went on to tell Orwell about the sixth tooth Richard had just acquired, and how proud she'd been when he didn't make a sound as a doctor injected him against whooping cough. This complete letter is reproduced in the Appendix, on page 419.

Eileen's last letter to Orwell, written on the morning of the day she died, 29 March 1945.

Just as Eileen was writing this letter, Orwell was being admitted to a hospital in Cologne with yet another serious lung eruption, telling a friend later, 'I thought at one time it was all up with me.'[115] He was still in the hospital when he received the telegram from Eileen asking his permission for the operation, and he telegraphed back his consent.

Eileen's handwriting trailed off as the morphine took effect.

Eileen entered the Fernwood House nursing home all alone on Wednesday, ahead of the Thursday morning operation. She had written to Lettice the week before asking only, 'If you could write a letter that would be nice,' but she didn't hear back. Eileen also told Inez that she would like to hear from her before she went into the operating room, but Inez decided, much to her regret, that Eileen 'would rather have letters and telegrams [after] she had had the operation'. Another friend from the Ministry of Food told Inez, sadly, that 'Eileen was rather alone and many people had received letters and so on, but in fact very little was done.'[116] Eileen put on a brave face even though she received no mail from the friends she'd asked to write. She had decided not to ask Lettice to go to the hospital with her, but she did manage to honestly confess in her letter, 'Theoretically I don't want any visitors; . . . in practice I'll probably be furious that no one comes.'[117] Because of the mail delays during the war, Lettice didn't receive this anxious letter in time, and she was devastated: 'If I had known about the serious operation and that she was going into Newcastle alone, by bus, to have it, with no one there, I should have gone up to her, but I heard too late.'[118] Of all her probable letters from Eileen, this was the only one Lettice chose to save.

In her final letter to Orwell just before they wheeled her in for the operation, Eileen was still able to joke a bit, telling him she was 'already enema'd, injected (with morphia in the *right* arm which is a nuisance), cleaned & packed up like a precious image in cotton wool & bandages'. And, she told him shockingly, 'I haven't seen Harvey Evers since arrival & apparently Gwen didn't communicate with him & no one knows what operation I am having! They don't believe that Harvey Evers really left it to me to decide . . . But I must say I feel irritated though I am being a <u>model</u> patient.' Then, as the morphine took effect, her handwriting slurred together and the letter trailed off. 'This is a nice room – ground floor so one can see the garden. Not much in it except daffodils and I think arabis but a nice little lawn. My bed isn't near the window but it faces the right way. I also see the fire and the clock.'[119] And there it ended, the last letter Eileen would ever write. It was discovered on the table beside her bed.

Eileen was then wheeled into the operating room, having never received any last-minute assurances from Dr Evers, the man supposedly so well-loved by his patients. She did not even mention getting a blood transfusion, which she and others had assumed she would receive before the operation started. Dorothy Hopkinson, the anaesthetist, left a devastating description of what happened next. She applied a mixture of 'about two ounces of ether, one and a half drachms of chloroform, and also oxygen . . . in drops by the open method' – through a cloth placed over Eileen's mouth and nose – as she monitored her pulse and respiration. But, contrary to what everyone, including Orwell himself, was led to believe by the wording on her death certificate, Eileen did not die immediately from the anaesthesia before the operation had even begun. Instead, her 'abdomen was opened and the uterus had been lifted out to be prepared for removal', the coroner's report states. Then, just before the actual excision, Eileen's 'colour changed and her respiration became very shallow'. One minute later her heart stopped beating. For forty minutes afterwards, Eileen's heart was massaged and artificial respiration was attempted, during which time injections of Coramine (a circulatory stimulant, now banned) and Lobeline (a respiratory stimulant) were administered, all to no avail. Eileen could not be revived. Her heart had failed.[120]

During the inquest, the anaesthetist completed a lengthy report and interview, and it was decided, in a carefully worded conclusion, that Eileen had died of 'cardiac failure whilst under an anaesthetic of ether and chloroform skilfuly and properly administered for operation for removal of the uterus'.[121] No one was found guilty of any wrongdoing.

But, amazingly, there is no record of Dr Evers being present at the inquest or even being interviewed. Might he not have performed the operation himself? George Mason showed up later that day to identify Eileen's body. And someone did add a haunting note to the last page of the report: 'The deceased was in a very anaemic condition,' it appears to say. So the anaesthesia had been properly administered. Eileen was just too frail to withstand such an invasive operation. But Harvey Evers was never charged.

O rwell was still in the hospital in Cologne when the second telegram arrived. He took eight M. and B. tablets – an antibacterial medicine he had recently found helpful but no longer used for humans – and checked himself out of the hospital, then somehow found a military plane to fly him back to London.[122] He went straight to Newcastle, arriving on Saturday, 31 March. Avril said that she 'always thought it very strange that the anaesthetist and surgeon refused to see Eric when he arrived.'[123] He stayed in Newcastle with George Mason until he had found a burial spot in St Andrew's and Jesmond Cemetery, which was nearby. He then ordered a gravestone on which he approved a simply worded engraving, similar to the one he later requested for himself: 'Here Lies Eileen Maud Blair, Wife of Eric Arthur Blair, Born Sept. 25th 1905; Died March 29th 1945.' It's far too late now to be able to uncover more of the dreadful details. The funeral took place on 3 April, apparently a very informal affair, though Orwell did find time to plant some Polyantha roses in her memory. Orwell returned to Germany immediately afterwards, the only way he felt he could endure the next months. He didn't bother waiting for the coroner's report. There was no way Eileen could be brought back to him. In his payments book, he drew a black line across the page right after the last entry before Eileen's death.

Eileen died almost exactly ten years after she had overwhelmed Orwell with her charm and sparkling intelligence at the first party he'd ever given, in March 1935. We have these last long letters to Orwell to cherish because one of them arrived in London after he'd left for the Continent and two others didn't reach Paris before he'd returned to England. He didn't read them himself until Eileen had died. If he'd got them any earlier, he might have tossed them away as he ordinarily did.

Just as she threw away all the letters he'd sent her from Germany. That was their unfortunate habit.

During the next years Orwell continued to dwell on this agonising long weekend, choosing to honour Eileen by giving his most famous novel, *Nineteen Eighty-Four*, a title reflecting the title of the poem she had published the year before they met. Then he had the novel begin on 4 April, the day after he had buried Eileen. And he reprised the word 'clock', the last word in Eileen's last letter to him, as one of the first words in his great novel. The secret bedroom above the junk shop, where Julia and Winston make love, can be seen as a re-creation of Orwell's fond memories of the cottage he happily shared with Eileen just after they were married. On the ground floor was their shop of miscellaneous odds and ends, and right above it was the bedroom they shared during some of the happiest months of his life. Perhaps Orwell felt that Eileen had betrayed him by dying, just as he depicted Julia betraying Winston in the novel. Although Orwell disappointed some people with his reticence to mourn Eileen's loss in feeble words, he never forgot her.

Epilogue

Orwell Without Eileen

Poor Orwell. Just on the verge of happiness again. He believed he was about to fulfil all his dreams for recreating the best months of his life with Eileen. She'd given up her job to be a full-time mother, and they'd found an even more remote and primitive paradise on the island of Jura, with the peace and isolation he needed in order to concentrate solely on writing. He planned at last to begin work in earnest on the novel that had been in the back of his mind for years – the novel he and Eileen knew could be the literary masterpiece he was capable of. And just at the very moment that dream was about to come true, he had been shocked at the news of Eileen's sudden and completely unexpected death. After spending a few days in Newcastle arranging for her burial, then putting Richard in Doreen Kopp's care in London, he rushed back to Germany for a while. 'I felt so upset at home I thought I would rather be on the move for a bit,' he explained to a friend.[1]

Many people received letters from Orwell during the next months, and for the most part he repeated variations of 'It was a terribly cruel and stupid thing to happen'[2] and 'Things were just beginning to get better.'[3] And he kept insisting, wrongly, that '[N]either of us had expected the operation to be very serious.'[4] His matter-of-fact letters made some people conclude that Orwell hadn't felt intense grief at Eileen's death. But his family members and friends heard more details. 'Eric wrote to me at some length of Eileen's death and appeared to me to be very grieved about it . . . Those days for him must have been pretty strenuous and ghastly,'[5] his Aunt Nellie said. And when Crick interviewed Avril, she told him she had a letter from her brother 'and he seemed to me to be rather distraught'. Crick told her that he had 'come across several people who described [Orwell] as near to breakdown.'[6]

Orwell returned to London at the end of May, and his old friend Geoffrey Gorer felt Orwell was 'mourning very deeply'; he used Gorer as a confidant, asking often for his company during the next weeks. He 'seemed to want to talk to me about his grief . . . He kept on remembering little things about her – oh, how she would boil an egg,'[7] Gorer said. Another friend believed that 'Eileen's death was a blow to him from which in his personal life he never fully recovered.'[8] Others remembered hearing Orwell call a few women 'Eileen' by mistake during the months after she died. Orwell also told Gorer that he and Eileen had been hoping to have another baby, apparently under the colloquial belief that women do sometimes get pregnant shortly after they've adopted a child.[9] Orwell might also have naïvely hoped that what he believed was a minor operation would remove whatever obstacle was preventing Eileen from getting pregnant.

Richard, their one-year-old son, was now a huge concern for Orwell, and many friends advised him to give the child up. But Orwell was adamant that he intended to keep him. Many gorgeous photos have survived of a slightly weathered Orwell pushing a bright, curious Richard around his London neighbourhood. Part of the Jura dream that he and Eileen had shared was to have a home where Richard could 'run in and out of the house all day with no fear of traffic,'[10] and Orwell began to make definite plans to stop all book reviewing in May

1946 and move to Barnhill, with a nursemaid for Richard, and Avril as his Eileen substitute. The fact that *Animal Farm* was bringing in unexpected profits made this decision much easier. Orwell intended 'to sort out the furniture and books' at the cottage and have everything sent to Jura, but 'I have been putting it off because last time I was there it was with Eileen and it upsets me to go there,'[11] he told a friend.

While visiting Scotland near the end of May, Orwell spent some time at Eileen's gravesite in Newcastle. The Polyantha roses that he had planted on her grave the year before had all rooted well, he noted in his diary. And that day, he planted six new varieties of flowers, hopeful they would all take root.[12] A visitor to the cemetery in 2012 discovered, with some difficulty, Eileen's uncared-for gravestone with the extremely simple engraving he chose for her – a sharp contrast to the words on the gravestone right next to hers, which began more typically: 'In loving memory of my beloved wife'. And of course there was no sign of the flowers Orwell left in Eileen's memory seventy years earlier, only scrubby weeds and baked mud. Until quite recently hardly anyone even knew where Eileen's grave was. Happily, her gravesite is now being better cared for.

Some months after living on Jura with Richard and Avril, Orwell realised what he really missed having was a wife. And during the next two years he asked at least four different women to marry him, always reassuring them that sex wasn't his main objective, realising honestly that his age and illness might be a deterrent. He wanted Richard to have a mother after he was gone, and he also wanted someone to act as his literary executor, he told the women. But he was more honest with at least one of them, telling her, 'It's only that I feel so desperately alone sometimes. I have hundreds of friends, but no woman who takes an interest in me and can encourage me'[13] – an admission in an indirect way of how much he had always needed, and now profoundly missed, Eileen's constant 'encouragement'. We can assume that Eileen would have approved of his finding another wife and would have encouraged his quest. But all the women rejected him.

Another considerable problem with Avril as Eileen's replacement was that she couldn't type. So Orwell had to make other arrangements. He had made a start on his new novel, *Nineteen Eighty-Four*, during the summer of 1946, and when Miranda Wood, an experienced typist, sublet his Canonbury Square flat again in the summer of 1947, Orwell began mailing her parts of his manuscript for retyping, which she continued to do until late in the year. A poignant footnote to this part of the story is that, while working on *Nineteen Eighty-Four*, Wood used a typewriter she found in the flat that she believed had been Eileen's.

Between serious bouts of illness, Orwell managed to finish writing *Nineteen Eighty-Four* near the end of 1948, but Wood was no longer available for retyping. Orwell then tried desperately to get a typist to visit Barnhill, but he was unable to find anyone willing to travel to the wilds of Jura in the middle of winter to finish typing the final draft. In the end, Orwell made the fateful decision to stay in Jura for the winter and do the 'grisly job' himself. Propped up in bed with a fever, typing 5,000 words a day, he pushed himself well beyond his limits until the job was finished. Collapsing at the end, he was forced to suddenly depart for a sanatorium in January 1949, never to return to Jura. Orwell's last novel was published in June 1949, but by then he was permanently confined to a hospital.

One very sad endnote was the sudden discovery, by his childhood friend Jacintha, that her old lover Eric Blair, with whom she had lost touch for thirty years, was in fact the famous author George Orwell. She wrote to him at the sanatorium in February 1949, less than a year before he died, and he replied immediately with tender memories, saying 'as soon as I get back to London I do so want us to meet again.' Perhaps he was even thinking of asking her once again to be his wife when he wrote, 'I would like you to see Richard . . . Are you fond of children? I think you must be.'[14] But, no doubt wary of being rejected by her for the second time, he never got up the nerve. This would have been the perfect romantic ending for Orwell. And marriage to Jacintha might very well have made him happy enough to prolong his life for a while. Unfortunately, this second chance at a happy ending was denied him. He was never again well enough to walk the London streets, and they never managed to meet. If only he'd known, as Jacintha would confess later, that she had suffered 'a lifetime of ghosts and regret at turning away the only man who ever really appealed on all levels'.[15] Jacintha chose never to get married.

Instead, in September Orwell was moved to a hospital in London, and surprised everyone by marrying Sonia Brownell, a much younger woman who had rejected an earlier proposal. The marriage took place in his hospital room, on 13 October, and a luxurious wedding menu has survived, signed by Sonia and all their friends. However, Orwell wasn't well enough to attend the luncheon himself, which was served to all the others at the Ritz. The couple planned to go to Switzerland at the end of January, where the mountain air was believed to relieve tuberculosis symptoms. But Orwell didn't survive long enough to fulfil that dream.

How might this all have changed if Eileen had survived her operation? First of all, she most definitely would have typed *Nineteen Eighty-Four* for him, although in those circumstances the book might have been given quite a different title. And it might even have been a bit less morbid. Orwell managed to survive almost five years without Eileen, but she most likely would not have been able to control his self-destructive impulses in Jura any more than Avril could. However, it's easy to surmise that he might have gained a year or two of life with her devotion, enough time to write at least one more of the books he was still planning. This possible extension of Orwell's life would have proved exceedingly important in another way. Although in his last months he had been treated with the newest drugs available, Orwell had an extreme allergic reaction to them, partly because the proper dosage had not been perfected. Two years later, with more research, those same drugs might have indeed helped him get to the Swiss Alps. We know he definitely didn't want to die, as some have mistakenly speculated, since he told Avril that he hoped to be around until Richard was fourteen.[16] And no one would have accused him of a death wish if Eileen had still been at his side.

But this is all useless, wishful thinking. Orwell did indeed die suddenly in the middle of the night of 21 January 1950. He was all alone in his hospital bed when he was overwhelmed by a massive haemorrhage of his lung. His luck had finally run out.

Appendix

Two Complete Letters by Eileen

Throughout this biography I've used selections from many of Eileen's letters, but the excerpts often fail to show adequately the liveliness and easy flow of her letters, which Eileen seems to type as quickly as she thinks of what to say. These two complete letters give a much better flavour of Eileen's whimsical yet serious personality and the intensity of her approach to life.

The first letter was written to Norah Symes Myles, a close friend from Oxford University, on 1 January 1938. This text is from Peter Davison, *The Lost Orwell*, pp. 70–74.

New Year's Day, 1938.

[no salutation]

You see I have no pen, no ink, no glasses and the prospect of no light, because the pens, the ink, the glasses and the candles are all in the room where George is working and if I disturb him again it will be for the fifteenth time tonight. But full of determined ingenuity I found a typewriter, and blind people are said to type in their dark.

I have also to write to a woman who has suddenly sent me a Christmas present (I think it may be intended for a wedding present) after an estrangement of five or ten years, and in looking to see whether I had any clues to her address I found a bit of a letter to you, a very odd hysterical little letter, much more like Spain than any I can have written in that country. So here it is. The difficulty about the Spanish war is that it still dominated our lives in a most unreasonable manner because ~~Eric~~ George (or do you call him Eric?) is just finishing the book about it and I give him typescripts the reverse sides of which are covered with manuscript emendations that he can't read, and he is always having to speak about it and I have returned to complete pacifism and joined the P.P.U. [Peace Pledge Union] party because of it. (Incidentally, you must join the P.P.U. too. War is fun so far as the shooting goes and much less alarming than an aeroplane in a shop window, but it does appalling things to people normally quite sane and intelligent – some make desperate efforts to retain some kind of integrity and others like Langdon-Davies make no efforts at all but hardly anyone can stay reasonable, let alone honest.) The Georges Kopp situation is now more Dellian than ever. He is still in jail but has somehow managed to get several letters out to me, one of which George opened and read because I was away. He is very fond of Georges, who indeed cherished him with real tenderness in Spain and anyway is admirable as a soldier because of his quite remarkable courage, and he is extraordinarily magnanimous about the whole business – just as Georges was extraordinarily magnanimous. Indeed they went about saving each other's lives or trying to in a way that was almost horrible to me, though George had not then noticed that Georges was more than "a bit gone on" me. I sometimes think no one ever had such a sense of guilt before. It was always understood that I wasn't what they call in love with Georges – our association progressed in little leaps, each leap immediately preceding some attack or operation in which he would almost inevitably be killed, but the last time I saw him he was in jail waiting, as we were both confident, to be shot, and I simply couldn't explain to him again as a kind of farewell that he could never be a rival to George. So he has rotted in a filthy prison for more than six months with nothing to do but remember me in my most pliant moments. If he never gets out, which is indeed most probable, it's good that he has managed to have some thoughts in a way pleasant, but if he does get out I don't know how one reminds a man immediately he is a free man again that one has only once missed the cue for saying that nothing on earth would induce one to marry him. Being in prison in Spain means living in a room with a number of others (about fifteen to twenty in a room the size of your sitting-room) and never getting out of it; if the window has steel shutters, as many have, never seeing daylight, never having a letter; never being charged, let alone tried; never knowing whether you will be shot tomorrow or released, in either case without explanation; when your money runs out never eating anything but a bowl of the worst imaginable soup and a bit of bread at 3 p.m. and at 11 p.m.

On the whole it's a pity I found that letter because Spain doesn't really dominate us as much as all that. We have nineteen hens now – eighteen deliberately and the other by accident because we bought some ducklings and a hen escorted them. We thought we ought to boil her this autumn so we took it in turns to watch the nesting boxes to see whether she laid an egg to justify a longer life, and she did. And she is a good mother, so she is to have children in the spring. This afternoon we built a new henhouse – that is we put the sections together – and that is the nucleus of the breeding pen. There is probably no question on poultry-keeping that I am not able and very ready to answer. Perhaps you would like to have a battery (say three units) in the bathroom so that you could benefit from my advice. It would be a touching thing to collect an egg just before brushing one's teeth and eat it just after. Which reminds me that since we got back from Southwold, where we spent an incredibly family Christmas with the Blairs, we have eaten boiled eggs almost all the time. Before we had only one eggcup from Woolworths' – no two from Woolworths' and one that I gave George with an easter egg in it before we were married (that cost threepence with egg). So it was a Happy Thought dear, and they are such a nice shape and match your mother's butter dish and breadboard, giving tone to the table.

We also have a poodle puppy. We called him Marx to remind us that we had never read Marx and now we have read a little and taken so strong a personal dislike to the man that we can't look the dog in the face when we speak to him. He, the dog, is a French poodle, supposed to be miniature and of prize-winning stock, with silver hair. So far he has black and white hair, greying at the temples, and at four and a half months is rather larger than [his] mother. We think however he may take a prize as the largest miniature. He is very appealing and has a remarkable digestion. I am proud of this. He has never been sick, although almost daily he finds in the garden bones that no eye can have seen these twenty years and has eaten several rugs and a number of chairs and stools. We weren't going to clip him, but he has a lot of hairs which are literally dripping mud on the driest day – he rolls on every cushion in turn and then drips right through my lap – so we thought we would clip him a little. But now we shall never get him symmetrical till we shave him. Laurence (it is a dreadful thing that you have never seen Laurence) bears with him in a remarkable way and has never scratched even his nose.

I went to stay with Mary. You will have heard about the domestic changes. She went to stay with that pregnant cousin and read a book on infant feeding, from which she discovered that <u>everything</u> Nanny did was wrong. So of course she had to come home and tell her so, because otherwise she would have killed the children. Now they have a Norwegian nurse. I think she is better but it's bad luck for David who was hopelessly spoilt by fat Nanny and is not approved of by the Norwegian – who never raises her voice but puts him in the corner. Mary herself has become a good mother – when the children are there, I mean. She is perfectly reasonable with them. I don't know what happened. David is very intelligent and makes me slightly jealous because I should like a son and we don't have one. Mary and I summed up human history in a dreadful way when I was there – I was in the throes of pre-plague pains, which had happened so late that I was wondering whether I could persuade myself that I felt as though I were not going to have them, and Mary wasn't having any pre-plague pains at all and was in a fever and going to the chemist to try to buy some ergot or other corrective. We had two parties – we went to see Phyl Guimaraens and the MAMMETT CAME TO TEA. She might just as well have been in Girl Guide uniform but now she organises play-readings, when all the old St. Hugh's girls go to her house and read *Julius Caesar*. Mary went once but she thought they would be given something to eat and they weren't, not even a bun or a cup of tea, so she is embittered and not being a good old girl any more. David and the Mammett had a nice conversation. David had told me earlier in the day that she was coming to tea and he knew her very well, so I repeated this to her and she was delighted. When he was brought into the room this happened:

> "Well, little David (holding out the hand), and do you think you know who I am?"
>
> "Yes – you're granny" (with complete confidence, allowing his hand to be held and stroked).
>
> "No (ever so kindly), I'm not granny."
>
> "Oh? What are you then?"

Phyl is just the same as she used to be in her most charming moments. It was fun seeing her again. I think perhaps we might have a proper reunion some day. Couldn't you come and stay with her and while she is at the office eat potato crisps at the Criterion (Mary and I did this as much for old times' sake as because it was cold)? It seems to me superlatively clever for anyone to keep herself on the

Stock Exchange, as she says she does. I wonder about it all the time I'm with her.

The last candle is guttering, and there isn't any good way out of this letter. But perhaps it has broken a spell. Does yours mean that June is at Oxford? I just didn't know. Anyway she can't be more than fifteen. Norman? John? Elisabeth? Jean? Ruth? Your mother? Your father? I don't think I want any news of you and Quartus because I am quite sure I know all about you and it would be so dreadful to hear something quite different. The only thing I can do is to come and see. I am supposed to be having a holiday when the book is finished, as it will be this month, only we sh'n't have any money at all, and we were so rich. When are you coming to the sales? Or are you? I don't know whether I can get away even for a day because the book is late and the typescript of the final draft is not begun and Eric [Eileen's brother] is writing a book in collaboration with a number of people including a German and I keep getting his manuscript to revise and not being able to understand anything at all in it – but if you <u>were</u> coming to the sales these things would all be less important to

Pig.

Did I wish you a happy new year?

Please wish all your family a happy new year from me.

Eric (I mean George) has just come in to say that the light is out (he had the Aladdin lamp because he was Working) and is there any oil (such a question) and I can't type in this light (which may be true, but I can't read it) and he is hungry and wants some cocoa and some biscuits and it is after midnight and Marx is eating a bone and has left pieces in each chair and which shall he sit on now.

The second letter was written to Orwell on 25 March 1945. It was handwritten, and transcribed later by Sheila and Peter Davison. This text is from Peter Davison, *The Complete Works of George Orwell*, Vol. 17, pp. 107–9. Although Eileen had downplayed to Orwell the seriousness of the operation she was about to undergo four days later, she obviously feared she would not survive it. And the tragedy is: she was right.

Greystone,
Carlton,
Stockton-on-Tees.

Dearest   I'm trying to get forward with my correspondence because I go into the nursing home on Wednesday (this is Sunday) & of course I shan't be ready. It's impossible to write or do anything else while the children are up. I finish reading to Laurence about a quarter to eight (tonight it was five to eight), we have supper at 8 or 8.15, the 9 o'clock news now must be listened to & lasts till at least 9.30 (the war reports the last two nights have been brilliant) & then it's time to fill hotwater bottles etc. because we come to bed early. So I write in bed & don't type. Incidentally I did while explaining the poaching laws as I understand them to Laurence make my will—in handwriting because handwritten wills are nearly always valid. It is signed & witnessed. Nothing is less likely than that it will be used but I mention it because I have done an odd thing. I haven't left anything to Richard. You are the sole legatee if you survive me (your inheritance would be the Harefield house [the house Eileen inherited from her mother] which ought to be worth a few hundreds, that insurance policy, & furniture). If you don't, the estate would be larger & I have left it to Gwen absolutely with a note that I hope she will use it for Richard's benefit but without any legal obligation. The note is to convince Richard that I was not disinheriting him. But I've done it that way because I don't know how to devise the money to Richard himself. For one thing, there has been no communication from the Registrar General so I suppose Richard's name is still Robertson. For another thing he must have trustees & I don't know who you want & they'd have to be asked. For another, if he is to inherit in childhood it's important that his trustees should be able to use his money during his minority so that he may have as good an education as possible. We must get all this straightened out properly when you come home but I thought I must cover the possibility that you might be killed within the next few days & I might die on the table on Thursday. If you're killed after I die that'll be just too bad but still my little testament will indicate what I wanted done. Gwen's results in child-rearing have not been encouraging so far but after the war she will have a proper house in the country containing both the children & herself, she loves Richard & Laurie adores him. And all the retainers love him dearly. I'm sure he would be happier in that household than with Marjorie though I think Marjorie would take him on. Avril I think & hope would not take him on anyway. That I couldn't bear. Norah & Quartus would have him & bring him up beautifully but you've never seen either of them. Quartus is in India & I can't arrange it. So in all the circumstances I thought you would agree that this would be the best emergency measure.

RICHARD HAS SIX TEETH. Also he got hold of the playpen rail when I was putting him in & stood hanging on to it without other support. But he doesn't really know at all how to pull himself up so don't expect too much. Yesterday Nurse & I took all three to the doctor for whooping cough injections. He lives about 2½–3 miles away, partly across fields. We got lost & had to cross ploughland. The pram wouldn't perambulate & neither would Mary. She sat in a furrow & bellowed until carried. Laurence cried to be carried too . . . Laurence however didn't cry when the needle went in but Mary did *and* made an enormous pool on the surgery floor. Richard was done last. He played with a matchbox on my knee, looked at the doctor in some surprise when his arm was gripped & then turned to me in astonishment as though to say "Why is this apparently nice man sticking needles into me? Can it be right?" On being told it was he looked up at the doctor again rather gravely—& then smiled. He didn't make a sound & he was perfectly good all day too, though his arm is sort of bruised. The other two unfortunately remember that they'd been injected & screamed in agony if either arm was touched. It was a happy day.

But Richard did a *terrible* thing. He will *not* use his pot, nearly always goes into a tantrum when put on it & if he does sit on it does nothing more. The tooth upset his inside a bit too. After lunch I sent the other two to bed & left Richard in his playpen while I helped wash up. Then there were cries of agony. He had done what Mary calls tick-tocks for the third time, got his hands in it & *put his hands in his mouth.* I tried to wash his mouth out, hoping he'd be sick. But no. He seemed to swallow most of the water I poured in, so it was worse than useless. In the end I scoured his mouth with cotton wool, gave him some boiled water & hoped for the best. And he is very well. Poor little boy. And I was sorry for myself too. I *was* sick. Blackburn however says a lot of children do this every day – – – – –

I haven't had a copy of Windmill & I haven't had a proof. Surely you said they were sending a proof. And I failed to get the Observer one week which must have been the relevant one. I've also failed to get today's but shall get it I hope.

Your letter with the Animal Farm document came yesterday & I've sent the enclosure on to Moore. He will be pleased. This is much the quickest exchange we've had.

I suppose I'd better go to sleep. By the way the six teeth are 3 top & 3 bottom which gives rather an odd appearance, but I hope the fourth top one will be through soon.

All my love & Richard's
E.

Notes

Abbreviations for some reference books and archives:

Orwell.rem: Audrey Coppard and Bernard Crick (eds), *Orwell Remembered*, BBC, London, 1984.

Wadhams: Stephen Wadhams (ed.), *Remembering Orwell*, Penguin Books, Markham, Ontario, Canada, 1984.

Jackson article: Elisaveta Fen, 'George Orwell's First Wife,' *The Twentieth Century Magazine*, Volume 168, August 1960. (She used the name Lydia Jackson in London.)

Jackson book: Elisaveta Fen, *A Russian's England*, Paul Gordon Books, Warwick, 1976.

Crick Archive: Birkbeck Library, University of London. Extracts from the papers of the late Professor Sir Bernard Crick are used by kind permission of his literary executors at the Birkbeck University Archive, with thanks to Oliver Crick.

Orwell Archive: Special Collections, University College London. The written material and images from the Orwell Archive are supplied courtesy of Bill Hamilton, and of Amanda Wise, UCL Library Services, Special Collections.

Davison, *Lost*: Peter Davison, *The Lost Orwell*, Timewell, London, 2006. The six recently discovered letters from Eileen to Norah Symes Myles are printed in full here.

Davison, *Complete Works*: Peter Davison (ed.), *The Complete Works of George Orwell*, Secker & Warburg, London, 2000–1, 20 volumes in total.
Volume 10: *A Kind of Compulsion, 1903-1936*.
Volume 11: *Facing Unpleasant Facts, 1937-1939*.
Volume 12: *A Patriot After All, 1940-1941*.
Volume 13: *All Propaganda Is Lies, 1941-1942*.
Volume 14: *Keeping Our Little Corner Clean, 1942-1943*.
Volume 15: *Two Wasted Years, 1943*.
Volume 16: *I Have Tried to Tell the Truth, 1943-1944*.
Volume 17: *I Belong to the Left, 1945*.
Volume 18: *Smothered Under Journalism, 1946*.
Volume 19: *It Is What I Think, 1947-1948*.
Volume 20: *Our Job Is to Make Life Worth Living, 1949-1950*.

Some biographies of George Orwell:

Stansky and Abrahams bio: Peter Stansky and William Abrahams, *Orwell: The Transformation*, Constable, London, 1979.

Crick bio: Bernard Crick, *George Orwell: A Life*, Little, Brown, Boston, 1980.

Fyvel bio: T. R. Fyvel, *George Orwell: A Personal Memoir*, Weidenfeld and Nicholson, London, 1982.

Shelden bio: Michael Shelden, *Orwell: The Authorized Biography*, Harper Collins, New York, 1991.

Meyers bio: Jeffrey Meyers, *Orwell: Wintry Conscience of a Generation*, W. W. Norton, New York, 2001.

Bowker bio: Gordon Bowker, *Inside George Orwell*, Palgrave Macmillan, New York, 2003.

Taylor bio: D. J. Taylor, *Orwell: The Life*, Henry Holt, New York, 2003.

Chapter 1: A Complicated Ancestry

1   Rosalind Obermeyer letter, 12 November 1974, Crick Archive.

2   Lettice Cooper, 'Eileen Blair', *The PEN: Broadsheet of the English Centre of International PEN*, No. 16, Spring 1984. This is listed incorrectly as No. 17, Autumn 1984, in many places.

3   George Orwell, 'The Development of William Butler Yeats', *Horizon*, January 1943.

4   Jackson article, p. 116.

5   Email from Catherine Moncure to the author, 9 July 2014.

6   James P. Hynes, *The O'Shaughnessys*, independently published, 1987, James.Patrick@Hynes.net.

7   *Slater's National Commercial Directory of Ireland 1846* lists a Lawrence O'Shaughnessy as Master of Courtenay's School, on Limerick Road, in Newcastle, Ireland. (A 'w' is often used in the name 'Laurence', but the men in Eileen's family spelled it with a 'u'.)

8   The National Archives, Kew. Contains public sector information licensed under the Open Government Licence v3.0: http://www.nationalarchives.gov.uk/doc/open-government-licence/version/3/

9   Thomas Fennell, *The Royal Irish Constabulary*, University College, Dublin, Press, 2003.

10 Tim Herlihy, *The Royal Irish Constabulary*, Four Courts, Dublin, 1997.

11 Neil Simpson, museum@psni.police.uk.

12 Transcribed by Mary Ann Schloegl, rootsweb.com.

13 Neil Simpson, museum@psni.police.uk.

14 Fennell, *Royal Irish Constabulary*, p. 9.

15 *Guys Directory of Munster*, 1893.

16 Lizzie and her family were living at 'Cable Terrace', Valentia, in 1905, when old Mrs O'Shaughnessy died, and another of her children, Michael, then living in London, was listed as a witness on her death certificate. It's not clear when Lizzie and her family left Valentia Island, but by 1938, when her sister Margaret died, Lizzie and her husband were living at 2 Grasmere Avenue, Merton Park, in Morden, part of Greater London. Aunt Lizzie died on 18 January 1946, aged eighty-three. This large family kept in touch, and no doubt Eileen, and later Orwell, had some opportunities to visit these Irish aunts and uncles through the years, though unfortunately Eileen left no specific record.

17 Sister Margaret Patrice Slattery, C.C.V.I., *Promises to Keep: A History of the Sisters of Charity of the Incarnate Word*, San Antonio, TX, 1995, p. 136.

18 Sister Mary Helena Finck, M.A., *The Congregation of the Sisters of Charity of the Incarnate Word of San Antonio, Texas: A Brief Account of Its Origin and Its Work*, Dissertation, Catholic University of America Press, Washington, DC, 1925.

19 *Ibid.*, p. 188.

20 Slattery, *Promises to Keep*, p. 136.

21 Finck, *The Congregation*, p. 131.

22 *Ibid.*, p. 212.

23 *Ibid.*, p. 187.

24 Slattery, *Promises to Keep*, p. 149.

25 *Ibid.*, p. 216.

26 www.irishnewsarchive.com, Saturday, July 2, 1938.

27 Patricia Siegel, a certified document examiner and consultant for handwriting identification, handwriting analysis, and the study of handwriting, in the USA.

28 Michael Macdonagh, *The Reporters' Gallery*, Hodder and Stoughton, London, 1913.

29 Elizabeth Johnson, Administrator, Parliamentary Press Gallery, emails to the author, 16 and 19 June 2014.

30 *Irish Independent*, 1 January 1905.

31 *Ibid.*, 19 July 1905.

32 *Ibid.*, 20 July 1905.

33 *Ibid.*, 22 July 1905.

34 *Ibid.*, 19 July 1905.

35 *White's History, Gazetteer and Directory of Norfolk*, 1883.

36 The couple stayed in Nottingham, living at 21 Northcote Terrace in 1891 and at 3 Somerset Terrace in 1901.

37 Peter Hammond, Nottinghamshire Archives.

38 This building, in 1891, had housed three men, two of them 'civil servants Custom House'. Eileen's mother may have moved there to begin teaching at a new school, but more likely she moved to an area her husband-to-be was familiar with in order to prepare for her wedding.

39 Robert H. Hiscock, *A History of Gravesend*, Phillimore, 1981.

40 Although Laurence had been the witness at his brother Edward's wedding, in 1891, Edward did not perform that function here. Instead, Laurence's witness was Lionel O. V. Cox, aged thirty-four, a clerk in the London Postal Service. At the time he was a single man living at 485 Kings Rd, Chelsea, London, but his family was from Ireland and they were living in Gravesend in 1881 and for some time after that. Mary Westgate's witness was Frederick Mickleboro', a Mickleburgh relative from Norwich. The wedding certificate lists her father's name as 'Edward Westgate'. This is probably a transcriber's mistake, a repeat of Laurence's father's first name, although Mary might not have remembered her own father's real name. His occupation is listed as 'Gentleman', suggesting that Mary either had been brought up with that understanding or had given false information.

41 Shetland Archives.

42 J. J. Haldane Burgess, *Some Shetland Folk*, Thomas Mathewson, Lerwick, 1902, p. 32.

43 Callum Brown, *Up-helly-aa: Custom, Culture and Community in Shetland*, Manchester University Press, Manchester, 1998.

44 The letter continues: '*but I had moreover arranged with the Collector at Newcastle that he should send a II cl clerk from N'cle to assist at SoShields, should any unforeseen crisis arise – the 2nd officer Mr A Rhind acting as Collector.*

    On arrival in London early on the morning of the 20th I learned that the funeral could not take place until the 22nd, and I accordingly made the application on Enc No 1 for five days leave of absence, although it was my intention to return to duty as soon as possible, in order that my absence should not interfere seriously with the leave arrangements of the staff at SoShields or Newcastle.

    Under the circumstances, I regret that I was unable to give any longer notice of my proposed absence & that inconvenience should thereby have been caused. The fact of spending two nights in travelling to & from London coupled with the harassing time there, practically without any rest, will, I trust, show your Honours that I was anxious that as little inconvenience as possible should have arisen from my absence & that I was prepared to set aside my own personal feelings of comfort in the matter.' The National Archives, Kew, *Collectors Manual*. Contains public sector information licensed under the Open Government Licence v3.0: http://www.nationalarchives. gov.uk/doc/open-government-licence/version/3/

Chapter 2: Head Girl at High School

1   Stansky and Abrahams bio.

2   *Kelly's Directory*.

3   Gary Wilkinson, a South Shields photographer, email to the author.

4   *Burgess Rolls*.

5   David Harland, present owner, to Gary Wilkinson, relayed in email to the author.

6   Patricia Siegel, certified document examiner and consultant for handwriting identification, handwriting analysis, and the study of handwriting, in the USA.

7   *South Shields Ledger*, 16 December 1905.

8   *Ibid.*, 1 October 1906.

9   Catherine Moncure, Gwen O'Shaughnessy's adopted daughter, email to the author.

10 Patricia Siegel.

11 *Irish Independent*, 20 July 1905.

12 Jackson book, p. 345.

13 *Ibid.*, p. 344.

14 *Kelly's Directory*, 1914.
15 *Ibid.*
16 *Ibid.*
17 Miss D. Johnson, book of picture postcards of old South Shields, South Shields Library.
18 *The Shields Daily Gazette and Shipping Telegraph*, 27 January 1916.
19 Obituary of Eric O'Shaughnessy, *British Medical Journal*, 15 June 1940.
20 *Irish Independent*, 18 January 1937, p. 10.
21 Shelden bio, p. 207.
22 *Kelly's Directory*, 1914.
23 Audrey B. Sayers, *Sunderland Church High School for Girls: A Centenary History*, Sunderland Church High School, 1984, p. 23.
24 *Ibid.*, p. 28.
25 *Ibid.*, p. 32.
26 *Ibid.*, p. 42.
27 *Ibid.*, p. 35.
28 *Chronicle*, Sunderland Church High School Magazine, June 1922.
29 *Ibid.*, November 1923.
30 Amanda Ingram, Archivist, St Hugh's College, University of Oxford, personal communication.

Chapter 3: Honours at Oxford

1   Kathleen Mary Hobbs, St Hugh's Archives (SHA from now on), original submissions to the assistant to the editor of *St Hugh's: One Hundred Years of Women's Education in Oxford*, Palgrave Macmillan, 1986. By kind permission of the Principal and Fellows of St Hugh's College, Oxford.
2   Esther M. Power, SHA.
3   Hobbs, SHA.
4   Penny Griffin, (ed.), *St Hugh's: One Hundred Years of Women's Education in Oxford*, Palgrave Macmillan, 1986.
5   Hobbs, SHA.
6   Renée Haynes, *Neapolitan Ice*, Dial Press, New York, 1929, p. 17.
7   Personal communication with the author.
8   Janet Howarth, 'Women', in Brian Harrison (ed.), *The History of the University of Oxford: Volume VIII, The Twentieth Century*, pp. 345–77.
9   *The Times*, 15 October 1920.
10 Griffin, *St Hugh's*, p. 50.
11 *Ibid.*, p. 57.
12 *The Oxford Magazine*, 6 March 1924, p. 348.
13 Griffin, *St Hugh's*, p. 92.
14 G. M. B. Williams, SHA.
15 Hobbs, SHA.
16 Elaine Martin, PA to Head/Registrar, Sunderland High School, 2012.
17 Amanda Ingram, Archivist, St Hugh's College, University of Oxford, personal email.
18 Bowker, information given personally to the author.
19 Griffin, *St Hugh's*, p. 97.
20 Hobbs, SHA.
21 Haynes, SHA.
22 Joyce Robertson, SHA.
23 Power, SHA.
24 *Ibid.*
25 Griffin, *St Hugh's*, p. 95.
26 Laura Schwartz, *A Serious Endeavour: Gender, Education and Community at St Hugh's, 1886–2011*, Profile Books, London, 2011, p. 57.
27 Haynes, SHA.
28 Doris Saunders, SHA.

29 John Mullan, 'Jane Austen is not that soothing', *Guardian* books blog, 11 July 2013. https://www.theguardian.com/books/booksblog/2013/jul/11/jane-austen-fiction-not-anaesthetic.
30 M. A. Rice, 10 November 1940.
31 *London Evening News*, 15 November 1926.
32 D. Taylor, SHA.
33 Georgina Arrowsmith, SHA.
34 Power, SHA.
35 Robertson, SHA.
36 Flora Welch, SHA.
37 Hobbs, SHA.
38 Robertson, SHA.
39 Hobbs, SHA.
40 Robertson, SHA.
41 Hobbs, SHA.
42 Frances Crossfield, SHA.
43 Griffin, *St Hugh's*, p. 93.
44 Orwell Archive.
45 *Ibid.*
46 Anon, SHA.
47 Welch, SHA.
48 *Ibid.*
49 Hobbs, SHA.
50 *Ibid.*
51 Robertson, SHA.
52 *Ibid.*
53 Hobbs, SHA.
54 Power, SHA.
55 Hobbs, SHA.
56 Minutes Book, SHA.
57 *Isis*, 24 November 1926.
58 oxfordjournals.org.
59 Power, SHA.
60 *Ibid.*
61 Haynes, SHA.

Chapter 4: Between Oxford and Orwell

1   Jackson book, p. 343.
2   Nigel Smales, personal email. The school continued to function until about a decade ago, when a day nursery took its place.
3   Jackson article, p. 115.
4   Catherine Moncure, personal email to the author.
5   Lambeth Palace Library, LC151, p. 161.
6   Jackson book, p. 343.
7   W. B. Gurney is still in business, but the company has no records of employees in 1930.
8   Jackson article, p. 115.
9   *Ibid.*
10 Jackson book, p. 343.
11 *Ibid.*
12 *Ibid.*, p. 465.
13 Edna Bussey, Letter to Ian Angus, 19 September 1968, Ian Angus Archive, UCL.
14 *Ibid.*
15 H. C. Squires, *The Sudan Medical Service: An Experiment in Social Medicine*, William Heinemann, London, 1958, p. 52.

16   *Ibid.*
17   *Ibid.*, p. 120.
18   Obituary of Gwen O'Shaughnessy, *British Medical Journal*, 9 November 1964.
19   Squires, *Sudan*.
20   Jackson book, p. 344.
21   *Chronicle*, Sunderland Church High School Magazine, 1934.
22   Letter to Orwell, 21 March 1945, in Davison, *Complete Works*, vol. 17, p. 99.
23   Jackson book, p. 332.
24   Stansky and Abrahams bio, p. 107.
25   Jackson book, p. 341.
26   *Ibid.*, p. 332.
27   *Catalogue: Faculties of Arts and Science*, pp. 86–88, with many thanks to Robert Winckworth,
     UCL Special Collections.
28   *Annual Reports*, Workers' Educational Association, 1935 and 1936.
29   Jackson book, p. 341.
30   Letter in Crick Archive.
31   Jackson book, p. 341.
32   Stansky and Abrahams bio, p. 108.
33   Letter in Crick Archive.
34   Jackson book, pp. 341–2.
35   *Ibid.*, p. 348.
36   Jackson article, p. 118.
37   Jackson book, p. 342.
38   Jackson article, p. 116.
39   Jackson book, p. 344.
40   Patricia Siegel.
41   Jackson book, p. 343.
42   Jackson article, p. 115.
43   Jackson book, p. 343.
44   *Ibid.*, p. 345.
45   Jackson article, p. 116.
46   Catherine Moncure, personal email to the author, 24 July 2013.
47   Jackson book, p. 344.
48   *Evening News*, 5 June 1940.
49   *British Medical Journal*, 15 June 1940.
50   Letter to Norah Myles (née Symes), December 1938, Davison, *Lost*, p. 76.
51   Jackson book, p. 342.
52   *Ibid.*, p. 344.
53   *Ibid.*, p. 351.
54   Lydia Jackson, personal diary, 11 November 1979, with kind permission of Pamela Davidson.
55   Moncure, personal email, 24 July 2013.
56   Jackson book, p. 350.
57   Karl Schnetzler, letter to Ian Angus, 14 June 1967, Crick Archive.
58   Orwell, letter to Brenda Salkeld, 14 November 1934, in Davison, *Lost*, p. 95.
59   Rosalind Obermeyer, letter to Bernard Crick, Crick Archive.

Chapter 5: A Whirlwind Courtship

1   Jackson book, p. 345.
2   Masha Karp, member of the Orwell Society.
3   George Orwell, *Horizon*, January 1943.
4   Rosalind Obermeyer, Crick Archive.
5   Catherine Moncure, personal email to the author.
6   Jackson article, p. 116.

7   Richard Rees, *George Orwell: Fugitive from the Camp of Victory*, Southern Illinois University Press, Carbondale, IL, 1962, p. 39.

8   Lettice Cooper, 'Eileen Blair,' *The PEN: Broadsheet of the English Centre of International PEN*, No. 16, Spring 1984. This is credited incorrectly as No. 17, Autumn 1984, in many places.

9   Eileen Blair, Letter to Orwell, 21 March 1945, in Davison, *Complete Works*, vol. 17, p. 99.

10 Rosalind Obermeyer letter, 12 November 1974, Crick Archive.

11 Stansky and Abrahams bio, p. 110.

12 Geoffrey Gorer, letter to Orwell, 16 July 1935, Orwell Archive.

13 Cyril Connolly, *The New Statesman and Nation*, 6 July 1935.

14 Rosalind Obermeyer, Crick Archive.

15 Lettice Cooper, Crick Archive.

16 Richard Rees, Orwell.rem, p. 125.

17 Geoffrey Gorer, Crick Archive.

18 Cyril Connolly, Crick Archive.

19 Lydia Jackson, Wadhams, p. 67.

20 Lettice Cooper, Crick Archive.

21 George Woodcock, Wadhams, p. xiii.

22 Davison, *Complete Works*, vol. 12, p. 56.

23 Geoffrey Gorer, Crick Archive.

24 Avril Blair, Orwell.rem, p. 27.

25 Rosalind Obermeyer, Crick Archive.

26 Stansky and Abrahams bio, p. 125.

27 Jackson article, pp. 115–16.

28 Crick Archive.

29 Melvyn Bragg, BBC *Omnibus*, 1970, paragraph 3423.

30 Denys King-Farlow, Crick Archive.

31 Meyers bio, p. 123.

32 Henry Dakin, personal conversation with the author, 2015.

33 Rayner Heppenstall, Crick Archive.

34 Sonia Orwell, Crick Archive.

35 Jackson book, p. 345.

36 Mabel Fierz, Orwell.rem, p. 95.

37 Geoffrey Gorer, Crick Archive.

38 Malcolm Muggeridge, Introduction to George Orwell, *Burmese Days*, Time Inc., New York, 1962, p. xiii.

39 Mabel Fierz in an interview with Bernard Crick, 19 January 1973.

40 Sonia Orwell, Crick Archive.

41 Jack Denny, Orwell.rem, pp. 83–4.

42 Family tailor, Wadhams, p. 28.

43 Brenda Salkeld, Crick Archive.

44 Kay Ekevall, Wadhams, p. 57.

45 Frances Wilson, *The Ballad of Dorothy Wordsworth*, Faber and Faber, London, 2008, p. 101.

46 Fyvel bio, p. 104.

47 Brenda Salkeld, Crick Archive.

48 Davison, *Complete Works*, vol. 10, p. 386.

49 Brenda Salkeld, Crick Archive.

50 *Ibid.*

51 Bowker bio, p. 190.

52 Kay Ekevall, Wadhams, p. 56.

53 Bowker bio, p. 176.

54 Kay Ekevall, Wadhams, p. 58.

55 Kay Ekevall, Orwell.rem, p. 101.

56 Rayner Heppenstall, *Four Absentees*, Barrie & Jenkins, London, 1960.

57 Dione Venables, 'Postcript', Jacintha Buddicom, *Eric & Us*, Finlay, Chichester, 2006, p. 182.
58 Rayner Heppenstall, Orwell.rem, p. 111.
59 Rayner Heppenstall, Crick Archive.
60 Jackson book, p. 345.
61 Kay Ekevall, Orwell.rem, p. 102.
62 Jackson article, p. 116.
63 Jackson book, p. 349.
64 *Ibid.*, p. 345.
65 Davison, *Complete Works*, vol. 10, p. 394.
66 *Ibid.*, p. 399.
67 Tosco Fyvel, 'A Writer's Life', *World Review*, June 1960, p. 15.
68 Davison, *Complete Works*, vol. 10, p. 381.
69 *Ibid.*, p. 387.
70 *Ibid.*, p. 401.
71 *Ibid.*
72 *Ibid.*, p. 479.
73 *Ibid.*, p. 470.
74 Bowker bio, p. 187.
75 Davison, *Complete Works*, vol. 10, p. 445.
76 *Ibid.*, p. 404.
77 *Ibid.*
78 Jackson book, p. 345.
79 *Ibid.*, p. 346.
80 Kay Ekevall, Wadhams, p. 58.
81 Jackson book, p. 346.
82 Rayner Heppenstall, Orwell.rem, p. 108.
83 Bowker bio, p. 173.
84 Personal visit to house.
85 Orwell.rem, p. 113.
86 Davison, *Complete Works*, vol. 10, p. 383.
87 Cyril Connolly, Crick Archive.
88 Jackson book, p. 347.
89 Shelden bio, p. 209.
90 Jackson book, pp. 349–50.
91 *Ibid.*, p. 350.
92 *Ibid.*
93 Stansky and Abrahams bio, p. 110.
94 Orwell.rem, p. 111.
95 Orwell's mother's diary, Monday, 6 February 1905, in Crick bio, p. 8.
96 Geoffrey Gorer, Crick Archive.
97 Muggeridge, Introduction to *Burmese Days*, p. xii.
98 Geoffrey Gorer, Crick Archive.
99 Cyril Connolly, Crick Archive.
100 Brenda Salkeld, Crick Archive.
101 Rayner Heppenstall, Orwell.rem, p. 107.
102 Muggeridge, Introduction to *Burmese Days*, p. xiv.
103 Davison, *Complete Works*, vol. 10, p. 489.
104 Lettice Cooper, 'Eileen Blair', *The PEN: Broadsheet of the English Centre of International PEN*, No. 16, Spring 1984. This is credited incorrectly as No. 17, Autumn 1984, in many places.
105 Davison, *Lost*, p. 65.
106 Fyvel bio, p. 58.
107 Lettice Cooper, 'Eileen Blair', *The PEN: Broadsheet of the English Centre of International PEN*, No. 16, Spring 1984. This is credited incorrectly as No. 17, Autumn 1984, in many places.

108 John McNair, *Spanish Diary*, Independent Labour, Manchester, 1975, p. 14.
109 Crick bio, p. 173.

Chapter 6: Orwell in Love

1 Letter in Crick Archive.
2 George Orwell, *Keep the Aspidistra Flying*.
3 Bowker bio, p. 169.
4 *Ibid.*
5 *Ibid.*, p. 180.
6 Frances Wilson, *The Ballad of Dorothy Wordsworth*, Faber and Faber, London, 2008, p. 51.
7 *Ibid.*, p. 54.
8 Christopher Hitchens, Introduction to Peter Davison (ed.), *George Orwell Diaries*, Liveright, New York/London, 2012, p. xvi.
9 Davison, *Complete Works*, vol. 10, p. 442.
10 'The Road to the Left', BBC *Omnibus* Programme on Orwell, Melvyn Bragg, 1970.
11 *Ibid.*
12 Davison, *Complete Works*, vol. 10, p. 426.
13 *Ibid.*, p. 442.
14 *Highways and Byways in Hertfordshire*, travel booklet, 1902.
15 Davison, *Complete Works*, vol. 10, p. 468.
16 Shelden bio, p. 236.
17 Davison, *Complete Works*, vol. 10, p. 468.
18 *Ibid.*, p. 472.
19 Patricia Donahue, Wadhams, p. 118.
20 Davison, *Complete Works*, vol. 10, p. 468.
21 Jim Coutts Smith, *George Orwell in Wallington*, Mardleybury, 2010, p. 1.
22 Davison, *Complete Works*, vol. 10, p. 468.
23 Liz Kennedy, personal email to the author, 3 April 2012.
24 These actual measurements were kindly supplied to the author by Graham Lamb, the current owner, on 26 June 2019.
25 Davison, *Complete Works*, vol. 10, p. 472.
26 *Ibid.*, p. 479.
27 *Ibid.*, p. 471.
28 *Ibid.*, p. 485.
29 Orwell.rem, p. 143.
30 Davison, *Complete Works*, vol. 10, p. 482.
31 *Ibid.*, p. 470.
32 *Ibid.*, p. 471.
33 *Ibid.*, p. 474.
34 *Ibid.*, p. 484.
35 Bowker bio, p. 189.
36 Avril Blair, Crick Archive.
37 Davison, *Complete Works*, vol. 10, p. 482.
38 Jackson book, p. 347.
39 *Ibid.*, p. 348.
40 *Ibid.*
41 Davison, *Lost*, p. 64.
42 Davison, *Complete Works*, vol. 10, p. 479.
43 *Ibid.*, p. 483.
44 St Mary's Church, booklet, 2007.
45 Davison, *Complete Works*, vol. 10, p. 485.
46 *Ibid.*

Chapter 7: Six Happy Months of Marriage

1 Jackson article, p. 115.
2 Jim Coutts Smith, *George Orwell in Wallington*, Mardleybury, 2010, p. 3.
3 Bowker bio, p. 189.
4 Orwell's last literary notebook, Davison, *Complete Works*, vol. 20, p. 210.
5 Jackson book, p. 348.
6 Orwell, Box of miscellaneous personal papers, British Library.
7 *Ibid.*
8 Orwell letter to Jack Common, 12 October 1938, in Davison, *Complete Works*, vol. 11, p. 222.
9 Jackson book, p. 348.
10 Davison, *Lost*, p. 65.
11 Box of miscellaneous letters to Orwell, British Library.
12 Davison, *Complete Works*, vol. 10, p. 483.
13 Davison, *Lost*, p. 64.
14 Malcolm Muggeridge, Introduction to *Burmese Days*, Time Inc., New York, 1962, p. xi.
15 Davison, *Complete Works*, vol. 20, p. 204.
16 Sonia Orwell, Crick Archive.
17 Richard Blair, Personal communication with the author.
18 David Astor, Crick Archive.
19 Jackson book, p. 377.
20 Mark Benney, *Almost a Gentleman*, Peter Davies, London, 1966, p. 107.
21 Crick bio, p. 172.
22 Wadhams, p. 40.
23 Stanksy and Abrahams bio, p. 154.
24 Geoffrey Gorer, Crick Archive.
25 'The Road to the Left', BBC *Omnibus* Programme on Orwell, Melvyn Bragg, 1970.
26 Geoffrey Gorer, Crick Archive.
27 Mabel Fierz, in Orwell.rem, p. 97.
28 Meyers bio, p. 123.
29 Orwell.rem, p. 164.
30 Margaret Branch, in Shelden bio, p. 243.
31 Fyvel bio, p. 58.
32 Dennis Collings, in Orwell.rem, p. 81.
33 Jackson book, p. 349.
34 Lydia Jackson, personal diary, 2 November 1979, with kind permission of Pamela Davidson.
35 Lydia Jackson, in Wadhams, p. 68.
36 Jack Common, Crick Archive.
37 Wadhams, p. 46.
38 Davison, *Lost*, p. 70.
39 Shelden bio, p. 209.
40 *Ibid.*, p. 245.
41 *Ibid.*
42 Bowker bio, p. 190.
43 Patricia Donahue, in Wadhams, p. 119.
44 Denys King-Farlow, Crick Archive.
45 Wadhams, p. 115.
46 Dan Pinnock, personal visit, 2012.
47 Monica Bald, in Wadhams, p. 115.
48 Stansky and Abrahams bio, p. 150.
49 Jackson book, p. 378.
50 Fyvel bio, p. 109.
51 Wadhams, p. 116.
52 Meyers bio, p. 122.

53 Jackson article, p. 118.
54 Jackson book, p. 378.
55 Davison, *Lost*, p. 64.
56 Davison, *Complete Works*, Vol. 10, p. 599.
57 Jackson book, p. 349.
58 Davison, *Lost*, p. 64.
59 Meyers bio, p. 195.
60 Jackson book, p. 349.
61 Esther Brookes, Crick Archive.
62 Jackson book, p. 378.
63 Jackson article, p. 117.
64 *Ibid.*
65 Jackson book, p. 377.
66 Jackson article, p. 117.
67 Jackson book, p. 378.
68 Patricia Donahue, Crick Archive.
69 Anthony Powell, Crick Archive.
70 Liz Kopp, email to the author, 26 July 2012.
71 Davison, *Complete Works*, vol. 20, pp. 286–99.
72 Orwell.rem, p. 59.
73 Patricia Donahue, in Wadhams, p. 118.
74 Lettice Cooper, in Orwell.rem, p. 162.
75 Stansky and Abrahams bio, p. 177.
76 Davison, *Complete Works*, vol. 10, p. 496.
77 Anthony Powell, 'George Orwell, A Memoir', *Atlantic Monthly*, October 1967, p. 65.
78 Cyril Connolly, Crick Archive.
79 Orwell, Letter to Anne Popham, 18 April 1946, from Davison, *Complete Works*.
80 Jock Branthwaite, in Wadhams, p. 99.
81 George Orwell, in Stanley J. Kunitz (author), *Twentieth Century Authors*, H. W. Wilson, New York, 1942.
82 Wadhams, p. 41.
83 Brenda Salkeld, in Orwell.rem, p. 68.
84 During personal visit, 2015.
85 Mary Common, unsent letter to Eileen, 16 December 1938, Crick Archive.
86 Orwell.rem, p. 164.
87 Irene Stacey, in Ewan Foskett, *The Comet*, May 2011.
88 Irene Stacey, personal visit.
89 Esther Brookes, Crick Archive.
90 Wadhams, p. 47.
91 Jackson article, p. 118.
92 Patricia Donahue, in Wadhams, p. 118.
93 Orwell.rem, p. 114.
94 Davison, *Complete Works*, vol. 20, pp. 204–5.
95 Mabel Fierz, in Meyers bio, p. 127.
96 Bowker bio, p. 193.
97 *Keep the Aspidistra Flying.*
98 Richard Rees, *George Orwell: Fugitive from the Camp of Victory*, Southern Illinois University Press, Carbondale, IL, 1962, p. 139.
99 Davison, *Complete Works*, vol. 10, p. 507.
100 Richard Rees, Orwell.rem, p. 123.
101 Shelden bio, p. 218.
102 Denys King-Farlow, in Orwell.rem, p. 59.
103 Letter to Jack Common, 15 February 1937, Jack Common Archive, Special Collections, Newcastle University.

104 Davison, *Lost*, p. 65.
105 Davison, *Complete Works*, vol. 10, p. 527.
106 Davison, *Lost*, p. 64.
107 *Ibid.*, p. 68.
108 Preface to Ukrainian edition of *Animal Farm*, 1947, Davison, *Complete Works*, vol. 19, pp. 86–89.

Chapter 8: Escape from Catalonia

1   Jackson book, p. 417.
2   *Ibid.*
3   Jackson article, p. 119.
4   Philip Mairet, editor of *New English Weekly*.
5   Davison, *Complete Works*, vol. 10, p. 527.
6   Meyers bio, p. 141.
7   Davison, *Complete Works*, vol. 16, p. 403.
8   Peter Lewis, *George Orwell: The Road to 1984*, Harcourt, New York, 1981, pp. 55, 59.
9   Davison, *Complete Works*, vol. 11, p. 8.
10 *Ibid.*, p. 6.
11 Anthony Powell, 'George Orwell, A Memoir', *Atlantic Monthly*, October 1967, p. 65.
12 Davison, *Complete Works*, vol. 11, p. 10.
13 *Ibid.*, vol. 10, p. 528.
14 Davison, *Lost*, p. 68.
15 D. J. Taylor, 'Another Piece of the Puzzle', *Guardian*, 10 December 2005.
16 Davison, *Lost*, p. 68.
17 Davison, *Complete Works*, vol. 11, p. 11.
18 Philip Mairet, Crick archive.
19 Davison, *Lost*, p. 68.
20 Jackson book, p. 417.
21 *Ibid.*, p. 418.
22 Davison, *Lost*, p. 68.
23 *Ibid.*, p. 69.
24 Charles A. Orr, 'Homage to Orwell – As I Knew Him in Catalonia', unpublished pamphlet, 1984, p. 5.
25 *Ibid.*, p. 6.
26 Jon Kimche, Crick Archive.
27 Charles Orr, in Gerd-Rainer Horn, (ed.), *Letters from Barcelona: An American Woman in Revolution and Civil War*, Palgrave Macmillan, London, 2009, p. 138.
28 Lois Orr, Charles's wife, *Ibid.*, p. 148.
29 Davison, *Complete Works*, vol. 11, p. 13.
30 Letter to Leonard Moore, 12 April 1937, *Ibid.*, p. 17.
31 Letter to Eileen's mother, 22 March 1937, *Ibid.*, p. 13.
32 *Ibid.*
33 Davison, *Lost*, p. 71.
34 Davison, *Complete Works*, vol. 11, pp. 15–16.
35 *Ibid.*, p. 14.
36 Lois Orr, in Horn, *Letters from Barcelona*, p. 151.
37 Rob Stradling, 'The Spies Who Loved Them: The Blairs in Barcelona, 1937', *Intelligence and National Security*, October 2010.
38 Lois Orr, in Horn, *Letters from Barcelona*, p. 153.
39 Orr, *Ibid.*, p. 181.
40 Bob Edwards, in Shelden bio, p. 273.
41 Orr, 'Homage to Orwell', p. 10.
42 Marc Wildemeersch, *George Orwell's Commander in Spain: The Enigma of Georges Kopp*, Thames River Press, London, 2013, pp. 61, 76.

43 Jock Branthwaite, in Shelden bio, p. 272.
44 Lois Orr, in Horn, *Letters from Barcelona*, p. 128.
45 Davison, *Complete Works*, vol. 11, p. 14.
46 Wildemeersch, *George Orwell's Commander*, p. 61, KGB file: David Crook Report, Alba Collection.
47 Rosalind Obermeyer to Ian Angus, 30 January 1967.
48 31 January 1937, in Davison, *Complete Works*, vol. 11, p. 8.
49 *Homage to Catalonia*, Harcourt Brace, 1952, p. 83.
50 Bob Edwards, in Wadhams, p. 79.
51 'Looking Back at the Spanish Civil War', 1942?, *Complete Works*, vol. 13, p. 501.
52 Davison, *Complete Works*, vol. 11, p. 21.
53 Orr, 'Homage to Orwell', p. 7.
54 Stephen Koch, 'Barcelona on the Verge', *The Breaking Point*, Counterpoint, New York, 2005, pp. 178–84.
55 Orr, 'Homage to Orwell', p. 8.
56 *Homage to Catalonia*, p. 124.
57 Davison, *Complete Works*, vol. 11, p. 21.
58 *Homage to Catalonia*, p. 186.
59 *Ibid.*, p. 185.
60 Harry Milton, 'Fighting Back', radio programme.
61 *Homage to Catalonia*, p. 186.
62 Jock Branthwaite, in Wadhams, p. 90.
63 Davison, *Complete Works*, vol. 11, p. 24.
64 *Ibid.*, p. 25.
65 *Ibid.*, p. 23.
66 *Ibid.*, p. 24.
67 *Ibid.*, p. 25.
68 Letter to Cyril Connolly, 8 June 1937, *Ibid.*, p. 27.
69 *Ibid.*, p. 29.
70 Horn, *Letters from Barcelona*, p. 163.
71 Orwell.rem, p. 119.
72 *Ibid.*
73 *Homage to Catalonia*, p. 210.
74 Jackson book, p. 418.
75 Horn, *Letters from Barcelona*, p. 181.
76 *Homage to Catalonia*, pp. 204 and 211.
77 Davison, *Lost*, p. 71.
78 7 July 1937, Davison, *Complete Works*, vol. 11, p. 48.
79 Davison, *Lost*, p. 71.
80 Fenner Brockway, in Wadhams, p. 96.
81 *Homage to Catalonia*, p. 228.
83 Lettice Cooper, 'Eileen Blair', The PEN: Broadsheet of the English Centre of International PEN, No. 16, Spring 1984. This is listed incorrectly as No. 17, Autumn 1984, in many places.
83 *Homage to Catalonia*, pp. 229–30.

Chapter 9: From Overwork to Near Tragedy

1 Bowker bio, p. 228.
2 Davison, *Complete Works*, vol. 11, p. 23.
3 H. N. Brailsford, *Ibid.*, p. 119.
4 Charles Doran, *Ibid.*, p. 65.
5 *Ibid.*, p. 50.
6 Patricia Donaghue, Crick Archive.
7 Geoffrey Gorer, Davison, *Complete Works*, vol. 11, p. 69.

8 Davison, *Lost*, p. 71.
9 Jack Common, in Davison, *Complete Works*, vol. 11, p. 191.
10 Davison, *Lost*, p. 72.
11 *Ibid.*
12 *Ibid.*
13 Douglas Moyle, Wadhams, p. 100.
14 Davison, *Lost*, p. 72.
15 Jackson book, p. 449.
16 Davison, *Lost*, p. 72.
17 Davison, *Complete Works*, vol. 11, p. 53.
18 Wadhams, p. 101.
19 Davison, *Complete Works*, vol. 11, p. 46.
20 *Ibid.*, p. 53.
21 Davison, *Lost*, pp. 70–1.
22 Davison, *Complete Works*, vol. 11, p. 78.
23 *Ibid.*, p. 175.
24 Fyvel bio, p. 104.
25 Davison, *Complete Works*, vol. 11, p. 93.
26 *Ibid.*, p. 65.
27 *Ibid.*, p. 62.
28 *Ibid.*, p. 67.
29 *Ibid.*, p. 65.
30 *Ibid.*, p. 53.
31 *Ibid.*, p. 88.
32 Davison, *Lost*, p. 71.
33 Davison, *Complete Works*, vol. 11, p. 97.
34 *Ibid.*, p. 65.
35 Davison, *Lost*, p. 71.
36 Davison, *Complete Works*, vol. 11, p. 47.
37 *Ibid.*, p. 49.
38 *Ibid.*, p. 109.
39 Wadhams, p. 99.
40 *Ibid.*
41 Davison, *Complete Works*, vol. 11, p. 68.
42 Wadhams, p. 100.
43 Davison, *Lost*, p. 73.
44 *Ibid.*
45 *Ibid.*
46 Rayner Heppenstall, 'Orwell Intermittent', *The Twentieth Century*, May 1955, pp. 472–73.
47 BBC *Omnibus* Programme, Melvyn Bragg, 1970.
48 Lydia Jackson, personal diary, 2 November 1979, with kind permission of Pamela Davidson.
49 Davison, *Complete Works*, vol. 11, p. 62.
50 *Ibid.*
51 Heppenstall, Orwell.rem, p. 114.
52 Davison, *Lost*, p. 73.
53 *Ibid.*, p. 72.
54 *Ibid.*, p. 77.
55 *Ibid.*, pp. 70, 72, 74.
56 Jackson article, p. 120.
57 Davison, *Lost*, p. 73.
58 Davison, *Complete Works*, vol. 11, p. 111.
59 *Ibid.*, p. 116.
60 *Ibid.*, p. 123.

61 *Ibid.*, p. 121.
62 *Ibid.*, p. 122.
63 *Ibid.*, p. 115.
64 Rayner Heppenstall, *Four Absentees*, Barrie & Jenkins, London, 1960, pp. 145–6.
65 Davison, *Complete Works*, vol. 11, p. 122.
66 *Ibid.*, p. 127.
67 *Ibid.*, p. 128.
68 *Ibid.*, p. 129.
69 *Ibid.*, p. 127.
70 *Ibid.*, p. 129.
71 *Ibid.*

Chapter 10: Abandoned Again

1   Davison, *Complete Works*, vol. 11, p. 127.
2   *Ibid.*, p. 131.
3   *Ibid.*, p. 150.
4   Orwell Archive.
5   Denys King-Farlow, in Orwell.rem, p. 60. (This is mistakenly credited to Richard Rees.)
6   Victor Stacey, Crick Archive.
7   Davison, *Complete Works*, vol. 11, p. 134.
8   *Ibid.*, p. 171.
9   Jackson article, p. 120.
10 Crick bio, p. 245.
11 Davison, *Complete Works*, vol. 11, p. 135.
12 *Ibid.*, p. 133.
13 *Ibid.*, p. 175.
14 Richard Rees, *George Orwell: Fugitive from the Camp of Victory*, Southern Illinois University Press, Carbondale, IL, 1962, p. 65.
15 Davison, *Complete Works*, vol. 11, p. 155.
16 *Ibid.*, p. 180.
17 *Ibid.*, p. 158.
18 *Ibid.*
19 *Ibid.*, p. 169.
20 *Ibid.*, p. 170.
21 *Ibid.*, p. 158.
22 *Ibid.*, p. 129.
23 *Ibid.*
24 Bowker bio, p. 240.
25 Davison, *Complete Works*, vol. 11, p. 157.
26 *Ibid.*, p. 164.
27 *Ibid.*, p. 155.
28 *Ibid.*
29 *Ibid.*, p. 133.
30 *Ibid.*
31 *Ibid.*, p. 164.
32 *Ibid.*, p. 157.
33 *Ibid.*, p. 165.
34 *Ibid.*, p. 164.
35 Jackson article, p. 120.
36 Bowker bio, p. 230.
37 *Ibid.*, p. 239.
38 Davison, *Complete Works*, vol. 11, p. 169.
39 *Ibid.*, p. 154.

40 Crick bio, p. 248.
41 Davison, *Complete Works*, vol. 11, p. 242.
42 *Ibid.*, p. 175.
43 Rosalind Obermeyer, Crick Archive.
44 Victor Stacey, in Wadhams, pp. 107–8.
45 Jackson book, p. 419.
46 Lydia Jackson, personal diary, 20 November 1979, with kind permission of Pamela Davidson.
47 Crick bio, p. 248.
48 Davison, *Complete Works*, vol. 11, p. 177.
49 *Ibid.*, p. 184.
50 *Ibid.*, p. 165.
51 Shelden bio, p. 290.
52 Davison, *Complete Works*, vol. 11, p. 165.
53 Davison, *Lost*, p. 76.
54 Davison, *Complete Works*, vol. 11, p. 154.
55 Davison, *Lost*, p. 76.
56 *Ibid.*
57 Davison, *Complete Works*, vol. 11, p. 154.
58 Denys King-Farlow, Crick Archive.
59 Davison, *Complete Works*, vol. 11, p. 171.
60 *Ibid.*
61 *Ibid.*, p. 191.
62 *Ibid.*, p. 181.
63 *Ibid.*, p. 182.
64 *Ibid.*, p. 222.
65 Helen Darbishire, 'Ernest de Selincourt, 1870–1943', no date.
66 *Guardian*, 21 June 2004.
67 Davison, *Complete Works*, vol. 11, p. 181.
68 *Ibid.*
69 *Ibid.*, p. 182.
70 *Ibid.*, p. 187.
71 *Ibid.*, pp. 264–7.
72 Davison, *Lost*, p. 76.

Chapter 11: Coming Up for Air in Morocco

1   Davison, *Lost*, p. 76.
2   Davison, *Complete Works*, vol. 11, p. 198.
3   *Ibid.*
4   *Ibid.*
5   *Ibid.*, p. 345.
6   *Ibid.*, p. 199.
7   *Ibid.*, pp. 198–9.
8   *Ibid.*, p. 199.
9   *Ibid.*, p. 198.
10 Davison, *Lost*, p. 76.
11 Davison, *Complete Works*, vol. 11, p. 198.
12 *Ibid.*, p. 200.
13 *Ibid.*, p. 217.
14 *Ibid.*, p. 197.
15 *Ibid.*, p. 206.
16 Davison, *Lost*, p. 76.
17 *Ibid.*
18 Davison, *Complete Works*, vol. 11, p. 417.

19 *Ibid.*, p. 253.
20 Davison, *Lost*, p. 76.
21 Davison, *Complete Works*, vol. 11, p. 206.
22 Davison, *Lost*, p. 76.
23 Davison, *Complete Works*, vol. 11, p. 416.
24 Shelden bio, p. 302.
25 Davison, *Complete Works*, vol. 11, p. 276.
26 *Ibid.*, p. 285.
27 *Ibid.*, p. 211.
28 *Ibid.*, p. 271.
29 *Ibid.*, p. 283.
30 *Ibid.*, p. 315.
31 *Ibid.*, p. 307.
32 Davison, *Lost*, p. 77.
33 Davison, *Complete Works*, vol. 11, p. 218.
34 *Ibid.*, p. 199.
35 *Ibid.*, p. 206.
36 Ibid., p. 274.
37 Davison, *Lost*, p. 77.
38 Davison, *Complete Works*, vol. 11, p. 211.
39 *Ibid.*, p. 218.
40 *Ibid.*
41 *Ibid.*, p. 277.
42 *Ibid.*, p. 276.
43 *Ibid.*, p. 199.
44 *Ibid.*, p. 218.
45 *Ibid.*, p. 199.
46 *Ibid.*, p. 249.
47 Davison, *Lost*, p. 77.
48 Davison, *Complete Works*, vol. 11, p. 281.
49 *Ibid.*, p. 250.
50 *Ibid.*, p. 222.
51 *Ibid.*, p. 277.
52 *Ibid.*, p. 250.
53 *Ibid.*, p. 279.
54 *Ibid.*, p. 262.
55 Davison, *Lost*, p. 76.
56 Davison, *Complete Works*, vol. 11, p. 249.
57 Davison, *Lost*, p. 78.
58 Davison, *Complete Works*, vol. 11, p. 287.
59 Davison, *Lost*, p. 78.
60 Davison, *Complete Works*, vol. 11, p. 261.
61 *Ibid.*, p. 262.
62 Davison, *Lost*, p. 76.
63 Davison, *Complete Works*, vol. 11, p. 249.
64 *Ibid.*, p. 253.
65 *Ibid.*, p. 321.
66 Davison, *Lost*, p. 76.
67 Bowker bio, p. 244.
68 Jackson article, p. 119.
69 *Ibid.*
70 Lettice Cooper, 'Eileen Blair', The PEN: Broadsheet of the English Centre of International PEN, No. 16, Spring 1984, p. 19.

71 Richard Rees, *George Orwell: Fugitive from the Camp of Victory*, Southern Illinois University Press, Carbondale, IL, 1962, p. 69.
72 *Ibid.*, p. 77.
73 *Ibid.*, p. 79.
74 Davison, *Complete Works*, vol. 11, p. 221.
75 *Ibid.*, p. 261.
76 *Ibid.*, p. 318.
77 *Ibid.*, p. 338.
78 *Ibid.*, p. 345.
79 *Ibid.*, p. 231.
80 Crick bio, p. 251.
81 Davison, *Complete Works*, vol. 11, p. 231.
82 *Ibid.*, p. 331.
83 *Ibid.*, p. 345.
84 *Ibid.*, p. 331.
85 *Ibid.*, p. 337.
86 *Ibid.*, p. 205.
87 *Ibid.*, p. 206.
88 *Ibid.*
89 *Ibid.*, p. 205.
90 *Ibid.*, p. 285.
91 *Ibid.*, p. 346.
92 *Ibid.*, p. 212.
93 *Ibid.*, p. 240.
94 *Ibid.*, p. 341.
95 *Ibid.*, p. 206.
95 *Ibid.*, p. 218.
97 *Ibid.*, p. 215.
98 *Ibid.*, p. 216.
99 *Ibid.*, p. 205.
100 *Ibid.*, p. 212.
101 *Ibid.*, p. 237.
102 *Ibid.*, p. 318.
103 *Ibid.*, p. 321.
104 *Ibid.*, p. 320.
105 *Ibid.*, p. 206.
106 *Ibid.*, pp. 248–49.
107 *Ibid.*, p. 249.
108 *Ibid.*, p. 340.
109 *Ibid.*, p. 242.
110 *Ibid.*, p. 332.
111 *Ibid.*, p. 262.
112 *Ibid.*, p. 319.
113 *Ibid.*, p. 325.
114 *Ibid.*, p. 321.
115 Harold Acton, *More Memoirs of an Aesthete*, Faber & Faber, London, 1980, p. 153.
116 Fyvel bio, p. 109.
117 Meyers bio, p. 185.
118 Davison, *Complete Works*, vol. 11, p. 325.
119 *Ibid.*, p. 326.
120 *Ibid.*, p. 331.
121 *Ibid.*, p. 206.
122 *Ibid.*, p. 230.

123 *Ibid.*, p. 193.
124 *Ibid.*, p. 318.
125 *Ibid.*, p. 338.
126 *Ibid.*, p. 345.
127 *Ibid.*, p. 261.
128 *Ibid.*, p. 339.
129 Davison, *Lost*, p. 76.
130 Davison, *Complete Works*, vol. 11, p. 210.
131 Davison, *Lost*, p. 76.
132 Davison, *Complete Works*, vol. 11, p. 337.
133 Postscript by Eileen, *Ibid.*, p. 338.
134 *Ibid.*, p. 344.
135 *Ibid.*, p. 336.
136 Jackson book, p. 430.
137 Davison, *Complete Works*, vol. 11, p. 345.
138 *Ibid.*
139 *Ibid.*, p. 347.
140 *Ibid.*, p. 420.
141 Jackson article, p. 121.

Chapter 12: War Ends the Wallington Experiment

1   Davison, *Complete Works*, vol. 11, p. 348.
2   Jane Morgan, personal phone call with the author, 2012.
3   Davison, *Complete Works*, vol. 11, p. 348.
4   Jackson book, p. 431.
5   Davison, *Complete Works*, vol. 11, p. 349.
6   *Ibid.*, p. 350.
7   Letter to Mary Common from Eileen, *Ibid.*
8   *Ibid.*
9   *Ibid.*, p. 351.
10 Arthur Koestler, 'George Orwell', BBC Third Programme, November 1960.
11 Davison, *Complete Works*, vol. 11, p. 350.
12 *Ibid.*
13 *Ibid.*, p. 351.
14 *Ibid.*, p. 430.
15 *Ibid.*, p. 432.
16 *Ibid.*, p. 353.
17 Orwell.rem, p. 60.
18 Ruth Pitter, *Ibid.*, pp. 74–5.
19 Davison, *Complete Works*, vol. 11, pp. 433–4.
20 London Metropolitan Archives, personal email to the author, 4 March 2015.
21 Bowker bio, p. 249.
22 Munk's Roll, Royal College of Physicians.
23 Davison, *Complete Works*, vol. 11, p. 434.
24 *Ibid.*
25 *Ibid.*, p. 438.
26 *Ibid.*
27 *Ibid.*, p. 440.
28 *Ibid.*, p. 352.
29 *Ibid.*, p. 355.
30 T. R. Fyvel, 'A Writer's Life', *World Review*, June 1950.
31 R. D. Charques, 'Cracking World', *Times Literary Supplement*, June 17, 1939.
32 Davison, *Complete Works*, vol. 11, p. 358.

33 Mabel Fierz, in Orwell.rem, p. 97.
34 Ralph Strauss, *Sunday Times*, June 25, 1939.
35 Davison, *Complete Works*, vol. 11, p. 365.
36 Richard Rees, in Orwell.rem, p. 118.
37 Davison, *Complete Works*, vol. 11, pp. 442–3.
38 Jackson article, p. 121.
39 Patricia Donahue, letter to Bernard Crick, 10 January 1978, Crick Archive.
40 Jackson book, p. 377.
41 Shelden bio, p. 237.
42 Patricia Donahue, Wadhams, p. 118.
43 Lettice Cooper, *Ibid.*, pp. 116–17.
44 Jackson book, p. 431.
45 Lydia Jackson, personal diary, 30 October and 20 November 1979, with kind permission of Pamela Davidson.
46 Letter to Lydia Jackson from Bernard Crick, 7 December 1974, Crick Archive.
47 Letter to Bernard Crick from Lydia Jackson, 27 November 1974, Crick Archive.
48 Letter to Lydia Jackson from Bernard Crick, 7 December 1974, Crick Archive.
49 Georges Kopp to George Orwell, 12 August 1939, Orwell Archive.
50 Jackson book, p. 432.
51 Davison, *Complete Works*, vol. 20, p. 204.
52 Jackson book, p. 432.
53 Orwell.rem, p. 97.
54 Davison, *Lost*, p. 96.
55 Bowker bio, p. 252, letter to Brenda Salkeld from Orwell, 25 June 1940.
56 Jackson book, p. 432.
57 *Ibid.*
58 Davison, *Complete Works*, vol. 11, p. 351.
59 *Ibid.*, p. 365.
60 *Ibid.*, p. 393.
61 *Ibid.*, p. 365.
62 *Ibid.*, p. 361.
63 *Ibid.*, p. 452.
64 *Ibid.*, pp. 400, 402.
65 *Ibid.*, p. 403.
66 *Ibid.*, p. 399.
67 Jackson book, p. 449.
68 Obituary, *British Medical Journal*, 15 June 1940.
69 Jackson book, p. 448.
70 *Ibid.*
71 *Ibid.*, p. 449.
72 Jackson article, p. 121.
73 Jackson book, p. 449.
74 Jackson article, p. 121.
75 Davison, *Complete Works*, vol. 12, p. 7.
76 The National Archives, Kew. Contains public sector information licensed under the Open Government Licence v3.0: http://www.nationalarchives.gov.uk/doc/open-government-licence/version/3/
77 *Ibid.*
78 Davison, *Complete Works*, vol. 11, p. 402, 'Private note,' added to Orwell's 29 August 1939 War Diary.
79 *Nineteen Eighty-Four*, Penguin, London, 2008, pp. 5–6.
80 Ministry of Information files, The National Archives, Kew. Contains public sector information licensed under the Open Government Licence v3.0: http://www.nationalarchives.gov.uk/doc/open-government-licence/version/3/

81 Lord Birkenhead, *Walter Monckton*, Weidenfeld and Nicolson, London, 1969, p. 184.
82 Ministry of Information files, The National Archives, Kew. Contains public sector information. licensed under the Open Government Licence v3.0: http://www.nationalarchives.gov.uk/doc/open-government-licence/version/3/
83 Davison, *Complete Works*, vol. 17, p. 479.
84 *Ibid.*, vol. 12, p. 515.
85 *Ibid.*, vol. 11, pp. 453–4.
86 *Ibid.*, p. 458.
87 *Ibid.*, p. 456.
88 *Ibid.*, p. 413.
89 *Ibid.*, p. 422.
90 *Ibid.*, vol. 20, p. 204.
91 *Ibid.*, vol. 12, p. 318.
92 *Ibid.*
93 *Ibid.*, p. 320.
94 *Ibid.*
95 *Ibid.*, p. 138.
96 Shelden bio, p. 322.
97 Davison, *Complete Works*, vol. 12, p. 138.
98 *Ibid.*, p. 137.
99 *Ibid.*, p. 139.
100 *Ibid.*, p. 148.
101 Fyvel bio, p. 135.
102 *Ibid.*, p. 103.
103 Davison, *Complete Works*, vol. 12, p. 160.
104 Lettice Cooper, 'Eileen Blair', The PEN: Broadsheet of the English Centre of International PEN, No. 16, Spring 1984. This is listed incorrectly as No. 17, Autumn 1984, in many places.
105 Davison, *Complete Works*, vol. 12, p. 169.
106 Crick bio, p. 263.
107 The London Picture Archive, collage.cityoflondon.gov.uk.
108 Westminster Archives Centre, 10 St Ann's St, London.
109 John Thompson, *Orwell's London*, Schocken Books, New York, 1985, p. 54.
110 *Daily Express*, 31 May 1940.
111 Davison, *Complete Works*, vol. 12, p. 169.
112 *Ibid.*
113 *Ibid.*, p. 170.

Chapter 13: The Worst Years of Her Life

1   *Daily Express*, 31 May 1940.
2   Davison, *Complete Works*, vol. 12, p. 174.
3   Jackson article, p. 122.
4   Catherine Moncure, personal email to the author.
5   Richard McNab, *Retreat from Riviere: The Dunkirk Diary of Major George McNab*, Digital Print Media, Great Britain, 2013.
6   *Ibid.*, p. 5.
7   *Ibid.*, p. 115.
8   Richard McNab, personal email to the author.
9   McNab, *Retreat*, p. 134.
10 *Ibid.*
11 Jackson article, p. 122.
12 Davison, *Complete Works*, vol. 12, p. 513.
13 Fyvel bio, p. 105.
14 *Ibid.*, p. 135.

15 Davison, *Complete Works*, vol. 12, p. 182.
16 *Ibid.*, p. 183.
17 *Ibid.*, p. 197.
18 Virginia Nicholson, *Millions Like Us*, Penguin, London, 2012, p. 63.
19 Bowker bio, p. 266.
20 Georges Kopp, letter to Eileen, 8 September 1940, Orwell Archive.
21 Davison, *Complete Works*, vol. 12, p. 187.
22 Catherine Moncure, personal email to the author.
23 Hilton Als, 'Three on a Match', *The New Yorker*, 11 November 2013, p. 86.
24 Davison, *Complete Works*, vol. 12, p. 197.
25 Victor (V. S.) Pritchett, in Orwell.rem, p. 167.
26 Jackson article, p. 122.
27 *Ibid.*, p. 124.
28 Davison, *Lost*, p. 82.
29 Davison, *Complete Works*, vol. 12, p. 245.
30 *Ibid.*, p. 246.
31 *Ibid.*
32 *Ibid.*, p. 255.
33 *Ibid.*, p. 268.
34 Amy Helen Bell, *London Was Ours*, I. B. Tauris, London, 2008, p. 44.
35 Nicholson, *Millions*, p. 89.
36 Dione Venables, personal email to the author, 18 April 2015.
37 Bell, *London*, pp. 34–5.
38 Davison, *Complete Works*, vol. 12, p. 468.
39 *Ibid.*, p. 268.
40 Nicholson, *Millions*, p. 94.
41 Lettice Cooper, *Black Bethlehem*, Macmillan, New York, 1947, pp. 162, 189. Reprinted by permission of Peters Fraser & Dunlop (www.petersfraserdunlop.com) on behalf of the estate of Lettice Cooper.
42 Davison, *Complete Works*, vol. 12, p. 273.
43 Davison, *Lost*, p. 82.
44 Crick Archive.
45 Wadhams, p. 117.
46 *Ibid.*, p. 115.
47 Davison, *Complete Works*, vol. 12, p. 250.
48 Davison, *Lost*, p. 82.
49 Davison, *Complete Works*, vol. 12, p. 490.
50 *Ibid.*, p. 263.
51 Julian Symons, in Shelden bio, p. 329.
52 Jackson article, p. 123.
53 Patricia Donahue, Crick Archive.
54 Lettice Cooper, Orwell.rem, p. 163.
55 Davison, *Lost*, p. 79.
56 *Ibid.*, p. 80.
57 *Ibid.*, pp. 79–80.
58 Monica Hunton, Gwen O'Shaughnessy's sister-in-law, via Liz Kopp email, 4 June 2012.
59 Lettice Cooper, in Orwell.rem, p. 163.
60 Jackson book, p. 449.
61 Davison, *Complete Works*, vol. 12, p. 202.
62 *Ibid.*, p. 187.
63 Davison, *Lost*, p. 80.
64 Davison, *Complete Works*, vol. 12, p. 196.
65 *Ibid.*, p. 197.

66 Davison, *Complete Works*, vol. 11, p. 331.
67 Jackson article, p. 122.
68 Davison, *Lost*, p. 80.
69 Davison, *Complete Works*, vol. 12, p. 452.
70 Davison, *Lost*, p. 82.
71 Davison, *Complete Works*, vol. 12, p. 452.
72 Davison, *Lost*, p. 82.
73 Letters in Orwell collection, British Library.
74 Davison, *Lost*, p. 82.
75 Mark Benney, *Almost a Gentleman*, P. Davies, London, 1966, p. 167.
76 William J. West (ed.), *George Orwell: The Lost Writings*, Avon Books, New York, 1985, p. 17.
77 Davison, *Complete Works*, vol. 12, p. 457.
78 *Ibid.*, p. 479.
79 *Ibid.*, p. 480.
80 Lettice Cooper, 'Eileen Blair', *The PEN: Broadsheet of the English Centre of International PEN*, No. 16, Spring 1984, p. 19. This is credited incorrectly as No. 17, Autumn 1984, in many places.
81 Davison, *Complete Works*, vol. 12, p. 480.
82 Davison, *Lost*, p. 82.
83 Davison, *Complete Works*, vol. 12, p. 443.
84 *Ibid.*, p. 480.
85 *Ibid.*, p. 263.
86 *Ibid.*, p. 480.
87 *Ibid.*, p. 370.
88 *Ibid.*, p. 480.
89 Patricia Donahue, Wadhams, p. 118.
90 Meyers bio, p. 199.
91 Benney, *Almost a Gentleman*, p. 166.
92 Henry Dakin, personal letter to the author.
93 Shelden bio, p. 328.
94 Patricia Donahue, Wadhams, p. 118.
95 Davison, *Complete Works*, vol. 12, pp. 495–6.
96 Lettice Cooper, Orwell.rem, p. 164.
97 Lettice Cooper, Wadhams, p. 132.
98 Lettice Cooper, letter in Crick Archive.
99 Benney, *Almost a Gentleman*, p. 166.
100 *Ibid.*, p. 167.
101 Wadhams, p. 68.
102 Davison, *Complete Works*, vol. 12, p. 515.
103 Fyvel bio, p. 118.
104 W. J. West (ed.), *George Orwell: The War Broadcasts*, Penguin, Harmondsworth, 1987, p. 16.
105 *Ibid.*, p. 19.
106 Davison, *Complete Works*, vol. 13, p. 4.
107 *Ibid.*, p. 229.
108 Personal communication.
109 Henry Swanzy, Wadhams, p. 125.
110 *Ibid.*
111 Davison, *Complete Works*, vol. 13, p. 56.
112 *Ibid.*, p. 172.
113 William Empson, in Miriam Gross (ed.), *The World of George Orwell*, Simon and Schuster, New York, 1971, p. 97.
114 Obituary, *British Medical Journal*, 15 June 1940.
115 Davison, *Complete Works*, vol. 13, p. 366.

Chapter 14: Coming into Her Own at Last

1 The Earl of Woolton, *The Memoirs of the Rt. Hon. the Earl of Woolton*, Cassell & Co, London, 1959, p. 250.

2 BBC Written Archives, Reading, 8 May 1941. BBC copyright content reproduced courtesy of the British Broadcasting Corporation. All rights reserved.

3 The National Archives, Kew, RG 23/3. Contains public sector information licensed under the Open Government Licence v3.0: http://www.nationalarchives.gov.uk/doc/open-government-licence/version/3/

4 Davison, *Complete Works*, vol. 12, p. 7.

5 Letter from A. R. Nilson, 5 December 1983, Crick Archive.

6 A. R. Nilson, 'An Account of My Work at the Ministry of Food from 1943 to 1946'.

7 Lettice Cooper, 'Eileen Blair', The PEN: Broadsheet of the English Centre of International PEN, No. 16, Spring 1984, p. 19.

8 Wadhams, p. 130.

9 Orwell.rem, p. 166.

10 Wadhams, p. 130.

11 Lettice Cooper, in Orwell.rem, p. 166.

12 Lettice Cooper, 'Eileen Blair', The PEN: Broadsheet of the English Centre of International PEN, No. 16, Spring 1984, p. 19.

13 Woolton, *Memoirs*, p. 245.

14 Lettice Cooper, 'Eileen Blair', The PEN: Broadsheet of the English Centre of International PEN, No. 16, Spring 1984, p. 19.

15 Wadhams, p. 130.

16 Lettice Cooper, Crick Archive.

17 Woolton, *Memoirs*, p. 251.

18 All quotes are from the Mabel Constanduros files at the BBC Written Archives. BBC copyright content reproduced courtesy of the British Broadcasting Corporation. All rights reserved.

19 Typed copies of all the *Kitchen Front* scripts are preserved at the National Archives, with microfilm copies at the BBC Written Archives, Reading. BBC copyright content reproduced courtesy of the British Broadcasting Corporation. All rights reserved.

20 Nell Heaton, *The Complete Cook*, Faber, London, 1948.

21 Lettice Cooper, in Wadhams, p. 130.

22 Crick bio, p. 298.

23 Personal letter to Bernard Crick, 3 April 1977, Crick Archive.

24 Davison, *Complete Works*, vol. 20, p. 299.

25 All *Kitchen Front* letters are in the BBC Written Archives, Reading. BBC copyright content reproduced courtesy of the British Broadcasting Corporation. All rights reserved.

26 Davison, *Complete Works*, vol. 13, p. 288.

27 Marianne Colloms and Dick Weindling, *The Greville Estate*, Camden History Society, London, 2007, map, p. 83.

28 Anthony Powell, 'George Orwell: A Memoir', *Atlantic Monthly*, October 1967, p. 65.

29 Fyvel bio, p. 136.

30 Orwell.rem, p. 187.

31 Powell, 'George Orwell'.

32 Henry Dakin, phone conversation with the author, 2012.

33 Personal letter from Henry Dakin to the author.

34 Crick bio, p. 296.

35 Personal letter from Henry Dakin to the author.

36 Henry Dakin, phone conversation with the author, 2012.

37 Jane Morgan, phone conversation with the author, 2 November 2016.

38 Catherine Moncure, email to the author, 22 October 2016.

39 David Astor, in Bowker bio, p. 296.

40 David Astor, in Shelden bio, p. 359.

41 Davison, *Complete Works*, vol. 13, p. 443.
42 Orwell.rem, p. 187.
43 Davison, *Complete Works*, vol. 14, p. 152.
44 *Ibid.*, p. 307.
45 *Ibid.*, p. 342.
46 David Astor, Crick Archive.
47 Orwell.rem, p. 187.
48 Orwell, in Gangulee file, 27 May 1943, and Eileen, in Mrs. L. E. Jackson file, 17 December 1943, both at the BBC Written Archives. BBC copyright content reproduced courtesy of the British Broadcasting Corporation. All rights reserved.
49 Jane Morgan, Orwell.rem, p. 87.
50 *Ibid.*, p. 89.
51 Davison, *Complete Works*, vol. 13, p. 520.
52 *Ibid.*, vol. 14, p. 213.
53 *Ibid.*, pp. 272–3.
54 T. S. Eliot correspondence, Orwell Archive.
55 Lettice Cooper, Crick Archive.
56 *Ibid.*
57 Davison, *Complete Works*, vol. 17, p. 99.
58 Orwell.rem, p. 133.
59 Michael Meyer, Crick Archive.
60 Wadhams, p. 135.
61 *Ibid.*, pp. 135–6.
62 Inez Holden, 'Orwell or Wells?' *Listener*, 24 February 1972.
63 Crick Archive.
64 Davison, *Complete Works*, vol. 13, p. 250.
65 Michael Meyer, *Listener*, 2 March 1972.
66 Inez Holden, *Listener*, 9 March 1972.
67 Inez Holden diary, 28 April 1942, Crick Archive.
68 27 March 1942, Davison, *Complete Works*, vol. 13, p. 249.
69 Jane Morgan, in Orwell.rem, p. 89.
70 Patricia Donahue, Crick Archive.
71 Michael Meyer, Crick Archive.
72 Davison, *Complete Works*, vol. 13, p. 370.
73 Ruth Pitter, in Orwell.rem, pp. 74–5.
74 *Ibid.*
75 Davison, *Complete Works*, vol. 14, p. 5.
76 Orwell.rem, p. 165.
77 Jackson article, p. 123.

Chapter 15: But Smooth Sailing Was Never an Option

1   All *Kitchen Front* letters are at the BBC Written Archives, Reading. BBC copyright content reproduced courtesy of the British Broadcasting Corporation. All rights reserved.
2   Davison, *Complete Works*, vol. 14, p. 250.
3   *Ibid.*, pp. 250–2. This script is marked 'As broadcast'. The actual recording did not survive.
4   W. J. West (ed.), *George Orwell: The War Broadcasts*, Penguin, Harmondsworth, 1987, p. 48.
5   Davison, *Complete Works*, vol. 15, p. 118.
6   Sunday Wilshin, in Wadhams, p. 126.
7   'The Road to the Left', BBC *Omnibus* Programme on Orwell, Melvyn Bragg, 1970.
8   Letter to Anne Popham, 18 April 1946, in Davison, *Complete Works*, vol. 18, p. 249.
9   Orwell.rem, p. 163.
10 Patricia Donahue, in Wadhams, p. 119.
11 Lettice Cooper, Crick Archive.

12 Kay Dick, Crick Archive.
13 Bowker bio, p. 278.
14 Celia Goodman, Crick Archive.
15 Sonia Orwell, Crick Archive.
16 Frances Spalding, *Stevie Smith*, Faber and Faber, London, 1988, p. 154.
17 Kay Dick, Crick Archive.
18 Malcolm Muggeridge, in Meyers bio, p. 221.
19 Anthony Powell, *Ibid.*
20 Sonia Orwell, Crick Archive.
21 Lydia Jackson, Crick Archive.
22 Lydia Jackson, personal diary, 20 November 1979, with kind permission of Pamela Davidson.
23 Orwell.rem, p. 163.
24 Lettice Cooper, Crick Archive.
25 *Ibid.*
26 Celia Paget Goodman, in Shelden bio, p. 383.
27 Davison, *Complete Works*, vol. 17, p. 88.
28 Obituary, *London Times*, 4 January 1997, p. 19.
29 Susan Watson, Crick interview, 20 October 1975, Crick Archive.
30 Letter from Georges Kopp to George and Evelyn Mason, 17 December 1941, The National Archives, Kew, HS9/858/8. Contains public sector information licensed under the Open Government Licence v3.0: http://www.nationalarchives.gov.uk/doc/open-government-licence/version/3/
31 Davison, *Complete Works*, vol. 13, pp. 482–3.
32 *Ibid.*, vol. 15, pp. 175–6.
33 *Ibid.*, p. 176.
34 Quentin Kopp, email to the author, 18 November 2015.
35 *Ibid.*, 21 September 2016.
36 Catherine Moncure, email to the author.
37 Bowker bio, p. 284.
38 Letter to Anne Popham, in Davison, *Complete Works*, vol. 18, p. 249.
39 Patricia Donahue, Crick Archive.
40 Shelden bio, p. 362.
41 *Ibid.*
42 Orwell.rem, p. 29.
43 Lettice Cooper, Crick Archive.
44 All quotes are directly from Lettice Cooper, *Black Bethlehem*, Macmillan, New York, 1947. Reprinted by permission of Peters Fraser & Dunlop (www.petersfraserdunlop.com) on behalf of the estate of Lettice Cooper.
45 Lettice Cooper, 'Eileen Blair', The PEN: Broadsheet of the English Centre of International PEN, No. 16, Spring 1984. This is listed incorrectly as No. 17, Autumn 1984, in many places.
46 Fyvel bio, p. 136.
47 Lettice Cooper, Crick Archive.
48 Patricia Donahue, Crick Archive.
49 Lettice Cooper, Crick Archive.
50 Wadhams, p. 130.
51 Lydia Jackson, 27 November 1974, Crick Archive.
52 Lettice Cooper, Crick Archive.
53 Davison, *Complete Works*, vol. 15, p. 206.
54 21 March 1945, in Davison, *Complete Works*, vol. 17, p. 99.
55 *Ibid.*
56 Letter to Anne Popham, 15 March 1946, in Davison, *Complete Works*, vol. 18, p. 153.
57 *Ibid.*
58 Davison, *Complete Works*, vol. 16, p. 126.

59 *Ibid.*, p. 269.
60 *Ibid.*, vol. 15, p. 186.
61 Meyers bio, p. 248.
62 Orwell, letter to Glen Struve, in Davison, *Complete Works*, vol. 16, p. 99.
63 Michael Meyer, Wadhams, p. 134.
64 Lettice Cooper, Wadhams, p. 131.
65 Lettice Cooper, Crick Archive.
66 Jackson article, p. 123.
67 Fyvel bio, p. 134.
68 *Ibid.*, pp. 137–8.
69 Wadhams, p. 131.
70 Ian Angus, Letter to Edna Bussey, 1 October 1968, Orwell Archive.
71 Peter Davison, *George Orwell: A Literary Life*, Palgrave Macmillan, London, 1996, p. 129.
72 Fredric Warburg, *All Authors Are Equal*, Hutchinson, London, 1973, p. 56.
73 Sonia Orwell, Crick Archive.
74 Quentin Kopp, personal email to the author, 25 August 2015.
75 Catherine Moncure, personal email to the author, 28 August 2015.
76 Davison, *Complete Works*, vol. 18, p. 115.
77 Meyers bio, p. 248.

Chapter 16: Nearly a Happy Ending

1   Davison, *Complete Works*, vol. 16, p. 126.
2   *Ibid.*, p. 269.
3   *Ibid.*, vol. 18, p. 123.
4   *Ibid.*, vol. 16, p. 174.
5   *Ibid.*, p. 156.
6   Orwell, letter to Dwight Macdonald, December 1946, Orwell Archive.
7   Fyvel bio, p. 136.
8   Shelden bio, p. 372.
9   Fredric Warburg, *All Authors Are Equal*, Hutchinson, London, 1973, pp. 47–8.
10 Meyers bio, p. 227.
11 Letter to Anne Popham, Davison, *Complete Works*, vol. 18, p. 249.
12 Davison, *Complete Works*, vol. 16, p. 160.
13 *Ibid.*, p. 230.
14 Jackson book, p. 378.
15 Lettice Cooper, 'Eileen Blair', The PEN: Broadsheet of the English Centre of International PEN, No. 16, Spring 1984, p. 19.
16 Mabel Fierz, Orwell.rem, p. 97.
17 Susan Watson, 20 October 1975, Crick Archive.
18 Lettice Cooper, 'Eileen Blair', The PEN: Broadsheet of the English Centre of International PEN, No. 16, Spring 1984, p. 19.
19 Lettice Cooper, Orwell.rem, p. 165.
20 Davison, *Complete Works*, vol. 16, p. 295. Richard's horoscope is in a letter to Orwell from Heppenstall, 14 October, 1944, Orwell Archive.
21 *Ibid.*, p. 487.
22 *Ibid.*, vol. 17, p. 38.
23 Jackson article, p. 124.
24 *Ibid.*
25 Lettice Cooper, Crick Archive.
26 Inez Holden, Crick Archive.
27 Patricia Donahue, Crick Archive.
28 Davison, *Complete Works*, vol. 16, p. 324.
29 *Ibid.*

30 Patricia Donahue, Crick Archive.
31 Lettice Cooper, Crick Archive.
32 Catherine Moncure, email to the author, 10 September 2015.
33 Quentin Kopp, conversation with the author.
34 Catherine Moncure, email to the author, 10 September 2015.
35 Quentin Kopp, email to the author, 21 September 2016.
36 Davison, *Complete Works*, vol. 12, p. 188.
37 Wadhams, p. 170.
38 Richard Rees, *George Orwell: Fugitive from the Camp of Victory*, Southern Illinois University, Carbondale, IL, 1962, p. 140.
39 Margaret Nelson, owner of Barnhill, 2 September 1976, Crick Archive.
40 Davison, *Complete Works*, vol. 17, p. 97.
41 *Ibid.*, p. 99.
42 *Ibid.*, p. 100.
43 *Ibid.*, p. 98.
44 *Ibid.*, vol. 16, p. 325.
45 *Ibid.*, p. 425.
46 *Ibid.*, pp. 445–6.
47 Mrs Miranda Wood's Memoir, Davison, *Complete Works*, vol. 20, pp. 300–6.
48 Bowker bio, pp. 317–18.
49 Wood's Memoir, Davison, *Complete Works*, vol. 20, pp. 300–6.
50 William Empson, in Orwell.rem, p. 182.
51 Meyers bio, p. 229.
52 George Woodcock, 'Recollections of George Orwell', *Northern Review*, Montreal, 1954, p. 20.
53 Celia Goodman, Crick Archive.
54 Wood's Memoir, Davison, *Complete Works*, vol. 20, pp. 300–6.
55 Davison, *Complete Works*, vol. 17, p. 43.
56 Paul Potts, 'Don Quixote on a Bicycle', *Dante Called You Beatrice*, Eyre & Spottiswoode, London, 1960, pp. 72–3.
57 Davison, *Complete Works*, vol. 16, p. 437.
58 *Ibid.*, vol. 17, p. 100.
59 *Ibid.*, p. 104.
60 *Ibid.*, p. 105.
61 *Ibid.*, vol. 16, p. 446.
62 Lettice Cooper, 'Eileen Blair', The PEN: Broadsheet of the English Centre of International PEN, No. 16, Spring 1984, p. 19.
63 Jackson article, p. 124.
64 Lettice Cooper, Crick Archive.
65 Shelden bio, p. 363.
66 Jackson article, p. 124.
67 Lettice Cooper, Crick Archive.
68 Wadhams, p. 196.
69 Richard Blair, email to the author, 21 September 2016.
70 Crick bio, p. 321.
71 Celia Goodman, Crick Archive.
72 Davison, *Complete Works*, vol. 16, pp. 358, 419.
73 Peter Lewis, *George Orwell: The Road to 1984*, Harcourt, New York, 1981, p. 102.
74 Cyril Connolly, in Davison, *Complete Works*, vol. 17, p. 111.
75 Jackson article, p. 124.
76 Jane Morgan, in Orwell.rem, p. 87.
77 Davison, *Complete Works*, vol. 17, p. 99.
78 Avril Blair, Crick Archive.
79 Shelden bio, p. 360.

80 David Astor, in Orwell.rem, p. 186.
81 Davison, *Complete Works*, vol. 17, p. 111.
82 *Ibid.*, p. 38.
83 *Ibid.*, pp. 42–3.
84 Bowker bio, p. 325.
85 *Ibid.*, p. 328.
86 Davison, *Complete Works*, vol. 17, p. 97.
87 *Ibid.*, p. 98.
88 *Ibid.*, p. 46.
89 *Ibid.*, p. 109.
90 *Ibid.*, p. 97.
91 Lettice Cooper, in Wadhams, p. 131.
92 Lettice Cooper, 'Eileen Blair', The PEN: Broadsheet of the English Centre of International PEN, No. 16, Spring 1984, p. 19.
93 Davison, *Complete Works*, vol. 17, p. 81.
94 Jackson article, p. 125.
95 *Ibid.*
96 Davison, *Complete Works*, vol. 17, p. 104.
97 Inez Holden, diary, 30 March 1945, Crick Archive.
98 Davison, *Complete Works*, vol. 17, p. 99.
99 *Ibid.*, p. 96.
100 *Ibid.*, p. 104.
101 *Ibid.*, p. 95.
102 Obituary, *British Medical Journal*, 7 July 1979, p. 45.
103 Davison, *Complete Works*, vol. 17, p. 105.
104 *Ibid.*
105 *Ibid.*, p. 97.
106 *Ibid.*, p. 105.
107 *Ibid.*, p. 96.
108 *Ibid.*
109 *Ibid.*, p. 99.
110 *Ibid.*, p. 100.
111 *Ibid.*, p. 105.
112 *Ibid.*, p. 98.
113 Cyril Connelly, *Ibid.*, p. 111.
114 *Ibid.*, p. 108.
115 Meyers bio, p. 237.
116 Inez Holden, diary, Crick Archive.
117 Davison, *Complete Works*, vol. 17, p. 105.
118 Lettice Cooper, Crick Archive.
119 Davison, *Complete Works*, vol. 17, p. 112.
120 Coroner's Report for Eileen Blair.
121 Eileen Blair, Death certificate.
122 Inez Holden, diary, Crick Archive.
123 Avril Blair, Crick Archive.

Epilogue: Orwell Without Eileen

1 Anthony Powell, in Davison, *Complete Works*, vol. 17, p. 124.
2 Dorothy Plowman, *Ibid.*, vol. 18, p. 115.
3 Powell, *Ibid.*, vol. 17, p. 124.
4 Stafford Cottman, *Ibid.*, vol. 18, p. 258.
5 *Ibid.*, vol. 17, p. 128.
6 Crick, conversation with Avril Blair, Crick Archive.

7   Geoffrey Gorer, Crick Archive.
8   Tosco Fyvel, in Davison, *Complete Works*, vol. 17, p. 121.
9   Geoffrey Gorer, Crick Archive.
10 Dorothy Plowman, in Davison, *Complete Works*, vol. 18, p. 115.
11 *Ibid.*
12 Davison, *Complete Works*, vol. 18, p. 311.
13 Anne Popham, *Ibid.*, p. 153.
14 Davison, *Complete Works*, vol. 20, p. 44.
15 Dione Venables, 'Postcript', in Jacintha Buddicom, *Eric & Us*, Finlay, Chichester, 2006.
16 Avril Dunn, 'My Brother George Orwell', *The Twentieth Century*, March 1961.

A Note of Appreciation

First I would like to give a special thank you to the many others like Eileen in the world, all the wives, husbands, and partners of celebrated people who have devoted their lives joyfully to assisting their talented partners in all their various needs, knowing all along that they would be underappreciated and often ignored, and yet never faltering in their dedication, or in their willingness to submerge their own personal talents into their partners' success.

Throughout the eight years it has taken me to get this book into bookshops, there are so many family members and friends to remember and thank, people who encouraged and supported me from the very beginning, in the spring of 2011, when I first started to seriously begin research for this book. I needed their support especially, since this is the first book I have written by myself, the first one I've worked on without Tuli Kupferberg, my partner of over fifty years – together we produced over thirty books, some collections of his original writing and drawings, and a number of books and magazines centered on subject matters of special interest to us both. I could never have gotten this far, of course, without the generous and so much appreciated support of those friends as well as of interested strangers, all named in the supporters list at the back of the book, all part of the 372 people who took a chance and ordered a copy of my book before publication, including three who offered quite special help: Richard Blair, and two friends of many years, Marie Brown and Richard Sisk. I especially want to thank my daughter Samara Kupferberg and my good friends Julia Röhl and Mike Byrne, all of whom read carefully through early versions of the whole book and helped me continue in the right direction. And then, when I had a final manuscript ready for publication, my son Noah Kupferberg carefully edited the chapters, always making excellent suggestions for improvement.

In the spring of 2012, I went to the first meeting of the newly formed Orwell Society, held in the Senate House, in London. There I met many Orwell family members and scholars, including Quentin Kopp, a close relative of Eileen's, and his wife, Liz, who told me at that first meeting about Eileen's involvement in the creation of *Animal Farm*. We immediately became friends, and they constantly contributed much appreciated encouragement and advice. Later that year, Richard Blair, the son Eileen and Orwell had adopted as an infant, and his wife, Eleanor, thrilled me with an invitation to lunch at their home, where they shared an afternoon of fascinating memories with me. They also became good friends, always in touch whenever I asked for anything. Some time later, I met Catherine Moncure in Washington, D.C., the child Gwen O'Shaughnessy, the wife of Eileen's brother Eric, had adopted as an infant, and she brought along a load of photographs and information about Eileen as well as about Catherine's parents Eric and Gwen O'Shaughnessy. Catherine has always responded with great kindness to all my questions. Around the same time, I got to know many others who are closely connected to Orwell and Eileen, including Les Hurst, Masha Karp, Dione Venables, Richard Young, Neil Smith, Jason Crimp, Anita Coppola, Richard Keeble, Tim Crook, Desmond Avery, and Nathan Waddell, who were all extremely helpful and full of encouragement. I'm so proud to have become friends with them.

During my research, I was welcomed by the two most recent Orwell biographers, David Taylor, who made lunch for me in his Norfolk home and told me about the recently found letters Eileen had written to her Oxford friend Norah, and Gordon Bowker, who invited me to his London home and gave me many leads to Eileen's studies at Oxford and University College London. I reached out by email to Peter Stansky, Michael Shelden, Jeffrey Meyers, and Steve Wadhams. These Orwell biographers were enthusiastic about my interest in the elusive Eileen, and three of them kindly wrote blurbs for the back cover of this book. Peter Davison, the prolific Orwell authority, then near retirement, was always immediately responsive to my emails and full of praise for my efforts, and he kindly wrote a wonderful foreword for this book.

On my first visit to South Shields, I met Gary Wilkinson and Tom Kelly, both of whom were excited to learn that Eileen had grown up in their hometown and were extremely helpful in showing me around the town. Gary took photos of important sites and later made a wonderful short film, 'Wildflower', about Eileen, and he is now helping to get a Blue Plaque placed on Eileen's childhood home in South Shields in March 2020. Tom wrote a lovely poem celebrating Eileen called 'You, You, You', and a recording of him reading it in his lovely lilting accent can be found at unbound.com/books/eileen/updates/you-you-you-by-tom-kelly. My friend Frank Hunter, who lives in Sunderland, managed with some effort to get the original coroner's report for Eileen, and, as we had expected, it seemed to contradict some of the information on Eileen's death certificate. A few years ago, I was excited to hear from Richard McNab, whose father had been a doctor along with Eric O'Shaughnessy at Dunkirk. Richard shared his father's diary, with shocking details about Eric's death there. Another friend, Mike Watson, searched the Arthur Koestler Archive in Edinburgh for any new material about Eileen.

Throughout my years of research and initial drafts of chapters, I travelled to some of the places where Eileen had lived or visited—

South Shields, Sunderland, Oxford, London, Wallington, Barcelona, Windermere, Greystone, and Newcastle, where her grave is. On the first Orwell Society trip to Barcelona, Alan Warren drove me and Quentin and Liz up to the front where Orwell had fought in the Spanish Civil War, and showed us Eileen's hotel and workplace with the Independent Labour Party in Barcelona. When I was in Windermere, I enjoyed lunch in nearby Keswick with Orwell's nephew, Henry Dakin, and his two nieces, Jane Morgan and Lucy Bestley, all in their eighties. Henry and Jane had actually met Eileen, unfortunately two of the very few left who had, and Henry gave me some typed pages of his fascinating memories of Eileen. On my three previous visits to Wallington, I was never able to get permission to go inside the cottage, although Dan Pinnock, who scheduled tours of the village, welcomed me each time, showing me all the interesting sites connected to Eileen and Orwell. But finally, this past June, I was thrilled to be in a group of Orwell Society members whom the current owners, Graham and Dawn Lamb, allowed to enter the cottage. At last I got to breathe the inside air, and walk through their tiny downstairs rooms, one of which had been set up as a store just after they moved in. Sadly, the precarious winding staircase is no longer used, but a modern staircase took us up to Orwell's study and the two upstairs bedrooms, a years-long dream fulfilled.

I visited many archives as I collected material, and all the archivists gave me excellent assistance in my research, keeping in close touch through the years. I especially want to thank Gill Furlong and Amanda Wise and the staff at the Orwell Archive, part of the University College London Special Collections. Throughout my many visits, they set out boxes of material concerning Eileen and cheerfully answered all my requests. Robert Winckworth, also with the UCL Special Collections, was very helpful with information about Eileen's psychology classes there. Dr Aubrey Greenwood and Jackie Madden, librarians at the Bernard Crick Archive, at Birkbeck College, in London, welcomed me for many days as I searched through their huge collection. Louise North, archivist at the BBC Written Archives, in Reading, kindly copied hundreds of pages of Eileen's letters and other documents from her years at the Ministry of Food. Amanda Ingram, archivist at St. Hugh's College, in Oxford, provided wonderful group photos of Eileen's classes as well as tutors reports that had survived all those years, and on my visits she showed me all the student journals Eileen had worked on as well as other fascinating documents. Elaine Martin, PA to Head/ Registrar at Eileen's Sunderland High School, found a huge amount of wonderful material concerning Eileen for me to browse through. Anne Sharp, librarian of the South Shields Library, was just starting to collect information about Eileen as I arrived there in 2012.

After a few years it was time to look for an agent, and I was thrilled to find Bill Hamilton, of A. M. Heath, willing to take me on. Bill patiently directed me through several drafts of the book, suggesting many important areas to expand on. When he decided it was time to find a publisher, Bill contacted Phil Connor, at Unbound, and Phil's suggestion of *Eileen: The Making of George Orwell* as a title seemed perfect to me. At Unbound, Phil and Georgia Odd helped me set up the website, with a charming video about the book, where people were invited to buy advance copies, and they guided me through the early editing and production steps. More recently, Ella Chappell became my editor. I have thoroughly enjoyed working with Ella, who has tirelessly directed me through copyediting, cover design, selection of illustrations, book design, reference notes, permissions, and last-minute production steps, ending with the final product in your hands. At the last moment, Ella even took her camera to Greenwich to photograph Eileen's home for the book.

And I don't want to forget the many anonymous people who kindly offered extra special assistance through the years: the woman I approached at the exit to the Jesmond Metro station, in Newcastle, who, when I asked for directions to Fernwood House, where Eileen died, as well as to the St. Andrew's and Jesmond Cemetery, where she was buried, suggested I hop in her car as she delivered me to both places. In South Shields, as I searched for the now non-existent

Wellington Terrace where Eileen grew up, I asked a woman in charge of the taxi stand for help, and when she had never heard of that street herself, she called a few of the older cabbies in case they remembered it, reporting back that no one did. Then there was the man at the door to the Langford Court apartment building in London who took me up in the lift to the top floor so I could see the door to Eileen and Orwell's apartment number 111. And, as I stood in the street taking photos of 50 Lawford Road, where Orwell had lived for a few months with two friends while he was courting Eileen, a woman in the front garden became curious, then offered tea in the back garden with her housemate, and a most welcome tour of Orwell's top-floor flat. And of course there were many others.

I feel most fortunate to have met and talked with all these people through the eight years. I could never have completed this book without the kindness shown to me by every one of them. I am so happy that you as a reader now have my book in your hands!

Index

Note: EMB denotes Eileen Maud Blair; GO denotes George Orwell.

Unbound is the world's first crowdfunding publisher, established in 2011.

We believe that wonderful things can happen when you clear a path for people who share a passion. That's why we've built a platform that brings together readers and authors to crowdfund books they believe in – and give fresh ideas that don't fit the traditional mould the chance they deserve.

This book is in your hands because readers made it possible. Everyone who pledged their support is listed below. Join them by visiting unbound.com and supporting a book today.

Geoffrey Abrams
Debby Accuardi
Adamos Adamou
Amy Adams
ADW Decorators
Ali Ambridge
Christopher Anderson
Judy Andraski
Christopher Angel
Steve Antoniewicz
Joe Armstrong
Richard Atkinson
Desmond Avery
M Bagge
David Baillie
Debby Baker
Karen Baker
Richard Baker
Emerald Balzer
Phil Barker
Lynne Barnsley
Zena Barrie
Roy Bartley

Dennis Bates
Helen Bates
Sue J Beley
Aimee Bell
Laura Bell
A. Benattar
Ann Benattar
Phillip Bennett-Richards
Henry Benoit
Miquel Berga
Suchada Bhirombhakdi
Carol Biederstadt
Allan Bilsky
Terry Bisbee
Norman Bissell
Alastair, Taryn, Grace & Matilda Blair
Richard Blair
Thelma Blitz
Mary Boase
Sacha Boegem
Charles Boot
Anne Booth
Francois Bordes

Philip Bounds
Jonathan Bradley
John E. Branch Jr.
Joan Brooks
Robert Brooks
Marie Brown
Nicky Brown
Zack Brown
Nigel Bryant
Barbara Burge
Helen Bush
Mike Byrne
Katie Calautti
Antonio Cantafio
Paul Carroll
Kevin Carter
James Cholakis
Georgia Christgau
Juan Christian
Brendan Clarke
Vanessa Cobb
Alison Colby
Sue Cole
Robert Colls
Sheila Connop
Anne Coper
David Coward
Robert Cox
John Crawford
Susan Crimmins
Jason Crimp and Anita Coppola
Professor Tim Crook
Bob Cullen
Ray Cyphers
Emoke Czako
Russ Davidson
Frank de Langen
Adam De Salle
Frederic Delaroche
Anna Dent
JF Derry
Peter Devine

Pete Dewhirst
Doug Dezzani
Jill Diamond
Mark Donoghue
Michael Dougall
Lawrence T Doyle
Sam Egerton
Carol Eicher
Birgit Einhoff
Michelle Eldredge
Brendan Evans
Margaret Evans
Ilona Fabian
Rachel Farrow
David Fenner
Scott Ferguson
Johnny Fewings
Diane Fisher
Molly Fletcher
Alan & Lynn Fliegel
David Ford
Alan Fremlin
Andrew Friedman
Liz Friend
Gillian Furlong
Simon Fussell
Roger Gaess
John Galazin
Mark Gamble
Alicia Garcia Lopez
Amro Gebreel
Ginger Gillespie
Philip Ginsbury
Robert Graf
Sam Graff
Joanne Greenway
Elizabeth Hale-Garland
Sky Hall
Richard Hallmark
Jocelyn Hanlon
David Harding
Alison Hardy

Laura Hartmann-Villalta
Moe Harvey
Tom Haushalter
Mark Haviland
David Hilborn
Michael Hilborn
Frances Hill
Beverly Hills
Kathryn Hilt
Peter Hirschmann
Michael Hobbs
Susan Hodgson
John Hodson
Roger Howe
Nick Hubble
Charlie Huisken
Michael Hunt
William Hunt
Frank Hunter
Martha Hurley
Leslie Hurst
Glenn Ibbitson
Stephen Ingle
Islay Book Festival
Philip Jackson
Gail Jaitin
Antti Jauhiainen
Simon Jerrome
Gary Jones
M. I. Jones
Nicholas Jones
Russ Jones
Yasemin Jones
Joseph Joyce
Tara Kainer
Eileen Kaner
Masha Karp
Richard Keeble
Andrew Kelly
Tom Kelly
Alistair Kemp
Douglas Kerr

Dan Kieran
Michael King
Huseyin Kishi
Richard Knott
Michaela Knowles
Jules Kohn
Quentin Kopp
Ann Kronbergs
Michael Kucz
Charlotte Kupferberg
Mercury Kupferberg
Noah Kupferberg
Samara Kupferberg
Nicole Laemmle
Mindi Laine
Patricia Lawlor
Nigel Lax
Mavis Le Page Leathley
Barbara Leckie
Judith Leckie
Rosemary Leckie
Steve Leckie
Dickey Lee
David Legg
Laurence Leigh
Nancy Lemon
Liana Lepingwell
Jeffrey Lewis
Penny Lewis
Flash Light
Mark Lodge
Michael Longacre
Isabell Lorenz
Susi Luss
Joe Luttrell
Nancy Lyn
Patty MacDougall
Stephen MacPhail
Mary Lyn Maiscott
Catherine Makin
Jane Mattley
Imbert Maurice

Stacy Schneider Boegem
Virginia Scott
Rose Seabury
Kathryn Shagas
Robina Shaw
Clare Shepherd
Maurice Sherlock
Rachel Shirley
Cindy Shove
Patricia Siegel
Doug Simmons
Duncan Simpson
Richard Sisk
Paul Skinner
Sandra Skoblar
Andreas Skyman
Iain Slack
Clive Smith
Neil Smith
Patricia (Tish) Smith
Michael Arthur Soares
Lili Soh
Greg Spiro
Lori Steiner
Gary Stocker
Barbara Storey
Pat Sullivan
Sarah Sullivan
Andrew Syvret
Robin Tatham
Johnnie Taylor
Jillian Tees
J.P. Tettmar-Saleh
Brian Thompson
Bruce Topp
Elizabeth Topp
John Topp

Leslie Topp
Sylvia Tracy
Leonardo Trevas
Helen Trippier
Jennifer Tubbs
Elizabeth Tunstall
Aleksy Uchanski
Martijn van Bloois
James Vavra
Dione Venables
Rob Verweij
Jonathan Vickers
Nathan Waddell
Steve Wadhams
Aidan Waine
Jan Walter
Nigel Ward
Alan Warren
Deirdre Watson
Harry Watson
Mike Watson
Sarah Watson-Saunders
Clare Wells
Mary Wheeler
Sheila Whiting
Rae Williams
Keith Williamson
Julian Willis
Ludger Wilmott
Jon Wilson
Stephen Wood
William Wykhuis
Ros Wynne-Jones
Richard Young
Patricia Zaffino
Rebekah Zammit
Elizabeth Zimmer